LIFE

IN

ANCIENT INDIA

LIFE
IN
ANCIENT INDIA

MRS. SPEIR.

ILLUSTRATED BY

GEORGE SCHARF, JUN., F.S.A.

GYAN

Published by

Gyan Publishing House
5, Ansari Road
Daryaganj, New Delhi-110002
Phone: 011-47034999, 9811692060
E-mail: books@gyanbooks.com

Distribution Network
gyanbooks.com
India, USA, Canada, UK, Australia, France

ISBN: 978-81-212-8608-4 (PB)
First Published, 1856

2nd Impression 2023

Printed at: Gyan Press, Delhi.

LIFE IN ANCIENT INDIA
Author: Mrs. Speir

Life in Ancient India.

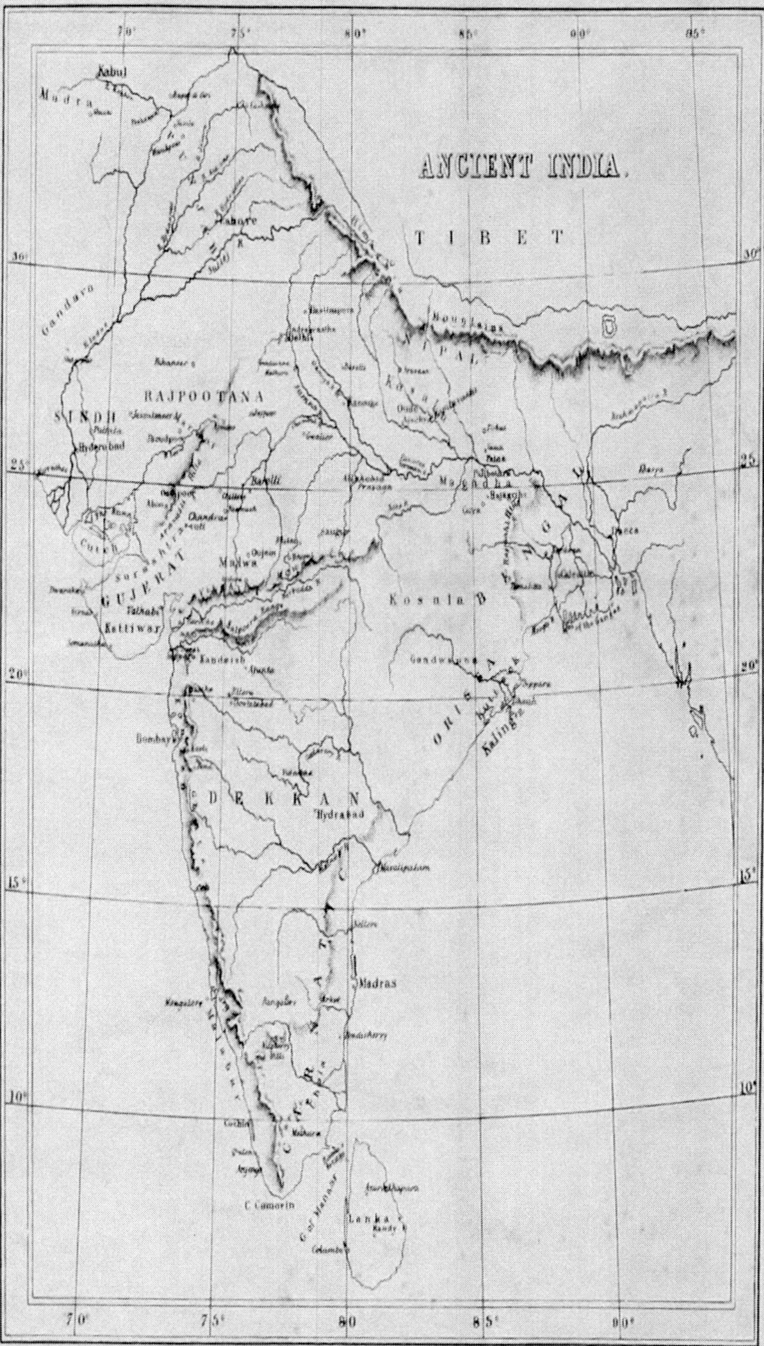

J & C Walker Litho

LIFE

IN

ANCIENT INDIA.

BY

MRS. SPEIR.

With a Map, and Illustrations drawn on Wood by

GEORGE SCHARF, JUN., F.S.A.

"Es ist immer das Land der Sehnsucht gewesen, und erscheint uns noch als ein Wunderreich, als eine verzauberte Welt."—HEGEL, *Philosophie der Geschichte: Indien.*

LONDON:

SMITH, ELDER, AND CO., CORNHILL.

SMITH, TAYLOR, AND CO., BOMBAY.

1856.

TO

H. H. WILSON, M.A., F.R.S.,

BODEN PROFESSOR OF SANSKRIT IN THE UNIVERSITY OF OXFORD,

This Volume is Dedicated

AS A

MARK OF RESPECT AND OBLIGATION.

PREFACE.

THE idea of writing a little Book on Ancient India first occurred to me whilst residing for a few years with my late husband in Calcutta. The interest we felt in the country and its inhabitants led us to study this subject in standard European works; but from day to day discoveries were being made of coins, inscriptions, and manuscripts, which quite changed the leading features of all extant histories, and at the same time translations from Eastern sources continually appeared, attracting English readers to their study. Since that period the 'Indische Alterthumskunde' of Professor Lassen has brought under review the researches of the present age in Indian Archæology; but whilst voluminous in facts and rich in scientific analysis, his volumes offer no specimens or translations of the ancient literature of India, the charm of which has induced some of the first European scholars to devote their lives to its study and elucidation. When therefore, after an interval of many years, I recurred to the studies which I had formerly shared with Mr. Speir, I did not attempt to translate Lassen's Work, but aimed rather at making generally known whatever had been most attractive to myself, hoping thus to diffuse the interest I felt, and notify the sources from which further information might be drawn.

In fulfilling this design many friends have assisted me; and although I can mention here but few of those friends, I trust that all will believe me thankful. From the Libraries of the Asiatic Society and the East India House I have been liberally supplied with books for reference. To the kindness of Mr. H. T. Prinsep, Dr. Royle, and Mr. Norris I am indebted for encouragement and assistance in various ways; and for the valuable information, advice, and correction which Professor Wilson has most kindly given, I can but imperfectly express my thanks.

My obligations to amateur artists are more obvious, and will be especially acknowledged by all those who appreciate the sketches of my accomplished friend Mr. William Prinsep.

C. S.

Gloucester Terrace, Hyde Park,
August, 1856.

CONTENTS.

CHAPTER IV.

CHAPTER V.

CHAPTER VI.

CHAPTER VII.

CHAPTER VIII.

CHAPTER IX.

BOOK II.

Buddhism.

CHAPTER I.

CHAPTER II.

CHAPTER III.

CHAPTER IV.

CHAPTER V.

BOOK III.

CHAPTER I.

CHAPTER II.

CHAPTER III.

CHAPTER IV.

CHAPTER V.

CHAPTER VI.

ILLUSTRATIONS,

DRAWN ON WOOD BY GEORGE SCHARF, JUN., F.S.A., FROM ORIGINAL SKETCHES, PAINTINGS, ETC.

INTRODUCTION.

"To the east a lovely country wide extends,
India, whose borders the wide Ocean bounds:
On this the Sun, new rising from the main,
Smiles pleased, and sheds its radiant beam."

INDIA, the land of gold and sunshine, has ever been regarded as a region of Romance. In the tales of our childhood magicians and jugglers move amid scenes oppressed by the luscious scents, gay with the flowers, and sparkling with the precious gems and fabrics of India. In the classic page, India is the mysterious bourn to which point the fabulous expeditions of Bacchus and Sesostris; and when history emerges from primeval haze, we see India as the gorgeous eastern boundary of Earth, where princes enthroned on elephants offer tribute in solid gold. Nor is there less romance in India's natural history and geography; in the golden ant-hills of Herodotus, in the tree he notes as sheltering ten thousand troops, or his rivers too wide for the eye to reach across. Romance is inherent in the country, steeping even the science, metaphysics, and mythology of this wonderful country in its rainbow-tinted hues.

The name India is not that by which it is known to its own inhabitants, but is first met with in Herodotus and other Greek writers. It comes from the Sanskrit, *Sindhu*, ocean. First, the name was transferred from the ocean to the river, and then to the country and the people bordering the river, on the banks of which the first Hindu settlements were made. Indus, Ind, or Sindh, therefore signifies the river and adjacent country forming the western boundary of India. The Persians wrote the word with an H, but the Greeks omitted the aspirate; and at present we use both forms, only geographers and historians consider it more correct to limit Hindustan to that part of the country which lies to the north of the Vindhya Mountains, and to apply the name of India to the country north and south, from the Himalaya to Cape Comorin. The Arabians, not aware that Sindh and Hind were the same word in different languages, thought they were two descendants of Noah, who extended their settlements in this direction, and gave each his name to his own respective territories.*

To the north, India is bounded by the Himalaya Mountains, to the west by the Indus, and to the east by the Brahmaputra, but not strictly, for some of the Bengal pro-

* Lassen, 'Indische Alterthumskunde,' vol. i. pp. 2, 3.

vinces stretch beyond; to the south it is a peninsula jutting out into the ocean. This vast territory is exceedingly varied, and details of its physical features, inhabitants, and governments, would furnish most interesting subjects for investigation; but a very slight sketch is alone admissible at present, and, in making this, we find it an assistance to separate India into four sections.

I. The Punjaub, Sindh, Rajputana, Malwa, Guzerat, and the Nerbudda River.

II. The Peninsula.

III. Plains of the Ganges.

IV. Bengal.

This must be acknowledged to be a somewhat arbitrary proceeding, but it has the advantage of introducing us, first, to the earliest haunts of the Sanskrit-speakers; second, to the coasts and forests earliest known to Hindu commerce and literature; third, to the scenes of most ancient Brahmanical celebrity; and fourth, to the focus of modern British wealth and government.

It might assist us in remembering these divisions, if we imagined India sketched out as the rude outline of a human figure; such a figure as that, for instance, of Orion or Aldebaran, in the maps of the stars. The Himalaya Mountains would be the head; Sindh, Malwa, etc. would be a bare right arm, with projecting ornaments and weapons; the Peninsula would give the bony legs, partially visible, as the Ghats of Southern India; the basin of the Ganges would represent smooth folds of drapery falling over the left arm; and, lastly, Bengal, with the Ganges divided into many streams, would be the hand of our figure, with extended fingers.

I. The Punjaub down to the Nerbudda.

We begin then with the Punjaub, the border-land between India and many other countries; as India and Assyria, India and Persia, India and Bactria, and, we may almost say, between India and Tartary. At the present day it is occupied by a border population, made up of many races, with a mixed religion, half Hindu and half Mohammedan. The name Punjaub comes from *punj*, five, and *ab*, waters,—five rivers flowing through this district. Below the Punjaub the five streams unite as the Indus, which flows through Sindh, attended by a border of fertility, and forming a productive delta at its junction with the sea. Barren sand is however the characteristic not only of Sindh but of the contiguous countries towards the East. Here we find Jessalmere shining out as a green favoured island, and the fertile strip of Cutch stretching like a bridge between Sindh and Guzerat. A salt river, called the Looni, enriches Marwar, and, after a course of three hundred miles, is lost in the Run of Cutch, a fen formed by its deposits and those of other salt streams from the desert of Dhat. This Run, or marsh, which is a hundred and fifty miles in length and about seventy in breadth, has but one green spot for the refreshment of travellers or their camels. In the dry season it is one great glaring sheet of salt, full of quicksands, and subject to mirage, called "winter castles" by the Rajpoot inhabitants. During the rains the dazzling crystal melts, and presents a dreary spectacle of dirty water, through which the camels wade, even to their saddle-girths.

To the eastward again of these deserts we find the

Aravalli Hills, and "immediately in front of the broadest part stands the noble mountain of Aboo, rising as abruptly from the sandy plain," says Mr. Fergusson, "as an island from the ocean. It seems," he continues, "one vast bubble of granite, that has boiled up from the bottom of what then was the sea, the summit of which, in cooling, has sunk back on itself, forming a valley on its summit, six or eight miles long, which offers a most enchanting contrast to the deserts below." Our author doubts, indeed, if the whole world contains another spot so exquisitely beautiful as the little "Jewel Lake" on the summit of Mount Aboo.*

Sir John Malcolm has gathered all the lands immediately eastward of Sindh into a group, which he calls Central India. It comprehends nearly eight degrees of latitude and nine of longitude, and has a superficial area of 350,000 square miles. Jessalmere and Marwar are the level portions, whilst Ajmere, Oodeypore, and Malwa, etc., form a table-land 2000 feet above the level of the sea, of which the Aravalli Hills are the western and the Vindhyas the southern rampart. This lofty plateau has two declivities; one from west to east, towards the Betwa River, and the other from south to north, towards the Jumna. The Aravalli chain, so distinguished a feature in Central India, is remarkable for its peaks of rose-coloured quartz, and the dazzling slates and schists, which furnish roofs for houses and temples. The insulated hills in the same district are formed of sandstone, capped with ironstone and basalt. Sangor, Chittore, Ajmere, etc., are natural fortresses of this description, requiring little aid from art beyond a low parapet round the top; and sandstone is so abundant, that

* Fergusson's 'Ancient Architecture of Hindustan,' p. 39.

whole towns may be seen in which the poorest houses are built of pure white freestone.

The climate of this lofty region is remarkable for salubrity, the air dry and invigorating, and the precious annual rains secured by intercepting hills and towns. From the earliest times Malwa has produced luxuriant crops of cotton, wheat, sugar, vegetable oils, and ginger; and to these may now be added tobacco and opium. In 1847–8 the produce of opium was 1,638,000 lbs., and in 1848–9 this quantity was nearly doubled, or about three million pounds.* But many as are the attractions of Central India, it was until lately but little known. Bishop Heber found many parts destitute of roads, or, if any road had been attempted, it was a mere track, impassable for wheeled carriages, and leading through such deep gullies and steep ravines, as rendered roads impossible. The perpetual warfare and lawless condition of its inhabitants presented yet greater difficulties to a traveller; and the country was becoming year by year more desolate, until, in 1818, Sir John Malcolm undertook its government. Then within five years the whole aspect of things changed: "it was made worth while to acquire industrious habits," and, says Bishop Heber, "from a wilderness it was changed into a garden."

The same happy effect has followed from good government in Mairwara, a district of Ajmere, lying in the Aravalli Hills, to the north of Mount Aboo. About one hundred miles in length and twenty-five or thirty in breadth, Mairwara, though small, has become justly celebrated as the theatre of noble and successful experiments. When first it came into the possession of the British, it was the abode and

* M'Culloch's Commercial Dictionary, article *Opium*.

resort of lawless freebooters,—a place in which female infants were destroyed, wives and widowed mothers sold by husbands and sons, and where life and property required the protection of arms and fortifications. In unequal portions it was divided between the East India Company, Jodpore, and Oodeypore, and the consent of the two native States was necessary before it could be placed under British management. Happily this was obtained, and Colonel Hall was appointed to the charge of the district in 1822. His first measure was to form a local battalion, in which the youthful Mairs learned discipline, and to attach themselves to a Government which treated them with confidence and kindness. This body of native troops, ready to coerce the refractory, added materially to Colonel Hall's good influence; predatory habits were reformed, infanticide ceased, and the slavery of women greatly decreased. One of Mairwara's chief misfortunes was deficiency of water; having no river, it depends entirely upon the annual rains, which come down from the hills in torrents. These were soon exhausted, and the crops, in consequence, most precarious. To remedy this evil, Colonel Hall had seven great tanks made or repaired; but in 1835 his labours were interrupted by ill-health, and he quitted India. His successor was Colonel Dixon, under whose beneficent superintendence improvements have yet more abounded. He induced the people to sink wells, to throw earthen embankments across hollows, to erect stone dykes to retain the rain-water on the soil, and to cultivate waste lands. Within twelve years jungles were cleared, one hundred and six new hamlets located in their place, a town called Nya Nugger built as a mart for commerce, an annual fair established, and wells and waterworks innumerable completed, some of these being works of considerable skill and expense. The contiguous little state of Ajmere has shared in these improvements, sympathy becoming established between the authorities and the cultivators, litigiousness ceasing, and industry generally prevailing; so that in 1848 Ajmeer was no longer an abode of banditti, but bidding fair to rival Mairwara in peace and prosperity. The minute attention here bestowed upon these districts is out of all proportion to the momentary glance given to larger territories; but the temptation is, that Malwa under Sir John Malcolm, and Mairwara under Colonel Dixon, stand out as most encouraging examples of what Anglo-Saxon government and Christian civilization can effect in the wildest parts of India.

We must now proceed to Guzerat, a province considerably varied in appearance. The eastern coast of Kattiwar is strewn with boulders of granite, rounded as by the action of water; amongst these some light-coloured granite peaks arise, which are supposed to mark the site of the celebrated missing city of Valabhi. After flourishing under the Gupta kings for some centuries since our era, it was swallowed up by the sea, and, owing to volcanic action, its remains are now discovered further inland than its original site.

Trees are deficient in this sandy district, the chief produce of which is the coarse kinds of grain, upon which horses thrive, the Kattiwar horses being much in demand for the British cavalry. In the western portion of this peninsula vegetation is luxuriant, and the banyan-trees gigantic, especially that famous specimen called the Cubbeer

Burr, which has a circumference measuring eighteen hundred feet. Mangoes are abundant, and particular ledges of rock at Girnar are named the "One Thousand" and the "Hundred Thousand," from the numbers of their mango-trees. Guzerat is also rich in cities and in a sea-coast favourable to commerce, and has such resources, that in the reign of the Emperor Akber (A.D. 1556 to 1586) it maintained 67,375 cavalry and 8900 infantry.

We have now arrived at the scenes of most interesting incidents in the Mahratta wars, and it is very tempting to touch upon modern history, but we must refrain; Ancient India is our appointed subject, and our present ramble is merely permitted as an introduction to the country in which old Veda worshippers, venerable Brahmans, and original Buddhists once lived and flourished. We want at present to learn geographical features, and must not therefore omit to note that the lord of the floods in Central India is the Chumbul, which, rising in Malwa, flows toward the north. It is at first much impeded by rocks and shallows, but, after breaking through the Mokundra range into Harrowti, it becomes a fine deep stream, and runs a course of above five hundred miles. Malwa is bounded to the south by the Vindhya Hills, which stretch all across the centre of India, separating the peninsula from Hindustan. This mountain-chain seldom rises higher than 2000 feet, and several cities in Malwa have been built nearly at this height, Indore being 1998 feet above the level of the sea, and Neemutch 1476 feet; but at the south the declivity is precipitous, and gives the hills the character of a buttress or rampart protecting Malwa, at the bottom of which flows the river Nerbudda (or Narmada, from *narma*, pleasure, and *da*, she who bestows). This is a beautiful stream, with wild romantic banks of white marble, sandstone, and other craggy rocks, which sometimes impede its course and send it foaming down in cataracts. The Nerbudda is much loved by the Hindus, and not being navigable, the superstitions attached to it remain unshaken by the tide of commercial enterprise. Colonel Sleeman, who was long resident at Jubbulpore, observed a marked difference between the degree of enlightenment of the natives worshipping the Nerbudda and those living near the Ganges, and observed that, whilst the Ganges yearly loses somewhat of its sacred character, the Nerbudda as constantly gains increase of sanctity, and the stories told seventy years ago by Forbes are repeated by Sleeman as the favourite traditions of the present period. One of these is not without beauty and interest, as exhibiting the playful fancy and vivid personification pervading the religious conceptions of the region. It is briefly as follows:—

The river Sone courted the Nerbudda in the high lands of Omerkuntuk, in which they both take their rise. The rivers slowly advanced to meet each other, when the Nerbudda, getting impatient, sent the little stream Jhola, the barber's daughter, to report upon the appearance of the bridegroom. The Sone supposed Jhola to be the bride, and fell in love with her accordingly, whereat the Nerbudda became enraged, and turning short round to the west, has flowed ever since in that direction, forming splendid cataracts sometimes four hundred feet in depth; at times she expands into a broad stream, and then again contracts herself within walls not more than a hundred feet apart. As she approaches the sea her turbulence is calmed, and, flowing placidly through Guzerat, she reaches the ocean in the Gulf of Cambay; whereas had she joined her false suitor, the Sone, she would with him have joined the Ganges near Patna, and thus have made her way to the Bay of Bengal. This river is still talked of and thought of by Hindus as a real being,—" not," Colonel Sleeman observes, " as a representation of Deity, but as itself a power and intelligence; and," he adds, " it is only in India that we can understand how every individual of a whole community of many millions can address a fine river as a living being, a sovereign princess, who hears and understands all they say, and exercises a kind of local superintendence over their affairs, without a single temple in which her image is worshipped, or a single priest to profit by the delusion."*

Both the Vindhya and the lower range called the Satpoora Hills contain extensive beds of coal and iron beneath sandstone, thus offering facilities for the spirit of engineering that distinguishes our era. The valleys are rich with a soil of decomposed basalt, much of which is unfortunately washed away each year by the rains and lost in the sea.

II. The Peninsula.

We have now entered upon our second section or division, the whole country below the Vindhya Hills being reckoned by geographers as the Peninsula. This is called by the Hindus themselves Dekkan, meaning in Sanskrit south (*Dakshin*); but in common European discourse the word Dekkan is now more frequently restricted to the high table-land, the centre of the peninsula between the river Tapti and the Kistnah. This peninsula, or Dekkan,

* Rambles and Recollections, vol. i. ch. 3.

is divided from the north by well-marked boundaries. We have already noticed the Vindhya Hills, and the river Nerbudda at their base. To the south of the Nerbudda rise the Satpoora Hills, and to the south of this second range flows the river Tapti, thus completing the fourfold girdle thrown around the waist of India. The Satpoora Mountains are scarcely so lofty as the Vindhya, and are similar in geological structure, but have a bolder outline, and rise into peaks, the highest of which, "about 2500 feet above the sea, consists of amygdaloid and greenstone (which composes more than half the hill), and at the top basalt."* This same formation of basalt, obtruded into older strata, extends from the Aravalli Hills, a little south of Agra, through Central India and the Peninsula, down to Cape Comorin.

It is a marked feature of Southern India that the coast on each side is bordered by lofty mountains, from 4000 to 6000 feet in height. They rise with abrupt declivities one above another, like a succession of walls or terraces, with bold well-defined outlines. This appearance of gigantic steps leading from the table-land of the interior down to the sea-coast, has given the hills the name of Ghats, because they resemble the handsome flight of steps called Ghats which are built on the banks of rivers and tanks for the convenience of Hindu daily worship. On the western coast the Ghats are higher, and here they approach within forty or fifty miles of the sea. The narrow strip of country thus left along the coast is divided into several distinct districts. From Surat to a distance below Bombay it is called the Northern and Southern Concans; below these we find

* Hamilton's Gazetteer, vol. ii. p. 510.

Canara, containing the famous Portuguese settlement of Goa. It is about this point, midway between Cambay and Travancore, that the hills attain their greatest elevation of 6000 feet; and in the alpine region of Coorg, above Mangalore, grows the finest sandal-wood, equally prized in modern as in ancient times. The Sandal is an elegant tree, which can be cultivated in the plains, where it attains a considerable size, but the wood is inferior, and has little scent compared with that produced upon the hills.

To the south of Canara the Malabar coast extends until it is lost in the district of Cochin; sometimes indeed the whole western coast is called Malabar, but not when aiming at geographical accuracy. The climate of this coast is delightfully cooled by sea-breezes; and Baroche, Surat, Bombay, Mangalore, Tellicherry, etc. are, in consequence, favourite places of European residence. Calicut and Ponani, in the south, are among the towns from which considerable exports are made, chiefly of pepper, which is extensively cultivated, the vines being trained over mango and jack-fruit trees on the lower ledges of the hills. In the plains rice is grown, and far up the mountains, at a height of from 2000 to 4000 feet, grows the best teak timber, far above any town or village, and difficult to remove after it has been felled. The woodcutters are obliged to spend the winter and the early part of the year in these lonely forests, that the timber may be ready for the rains of June and July, this being the only period at which the mountain-streams are sufficiently full to float it down. A break occurs in the hills at Ponani, through which the river Ponani takes its course, and is joined by many smaller streams and torrents which come directly from the teak district. The same forests produce a variety of other large timber-trees the names and qualities of which are not fully known, although some of them are occasionally used by the Calicut ship-builders; but the present opinion is that teak alone fully repays all the difficulty and expense of export to other countries.

South of Ponani the Ghats again rise, extending their chain through Cochin and Travancore to the extreme point of Cape Comorin. The scenery of this southern district is generally beautiful, but of Anjengo and Quilon Forbes* writes in perfect raptures: the hills, the woods, the flowers, all contributing to the enchantment, and even the abundance of land-crabs and of lizards, with bright scarlet caps, assisting to give it a peculiar character. Amongst flowers Forbes particularly mentions the *Gloriosa superba* as growing everywhere like a weed which cannot be exterminated. This magnificent creeper is found in the forests of the Western as well as of the Eastern Ghats; its flowers, when first blown, are of a pale greenish colour, which the next day changes to a splendid scarlet. Although a lily, with reflex petals like the Turk's-cap, it climbs to the tops of lofty trees, and is one of the most striking objects in an Indian forest.

The ports of Cochin and Allapee are chiefly important owing to their ship-building and exportation of teak timber. These are the only towns of any consideration in the extreme south, over which great forests full of elephants and other wild animals appear and spread; but less is known of this corner of the land than even of other parts of India.

Returning then to Ponani, we shall find that where the

* Forbes, 'Oriental Memoirs.'

Western Ghats break away from the south they retreat, as it were, backwards, and join the hills which have come down the eastern coast of the peninsula, as if Ponani had once been intended to be the southern limit of India, or as if an earthquake had broken off Cape Comorin and patched it on again below the Nilgherry and Wynaad Mountains, which form the southern extremity of the Eastern Ghats. These hills are further removed from the sea than those on the west coast, and leave room for the plains of the Carnatic, which are hotter than any other place in India; but as they present a soil peculiarly favourable for the cultivation of rice, they were early inhabited by Hindus from Northern India, and the whole country is rich in ruins of ancient magnificence, which existed many centuries before the unfortunate Nabobs of Arcot and Nellore had commenced the acquisition or display of that distinguished wealth which caused their ruin.

To the south-east of the Carnatic lies the island of Ceylon, said to be composed almost exclusively of primitive rocks, and to show no traces of a volcano; it abounds in rivers, and is celebrated for its cinnamon gardens and for the size and profusion of its cocoas and talipot palms. The climate is so moderate that roses, mignonette, and pinks are almost as sweet as in England, whilst all the splendid lilies of the tropics grow wild. Coffee plantations succeed well, and coffee-trees of great age and size are numerous: they were introduced into the island by the Dutch, and were at first cultivated for their flowers.

In the earliest days Ceylon was celebrated for its pearl-fishery, the pearls being whiter than those in the Gulf of Ormuzd; but for eight years past there have been no pearls, and apparently in consequence of what was intended as a boon. Between Ceylon and the coast of India runs a reef of rocks, some of which being below water, allow unloaded ships to sail over them; but since it was very inconvenient to unload and reload, or to make the circuit of the island, instead of going through the Straits of Manaar, it was proposed to blast the rocks and deepen the passage. This commenced, and the oysters appeared to receive it as a signal to quit, for never since have pearls been found on Rama's Bridge; but a more matter-of-fact interpretation is that the fisheries had been too frequent, and the exhausted oysters ceased in consequence to form pearls. Three years is ascertained to be the shortest allowable interval; and so long as this rule is adhered to, it is not believed that the passage of ships through the Straits will at all interfere with the prosperity or productiveness of the oyster colony.

To the north of Madras and Nellore is the mouth of the Kistnah, the river upon which Haiderabad is placed; and above this flows the Godavery, the source of which is far away on the other side of India, making the town of Nassik a place of peculiar sanctity. To the north of Godavery extends the province of Orissa, in which we shall find the black pagodas and the temple of Juggunnat; and to the west of Orissa, on the high land between the Ghats, is the province of Gondwana, a great part of which consists of dense forests yet unreclaimed. From Gondwana we pass into Bundelkund, a division of Allahabad, and thus we arrive at the third of our arbitrary sections of India.

But before entering upon the more open, civilized, and cultivated lands of Upper India and Bengal, we must notice the remnants of primitive inhabitants which still linger in the woods and fastnesses of Central India and the Peninsula. Schlegel observes that "in the background of old, mighty, and civilized nations we can almost always trace the primeval inhabitants of the country, who, dispossessed of their territory, have been reduced to servitude by their conquerors, or have gradually been incorporated with them. These primitive inhabitants, when compared with their later or more civilized conquerors, appear in general rude and barbarous; though we find among them a certain number of ancient customs and arts which by no means tend to confirm the notion of an original and universal savage state of nature." Such people may still be seen in India, sometimes half hidden by the hills and forests, "hanging like a fringe," as Professor Lassen says, "upon the borders of the cultivated plains." Small in stature, with little eyes and flat noses, they have no caste, although extensively divided and subdivided into clans and tribes, and no idols, although their superstitions are various. They are not without industry and ingenuity, and their mountain-huts often possess a considerable air of comfort. They are a people without a history and without a formed language; and, having been obliged to recede before the superior force and intelligence of the Hindus, or Aryan race, they have taken refuge in dense forests or on barren rocks, and have fallen in many cases far below the grade to which they had previously attained. This race is now widely scattered and divided, and the Gonds, the Bheels, the Koolies, and the other people of whom it is composed, have nothing in common, and cannot understand each other's dialect or jargon. The Koolies in Guzerat are a tall, athletic race particularly black. The Bheels in Malwa are also black, but short in stature, with thick rugged hair and beards. The Bheels are the most important and numerous of all the aboriginal tribes, and are mentioned by Sir John Malcolm* with much consideration. He regrets that their dispersion over "rugged mountains, their extreme ignorance and prejudices, and their repugnance to confidential intercourse with all but their own tribe," have prevented our obtaining any full or correct knowledge of their history. When conquered and driven south by the Rajputs, some became desperate freebooters; but others quietly submitted, and live now amongst their conquerors, partly as cultivators of the soil and partly as village watchmen. Their chief religion seems to consist in propitiatory offerings and sacrifices to the minor Hindu deities, whom they especially invoke to save them from small-pox. They eat the flesh not only of buffaloes, but also of cows when it can be obtained, and are particularly fond of intoxicating drinks; often however both food and drink are wholly derived from the flowers and fruit of the Mahua-tree (*Bassia latifolia*), a timber-tree of moderate size, which abounds in the forests of Malwa. The flowers are of a pale pink colour, and when dried resemble raisins in flavour and appearance. The fruit—a small nut, containing an astringent oil—is palatable when roasted, and the fleshy calyx is pressed and fermented into a spirituous liquor.† The Bheels have among themselves many traces of former importance, and assert that their leaders have been as much distinguished by character as by wealth. At Neemuch, Bishop Heber says, the Rajputs virtually acknowledge that most of their principal cities and fortresses were founded

* Malcolm's Central India.

† Elphinstone's History of India, pp. 6, 193.

by Bheel chiefs; and a custom is said to exist, by which a Rajput on attaining power or office is marked in the forehead with blood taken from the heel or thumb of a Bheel. Owing to various changes in their condition they are now divided into several classes, more or less civilized. Some lead a half-savage life, shooting from amongst the long grass with bows and arrows, which they hold with their feet. Their bows are made of split bamboos, and the arrows are the same, but with iron heads; of bamboos also they construct their huts, with neat projecting roofs, and doors with hinges similar to the lid of a basket. Although very uncultivated, and often a drunken, thievish set, Sir John Malcolm gives them credit for some virtues in which the polished Hindus are deficient: their word is more to be depended on, and the position of their women is superior. In all the recent reforms the Bheel women have acted a prominent part, and have invariably been the advocates of order and industry. In Guzerat Bheels and Koolies are uniformly preferred for the service of the police, and as *durwans* to watch at the gates of gentlemen's houses and gardens. There are Bheels also in Candeish, south of the Nerbudda; and this tribe had the good fortune, between 1825 and 1835, to be under the civilizing influences of Colonel Outram, who, after sufficient severity to convince them of British strength, went amongst them unarmed, and excited their enthusiasm by his skill and activity in hunting; and lastly, in conjunction with Colonel Ovens, he taught them to obey law, and submit to be trained into a regularly organized local militia.

In Gondwana and south of the Nerbudda we find the

Gonds, who inhabit the rocky banks of rivers and forests which are almost inaccessible. They are jet-black, dirty, and forbidding in appearance, short in stature, with small noses, thick lips, broad foreheads, and little deep-set red eyes, black teeth and hair, which is described as in some cases long and black, but occasionally red, and almost woolly; making a near approach to the Negro type of the Austral-Indians and the natives of the Andaman Islands. Some of the Gonds are quite uncovered, others, living in the neighbourhood of a more advanced people, become a little civilized; but in general they lead a life of poverty, dwelling in miserable huts, surrounded by their swine, and buffaloes if so fortunate as to possess them, and poultry, in the rearing of which they excel. They are said to be a quiet people, inoffensive, with the exception of their occasional custom of child-stealing; their rude perverted notion of religion seeming to consist in nothing beyond the worship of demons, to whom children were supposed to be a necessary offering. They have no priests, and pay no reverence to Brahmans.

Gondwana verges on Orissa, parts of which are inhabited by three different tribes of Aborigines,—Khonds, Koles, and Sourahs. With the Khonds of the hills the British Government first came into close contact in 1835, when waging war with the rebellious Rajah of Goomsur. When the war ceased, Captain Macpherson was employed to make surveys; and being at a subsequent period appointed to suppress human sacrifices amongst the Khonds, he was enabled to acquire accurate and detailed information concerning their dreadful superstitions, and this he has embodied in a valuable contribution to the Royal Asiatic

Society's Journal, published in the spring of 1852. Captain Macpherson takes away all the softening veils which ignorance usually interposes between ourselves and the religious customs of rude heathens, and exhibits human sacrifice and female infanticide as parts of a long-established worship; recognizing first a Supreme Deity, and secondly, a female spirit created by the Supreme Deity, but which had turned evil, had rebelled herself, and had induced mankind to rebel, and to worship her with human sacrifice. The victims offered to this evil goddess are called Meriahs: they must be the absolute property of those who offer them, and are usually stolen, or bought whilst children from other aboriginal tribes, or from impoverished Hindus; but some instances occur in which the Khonds themselves sell their children. The victims are led blindfold into the village, and lodged at the house of the chief—in fetters, if grown-up, but if children they are allowed to go free; and there are usually so many of them as to give each a reasonable hope that he may never be required in sacrifice. These unfortunate youths are reared with every indulgence, being considered as more divine than human, and few cases occur of their attempting to escape; because whilst the chances are fearfully against success, they are taught that if they die as victims they are certain of happiness hereafter, but if they escape they are certain to die by dire disease and to have no future bliss. These horrid sacrifices are only made on occasions of unusual calamity: they are accompanied by drunken feasting and frantic dances; and "in some parts of Goomsur where this practice prevails, small rude images of beasts and birds in clay and wood are made in great numbers for this festival and stuck on poles,—a practice the origin or meaning of which is not at all clear."*

The "Meriahs," or victims, may be either boys or girls, and of any race, except, Captain Macpherson thinks, Brahmans, who are supposed to have been already devoted to the gods. Many of the pleasing, intelligent little girls in Mrs. Wilson's Orphan Refuge School, near Calcutta, had been rescued by the British army from this dreadful fate, and the daring escape of others has been the theme of song. One sect amongst the Khonds abhors human sacrifice, but equally with the other tribes believes in Boora Pennu, the supreme god; and in Tari Pennu, the perverse earth-goddess, who is jealous of the human race, impedes the government of Boora Pennu, causes every description of evil, and must be invoked with deep awe and reverence.

More gentle forest tribes are described as inhabiting the southern extremity of the Peninsula. Mr. Taylor, of Madras, mentions several in the Dindigul district who possess bows and arrows, but appear to live chiefly on roots, honey, and reptiles; and the eminent botanist Roxburgh alludes to equally poor denizens of the neighbouring Wynaad hills, whose clothing is made from the bark of a tree named *Sterculia guttata.*† But the most interesting and pleasing of all the Indian aborigines are the Tudas, inhabiting the Nilgherry Hills, where they were discovered about thirty years ago. The unwholesome jungle at the base of these hills probably prevented their being earlier explored, for although in 1819 Mr. Leschenhault succeeded in ascending from the Coimbatore side to the west near Ponani, he speaks of the route as scarcely practicable, owing to thorny shrubs, tigers, bears, and wild dogs.

* J. R. A. S. vol. xiii. part 2, p. 247.

† Roxb. vol. iii. p. 148.

Having once got through these savage lines of defence, he no sooner found himself in the upper regions than he was astonished, as all other travellers have been, by "the noble race of natives" inhabiting the Naad district. They are called Tudas, or Tomwars, or Thodawars. They are a tall, athletic people, with fine symmetric features, described as Roman, but some amongst them are said to have a Jewish cast of features.* Dwelling at a height of 7000 or 8000 feet above the level of the sea, in an atmosphere cooled and refreshed by the monsoon, they enjoy a climate of perpetual spring; and the consequent great salubrity is supposed to account, in some degree, for their superior physical appearance, which is unexampled amongst tribes not boasting of Sanskrit (Aryan or Hindu) origin. Unfortunately the tribe is very small, and constantly diminishing, and does not appear to number above six hundred men. They keep flocks and herds, the men attending to the dairy; and they till the ground, raising crops of wheat, barley, oats, and several other kinds of grain.

Other travellers speak of the Tudas as having large full speaking eyes, pleasing form, and long fine hair, parted on the crown of the head and falling on all sides in natural locks, a grave, composed bearing, cheerful temper, and herculean strength.† The Chola and other Nilgherry tribes look up to the Tudas as their lords and superiors; and the Curumbars, who are a wretched-looking people, of small stature, thin hair, and watery eyes, are said to be nearly allied in race, and to derive their present abject appearance from misery caused by the oppression of more fortunate tribes. The Curumbars thus exhibit the condition of a people fallen from comparative civilization, which

* Hough's Letters, p. 63.

† Harkness.

is the worst fate that history depicts, for people thus fallen are usually exhausted and hopeless; and this is in general true of all the aboriginal tribes in India. One peculiarity observed amongst the Tudas is their tumuli, of which we shall have occasion to speak hereafter: some of these are marked by circles of rude stones on a level with the ground, whilst around others the stones are larger, and raised two or three feet; similar tombs are often met with, where there is no remnant of either people or towns to which they can be traced, and we can only suppose that they are monuments of races in some degree allied to the yet existing Gonds and Tudas. There are still current in the Peninsula of India several languages which, although largely intermixed with Sanskrit terms in consequence of Hindu conquest and civilization, are nevertheless of a distinct family of language. They are chiefly the Tamul, the Telinga, the Karnata, and the Malaya: collectively they are called Tamul languages; and the growing opinion of our guides in ethnology and philology is, that the rude remnant of hill and forest tribes, and the comparatively civilized inhabitants of Nagpore and the Malabar coast, etc., may be classed together as people who did not speak Sanskrit, and had not the Aryan and Indo-European conformation; people, in fact, more nearly allied with Scyths than with Hindus.

III. Plains of the Ganges.

But we are lingering too long in woods and wilds, and must hasten to travel up to the open country intervening between the Himalaya and the Vindhya Hills, where lie the fertile plains, which we ventured to represent as smooth folds of drapery, covering the left arm of our ideal India. These rich plains are well watered by the Ganges, its allies and tributaries, and are free comparatively from wood or jungle; although they have been under cultivation probably two thousand years, they are still luxuriant, and their productiveness requires little aid from art. Amongst the crops now raised are wheat and rice, indigo and ginger, sugar and cotton, roses, jessamine, and sweet grasses; and the trees are the oleander, magnolia, *Butea frondosa, Erythrina*, and others innumerable, of equal scent or beauty.

In these highly favoured plains, we do not look in vain for signs of ancient India's most prosperous towns, some of which were on sites now occupied by Oude, on the river Gogra; Kanoge, sixty-five miles west-north-west from Lucknow; Delhi, on the Jumna; and Allahabad, at the point where the Jumna and the Ganges join; and then descending the Ganges, we come to Benares, early celebrated as a school of learning, and a little lower down to Patna (the ancient Palibothra), not far from the junction of the Sone with the Ganges, and to Rajagriha in Bahar, a district famous for hot springs and holy shrines throughout Hindustan. One chief attraction of a town or village is a large and handsome tank, having in the centre of each side a wide flight of steps, surmounted by a portico. The porticoes are lofty covered gates, and with the steps attached are called Ghats, and are not only ornamental, but almost necessary to Hindu worship. Worshippers are required to bathe daily once or oftener, and after being exposed in the water to the full rays of a vertical sun, they seek the shelter of the portico to recite their prayers. To the Ghat also women come at noon and eventide, to fill their water-jars; and here they congregate, and enjoy a daily laugh and chat, so that a Ghat in India might almost be said to represent the village-green of England, as the place at which the neighbourhood holds its social gatherings or conversations. Amongst the singularities of Indian produce are the water-plants, which overspread the lakes and tanks; one of these, flowering in the rainy season, is called *Singhara*;* it has long stringy leaves and pure white flowers, which, like the *Victoria regina*, only expand late in the afternoon. The nuts or seeds of this plant are wholesome food, and so highly esteemed by the natives, that tanks in which it grows let for £10 or £14 per annum. The birds and flowers, the mountains, the animals, the rivers and the boats belonging to this region, are scarcely less interesting than its trees and towns. The little flycatcher sparkles in the sunshine as though its feathers were a glossy fabric shot with green and gold; peacocks flock into every cornfield, and in the same scene with birds of brilliant plumage, splendid flowers, sweet-scented grasses, and colossal trees, we have the elephant and the rhinoceros, the camel and the buffalo, and we might add the tortoise, the lizard, and the monkey. In the middle ground of our landscape stretches a dense line of forest, beneath which the fantastic epiphytes and air-plants sport their fairy forms; and above the forest, rising apparently in endless ranges, are seen the summits of the Himalaya, bearing their perpetual snowy mantles from 20,000 to 30,000 feet above the level of the sea.†

* Mrs. Hervey notices these plants as growing for miles together, in the lakes of Kashmir. *Sing*, she says, means horn, these water-nuts being horned.—Adventures in Tartary, vol. i. pp. 234–8. *Trapa bispinosa*, Roxb., vol. i. p. 428.

† Sleeman's 'Rambles and Recollections,' vol. i. p. 101.

IV. Bengal.

Gradually the plains of Hindustan lose their dry, free, open character. In Bengal, the Rajmahal Hills intrude, standing like piquets in advance of their main body, the Vindhya range; and here also the Ganges separates into several streams, three of which, the Jellinghy, the Bhagirathi, and the Martabanga, required at one time the constant attention of an engineer, who was called "Superintendent of the three Rivers," and whose annual occupation it was to repair the damage caused by the rains. The varying courses of the rivers is, indeed, one of the most striking features of Indian geography. In the rainy season a boat may sail over fields which but lately produced crops of cotton or indigo, and which the next season will probably produce the same; lands subject to inundation are even preferred for indigo-crops, although risk is run that the rains may come too soon and wash the whole away. Moisture, as well as heat, promotes the growth of this little trefoil; but the perfection of its seed requires a drier atmosphere than that of Bengal, and planters are in the habit of using seed ripened in the more westerly provinces. Below the Rajmahal Hills, Bengal is a perfect flat; and strictly speaking this district is not included in Hindustan, but still less does it belong to the Dekkan. It is a moist, alluvial soil, through which the Ganges flows in innumerable separate streams, one of these being the Hoogly, upon which Calcutta stands. All around the Bay of Bengal, for forty or fifty miles inland, the general character of the country is that of marshes, through which the mouths of the Ganges pour themselves into the sea. But these marshes are not like marshes in Europe, merely overgrown with reeds and rushes: the reeds of the Sunderbunds are bamboos, seventy feet high, lightly feathering above lofty trees of rich and heavy foliage, and thickly hemmed in below by an overgrown brushwood, infested by tigers. In some parts the ground is cleared for the manufacture of saltpetre and common salt, with which the whole soil is strongly impregnated, the basis being sand, with a substratum of clay and salt. Advancing inland, plantations of rice begin to appear, and the rivers, branching into numerous streams called Nullahs, make it easy to lay the fields periodically under water, and give the irrigation necessary for rice-crops. All vegetable produce is most abundant, and the lofty cocoa-nut, tamarind, jack-fruit, and many others, yielding the natives daily food, grow freely by the wayside. The plantain, with its broad leaves torn by the wind,* and the picturesque custard-apple, surround the native huts, whilst melons, gourds, and French beans overgrow the thatched roofs, and cover them with flowers. In Hindustan the native huts are built on open ground in compact towns or villages, and with tiled roofs; but in Bengal the roofs are covered with thatch, and whilst each cottage is separate, the whole village usually straggles through a jungle or thicket, the approach to which is by a narrow winding path, with high banks and hedges on each side, keeping out the little air that may be stirring, but so contrived apparently in order to prevent intrusion. These huts are very picturesque when seen singly, peeping from amongst their plantains and papaws and rose-apples, etc.; but in the outskirts of Calcutta, where they

* Called by the Arabs, ostrich feathers.

are necessarily crowded together, they look poor and comfortless, and are subject to continual conflagrations, which may be seen in the hot weather, illuminating the sky for seven or eight miles' distance.

Bengal is little mentioned in ancient Sanskrit literature; for the earliest Hindu merchants had their seaports on the eastern coast, and the earliest learned Brahmans held their schools or fixed their huts within sight of the mighty Himavat. Bengal cannot therefore boast of ancient buildings; but it has both temples and ruins in abundance, for a very few years will suffice to produce venerable-looking ruins in so moist an atmosphere; and these temples, some extensive, and others consisting of a single shrine, some shining in white plaster at the head of steps leading down to the river, and others placed in the picturesque seclusion of a grove, add greatly to the beauty of Bengal, which is a province by no means deficient in interest; but as it claims no special attention to archæology or ethnology, mineralogy or zoology, it leaves us free to note in passing the noble character of Indian trees. The most beautiful, and one of the best beloved both in ancient and modern times, is the *Jonesia Asoka,* which grows all over Hindustan, but may be seen in several gardens near Calcutta, and in the highest perfection in the Botanic Gardens, opposite Garden Reach.* It is the height of a moderate horse-chestnut, thick in foliage, and literally covered with heads of red flowers resembling the *Ixora;* only the colour is

* Mr. Fortune, in his second voyage to the East, saw the *Jonesia Asoka* in the Botanic Garden of Calcutta, and admired it more even than the splendid *Amherstia,* and is sure that, were it well known in England, fine specimens would be produced at our metropolitan flower-shows.—Tea Districts of China, p. 360.

more brilliant than even that of the *Ixora*, for it is not a fixed red, but every petal shades from scarlet into orange, and from the centre of each floret issue long red tassel-like anthers. The flowers are fragrant at night, which the Hindu poets do not fail to note, and they are so pre-eminently radiant, that for a gem to sparkle as the asoka-flower is not an uncommon image in Sanskrit poetry.

Another tree common all over India, bearing delicious-scented white flowers, is called by the natives Bakula, and by botanists *Mimusops Elengi*. It grows in many gardens near Calcutta, and also on the noble Barrackpore road made by Lord Wellesley, where splendid specimens of flowering-trees may be seen on either side. The *Adansonia*, celebrated as the largest tree the world produces, may also be seen in the Calcutta Botanic Gardens, where a tree not more than twenty-five years old was eighteen feet in circumference. These trees bear long flowers, snowy white, shaped like the *Datura*, but larger, which look most lovely, hanging as they do from the thick branches of a prodigious tree of soft wood, and of such awkward and clumsy aspect that the natives call it *gudd* (donkey). The teak, the sandalwood, the mahogany, and most of the trees for which India is famed, may be seen within the compass of this beautiful garden; but none of these timber-trees are indigenous in Bengal, and it seems doubtful whether so moist a climate will ever produce timber equal to that grown on the hills. Bengal is not, however, deficient in vegetation; and a Flora Bengalensis would be rich in trees and flowers of all shapes and sizes, from passion-flowers little larger than a wafer, up to the *Dillenia*, which may be said to look as a Spanish chestnut might if covered with a shower of magnificent white water-lilies.*

The banyan, which is, perhaps more than any other tree, characteristic of India, grows as freely in Bengal as elsewhere: its branches are usually the haunt of monkeys and the large bats called flying foxes, which feed upon its berries. A recollection of evening in Bengal brings these creatures to one's mind, flying in a single heavy file about a mile in length across the transient glow succeeding sunset.† The Peepal-tree is also of the fig tribe (*Ficus religiosa*), and is scarcely less noble in appearance. The leaf is heart-shaped, with a long taper point and a slender leaf-stalk, rustling in the wind. The roots of the peepal spread horizontally near the surface of the ground, and old peepal-trees often exhibit a great extent of bare roots, owing to the ground having been washed away; the trunks also lose their roundness with age, and become so full of ridges as to look like several trunks united: this tree is remarkable for the facility with which its seeds germinate, springing up in every crevice of brickwork, to which, if not speedily removed, their rapid growth causes great destruction. In India, in consequence, ruins and the peepal are as much associated in the mind as ruins and ivy are in England. And not only in brickwork does it spring unbidden, but its sprouts are often seen on other trees, and especially on

* To watch for the flowering of the trees, and observe the many freaks and endless varieties of vegetation, is one of the best pleasures of life in Calcutta, especially for those who have had the happiness of knowing the late Dr. Wallich, and have enjoyed the privilege of visiting the Botanic Gardens in his company.

† At a distance they might be casually mistaken for a flight of rooks; but their length of wing is much greater, six feet being sometimes the measure between the extended points.

the summit of the palmyra, where its berries or seeds are frequently dropped by birds. The peepal then sends its roots down outside the palmyra stem, round which they gradually form a case, until at length nothing is seen of the palmyra except the head, which appears to be growing in the midst of a peepal tree. When this occurs the joint tree becomes a very sacred object, modern Hindus regarding it as a divine marriage. Trees in India also grow together by simple contact, and trees half peepal and half banyan, or half peepal and half mango, are by no means uncommon; and in some cases the union is even purposely effected,—a notion at present prevailing in the central parts of India, that the fruit of a new mango plantation must not be tasted until an imaginary marriage has been performed between the mangoes and some other tree; and money must be spent and feasting carried on to as great an extent as if the marriage were a real one.*

Let us now imagine one of our countrymen making his first voyage to these Eastern territories, his mind well informed with all that the hints and the story-telling of classic and Indian history afford. As he enters the Bay

* Sleeman's 'Rambles and Recollections,' vol. i. pp. 41–43. The Peepal (*Ficus religiosa*) and the India-rubber tree (*Ficus elastica*) resemble the Banyan (which is *Ficus Indica*) in having a power of throwing out roots from the stem and branches. In the banyan these roots usually proceed from the outer branches, reach the ground, and become supports, giving occasionally to a single tree the effect of a little forest; in the peepal they are oftener seen dangling from the main stem; but both these and the India-rubber are alike in their tendency to throw out roots from the main stem as well as from the branches, and in the tendency which these roots have to run down the surface of the trunk and cohere either with it or with each other, giving a sculptural appearance which is extremely picturesque. This is described by the late lamented botanist, Mr. Griffith (of the East India Company's medical service), in a very interesting report on the caoutchouc

of Bengal he looks eagerly for the submerged city of Bali, and about thirty-five miles to the south of Madras a beautiful pagoda stands out upon a little peninsula of land. In passing the coast of Orissa he sees black specks, which he knows to be, first, the Temple of Juggunath, and secondly, the Black Pagoda; and he longs to see the more interesting and more ancient Temple of Bobaneswar, within fifteen miles of the town of Cuttack. The next land which meets the eye of the voyager is the island of Saugor, and then he knows that he has entered the broad mouth of the river Hoogly, and that the dark lines on the horizon are the heavy woods which fringe its banks. Immediately he feels transported into unreal life; scenes of a play, or dreams of Arabian Nights, or passages from Scripture, seem to be enacting in his presence. He sees Rebecca at the well, the sheep following the shepherd, two women grinding at one mill, etc. Presently signs of British wealth and energy appear: on his left hand the Botanic Garden, dear to all lovers of flowers as having been the residence of Roxburgh and Wallich, for a short time also of the lamented Griffith, and now of Dr. Thomson. Immediately

tree of Assam. "Very generally," he says, "this species, as well as some others, vegetates in other trees," the roots descend and form a network round the tree; "and at last a nearly solid and excessively firm cylinder is formed, which encloses, as it were in a case, the tree which originally protected the young seedling; in such a case the fig-tree has no trunk;" since what answers the purpose of a trunk "is an aggregation and coherence of roots, or growth in a descending direction. One may readily imagine such trees overtopping others, for if they vegetate on a tree sixty feet from its base, it is at once obvious that this distance is an actual gain in height over all the others. Such instances are perhaps the only ones in which epiphytes destroy the plants on which they grow." One of these trees measured seventy-four feet round the trunk, and was about one hundred feet in height.—*J. A. S. B.*, Feb. 1848.

above these gardens stands the Bishop's College, of which the learned Dr. Mill was Principal; and now the opposite bank is adorned with the beautiful villas of Garden Reach; then passing Kidderpore, the plain called the Maidan and its shaded, well-watered roads, to which every imaginable description of vehicle—barouche, palki, buggy, mail-coach, kranchy—bring their owners to enjoy the evening breeze, or "eat the air," in native phrase. Nor less varied are the boats, the panchways, dinghies, budgerows, schooners, cutters, steamboats, through which a ship from England makes (or used to make) its way, until the impatient passengers at length escaped, and, if they arrived in sunshine, were carried in palanquins up the steps of Chandpaul Ghat, having already caught sight of Government House, the Town-hall, the Cathedral, and the Ochterlony monument.

A former Governor-General is said to have declared that he had learned more of India during the one day spent in sailing up the Hoogly, than in all his previous years of Eastern study; and no doubt there is in India an atmosphere of richness, producing a tranquillity which can neither be expressed nor imparted. Quietude is as characteristic of the Hindu as activity of our northern races. To smoke the semi-intoxicating *bang*, or datura, is to them the highest happiness,—a professional story-teller, with dreamy eye, often entrancing the attention of a reclining audience, all smoking or chewing betel. Merchants, possessing stores of wealth, sit all day upon their shop-counters smoking hubble-bubbles. Native noblemen go about clothed in two wide strips of muslin, or rather they go little about, but sleep and smoke, and enjoy incense and perfumes within unfurnished palaces and formal gardens, content without newspapers or current literature, and often ignorant of political changes, even when living at the very seat of government. After dwelling for a time in India, it is discovered that although great capacity lies inherent in the Hindu character, and is shown at times in individuals, Hindus have not usually ready sympathy with Europeans and European modes of thought; and that the learned and generous Rammohun Roy, and the sagacious and open-minded Dwarkanath Tagore, are no more average specimens of Hindus than Robert Burns or Robert Bloomfield are of British ploughmen. The mass of the people appear inert, without wants and without energy, and a stranger is tempted to believe that their ideas have been stereotyped from generation to generation for countless ages past; but he remembers that these same Hindus are the people whose heroism was admired by Alexander the Great, and whose philosophy and manufactures are celebrated by Greek historians. He remembers also what he has read of the classic Sanskrit language and literature; and as soon as the dream of delight attending his first arrival has subsided, he seeks eagerly to learn which of all the motley groups around are real Hindus of ancient classical descent. Not the Mohammedans,—that point is easily determined, as their first incursion into the country was no earlier than A.D. 1000, a date too recent to admit of mystification. The same remark applies to those of Portuguese descent, at present numerous in Calcutta, and also to the Chinese; but besides these, some thick-featured, black-skinned people may be seen working in sewers, or serving as boats' crews, who are aborigines from the hills and forests; and, with these exceptions, he is told that all the native population he beholds may be considered generally as genuine Hindus. The Baboos, or native merchants, are Hindus; the Buneahs, or bankers, are Hindus; and the Zemindars and Ryots, who are respectively owners and cultivators of land, —the sepoys, or soldiers, and the Rajputs, and the up-country men who stand in pink or red turbans as durwans and chokeedars at the gates of gentlemen's houses,—these are all Hindus, and so also are Brahmans of every grade; those of highest rank who live in learned ease, those less wealthy or well-born who officiate in temples, and those still poorer who beg for a subsistence, are all descendants of the original Hindus,—the people who possess a language and a history, and whose ancestors at some remote and unknown period brought the religion of the Vedic Hymns from lands beyond the Indus. But to trace the thread of Hindu history, from the present period through the intermediate labyrinths, was found to be a task which Hindus themselves had not performed. Their genius ever increases the volume of the labyrinthine mazes, but gives no clue whereby to reach the solution of the mystery. Nor did our predecessors, the French, the Dutch, or the Portuguese, much concern themselves about antiquity; and consequently when in the middle of the last century the East India Company's factories became settled in Bengal, very little more was known of the country than had been related by the Greeks three hundred years before the Christian era; to the series of labours which then commenced we must now apply our best attention.

The first inquirers were little more than pioneers breaking up the ground for those who followed. Ruined cities, temples, and most astonishing excavations were discovered, the origin of which tradition vaguely hinted at as lost in periods too remote for history. The gods and goddesses of the existing idolatry were vainly compared with those of Greece and Egypt, and many theories were erected, to be as quickly overthrown; everywhere curiosity was excited, but nowhere could it meet with satisfaction. Chronicles and records were discovered, but they were all in Sanskrit, and Sanskrit was "the language of the gods," which it was sacrilege to communicate to foreigners and heretics. Added to the difficulty thus raised by superstition, was that of the very complex structure of the Sanskrit tongue; but difficulties only increased the ardour of the studious, and Adelung mentions that, in thirty years, seven hundred works were published upon this new subject.* But these labours did not resolve the difficulty, and, although the language was attained and the records explored, the search for history was baffled; in vain Sir William Jones and his fellow-labourers strove to reconcile dates and harmonize events, and it was at length discovered that, as a fancy artist deals with towns or churches, trees or hills, and places them near or far according to pictorial effect, so had the Hindu annalist treated events; and whilst picturesque remoteness was granted to one sovereign, the deeds of his posterity were grouped around another. The study of Sanskrit was not however abandoned, for the religious writings, although inaccurate in dates and names, gave indications of sublimity. The law-books bore internal evidence of antiquity, and offered most interesting pictures of manners and customs; the heroic poems shared this merit, and also proved themselves rich in poetry; the dramas and later effu-

* Hist. Sketch of Sanscrit Literature. (Talboys, Oxford.)

sions glittered with fanciful imagery, and only works comparatively modern were found encumbered by impure idolatry or puerile extravagance.

It is not surprising that, in the first enthusiasm of these discoveries, the merits of Sanskrit literature should have been exaggerated. Many learned Europeans expected a regeneration in letters similar to that produced by the revival of Greek in the fifteenth century; others hoped for the happiest effects from its religious spirit; and others again fixed their admiration rather on the language than on the literature it contained. One scholar after another proved its dates fictitious, and its facts enveloped in fable; but it dawned upon them that the very construction of the language itself would afford a date or fixed point, from which the successive variations of its forms and alphabets might be contemplated.

This hope has not been disappointed, for by researches into the structure and affinities of language, the learned have not only been assisted in their labour of marshalling Sanskrit writings into chronological groups, but they have become convinced that the Sanskrit language is the parent of all other classic tongues. Somewhere in Central Asia they place a primeval nursery, or great cradle, in which infant nations lisped in infant Sanskrit. From age to age emigrants or colonies wandered forth from this depôt, and, as centuries rolled on, were fashioned into Greeks, Latins, Slaves, Celts, etc., each developing its own peculiar language from the original Sanskrit germ. At length Persians and Hindus alone were left to cultivate their common language, and bear the name of *Aryan*,—a name which the Persians long retained, as may be seen in the inscriptions at Nakshi

Rustam. Lastly, the Hindus quitted the original *Aryavarta*, or home of Aryans, travelled to the East, and settled themselves in India.

Some years ago the possessors of the oldest *Aryan* language would have been allowed undisputed claim to the earliest civilization; but now Egypt claims a pre-Mosaic history, and Scythic Nineveh dates her prosperity as *previous to* 2231 B.C. India must therefore limit her pretensions to being the earliest heathen nation in the field of literature. Sanskrit hymns are extant in rude and rugged language, which the Pentateuch alone surpasses in antiquity; cut away from the mainland of Hindu literature, these collected hymns, called Vedas, loom out of the distance, like headland rocks which the sea has separated from the neighbouring coast. Much beauty or sublimity must not be expected in this unearthed, insular kind of literature, but it tells of customs and modes of worship nowhere else explained, and it is therefore indispensable to a right appreciation of the genius of antiquity.

Upon leaving the Vedas we must leap over several centuries, and then plunge into the Brahmanical literature so much admired by Sir William Jones. The ancient Brahmans are well known to have shown no small favour to class interests; but although selfish they were philosophic, full of deep thought, poetry, and a sublime belief in immortality. Beneath their jealous influence kings had little power, villages governed themselves, learning and the industrial arts flourished, and even religion possessed a freedom and energy unknown to India's later days. This subject will be treated in successive chapters, elucidating life in old Brahmanical India, by a reference to the literature which preceded the Macedonian invasion.

Book II. treats of Buddhism, a religion which bears an external perverted kind of resemblance to Christianity, giving a peculiar interest to the circumstances under which it was developed. Originating in India as a reform, it produced no general sensation until about three centuries after the death of its founder, when, during one long prosperous reign, it was adopted as the state religion. To Brahmans however we shall find it was utterly repulsive; through their influence it was ultimately banished from its native country, and to this day it is rejected by every Aryan nation.

Book III. returns to Brahmanism, giving a notice of the Poems, Dramas, and Puranas,—beautiful, absurd, fanciful,—which were produced subsequent to the era of Alexander the Great. This brings our review down to the time when the Mohammedans began their conquests in the country, at which period this Work concludes, after a short inquiry as to the success which attended Brahmanical regulations and Buddhist theories.

BOOK I.

INDIA PREVIOUS TO ALEXANDER THE GREAT.

"Zeus was not an invention of Homer, Jupiter was not borrowed from Greece. . . . Long before the Arians immigrated into Greece and Italy they worshipped the same God under the same name. . . . Brahmans who migrated towards the south invoked him along the rivers of the Punjab."—DR. MAX MÜLLER, *Edin. Review, Oct.* 1851.

CHAPTER I.

E'en the poor Pagan's homage to the Sun
I would not harshly scorn, lest even there
I spurn'd some element of Christian prayer,
An aim, though erring, at a world ayont:
Acknowledgment of good, of man's futility,
A sense of need and weakness, and indeed
That very thing so many Christians want—Humility.

THOMAS HOOD.

WHEN first the British went to India, religious Hindus thought it sacrilege to allow unbelieving Christians even to look upon their sacred books, and in consequence the Vedas long enjoyed that mysterious reputation which appertains to unseen authorities. Sir William Jones penetrated little beyond modern versions of particular passages; and even Mr. Colebrooke, who did much towards winning the confidence of the Pundits, was far from obtaining any complete knowledge of these works. Nevertheless up to a very recent period Mr. Colebrooke has been the first authority upon this subject, and his Essays are referred to and quoted by every writer on the Vedas, whether in India, Germany, France, or England. He has translated short fragments and made abstracts of larger portions, which are highly valued, as being accurate and free from unjust bias. He does not adopt Scripture language to convey the meaning of the Sanskrit words; nor does he, on the other hand, view these early religious impressions through the medium of European prejudice, an error of which the missionary author, Mr. Ward, cannot be acquitted. Gradually complete copies of these venerable books were obtained in India, and lodged in the public libraries of London, Oxford, France, and Germany, where, for a long series of years, they have in each country received the attention of distinguished scholars. The four Vedas were formerly supposed to be equally old and equally original; but now it is ascertained that whilst the hymns of which the Rig-Veda consists rank "as amongst the oldest extant records of the ancient world,"* the Sama Veda merely gives extracts from these hymns arranged for worship, the Yajur Veda contains hymns of later date, mixed with repetitions of the early specimens, and the Atharva Veda is a much later compilation, consisting of formularies required on certain rare occasions.

* Rig-Veda Sanhita, H. H. Wilson, Introd., p. xlviii.

The language used in the Vedas differs very considerably, as already noticed, from the Sanskrit of general literature; and Mr. Stevenson, of Bombay, noticed in the Sama Veda two thousand words not admitted in the second edition of Wilson's Sanskrit dictionary.* The use of an eight-syllable metre is also adduced as a sign of antiquity;† and for these and other reasons the age attributed to the Rig-Veda is 1200 or 1400 B.C. What religious opinions prevailed at so remote a period was long a mystery; but the early enthusiasts for Sanskrit conceived that monotheism was India's first belief. Sir William Jones was told that the daily prayer called *Gayatri* was an address to the Sun, taken from the Vedas; and obtaining a copy and explanations from a Pundit (or learned Hindu), he gave the following rendering, heading it—

"*The Indian Philosophers' Belief.*‡

"Let us adore the supremacy of that divine Sun (opposed to the visible luminary), the Godhead who illuminates all, who recreates all, from whom all proceed, to whom all must return, whom we invoke to direct our understandings aright in our progress towards his holy seat."

This may happily give the views of rare philosophers, such as the lamented Rammohun Roy, but it is not the doctrine of the ancient Vedas; and of this all students will soon be competent to judge, for translations of the several Vedas are in progress in England, France, and Germany.

Mr. Colebrooke gives the Gayatri thus:—

"Let us meditate on the adorable light of the divine Ruler (Savitri). May it guide our intellects! Desirous of food, we solicit the

* Mr. Stevenson's Introduction to the Sama Veda.

† Elphinstone, Hist. India, p. 37; Hist. Sketch of Sanskrit, 7, 69.

‡ Works of Sir W. Jones, vol. vi. quarto.

gift of the splendid Sun (Savitri), who should be studiously worshipped. Venerable men, guided by the understanding, salute the divine Sun (Savitri) with oblations and praise."*

Dr. Stevenson presents the following from the Sama Veda:—

"We are sustained by the superexcellent provisions furnished us by the resplendent Sun. May he prosper our sacred rites!"†

And lastly, Professor Wilson translates it:—

"Let us meditate on the sacred light of that divine Sun, that it may illuminate our minds."‡

And this last rendering may be considered as correct, both in text and translation, as human sagacity can make it. It recognizes spiritual light, but it is vague and indistinct. Sir William Jones assumed too much, and, amid the wilful confusion of the dates given to him by his Pundits, could not always distinguish the limits of India's first or Vedic era; but now correct translations and comments have thrown open the subject, and such inaccuracy would no longer be excusable.

Professor Wilson observes that the Sun, Surya or Savitri, occupies a less conspicuous place in Hindu worship than might have been anticipated; only three Suktas in the First Book are addressed to him individually, and these "convey no very strikingly expressive acknowledgment of his supremacy."§ But although Sun-worship was not prominent, the Hindus loved light and even warmth, and the Sun, the "ray-diffuser," and Agni, as light, heat, and fire, call forth their best affections. The expressions of the Hindu poets in their hymns to these deities show careful

* Colebrooke's Essays, vol. i. p. 30.

† Introduction to the Sama Veda.

‡ Oxford Lectures, p. 15.

§ Rig-Veda, Introd. p. xxxii.

and loving observation of Nature; "white as the sun" gives a truth which can scarcely be appreciated by those who have not experienced the striking absence of colour in the intense light of a summer day in India. The solar ray is called "deep-quivering, life-bestowing;" and the Sun is "bright-haired" and "golden-handed," that is, the giver of abundance. Agni is the "golden-haired," and both alike are regarded as emblems of purity. The Sun, Savitri, is said to come "from a distance, removing all sins;"* or the divine Sun is entreated to remove the "sickness of the heart" and "the yellowness of the body." The following address, translated by Mr. Griffith of Oxford, may be taken as a fair specimen of the higher spiritual perceptions proper to this era.

HYMN TO THE SUN.

I.

"Risen in majestic blaze,
Lo! the Universe's eye,
Vast and wondrous, host of rays,
Shineth brightly in the sky.
Soul of all that moveth not,
Soul of all that moves below;
Lighteth he earth's gloomiest spot,
And the heavens are all aglow!

II.

"See! he followeth the dawn,
Brilliant in her path above:
As a youth, by beauty drawn,
Seeks the maiden of his love!
Holy men and pious Sages
Worship now the glorious Sun;
For by rites, ordain'd for ages,
Shall a good reward be won.

* Hymn xxxv., p. 98.

III.

"Look! his horses, mounted high,
Good of limb, and swift and strong,
In the forehead of the sky,
Run their course the heavens along!
Praises to his steeds be given,
Racing o'er the road of heaven!

IV.

"Such the majesty and power,
Such the glory of the Sun:
When he sets at evening hour,
The worker leaves his task undone.
His steeds are loosed, and over all
Spreadeth Night her gloomy pall.

V.

"When he rides in noontide glow,
Blazing in the nation's sight,
The skies his boundless glory show,
And his majesty of light;
And when he sets, his absent might
Is felt in thickening shades of night.

VI.

"Hear us, O ye Gods, this day!
Hear us graciously, we pray!
As the Sun his state begins,
Free us from all heinous sins.
Mitra, Varun, Aditi!
Hear, O hear us graciously!
Powers of ocean, earth, and air,
Listen, listen to our prayer!"

The charm of a fresh morning after a night in India is expressed by a personification of Sunrise, or Dawn, as Ushas. "Born in the eastern quarter of the firmament, she displays a banner of rays of light;" "The noble and all-pervading Ushas has risen from darkness, bringing health to human habitations;" "The beloved Ushas scatters darkness from the sky;" "The many-tinted Dawn opens our doors, makes our riches manifest;" "The expansive Ushas has given back all regions."

> "She hath dwelt in heaven of old,
> May we now her light behold!
> Which, dawning brightly from afar,
> Stirreth up the harness'd car,
> Like as merchant-folk for gain
> Send their ships across the main.
>
> "Morning comes, the nurse of all,
> Like a matron, at whose call
> All that dwell the house within
> Their appointed task begin."*

More than once it is observed that the dawning of Ushas wakens the birds; and, lastly, it "causes the sacred fire to be kindled, and men to prepare for sacrifice." And this brings us to the reverence paid to fire in these hymns. The first act of a pious Hindu, when awakened in the morning, was to invoke "the smoke-bannered Agni (fire);" "The protector of the worship of the worshipper at the break of day." The earliest word for God, we must remember, expressed *light above,* and in accordance with this feeling we find "resplendent Agni" regarded as a type or form of deity. The sacrificial fire was kindled and cherished as heavenly light come down to dwell with man. "The Gods left Agni," says one of their hymns, "as a dear friend amongst the human races, present in the chamber of sacri-

* Specimens of Old Indian Poetry, by R. T. Griffith, vol. i., Hymn xlviii. of Rig-Veda.

fice."* Agni is like a "benevolent man:"† he gives "happiness in a dwelling like a son (newly born); he abides on earth like a prince with his faithful friends;" and "men sit in his presence like sons in the dwelling of a parent."‡ Agni is also more refined than many of the deities of this era. In purity he resembles an irreproachable and beloved wife, and with exquisite grace he is described as ornamenting the chamber of sacrifice as a woman adorns a dwelling.

But Agni, although much beloved, was nevertheless but a vague indefinite idea. Sometimes simply as *fire* he tosses about his flames like rushing rivers, and roaring like the resounding billows of the ocean; often he is a messenger between earth and heaven, sent as a prince who has become a friend sends an ambassador to his more powerful conqueror. At one time he sustains the earth, and studs the sky with constellations; at another he is born from dry wood, or created by rubbing one piece of wood upon another:—

"Thou to whom the wood gives birth,
Thou that callest Gods to earth,
Call them that we may adore them,
Sacred grass is ready for them.

"Messenger of Gods art thou;
Call them, Agni, call them now!
Fain our offerings would they taste;
Agni, bid them come in haste.

* Rig-Veda, vol. ii. pp. 11, 7; *Ibid.* vol. i. pp. 123, 78, 297.
† Wilson's Rig-Veda, vol. ii. p. 280.
‡ *Ibid.* vol. i. pp. 184, 194, 195, 179.

"Brilliant Agni! lo, to thee
Pour we offerings of ghee;
Oh, for this consume our foes
Who on demons' aid repose!

"Praise him in the sacrifice,
Agni, ever young and wise!
Glorious in his light is he,
Healer of all malady.

"Purifying, brilliant Fire!
Hear, great Agni, our desire!
Be thy care the Gods to bring
Hither to our offering."*

Agni was, as we have seen, a very variable character, sometimes acting the part of *Hotri*, as he calls the Gods to sacrifice; sometimes accepting offerings on his own behalf, but also indicating powers of purity, removing sin and granting health, and strengthening our affection for the Gods of Light.

Connected with Sun-worship are two hymns in honour of the Horse Sacrifice, called *Aswamedha*. The horse is a mystical horse, "sprung from the Gods," "fabricated from the sun." The actual sacrifice was probably a custom belonging to the Hindus' earlier home in Northern Asia, where the Scythians and Massagetæ are known to have offered horses to the sun; and later, when treated as an emblematic ceremony, the mythical horse typified the Sun, and the Sun typified the universal soul. The hymns describe the horse as "bathed and decorated with rich trappings, the variously-coloured goat going before him." Three times he is led round the sacrificial fire; he is bound

* Specimens of Old Indian Poetry, by R. T. Griffith.

to a post and immolated by an axe, and the flesh is roasted on a spit, boiled, made into balls and eaten, and finally—

> "The horse proceeds to that assembly which is most excellent:
> To the presence of his father and his mother (heaven and earth).
> Go (horse,) today rejoicing to the Gods, that (the sacrifice) may yield blessings to the donor."*

This ceremony was afterwards performed symbolically, and is alluded to in Upanishads and Brahmanas (which are treatises attached to the Vedas), as a ceremony of peculiar solemnity and deep significance, and one which is supposed to procure universal dominion. In the very much later writings called Puranas the rite is altogether travestied: a mortal rajah there performs the sacrifice in order to dethrone the God Indra; and it is upon this version of the story, that Southey constructed his 'Curse of Kehama,'—correctly enough, Professor Wilson observes, according to the authorities which he followed, "but the main object of the ceremony, the deposal of Indra from the throne of *Swarga* and the elevation of the Sacrificer after a hundred celebrations to that rank, are fictions of a later date, uncountenanced by the Veda."†

The worship of Light, with which this ceremony was first connected, began before the Hindus entered India; whereas Indra was a local deity of strictly Indian origin. Indra is a "personification of the phenomena of the firmament, particularly in the capacity of sending down rain." He personifies the sky or the atmosphere, and may be called the God of Clouds and Storms. He is invoked to strike the demon Vritra, who withholds the periodical rains, upon which the fertility of the country depends.

* Rig-Veda, vol. ii. p. 112. † *Ibid.*, vol. ii., Introd. p. xii.

In the month of May the heat in India becomes intense: vegetation is dried up, the crops cannot be sown, the cattle droop, and milk and butter become scarce. Famine or plenty depends upon the expected rains, and the daily gathering of the sky is watched with intense anxiety; but although the array of clouds is constantly enlarging, there is no rain until a rattling thunderstorm charges the ranks and the broken clouds let loose the impetuous showers "This," says the Veda, "is Indra, who comes 'loud shouting' in his car, and hurls his thunderbolt at the demon (or demon-shaped cloud, called) Vritra."

> "He strikes off the head of the earth-shaking Vritra with his rain-causing, hundred-spiked Vagra (thunderbolt). His might has been gloriously displayed, and Indra rolls up and spreads out both heaven and earth as men do a skin carpet."*

To do full justice to Indra's battle with Vritra a storm should be witnessed from a lofty hill in Western India, the thick black clouds coursing over the distant plains, the lightning darting into them from the electric vapour above, and the torrents of rain discharged in consequence. These beneficent storms are always preceded by sudden wind, announced by rushing sounds and whirlwinds of dust, which are Indra's attendant allies the Maruts, "at whose roaring every dweller upon earth shakes."

Indra recovered the cattle of the "Sacrificers" when the robber Vala had hidden them in a cave; and other rough deeds he performed for his worshippers, who praise him for being "strong as a twice-twisted rope:" they represent him as young and handsome, with a beautiful nose or chin,

* Stevenson, Sama-Veda, p. 251 *and note.*

wearing two golden earrings, ever joyous, and delighting in exhilarating draughts of the Soma-jüice.

"Rejoice, Indra! open thy jaws, set wide thy throat, be pleased with our oblations!

"Drinker of the Soma-juice, wielder of the thunderbolt! bestow upon us abundance of cows with projecting jaws!

"Thy swift horses, Indra, have uttered a loud sound announcing rain; the level earth anxiously expects its fall.

"The mighty Indra has shattered the guileful Vritra reposing in the cloud: heaven and earth shook, alarmed at the thundering bolt of the showerer. Drinking the Soma-juice, he (Indra) baffled the devices of the guileful Danava.

"Drink, hero, Indra, drink the Soma!

"Indra, hero, exulting in the solemn rites, quaff the Soma-juice, and, repeatedly shaking it from thy beard, repair to the drinking of the effused libation."

Some of the Vedic hymns would lead one to suppose that to *kindle* fire on the altar was the duty to which man first awoke; but other passages speak of fire as "constantly kindled" in the house of a pious worshipper, and it is therefore probable that he only gave "fresh vital air" to the flames at sunrise, and then made his offering of ghee or butter to whichever God he desired to invoke; but when the soma-juice was presented, a public ceremonial called a Soma-yága appears to have been held. On these occasions an additional fire was kindled, by means of a species of churn made of acacia, called *arani* wood: one piece of the wood was drilled into the other, and the upright piece pulled by a loose string, after the fashion by which Hindus make butter. In one address to Indra he is entreated to come "when they bind the churning-staff (with a cord), like reins to restrain (a horse)." A large shed was constructed, called the *Yajna-sálá*. Seven priests attended, each having a distinct title and office; the Rishi, or Raja, at whose expense the festival was given, acting as *Hotri,* or invoker. At a daily morning sacrifice only two persons are mentioned as officiating,—the Purohita, who superintended, and the Hotri, who invoked the Gods. The Sama-Veda gives hymns from the Rig-Veda, arranged in a ritual, to be used on these occasions, and the priests are exhorted to sing the birth of the Gods and the praise of the Gods in alternate lays, with a sound as regular as that of the dripping of the soma-juice. Very little allusion is made to animal sacrifices, but they were probably not unknown, for the priests are to make as much noise as "dogs driven away hungry from a sacrifice." The soma-juice was at any rate the more important portion of the offering; the plants were gathered on the hills by moonlight, and brought home in carts drawn by rams. "Indra," it is said, "found this treasure from heaven, hidden like the nestlings of a bird in a rock, amidst a pile of vast rocks, enclosed by bushes;" the stalks are bruised with stones, and placed with the juice in a strainer of goats'-hair, and are further squeezed by the priest's ten fingers, ornamented by rings of flattened gold. Lastly, the juice, mixed with barley and clarified butter, ferments, and is then drawn off in a scoop for the Gods, and a ladle for the priests, and then they say to Indra, "Thy inebriety is most intense, nevertheless thy acts are most beneficent."

Sometimes Indra is addressed in a more spiritual strain. "One man,"* says Agastya, "propitiates him with sacrifice, another worships with mind averted: to the first he is like a lake to a thirsty traveller; to the other, like an ever-

* Rig-Veda, vol. ii. p. 165.

lengthening road." Indra does not vary so much in character as Agni, but he also is sometimes recognized as Creator of the universe, as "he who fixed firm the moving earth, who tranquillized the incensed mountains, who spread the spacious firmament,"* or "fixed the heaven in unsupported (space)," and "measured the eastern (quarters) with measures like a chamber;"† but in this grand hymn the individuality of Indra is retained by the closing words of each verse: "In the exhilaration of the Soma, Indra has done these deeds."

Indra is occasionally called upon to share his "soma wine" and "sacrificial food" with his allies the Maruts (winds); but to this he objects, asking, "Who attracts them, wandering like kites in the mid-air?" "Sacred rites," Indra continues, "are mine; praises give me pleasure, libations are for me; I am fierce and strong and mighty, and have bowed down all mine enemies with death-dealing shafts;"—the Maruts assert that it was with their aid, and thus an innovation or dissent from the older worship is implied.‡

But whether presented to Indra alone, or to Indra and the Maruts conjointly, soma wine was the coveted offering, and this is an important fact in determining the locality of the Hindus in the time of the Rig-Veda. The Soma is a round, smooth, twining plant, not to be found in rich soils, as we learn from Dr. Royle, but is peculiar to the mountains in the west of India, the desert to the north of Delhi, and the mountains of the Bolan Pass.§ The Rig-

* Rig-Veda, vol. ii. p. 236. The scholiast explains that he "quieted the mountains, going hither and thither as long as they had wings: Indra cut them off."

† Rig-Veda, vol. ii. p. 245.

‡ *Ibid.*, vol. ii. p. 146.

§ Lecture on the Results of the Great Exhibition, p. 456, *note*.

Veda could not therefore have been composed upon the Ganges; its hymns tell moreover of dense forests through which a path is made by the "fierce-blazing Agni," who, rushing rapidly, "leaves a blackened track."

"Excited by the wind, and roaring loudly, Agni penetrates amongst the timber."

"He traverses the woods, and shears the hairs of the earth."

"The flame-weaponed and breeze-excited Agni, assailing the unexhaled moisture (of the trees), rushes triumphant like a bull; all are afraid of him as he flies along."*

Here we see newly-arrived settlers setting fire to the woods in North American fashion; and entering from the north-west, we imagine them to have made their way down the left bank of the Indus, and to have possessed themselves of lands stretching eastward to the Aravalli Hills, and southward to the sea: such a location appears to fulfil the conditions required by the hymns, where we have Prince Bhávya† "dwelling upon the banks of the Sindhu;" and within sight, undoubtedly, were mountains and caves not far distant, in which Vala hid the cows of the worshippers. Indra, in battle, wearing armour, is said to "shine like the peak of a mountain seen afar;" his impetuosity is compared to the "rush of waters down a precipice," and his golden thunderbolt, hurled against the foe, "slept not on the mountain;" the "graceful spotted deer" and "thirsty deer" also indicate the neighbourhood of hills, whilst the prominent place which these singers give to horses is accounted for by their possession of the level plains of Sindh and Kattiwar.‡ The Gods are compared to horses: "Indra

* Rig-Veda, vol. i. p. 156. † *Ibid.*, vol. ii. p. 17; vol. i. p. 320.

‡ The horse of the country along the Ganges is a very inferior animal, and never could have furnished the illustrations of the Veda.—H. H. W.

becomes furious as a horse's tail," or Agni goes to receive offerings, "delighted as a horse goes to battle;" and distinction is made between "rider-bearing steeds" and "quick-moving, prancing steeds, rapid as hawks," which fly through the air yoked to cars. Cars and chariots are continually mentioned, but we do not meet with official charioteers. Indra himself drives his "long-maned steeds," and Agni harnesses "his glossy-backed coursers;" whereas in later Sanskrit literature we find the king always accompanied by a driver, according to the Assyrian custom depicted on the marbles from Nineveh. One passage is thought to indicate that their horses had no saddles, and another that they had the Tatar practice of milking the mares. "A hundred vigorous steeds" is not an unusual present from a generous prince to a holy man, or Rishi; one of whom says "he accepted gold, horses, and bulls," and then proceeds, "Ten chariots drawn by bay steeds, and carrying my wives, stood near me;" "Forty bay horses harnessed to the chariots, lead the procession in front of a thousand followers:" and on this occasion the great man's kinsmen "rub down the high-spirited steeds, decorated with golden trappings."*

We observe a perpetual dread of enemies of a race unlike their own, for they not only call them "spider-like sons of Danu," and Dasyas (robbers), but a "*black*-sprung host" and "*black* Asuras:" these enemies had cities and kings, and worshipped a god, *Nirritti*, who is dreaded even by the "*white*-complexioned friends of Indra."

"Let not the most powerful and indestructible Nirritti destroy us: let her perish with our (evil) desires."

* Rig-Veda, vol. ii. p. 18; vol. i. pp. 210, 211, 214.

"Keep far from us Nirritti with unfriendly looks, and liberate us from whatever sin we may have committed."*

The Hindus call themselves *Aryas*, and although less is said of cities of the Aryas than of cities of the Dasyas, they were not a nomadic people, for they "measure the land with a rod," "plough the earth for barley," and "bring home the produce of their *fields* in *carts*."† We also find, through their poetical similes, that they practised many of the arts of civilized society. A holy man at the bottom of a well cries out, "Cares consume me, as a rat gnaws a weaver's threads." In other passages, "Day and night, like two famous female weavers, interweave the extended thread;"‡ or, "Night envelopes the extended (world) like (a woman) weaving a garment." Earrings and finger-rings, and wheels and yokes of chariots, are made of gold; and gold is the favourite simile for the rising sun, and for the hair of Agni; nor were they less acquainted with the use of iron, for a singer praises Indra as eagerly "as a carpenter bends the pliant metal round the wheel;" and when Vispalá, wife of Khela, had her foot cut off "like the wing of a bird in an engagement by night," the Aswins "gave her an iron leg that she might walk, the hidden treasure of the enemy being the object of the conflict."§

Nothing is said of money, but they seem to have used cowrie-shells as dice, a frightened man being compared to a gamester, who fears his adversary holding the four cowries, until they are thrown. Their riches they "hid in a chest, a hill, or a well." This is still the custom in Western India, and when the English took possession of Poonah, ten lacs of rupees belonging to the Peshwa were found built into

* Rig-Veda, vol. i. pp. 62, 107.

† *Ibid.*, vol. i. pp. 56, 284.

‡ *Ibid.*, vol. ii. p. 218.

§ *Ibid.*, vol. i. p. 311.

the side of a well. They transacted trade, and entreated Indra not to "take advantage" of his worshippers, "like a dealer." Merchants are also mentioned, "covetous of gain," whose ships "crowd the ocean;" but no foreign products appear to have been in use. Women are but casually mentioned, but enough is said to show that their condition was free and natural: the wife of a chief accompanies him to a midnight foray; the wife of a hunter "cuts up and divides the birds;" the first rays of morning come like a matron, awaking the household to their duties. From other passages we learn that women appeared in public, as where lightning is compared to a "splendidly attired wife of a man of rank," and the "bushes" are said to "wave to and fro like a woman in a chariot." A virtuous maiden who grows old in her father's house claims from him her support. "Thieves are frequently mentioned, debts and debtors are adverted to, and reverses of fortune." Another sign of social progress we gain from their knowledge of herbs and modes of medical treatment; "ambrosia," says a son of Kanwa, "is in the waters;" "all medicaments are in the waters;" thus anticipating some three thousand years ago the hydropathic doctrine of the nineteenth century. The sick man however expects the god Agni to co-operate with the waters: he exclaims, "Take away whatever sin has been found in me;" "May Agni abiding in the waters fill me with vigour!"* The virtue of herbs was also acknowledged; and praying to Rudra, called the chief physician amongst physicians, the worshipper says:—

> "Nourished by the sanatory vegetables bestowed by thee, may I live a hundred winters!"†

* Rig-Veda, vol. i. p. 58. † *Ibid.*, vol. ii. p. 290.

Rudra is an uncertain sort of deity, sometimes identified apparently with Indra; but in general, medicine is practised by two grotesque personages, called the Aswins; they are brothers, sons of the Sun; they travel in a three-cornered, three-wheeled car, drawn by asses, and with their long arms concern themselves in every odd legend of which the Veda makes mention: half-comic and half-serious, to a holy man who was beheaded for revealing to them forbidden science, they gave a horse's head, and stuck it on his shoulders in place of his own; the lame they enabled to walk, and the blind to see; an "aged man they restored to youth, as a wheelwright repairs a worn-out car;" one man they brought up from a well of water in which he lay like a jar of buried gold; "another, who was scorched by fire, they relieved with snow; an emaciated cow they made to give milk, and a field of barley they caused to be sown." For Vispalá they made an iron foot; to King Pedu they gave a white horse ensuring victory, and from the hoof of another steed they produced a hundred jars of wine. For their friend Divodasi they yoked the bull and the tortoise, and carried food and treasure to his dwelling in a car.* Not less strange was their manner of assisting Bhujyu, who "sailed in a hundred-oared ship:" he went to sea, and was nearly drowned; "when there was nothing to give support, nothing to rest upon, nothing to cling to," then went the Aswins, and brought him back "in vessels of their own, drawn by six horses along the dry bed of the ocean."† Our conclusion is, that these youthful professors of the healing art were the direct progenitors of the jugglers, magicians, barbers, and quacks, who in all ages have been celebrated

* Rig-Veda, vol. i., Hymns cxii. cxix.

† *Ibid.*, vol. i. p. 307.

for combining drollery and sleight of hand, with skill in surgery and knowledge of medicaments.

In poetry the Hindus undoubtedly excelled, but the misfortune is, that those who cannot read Sanskrit are by no means in a position to do them justice. The third book of the Rig-Veda is said to be incomparably the finest, and this Professor Wilson has not yet translated, besides which, this primitive poetry is said to have a peculiar facility of escaping under the process of translation: perhaps we need two versions, one given with critical accuracy, and another in the imaginative spirit of the original. To sing praises was early an official occupation, and to "recite like a bard" used as a simile. Sacred hymns however are composed by Rishis (holy men), chiefs, or patriarchs, whose families are noted in Sanskrit literature even down to the Puranas, two thousand years later, as Angiras and the Angirases, Kanwa and the Kanwas, Viswamitra, Vasishta, and others. These men were not Brahmans, nor even priests, for during the Rig-Veda period division of caste had not commenced. We find neither Kshatriyas, nor Vaisyas, nor Sudras; and although Brahmans are mentioned, they are merely one amongst seven orders of priests, who minister under a king or patriarch at a solemn sacrifice. Society is always said to consist of *five* classes of men, an expression which Brahmanical scholiasts explain to mean the Aborigines, in addition to the four Castes; but this is a gratuitous supposition, for the whole tone of the Rig-Veda implies a free condition of society, quite different from that which afterwards prevailed under Brahmanical regulation. We there find new settlers, surrounded by enemies of different race, remembering the deities and customs of their fatherland, though adopting modes of worship suited to their new locality. Languishing in the arid sands of Sindh, they rejoiced to discover the acid soma-plant upon the neighbouring hills; panting for rain, they entreated Indra to quaff the exhilarating beverage, and to rend the clouds asunder, and let loose the reviving floods. The blessings prayed for are chiefly, as expressed by Professor Wilson, "of a temporal and personal description,—wealth, food, life, posterity, cattle, cows, horses, protection against enemies" —selfish and often puerile petitions; but self-forgetting aspirations also find utterance, and a few indications there are "of a hope of immortality, hatred of untruth, and abhorrence of sin;"* and many an old Hindu, we may hope, has stood by his fire-altar at daybreak, offering up fervent adoration to the "God written in the heart," of which the altar flames were to him the beloved household representation.

* Rig-Veda, vol. i., Introd. p. xxv.

CHAPTER II.

> "Let wild creeds come and go . . .
> On nought but One, in Godhead infinite
> And infinite in might,
> Can deathless being lay its fever'd brow."—WILLIAMS.

SKETCHES of a nation's infancy bear some resemblance to a modern album or note-book, where many pages are blank, whilst others are crowded with graphic detail; where a few highly-finished drawings are found amongst numerous slight outlines, and where fragments of eloquent poetry are interspersed with dry, prosaic autographs. Or we may vary the image, and compare the earliest attainable views of Hindu life to a series of *tableaux vivans*, the first of which showed us the Patriarchs on the Indus writing hymns, invoking the Gods, and making war on their predatory neighbours;

whilst *five* classes of men filled up the frame. This five-fold division is not explained in the Veda, and commentators are not agreed upon the subject; but it was evidently headed by the patriarch kings or chieftains, who united in themselves the office of high-priest and sovereign; the second class was probably formed of warriors riding and driving horses; the third was in this case a class of priests; the fourth comprised those following agriculture, trade, and mechanics; and the fifth is supposed to have been the aboriginal race, who stole cattle, but who possessed fields, cities, and gold, tempting the intruders to aggression. We have no means of adding to what we may thus learn from the ancient hymns, for the Hindus have no other writings of the same era, and neither Persia nor China afford chronicles referring to contiguous countries of such remote antiquity; and consequently when the Rig-Veda lets the curtain fall, a pause ensues of about six centuries.

At length the same people, with their Vedas and their Sanskrit, come again upon the stage; but the scenery has changed, and we now behold them occupying the broad lands of the Ganges, and possessing important towns in Oude and Tirhut. But we cannot at present advert to their political acquisitions, for our attention is at once riveted by a group of venerable persons upon whom the chief light of the picture is made to fall. They are sitting upon sacred *kusa* grass; their hair is shaved, their looks composed, and they are clothed in religious raiment peculiar to themselves: kings humbly take off their tiaras as they bow to the feet of the holy men; the merchant class make obeisance at a respectful distance; and the fourth and lowest class sweep the roads, uphold umbrellas, and wave the fans and fly-flappers. In this second picture we note great changes to have taken place, and especially the sharp separation which has been effected between civil and religious offices. The King, no longer permitted to invoke the Gods, has resigned the first place of honour to the Brahmans, who are a new and sacred class, seeking to monopolize learning, power, and religion. The process by which this great change was effected remains hidden behind the scenes, and we can only conjecture that many struggles and failures occurred before Brahmans succeeded in establishing their claims to divine origin and the sole right of performing religious functions, and of exercising spiritual dominion. But at the same time, we believe that the very word Brahman originated in philosophical speculation. In a passage of great eloquence, Dr. Müller describes man in the hymns of the Rig-Veda striving to solve the riddle of this world. He stares at the tent of heaven and asks who supports it; he gives names to all the powers of nature; he invokes them; but still he feels that within his own breast there is a Power that wants a name, "a Power nearer to him than all the Gods of Nature; a Power that is never mute when he prays, never absent when he fears and trembles: it seems to inspire his prayers, and yet to listen to them; it seems to live in him, and yet to support him and all around him. The only name he can find for this mysterious power is *Brahme*, for *Brahme* means originally force, will, wish, and the propulsive power of creation." Brahmans we imagine to have been men distinguished by their knowledge of *Brahme*, who gradually became the most powerful section of the Hindu people. Colonel Sykes has shown that the word Brahman is not a mere designation of office, but signifies a race, family, or tribe, bearing peculiar characteristics; a family, or clan, we infer, who gained permanent ascendency by the force of their intellectual endowments. Although this ascendency was not accomplished in the period of the Rig-Veda, the intellectual meditation which led to it was then commenced; and "there are hymns, though few in number, in the Veda," says Dr. Müller, "so full of thought and speculation, that at this early period no poet in any other nation could have conceived them." It should however be stated that these hymns are confined to the 10th Mandala, the whole tenour of which shows that it was very long posterior to the other nine and to the complete organization of Caste. The following is from Colebrooke's translation of the 129th hymn of the tenth book :—

"Then there was no entity, nor nonentity,
No world nor sky, nor aught above it:
Nothing anywhere . . .
Nor water deep and dangerous.
Death was not,
Nor then was Immortality,
Nor distinction of the day or night;
But THAT breathed without afflation . . .
Darkness there was;
This universe was enveloped in darkness,
And was undistinguishable water. . . .
Who knows and shall declare whence and why
This creation (ever) took place?
The Gods are subsequent to the production of this world:
Who then can know from whence
This varied world uprose? . . .
He who in the highest heaven is ruler, does know,
But not another can possess that knowledge." *

* Colebrooke, Essays, vol. i. p. 33.

At this period of Brahmanical literature, the word That (*Tad*) is often used to indicate the Eternal Source of Being, as in the following hymn, or *Mantra*, from the Yajur-Veda :—

> " Fire is That : the Sun is That :
> The air, the moon, so also that pure Brahme,
> Waters and the Lord of creatures (Prajapati).
> * * * * *
> He, prior to whom nothing was born,
> And who became all beings . . .
> Produced the sun, moon, and fire.
> To what God should we offer oblations,
> But to Him who made the fluid sky and solid earth,
> Who fixed the solar orb . . . and framed the drops of rain ?
> To what God should we offer sacrifice
> But to Him whom heaven and earth
> Contemplate mentally ? . . .
> The wise man views that mysterious (Being)
> In whom the universe perpetually exists,
> Resting upon that sole support.
> In Him is this world absorbed ;
> From Him it issues ;
> In creatures is He twined and wove, in various forms.
> Let the wise man, conversant with holy writ,
> Promptly celebrate that immortal Being
> Who is the mysteriously existing, various abode." *

The hymn is continued in the same mystical strain, continually losing all idea of a Creator as separable from the world created, but including both ideas under the expressions Tad and Brahme.

The struggling forth of the universe from darkness and from water was a favourite idea of the Brahmans, who delighted in the sublimity of this primeval chaos, and knew that there was a "beginning," when "darkness was upon

* Colebrooke, vol. i. p. 57.

the face of the deep, and the spirit of God moved upon the face of the waters;" but it was the flash of an intuition, striking momentary light across dark and puerile speculation.

In the hymn which commences, "Waters alone there were," the Lord of creation moves in the waters, "assuming the form of a boar."* Sometimes the Supreme Spirit produces an egg, and from the egg the universe is evolved.† Another prevalent notion is, that the universal soul became manifest as a horse named Viraj, who is thus described:

"Morning is his head,
The sun his eye,
Air his breath, the moon his ear,
The world his intellect, the earth his feet;
The celebrated Veda is his speech."‡

And through the instrumentality of this horse Viraj, all human forms and animal beings were produced. But these are mere hints at Brahmanical accounts of the creation, for such passages as are translated contain many tedious repetitions, and a great many passages are left untranslated, because the translators feel the details to be too coarse and unpleasant to present to English readers. The approaches of these people towards God are intensely interesting, marking how much and how little man's unassisted reason can divine. They launch out conjectures upon the sublimest and abstrusest subjects, and sometimes, like rockets, their thoughts shoot up into infinity, and break into a thousand coruscations of coloured light; but when we pursue the thought after its transient brilliancy has passed, we find it

* Colebrooke, vol. i. p. 75.

† Cole, MS. ch. i.

‡ Colebrooke, vol. i. p. 62, and Ram. Roy, p. 32.

like the expiring rocket, a feeble spark tied to a dead stick, or we find the stick alone, and that dragged through the dirt.

Viraj figures in many of their histories of creation as a link connecting the darkness which preceded, with the visible world, at length produced; and they endeavour to express a vague feeling that *sacrifice* has been the immediate cause of life to men and animals. Viraj, or Prajapati (Lord of creatures), gave himself to be sacrificed by the Demigods, and the universe was created from his substance: thus, in one of the hymns translated by Mr. Colebrooke from the tenth book of the Rig-Veda, we read,—

"That victim who was wove with threads on every side
And stretched by the labours of one hundred and one gods,
The fathers, who wove and framed
And placed the warp and woof,
Do worship."*

And the hymn proceeds to state, that by that universal sacrifice was produced sages and men, the sun and moon, and the holy verse called Gayatri; and it concludes with saying that the seven inspired sages wisely practise the performance of sacrifice, in imitation of these primeval saints. In the earlier hymns, the usual offerings were butter, rice, and soma-juice, but animals were also offered upon certain rare occasions. It is probable that different tribes had different customs, and that whilst some were gentle and contemplative, and made vegetable offerings, others sacrificed horses and cattle.

Allusion is even made to human sacrifice, and the hymns by Sunahsepas are said to have been uttered whilst he

* Colebrooke, vol. i. p. 34.

was bound as a victim to the stake. No explanation is given in the Veda itself, but from an appended Brahmana we gather the following particulars.

A king, named Harischandra, had one hundred wives, but no son, and this was to him an intolerable affliction, because a sage named Narada assured him, that if he had no son he would have no existence after death, but that "a father who beholds the face of a living son discharges his debt (to his forefathers), and obtains immortality." The king therefore, acting under the advice of the sage, prayed to Varuna, and said, "Let a son be born unto me, and with him I will sacrifice to you." A son accordingly was born, and named Rohita, and Varuna claimed him as a sacrifice; but the father said he was yet too young, and Varuna consented to delay; but each year Varuna claimed the child, and the father still deferred, until his son, hearing of the fate intended for him, escaped to the woods, and the king, his father, was struck with leprosy in consequence. At length Rohita heard of the affliction which had befallen his father in consequence of his not fulfilling his vow of offering him in sacrifice, and instead of giving himself up as a victim, went to a distressed Brahman, named Ajigartta, and promised him a hundred cows if he would give one of his sons to be sacrificed in his place. Ajigartta agreed that he should have his second son, named Sunahsepas. Rohita then went to his father, saying, "Rejoice, father, for with this youth I shall redeem myself." The day for the sacrifice was appointed, and the ceremony commenced, but there was no one competent to the office of binding the victim to the stake; whereupon Ajigartta said, "If you will give me another hundred cows, I will perform the duty." This was done, the victim was bound, and the priests walked round him, bearing burning brands of sacred grass. But still there was no *immolator* amongst the ministering Brahmans, and Ajigartta, the father of the victim, once more said he would perform the service needed for another hundred cows, and his offer being accepted he went forth to sharpen his knife. In the interval thus afforded, the victim at the stake began to think of escape, and saying to himself, "These people will put me to death as if I were not a man, but an animal," he perceived that his only hope was in Divine succour, and praying heartily to all the Gods in turn, his bonds at length fell off, and he became free, and the king was cured of his complaint.

The most remarkable part of this story is the end, in which Sunahsepas refuses to return to his father, saying, "All present saw you with the instrument of immolation in your hand: such a sight was never beheld even amongst Sudras;" meaning, that even a Sudra would not sacrifice a son, but his father's officiating at all in the capacity of immolator showed a vile Sudra disposition, which Sunahsepas considered unpardonable, and he therefore renounced his own family, and became the adopted son of Viswamitra, who had officiated as chief-priest on the occasion. Fifty of Viswamitra's sons objected to this proceeding, and were in consequence degraded to the condition of the barbarous tribes, whilst the other fifty acceded to their father's wishes, and welcomed his newly adopted son, saying, "We give thee, Sunahsepas, precedence, and acknowledge ourselves to be subordinate to thee."* From this story we infer, first,

* On Human Sacrifices, by Professor Wilson; J.R.A.S., part i. vol. xiii. p. 96.

that Brahmans who could or would perform the office of immolator were few in number, and held in disrespect; secondly, that Brahmans generally regarded animal sacrifice as a vile Sudra practice, or a custom belonging to inferior races; and thirdly, that a difference of opinion on this subject gave rise to dissensions and divisions amongst the descendants of the Vedic patriarchs and sages.

Many similar legends occur in Brahmanical literature, the sacrifice never being proposed as a propitiation of evil beings, but merely as an offering to benevolent deities of an object precious to the worshipper; and a man is never sacrificed, but a substitute taken in his place. The horse-sacrifice was probably adopted by the Hindu race from the Scythians, before they crossed the Indus; and human sacrifice they probably witnessed amongst the inferior race whom they found as aborigines in India; but the Brahmans recoiled from both the customs, and as they could not at once sweep away the popular ceremonies and festivals, they endeavoured to invest them with symbolic meanings. Mr. Colebrooke gives this opinion of the *Aswamedha* (horse-sacrifice), and the *Purushamedha* (human sacrifice), as described in a Brahmana, or treatise, appended to the Yajur-Veda. For the first of these festivals, a certain number of animals were tied to posts, but after prayers had been offered up they were let loose without injury. In the second festival men were bound as victims, and prayers and hymns recited, alluding to the allegorical immolation of Viraj, in which solemn sacrifice "spring was the butter, summer the fuel, and sultry weather the oblation." As soon as the prescribed prayers and hymns were concluded, the victims were set free, and an offering of butter thrown upon the sacrificial fire.

Whether these mysterious, vague ideas received any impulse from recollections of primeval revelation we cannot determine, but the more obvious source is Brahmanical contemplation, striving to elevate religion from the less civilized views and customs prevailing in the country. For this object the Brahmanical philosophers withdrew from society and gave themselves up to religious contemplation: and such meditation under the skies and groves of India becomes an intense abstraction, scarcely to be conceived by the active inhabitants of northern climes. The glorious world on which they looked, and the unclouded sun on which man cannot look direct, convinced them that Power and Purity were not ephemeral, although these outward and visible signs would perish; and gradually they evolved the doctrine, that worldly views and practices could procure nothing beyond mere worldly advantages, but that man might reach the Eternal by casting the whole force of his thoughts and his affections upon the abstraction Brahme. "What is Brahme?" is the usual theme of their Upanishads. Bhrigu asked this question of Varuna; and Varuna answered, that food, mind, speech were Brahme, and that Brahme, in fact, is that by which all beings are produced and supported, and towards which they all tend. But Bhrigu is not satisfied until Varuna further explains that life, intellect, meditation, and joy are also Brahme.* On another occasion, five persons conversant with holy writ go from one authority to another, trying to determine the questions, "What is our soul?" and "Who is Brahme?" The only person capable of giving the necessary instruction is a king, called Aswapati, son of Kaikeya; and he would take no notice of them until they came in the humble guise

* Colebrooke, vol. i. p. 77.

of pupils, each bearing a log of fire-wood. The king then addressed his visitors in turn, saying, "Whom dost thou worship as the Soul?" The first said, "Heaven." "That," said the king, "is merely the head." The second said, "The Sun," and is told it is merely the eye. The third said, "Air," which is merely the breath; and a fourth answered, "Earth," which he is told is the feet of the universal Soul. Certain advantages are admitted to result from offerings to these individual objects of worship, but they are mere earthly benefits, and such offerings are like fuel thrown on ashes, whereas knowledge of the universal Soul is like the tip of dry grass cast into the fire.*

These Brahmanical notions are very different from the views usually expressed in the Rig-Veda, where the sun and fire are the highest symbols of the Godhead, and where on two occasions worshippers attain the condition of Gods without losing their individuality. In the first instance, men of the family of Bhrigu "cherished Agni" (fire), and in consequence were "born as gods;"† in the second case, the Ribhus retired to the forest, to perform penance and worship Savitri, and the effect of their devotion was, that "being yet mortals they acquired immortality."‡ Subsequent hymns represent both Bhrigus and Ribhus as associating with Indra and other celestials, and like them receiving offerings of praise and the usual oblations of butter and the soma-juice. Let us now observe the difference between these two stages of belief. In the Vedic hymns of about B.C. 1400 devout worshippers make offerings to the sun and fire, and receive "a divine birth," beyond which there is no happiness conceivable for mortals. In the

* Colebrooke, i. 84. † Rig-Veda, lviii. 6 ‡ *Ibid.*, cx. 1, 2.

Brahmanas and Upanishads of about B.C. 800 Brahmans look upon fire-worship as procuring a renewal of merely perishable life, and upon the Gods as enjoying merely a limited term of existence. Beyond Agni and beyond the sun they perceive a sublimer object of adoration in *Brahme*, the universal Soul. But Brahme had no personality, and could receive no worship. Brahme pervaded the universe, and in proportion as any individual succeeded in approaching to the state of Brahme, he also lost his personality. The Brahmans had no idea of God as the creator and governor of the world, their sublimest notion being that of eternal essence universally diffused; plants, animals, men, and gods, all partook of this effusion of soul; but all visible life was mere illusion, and that which was held in common by all existence was the only reality. Brahmanical philosophy, in fact, confuses and puts to flight ordinary notions of reality by the very vehemence with which it struggles to escape from illusion. Birth or life was the entanglement of a portion of Brahme within the net of illusion, and from this entanglement not even death was an escape, for no sooner did one illusory existence close than another equally illusory commenced. The portion of soul which was disengaged by death, took possession of some other earthly tenement, it might be of an infant man, but it might with equal ease and probability be that of an animal or vegetable form. This appeared to the philosophical Brahmans as a necessary and logical deduction from their doctrine of the universal Soul, and they did not shrink from admitting the fact, although not at once anticipating all the consequences. The doctrine of Transmigration is touched upon in the Upanishads, and, although further developed in the Code of Manu, does not appear in its full detail and extravagance earlier than the Buddhist Sutras, written chiefly since our era, and the Brahmanical Puranas of modern Brahmanism, commencing about A.D. 900. Moral retribution was from the first combined with transmigration; and it was assumed that whilst men of the highest devotion had a chance of absorption into Brahme, or of being born again as inferior gods, bad men would become beasts or reptiles, and that all would be born and reborn, until the necessary penance had been made and the necessary perfection acquired, and all that was finite became merged into the infinite.

An interesting illustration of these opinions will be found in the following abstract of the Katha Upanishad, which has been translated by that distinguished and learned native of India, the late Rammohun Roy:—

A learned Brahman, named Vajasravasa, performed a sacrifice, at which he distributed his whole property; but the cows which he presented on the occasion as fees to the ministering priests were old and infirm, and this greatly distressed his son, the young Prince Nachiketa, who knew that whoever gave worn-out cows to priests was carried to the mansion where there is no felicity whatever. He begged therefore that his father would consign *him* in lieu of the cows, and persisted in asking to *whom* his father would consign him. The father, provoked at the boy's importunity, said hastily he would give him to Yama. This astonished the dutiful Nachiketa, for Yama was God of Death, and he wondered whether his father had had a previous engagement to this effect, or whether he spoke unawares in anger; but when the father recovered his self-possession, and was afflicted to think of the words which he had used, Nachiketa would not allow him to retract, saying, "Life is too short to make it worth while to gain advantages by means of falsehood and breach of promise."

Nachiketa proceeded therefore to the habitation of Yama; but the God of Death being absent from his dwelling, the youth remained three days unnoticed. Yama then returned, and was told by his family that for three days a Brahman had been his guest without receiving hospitality. Such an accident usually involved families in misfortune, for a Brahman guest is like fire, and good householders extinguish his anger by offering water, a seat, and food. Yama is in haste to offer every reparation in his power, and, in order "that bliss may attend him," begs that his guest will allow him to grant three favours in atonement for the pain which he had caused him. Nachiketa is readily conciliated, and makes the first of his three wishes a request that his father's distress may be removed, and his anger extinguished. To this Yama replied, "Thy father shall have the same regard for thee as before; and being assured of thy existence, he shall, through my power, repose the remaining nights of his life free from sorrow." The young man next begs for knowledge respecting fire, by which heaven is attained, where, he says, "there is no fear, and where even thou, Yama, canst not always exercise thy dominion." Yama consents, and proceeds to explain the nature of fire as the support of the world and yet residing in the body, and gives also particulars of the bricks which are requisite in forming and preserving sacred fire. Yama, gratified at the attentive manner in which his instruction is received, promised that in future sacred fire should be called after the name of

Nachiketa, and presenting on the occasion with "a variously-coloured necklace," assured him that a wise worshipper of sacred fire attains the highest fruition after death, concluding, "Now, O Nachiketa, make thy third request." But the pupil's third request was to be instructed in the nature of the soul; and at this Yama demurred, saying, "Even Gods have doubted and disputed on this subject, which being obscure never can be thoroughly comprehended. Ask, O Nachiketa, some other favour instead of this." But Nachiketa replied that no other object was so desirable, and no instructor equal to Yama could be found. Still Yama begs him to withdraw this wish, and not to take advantage of his promise. "Request," says he, "sons and grandsons, each to live a hundred years; request cattle, elephants, gold, horses, long life, and empire upon earth," anything, in fact, however difficult of acquisition, in the mortal world. "Ask," Yama begins again, "for beautiful women, with elegant equipages, and musical instruments such as no man can acquire without our aid." But the young philosopher is not to be dissuaded, and replies calmly, that such enjoyments as Yama has been offering are short-lived, destroying the strength of the senses, and that the life even of the Gods is comparatively short. "Let therefore thy equipages and thy dancing and music remain with thee; no man can be satisfied with riches. . . . The only object I desire is what I have already begged of thee." "Do thou instruct us," he continues, "in that knowledge which removes doubts respecting existence after death; I, Nachiketa, cannot ask any other favour than this."

Yama, although God of Death, at length consents, saying, "Knowledge which leads to absorption is one thing, and rites which have fruition for their object another; each of these, producing different consequences, holds out to man inducements to follow it: the man who of these two chooses knowledge, is blessed; and he who for the sake of reward practises rites, is excluded from the enjoyment of eternal beatitude." Yama enlarges further upon this idea, and expresses admiration at Nachiketa's having refused to adopt practices which lead merely to riches and other perishable gratifications, to which men in general are attached; and he makes this curious confession, that he had himself performed the worship of the sacred fire in order to procure his present sovereignty of long duration, although he knew that all fruition obtained by means of rites was perishable. Yama then endeavours to explain the nature of the soul, saying, it is "that which is difficult to be comprehended, . . . veiled by the ideas acquired through the senses, . . . does not depart even in great danger, and exists unchangeable. A wise man, knowing the resplendent soul through a mind abstracted from worldly objects, . . . neither rejoices nor does he grieve." Yama endeavours further to explain the nature of the soul as "unborn, eternal," "not injured by the hurt which the body may receive: if any one ready to kill another imagine he can destroy his soul, and the other think that his soul shall suffer destruction, they both know nothing; for neither does it kill, nor is it killed." Some of Yama's assertions respecting the soul are given in antithesis, as, "The soul is the smallest of the small, and greatest of the great. The soul, although without motion, seems to go to furthest space; though it resides in the body at rest, yet it seems to move everywhere." * The soul moreover

* Referring to this passage, Dr. E. Röer remarks, that "the Upanishads

"resides in fire, walks on the earth, enters like a guest into sacrificial vessels; dwells in man, in gods, in sacrifices; moves throughout the sky, seems to be born in water." A man who has this knowledge escapes from grief, and acquires absorption; but those who are ignorant of the universal Soul are born again as animals or trees. This was not however the fate of Nachiketa, for he acquired the divine doctrine, became freed from the consequences of good and evil acts, and acquired in consequence absorption into Brahme.*

Thus vaguely do these interesting speculations terminate. To be absorbed into an infinite abstraction was the rare privilege of the few who attained the highest knowledge; but for men in general the promise of future life was, to be born again as trees or beasts, as kings or gods, but only for a time of short duration. It may be said that the Hindu gasped for immortality, and that at a distance he beheld the blessed vision; but when he strained every nerve to bring it near and realize it to himself, the vision changed, and it was not immortality, but transmigration. The Hindu's belief in immortality is chained to transmigration like the rocket to the blackened stick, and when it leaves the stick it explodes into total darkness. The Hindu believed, not that man shall live again, but that man shares in a soul which cannot die.

"Though a hundred bodies like iron chains hold me down," says one of their Upanishads, "yet like a falcon I quickly rise."†

generally represent the difficulty of understanding the infinite soul by assigning to it contradictory predicates."—Bibliotheca Indica, Brihad Aranyaka, p. 73.

* Rammohun Roy, 'Translation of Passages from the Vedas,' p. 59.

† Colebrooke, vol. i. p. 51, Aitareya Aranya.

CHAPTER III.

"As little children lisp and tell of heaven,
So thoughts beyond their thought to those high Bards were given."

KEBLE.

WHILST the narrow strip of land on the Saraswati was the especial residence of studious Brahmans, all the fertile plains of the Ganges, including in fact the whole country between the Himalaya and the Vindhya hills, was considered the fitting abode of Hindus under Brahmanical guidance. Between these mountains "lies the tract which the wise have named Aryavarta," says the Law-book; Aryavarta meaning the abode of *Aryas,* or respectable men. On a tributary of the Ganges, called the river Gogra, to the south-east of this district, was placed the oldest or earliest

Hindu city, Ayodhya, occupying nearly the same site as the modern city of Oude, where remains of the ancient buildings are yet visible.

The first king who reigned at Ayodhya was Vaivaswata, a descendant of the sun, called in consequence the founder of the Solar race. One of his posterity, named Ikshwaku, was Raja of Mithila, a kingdom nearly corresponding with the modern Tirhut; and other monarchs of the Solar line were established at Vesali, in the district now known as Little Tirhut. The branch of the royal family called the Lunar dynasty colonized more adventurously, beginning with Benares and extending their kingdoms across the Vindhya hills to Berar, along the Nerbudda to Guzerat, and thence northwards to Mathura on the Jumna, and to Hastinapura on the Ganges.* The Lunar dynasties however appear to have had more of Scythian manners, and less of Brahmanical civilization, than the Solar line of Ayodhya.

In the time of King Vaivaswata, Caste had not become hereditary, for it is reported that whilst some of his sons were Kshatriyas and kings, one founded a tribe of Brahmans, one was a Vaisya, and another a Sudra. Some of the early kings are distinguished as having themselves *established* Caste amongst their subjects, and instances are even recorded of Brahmanical families proceeding from Kshatriya races or families. By degrees however Brahmans propounded their scheme of Hereditary Caste with great authority, as recorded in their Law-book, called the Code of Manu. This Code is a later composition than the Upanishads, and adopts the same religious doctrine, with additions, giving new links to the chain by which they con-

* H. H. Wilson, Vishnu Purana, Introd., pp. lxvii.-lxix.

nect the visible world with the self-existent universal Soul. First, Brahme created the waters and placed in them a seed, which became an egg; and in that egg, "bright as gold and blazing like the luminary with a thousand beams,"* Brahmá was born; Brahmá being as it were an isolated portion of Brahme, assuming individuality in order to create the world; this was not however accomplished by any direct process, for Brahmá produced Viraj, and then retired into inactivity. Viraj in like manner produced Manu, and upon him devolved the further duty of creation. Manu produced the Rishis, or Sages, of the Rig-Veda, Angiras, Bhrigu, etc., ten in number. The ten Rishis produced semi-divine beings of various degrees, and the whole vegetable and animal creation, endowed with internal consciousness, and sensible of pleasure and pain by means of past actions.† The work of creation was thus nominally attributed to many agents; but practically the scheme of the Code makes Brahme give place to the more active Brahmá, and Viraj retire to make room for his successor, Manu.

This celebrated Law-book commences in the following strain of dignity:—"Manu sat reclined with his attention fixed; the divine sages approached, and making salutations delivered the following address: 'Deign, sovereign ruler, to apprise us of the sacred laws in their order, as they must be followed by the four classes.'" Thus solicited, Manu replied, that for the sake of preserving the universe Brahmá had produced four classes of men, and allotted separate duties to each. These four classes were Brahmans, Kshatriyas, Vaisyas, and Sudras, who sprang respectively from the mouth, the arm, the thigh, and the foot of Brahmá.‡

* Code of Manu, i. 9. † *Ibid.*, iv. 49. ‡ *Ibid.*, i. 87.

Manu makes no allusion to the *five* classes of the Rig-Veda, says nothing of any changes, nothing of Brahmá as a new object of worship, or of kings having once had equal rights with Brahmans to minister in sacrifice; but he enunciates Brahmanical supremacy as a fact coeval with creation. The duties of the four Castes are thus defined:—Brahmans are to read the Veda and to teach it, to sacrifice, to conduct sacrifices for others, to give alms if rich, and to receive gifts when poor; Kshatriyas are to defend the people, give alms, and read the Veda; Vaisyas are to keep cattle, carry on trade, lend at interest, and cultivate the land; whilst to Sudras one principal duty is assigned, namely, to serve the before-mentioned classes.

The education of the first three Castes is most sagaciously consigned to Brahmans, and a series of auspicious acts prescribed, which commence even before a child is born. In the first or third year of his infant life he must be tonsured; and in his eighth year for a Brahman, or later for the two other Castes, or at any age up to sixteen for Brahmans, and twenty-two and twenty-four for Kshatriyas and Vaisyas, he must be invested with the mark of the Caste to which he owes his birth.* This is a most important ceremony, conferring, in Brahmanical language, a second birth: it is performed by passing what is called a sacrificial thread about the neck and beneath one shoulder of the youth; whilst the Brahman teacher, called Acharya, pronounces the sacred Gayatri, preceded by the mysterious triliteral syllable *Om*, the import of which will be considered when the systems of Brahmanical philosophy become the object of our study. Until this investiture or second birth has taken place, the

* Code of Manu, ii. 26-36.

young man is unable to read the sacred Vedas, or to perform sacrifice;* and if investiture is delayed beyond the age of sixteen for a Brahman, or a few years later for the other classes, the youths become outcasts,† to whom Brahmans must not teach the Veda, and with whom they must have no connection. The sacrificial cord is in fact the distinction between a twice-born man and a Sudra; all who wear this token of having received Brahmanical instruction are of the privileged Castes, and all who are without it are Sudras. The term 'sacrificial cord' means a cord which entitles the wearer to the privilege of sacrifice. Certain ceremonies are performed for girls as well as boys, but neither girls nor women are invested with the cord, and have in consequence no right to sacrifice. The Brahman from whom a youth receives investiture becomes his Acharya, or teacher, and a pupil is taught to regard such a teacher with even greater reverence than his natural parents, "because a second or divine birth ensures life both in this world and hereafter eternally."‡ Even a little child teaching holy texts from the Veda to his uncles, is entitled to call them "little sons;" for holy sages have always said "Child" to an ignorant man, and "Father" to a teacher of Scripture.§ The sanctity attached in the Code to the Vedic hymns (or Veda Sanhita) is somewhat remarkable, for already the language in which they are written was becoming obsolete, the Vedic Gods superseded, and the organization of society entirely different. The Code never quotes them, although it refers with pride of ancestry to Angiras and Bhrigu and other Vedic Rishis; but the only text of which it shows any knowledge is the address to the divine light of the sun

* Code, ii. 721. † *Ibid.*, ii. 38. ‡ *Ibid.*, ii. 146–169. § *Ibid.*, ii. 151–153.

for guidance, which is the holy Gayatri still in daily use. Indeed Mr. Colebrooke's observations on the superstitious modes in which Hindus now repeat the Vedas seem to apply even to the early period of the Code. Pupils must learn accurately the name of the Rishi by whom the verses were first uttered; but the verses may be repeated backwards or forwards, joined or disjoined.* The sons of Rajas appear to have received instruction from a preceptor resident at courts, and the children of Kshatriyas and Vaisyas probably attended their teachers daily; but the sons of Brahmans went to reside with their spiritual father, and performed for him menial service, such as collecting wood for the holy fire, sweeping the floor, and fetching the water required for daily use. The noviciate of a young Brahman required abstinence from pleasure and luxury: he must refrain from honey, flesh-meat, perfumes, chaplets of flowers, black powder for his eyes, sandals, umbrellas, dancing, music, and gaming.† Brahman pupils still live with their teachers, and are still restricted to the simplest fare; but this appears now as much the dictate of necessity as of principle, for the teachers are usually extremely poor. The course of instruction indicated in the Code comprises the Upanishads, grammar, prosody, and astronomy; and whilst the teacher is advised to use sweet gentle speech and give no pain, of the pupil it is said,—

> "As he who digs with a spade comes to a spring of water, so the student who humbly serves his teacher attains the knowledge which lies deep in his teacher's mind."‡

The Code of Manu ranks reverence for Acharyas as one of the first of virtues, and requires a pupil "to stand

* Colebrooke, i. 20. † Code, ii. 177. ‡ *Ibid.*, ii. 218.

with the palms of his hands joined, looking at the face of his preceptor;" in his presence, to "keep his right arm uncovered, to eat less, to wear a coarser mantle," and show endless tokens of respect.

"When his teacher is nigh, let his couch or his bench be always placed low; when his preceptor's eye can observe him, let him not sit carelessly or at ease.

"Let him never pronounce the mere name of his tutor, even in his absence; nor even mimic his gait, his speech, or his manner.

"In whatever place either true but censorious, or false and defamatory, discourse is held concerning his teacher, let him there cover his ears or remove to another place.

"By censuring his preceptor, though justly, he will be born an ass; by falsely defaming him, a dog; by using his goods without leave, a small worm; by envying his merit, a larger insect or reptile."*

A pupil is forbidden to give presents during the period of residence in a teacher's house; but when the course of instruction is concluded, he may "give the venerable man some valuable thing to the best of his power,—a field, or gold, a cow, an umbrella, a pair of sandals, or even any very excellent vegetable: thus will he gain the affectionate remembrance of his instructor."†

The first duty of a twice-born man, who has performed his ablution with stated ceremonies and has returned home, is to espouse a wife of the same class with himself.‡ But he must not marry into a family "which omits prescribed acts of religion," nor into one remarkable for ill-health, be they ever so great, or rich in kine, goats, sheep, gold, or grain; nor must he marry a girl with reddish hair, . . . nor one immoderately talkative, nor one with inflamed eyes,

* Code, ii. 198–201. † *Ibid.*, ii. 246. ‡ *Ibid.*, iii. 4–10.

nor one with the name of a constellation, tree, river of a barbarous nation, a winged creature, a snake;

"But let him choose for his wife a girl whose form has no defect, . . . who walks gracefully, like a flamingo or a young elephant."

After a Brahman has married a wife of rank equal to his own, he is to spend this second portion of his life as a happy householder, making daily offerings to fire, with some additional ceremonies at the close of each fortnight, and a moonplant festival at the end of each year.* If he has not sufficient wealth, he may attend on cattle or apply himself to agriculture; but keeping herds is preferable, because "tillage gives pain to sentient creatures, and is dependent upon the labour of bulls."† Many occupations are specified as wholly inconsistent with Brahmanical sanctity; amongst these are playing with dice,‡ singing, striking his arm, and dancing,§ dealing in tila seeds, which produce oil required in holy rites, and holding them back in hope of greater gain.|| Strict warnings are given against holding intercourse with people who do not believe in the Veda, people "who subsist like cats," or "live like rapacious water-birds;"¶ he must not reside in a city governed by a Sudra king, nor "long upon a mountain,"** which looks very much as if the hill-tribes were then as now beyond Brahmanical control. One of the worst sins however which a Brahman could commit was to impart knowledge of sacrifice or of Scripture to Sudras, or to receive a present from a king not born in the Kshatriya Caste;†† this enactment being necessary to the preservation of strict hereditary caste. But beyond this a higher mark was

* Code, iv. 25.
† *Ibid.*, x. 81.
‡ *Ibid.*, iv. 74.
§ *Ibid.*, iv. 64.
|| *Ibid.*, x. 90.
¶ *Ibid.*, iv. 30.
** *Ibid.*, iv. 60, 61.
†† *Ibid.*, iv. 84.

aimed at, for according to the Code it degraded a Brahman to receive gifts from an avaricious or irreligious king; and even if the giver of the gifts were unexceptionable,* a Brahman must avoid the habit of taking them, "since by taking many gifts his divine light soon fades."†

"Let him, then, who knows the law be fearful of presents; . . . since an ignorant man, even by a small gift, may become helpless as a cow in a bog."

A Brahman was to be distinguished for learning and virtue; and if such a one pronounced texts for the sake of gain he was "a covetous wretch, who displays the flag of virtue, a pretender, a deluder of the people,"‡ and the giver of gifts to so hypocritical a person shared in this punishment, for—

"As he who tries to pass over deep water in a boat of stone sinks to the bottom, so those two ignorant men, the receiver and the giver, sink to a region of torment."§

In the translation of the Code by Sir William Jones, the word *priest* is used throughout as corresponding precisely with the term Brahman; but to this it is objected, that to perform the offices of religion was only *one* of a Brahman's occupations, and one which he considered inconsistent with

* Code, iv. 87. † *Ibid.*, iv. 186. ‡ *Ibid.*, iv. 191.

§ Code, iv. 194. Some of the acts forbidden to Brahmans are both curious and unaccountable, as "he must not gaze on the sun, whether rising or setting, or eclipsed or reflected in water." He must not "run whilst it rains." He must not "look on his own image in water." When he sees the bow of Indra in the sky, he must not show it to any man. He must not step over a string to which a calf is tied, and he must not interrupt a cow when she is drinking; and he must not wash his feet in a pan of mixed metal." These and many other curious particulars will be found in the fourth chapter of the Code.

the highest sanctity;* a wealthy Brahman always employing, therefore, professional priests to perform religious ceremonies or minister for him in sacrifice. To give instruction in the sacred books, to give political counsel, and to administer justice, were the occupations preferred by a Brahman during middle life. No asceticism is then required: he is even desired not to waste himself with hunger, nor to wear old and sordid clothes; but with his hair and beard properly trimmed, his passions subdued, and his mantle white, "let him carry a staff of *Venu*, a ewer with water in it, a handful of *kusa*-grass, or a copy of the Vedas, with a pair of bright golden rings in his ears."†

But when middle life is past, and he has paid, as the law directs, his debts to the Sages, to the Manes, and to the Gods, the Brahman may resign all to his son, and retire to some solitary place to meditate on the divine nature of the soul.‡

We need not suppose that this rule of retiring from active life in middle age was ever the universal custom of the Brahman caste; but, doubtless, those who aimed at great learning or spiritual perfection did adopt the practice, and through their self-denying struggles and mortifications obtained that paramount influence which is so remarkable a feature in early Sanskrit literature. The language of the Code upon this subject is so beautiful and expressive, that the quotation of a few verses from the commencement of the sixth chapter is irresistible:—

"Having thus remained in the order of a housekeeper as the law ordains, let the twice-born man who had before completed his

* Elphinstone, Hist. of India, pp. 13, 14, *and note*.

† Code, iv. 34, 35. ‡ *Ibid.*, iv. 257, 258.

studentship dwell in a forest, his faith being firm and his organs wholly subdued.

"When the father of a family perceives his muscles becoming flaccid and his hair grey, and sees the child of his child, let him then seek refuge in a forest.

"Abandoning all food eaten in towns and all his household utensils, let him repair to the lonely wood, committing the care of his wife to her sons, or accompanied by her.

"Let him take up his consecrated fire, and all his domestic implements for making oblations to it, and, departing from the town to the forest, let him dwell in it with complete power over his organs.

"With many sorts of pure food, such as holy sages used to eat, with green herbs, roots, and fruit, let him perform the five great sacraments. . . .

"Let him wear a black antelope's hide, or a vesture of bark; let him bathe evening and morning; let him suffer the hairs of his head, his beard, and his nails to grow continually.

"From such food as himself may eat, let him to the utmost of his power make offerings and give alms; and with presents of water, roots, and fruit, let him honour those who visit his hermitage.

"Let him be constantly engaged in reading the Veda; patient of all extremities, universally benevolent, with a mind intent on the Supreme Being; a perpetual giver, but no receiver of gifts; with tender affection for all animated bodies.

"Let him, as the law directs, make oblations on the hearth with three sacred fires, not omitting in due time the ceremonies to be performed at the conjunction and opposition of the moon."

The hermit's food, like that of a Brahman pupil, was considerably restricted: no honey, no flesh-meat, no mushrooms, no fruit or roots produced in a town; but green herbs produced in earth or water, oils formed in fruits, and "pure grains, the food of ancient sages." This pure grain, brought home by himself, he may boil or make into cakes, and, as the law ordains, present oblations.

"He may eat what is mellowed by fire, and he may eat what is ripened by time; and either let him break hard fruits with a stone, or let his teeth serve as a pestle.

"Either let him pluck enough for a day, or let him gather enough for a month, or let him collect enough for six months, or lay up enough for a year."*

By degrees the severity of the hermit's self-denial is increased, and absolute suffering is prescribed in order to subdue the bodily frame and enable the spirit to escape from time and mingle with eternity. "To slide backwards and forwards on the ground; to stand a whole day on tiptoe; to sit in the hot season exposed to five fires, and stand uncovered during the rains," are amongst the trials recommended; that by "enduring harsher and harsher mortifications, he may dry up his bodily frame," and enter upon the fourth and closing period of a Brahman's life, when,

"Having reposited his holy fires, as the law directs, in his mind, let him live without external fire, without a mansion, wholly silent, feeding upon roots and fruits."†

When the hermit assumes a state of silence and gives up the use of fire, he becomes a Sanyasi, who must eat little, and ask but once in the day for food.

"At the time when the smoke of kitchen fires has ceased, when the pestle lies motionless, when the burning charcoal is extinguished, when people have eaten, and when dishes are removed, let the Sanyasi beg for food.‡

"For missing it let him not be sorrowful, nor for gaining it let him be glad; let him care only for a sufficiency to support life."

Indifference is the state which he must endeavour to acquire, and "by the absence of hate and affection, and by giving no pain to sentient creatures," to become fit for immortality. His means of showing kindness towards living

* Code of Manu, vi. 17. This had been done by a Hermit in the Hitopadesa, but a rat discovers his little store. "Hiranyaka, the prince of mice," was for ever eating the food of Churakarna, a religious mendicant, who had accumulated a hoard in a hole.—Hitopadesa, ch. i., fables v., vi.

† Code, vi. 31. ‡ *Ibid.*, vi. 56, 57.

creatures are extremely limited; but for the sake of preserving minute animals, he must never walk without looking on the ground; and for fear of destroying insects, he must not drink water until it has been strained.*

The Sanyasi is pointedly warned against explaining omens and prodigies, or showing skill in palmistry or astrology, to which occupations his reputation for sanctity would expose him. He is even desired to clip his hair, his nails, and his beard, in order perhaps to excite less attention; and the only occupation suitable to his situation is meditation,†—meditation upon the transmigration of men caused by their sinful deeds; on their separation from those whom they love, and their union with those whom they hate; on their strength overpowered by old-age; on their bodies racked by disease, and their agonizing departure from this corporeal frame;‡ and on "the progress of this internal spirit through various bodies high and low," which is admitted to be a progress hard to be discerned "by men of unimproved intellect."§

We dwell with particular pleasure on the picture of a tranquil philosopher who attains equanimity towards all creatures, who can bear a reproachful speech with patience,|| and who wishes neither for life nor death, but expects his appointed time as a hired servant expects his wages;¶ and we could almost envy the Brahman the indifference with which he anticipates leaving his body, "a mansion with bones for its rafters and beams," a mansion "infested by age and sorrow, . . . incapable of standing long." "Such a mansion," says the Brahman, "let the vital soul cheerfully quit; as a tree leaves the bank of a river, or as a bird

* Code, vi. 68–46.
† *Ibid.*, vi. 50, 52.
‡ *Ibid.*, vi. 61.
§ *Ibid.*, vi. 73.
|| *Ibid.*, vi. 47.
¶ *Ibid.*, vi. 45.

leaves the branch of a tree . . . thus is he who leaves his body delivered from the ravening shark of the world."*

But we must not lose sight of the cutting line which these philosophers drew between what is good for this life, and what is good for life hereafter. Our Brahman thought it better to meditate upon eternity than to contend with the ravening shark of the world; but he never thought of taming the shark; or, supposing its ravening propensities unalterable, he never thought of defending society from its incursions, or of finding happiness and blessedness in promoting the happiness and blessedness of others. Nevertheless the Brahman's view of old-age and death is very beautiful, and, as far as we know, comes nearer to the pathos and sublimity of Hebrew Scripture than any other ante-Christian record.

Turning from the Brahmans to the Kings, we feel reminded that Brahmans were the authors of the Code; for alas! the earnest eloquence, ease, and graphic detail which we have been admiring, vanish when kings become the subject; and in pompous words a mere superficial view is given of what Brahmans apparently intended to be mere superficial authority. The very word for King in Sanskrit, *Raja*, signifies *to shine* as well as *to rule*, and the Brahmans took pains to make their king—

> "As glorious as the autumn's evening sky,
> Bright with the moon, and set with radiant stars."†

A part of his daily duty was to enter his hall, or hold his court in "decently splendid attire," and stand there to gratify his subjects with kind words and looks. In the afternoon he is to gratify his warriors in the same way, by going forth completely arrayed to review his troops, ele-

* Code, vi. 76–78.

† Hindu Theatre, vol. ii. p. 231.

phants, horses,* cars, etc. In fact, one reads of kings in the Code with a feeling that they are puppets in an imaginary pageant; but the regulations concerning them are nevertheless worth studying, for although never fully realized they are alluded to and partially recognized in general Sanskrit literature. The King is exhorted to conduct himself with humility towards Brahmans learned in the three Vedas, to avoid idleness and vice, and to appoint seven or eight ministers versed in the holy books, skilled in the use of weapons, and whose lineage is noble. He must also have a very learned Brahman as a confidential adviser, and various other ministers, usually Brahmans, who assist in the council which the King meets every morning; "ascending up the back of a mountain, or going privately to a terrace, a bower, a forest, or a lonely place," that he may consult them unobserved, for it is said that "that prince of whose weighty secrets all assemblies of men are ignorant, shall attain dominion over the whole earth." The secrecy required in these Brahmanical councils, in Ayodhya and the other early kingdoms of Hindostan, offers a striking contrast to the public assemblies of the Rajputs in Guzerat and at Mathura, as recorded in after-years. From this council 'with closed doors' the Code requires that all blind, deaf, and decrepit persons should be removed, because those who are suffering in this world for sins committed in previous births, are apt to betray counsel; and for the same reason talking birds, and above all, women must be excluded. An account of the subjects on which a council deliberates occupies a large portion of the chapter assigned to the King's duties. The whole question of war and negotiation is discussed, and the qualifications required in an ambassador:

* Code, vii. 145, 146, 222.

he must have a pure hand and a pure heart; he must be handsome, intrepid, eloquent, have an excellent memory, and be well acquainted with countries and times; but it is also essential that he understand external signs and hints, that he may discover the arts of a foreign prince through the acts of his confidential servants. By the aid of this illustrious ambassador and his secret negotiations the enemy is to be reduced by internal dissension, and by well-applied gifts all such leaders are to be gained as can be safely brought over. For this purpose spies of five descriptions are recommended; as, "active and artful youths, degraded anchorites, distressed husbandmen, decayed merchants, and fictitious penitents," who are all to be seen and paid in private. Intrigue is no disgrace, and prudence a cardinal virtue; the Code giving its highest commendation to the king who foresees the good and evil to ensue from his measures, and so arranges his affairs that no ally, neutral prince, or enemy, ever gets an advantage over him. On the other hand, there is no praise for heroic daring, or hopeless valour, or generous defence of country, home and hearth. The negative duty of not turning his face from battle is the only military duty inculcated upon kings and soldiers, and the rules of war in general are tame and dull; although they read very like rules for preserving peace, they do not excite respect and confidence, because they have the air of being drawn up in seclusion, by students who had never seen or felt the troubles and difficulties of actual warfare or political contention; and, on the other hand, one is irresistibly inclined to attribute them to learned men, anxious to be independent of the Military Caste. The most pleasing part of the subject is the mercy required in the choice of weapons, and also towards captives; these rules have fortunately been translated in metre, which gives a most opportune relief to this unusually prosaic prose:

> "Let the soldier, good in battle, never guilefully conceal
> (Wherewithal to smite the unwary) in his staff the treacherous steel;
> Let him scorn to barb his javelin; let the valiant ne'er anoint
> With fell poison-juice his arrows, ne'er put fire upon the point.
> In his car, or on his war-horse, should he chance his foe to meet,
> Let him smite not if he find him lighted down upon his feet;
> Let him spare one standing suppliant, with his closed hands raised on high,
> Spare him whom his long hair loosen'd blinds and hinders from to fly,—
> Spare him if he sink exhausted; spare him if for life he crave;
> Spare him crying out for mercy, 'Take me, for I am thy slave.'
> Still remembering his duty, never let the soldier smite
> One unarm'd, defenceless, mourning for one fallen in the fight;
> Never strike the sadly wounded; never let the brave attack
> One by sudden terror smitten, turning in base flight his back."*

The Law-book mentions so few names of places, kings, or kingdoms, that we may almost suspect it of wishing to avoid identifying itself with any particular time or place: it is written for all time and for all Hindus, and in consequence gives very few *data* enabliug us to judge how far Hindus and Brahmans had penetrated. They do not however appear to have been confined to the plains of the Ganges, which the Code calls Aryavarta, for allusions are made to most desirable forts on hills, which one hundred bowmen can defend against ten thousand. Such natural defences would be difficult to find near the Ganges; but Gwalior and Dowlatabad and other basaltic rocks of Malwa and Rajputana answer well to the description. Mathura is likewise mentioned; the men of Mathura being tall and light, and therefore good soldiers for the van of an army. The coun-

* R. T. Griffith, Specimens of Indian Poetry, p. 9.

try was divided into a number of small unequal states, of which the weaker sought the protection of the stronger; and the conquest of foreign States *appears* to be alluded to, for it is recommended that the deities and virtuous priests of a conquered country be respected, but we can only suppose that this refers to slight varieties amongst Hindu States. It may be a recommendation to kings of the Solar race to be tolerant towards the usages of the Lunar dynasties, or to Hindus settled in Oude to be liberal towards Rajputs in Malwa, or Saurashtrians in modern Guzerat; but it is not probable that despotic and exclusive Brahmans recommended positive toleration towards the religions of people whom they called Sudras, robbers, or barbarians. If they conquered Scythian tribes in the northern mountains, whom they called Hunas and Sakas, they did not attempt to hold them or govern them, because this was apparently impossible to the philosophic theories of the Brahmans, which affected the Court and capital, but made very little impression on the people as a nation. It may be for want of knowing how to extract the information required, but with mere ordinary apparatus for this purpose the Code is far from satisfactory upon the subject of the Kshatriya, or Military Caste: if it gave mere law we could not complain, but whilst we are told that a king's displeasure is worse than lightning, and consumes whole families by its destructive violence, and that Abundance rises on her lotus-leaf whenever a king is well pleased and gracious, we get no facts to show in what manner a king ever has or ever can exercise individual enterprise in promoting the welfare or improvement of his kingdom.

CHAPTER IV.

THE RAMAYANA.

"The lark soars upwards and is gone;
His voice is heard, but body there is none.
* * * *
So poets' songs are with us, though they die,
And earth inherits the rich melody."—HOOD.

HITHERTO we have been like voyagers sailing towards an unknown land, striving to catch glimpses through a telescope of the leading features of the country, but baffled by twilight when hoping to make more detailed observations. Now that we are about to look upon the graphic pages of epic poetry, we shall feel a change in our sensations, as if when nearing our port at dusk the coast should suddenly appear illuminated by a revolving lighthouse, and a palace, a procession, a sacrifice, or a tournament were for a moment visible in the rich red light, or in the succeeding clear white rays of the lofty beacon. Such are the transitory high-coloured views of life in Ancient India, which we get from the portions of the Sanskrit Epics which have been translated; and it is more especially upon the kings and courts, so slighted in the Code, that they delight to shed their glowing gleams.

The Ramayana is the more ancient, and also the more connected of these poems, and commences with the history of a King of Ayodhya, an ancient city on the river Gogra, then called the Srayu (tributary to the Ganges). King of Ayodhya is his title, although Ayodhya was merely the capital of the province of Kosala, corresponding nearly with the modern province of Oude. Ayodhya held in fact nearly the same position as the modern city of Oude, where remains of old buildings are still visible.* "The streets and alleys of this city were admirably disposed, and the principal streets well watered. It was beautified with gardens, fortified with gates, . . . crowded with charioteers and messengers furnished with arms, adorned with banners, filled with dancing girls and dancing men, crowded with elephants, horses, and chariots, merchants and ambassadors from various countries. It resembled a mine of jewels, or the residence of *Sri*, the walls were variegated with divers sorts of gems like the divisions of a chess-board,† the houses formed one continued row of equal height, resounding with the music of the tabor, . . . the twang of the bow, and the sacred sound of the Veda. It was perfumed with incense, chaplets of flowers, and articles for sacrifice, by their odour cheering the heart."‡

In this city of well-fed happy people no one practised a

* Oude is seventy-nine miles from Lucknow, and adjoins Fyzabad.

† This expression seems to indicate that in India, as in Assyria, walls were ornamented in mosaic. See Fergusson.

‡ Cary, vol. i. pp. 95–98.

calling not his own; none were without relations; the men loved their wives, the women were faithful and obedient to their husbands; no one was without earrings; no one went unperfumed; no Brahman was without the constant fire, and no man gave less than a thousand rupees to the Brahmans. This city was guarded by warriors as a mountain den by lions, filled with horses from Kamboja and other places, and elephants from the Vindhya and Himalaya mountains, and governed as Indra governs his city, by Dasaratha, chief of the race of Ikshwaku.*

This King was perfectly skilled in the Vedas and Vedangas, beloved by his people, a great charioteer, and constant in sacrifice. His courtiers were wise, capable of understanding a nod, and constantly devoted to him. Eight Brahmans are mentioned as chief counsellors, two as *chosen priests*, and these appear to have been his prime ministers; six others were also in office. "Surrounded by all these counsellors, learned, faithful, eminent, seeking by wise counsels the good of the kingdom, Dasaratha shone resplendent as the sun irradiating the world."†

But even Dasaratha, King of Ayodhya, had a grief,—he pined because he had no son; and consulting his Brahmans, they brought a Rishi, or eminent devotee, to court, to perform the Aswamedha, or horse sacrifice, supposed to ensure the boon desired by him who performs it with sufficient magnificence and liberality. The sacrifice succeeded, the divinities were propitiated, and the King's three wives became the mothers of four sons. The first and favourite

* The above is given nearly *verbatim*, with Cary's translation, only omitting repetitions and redundancies.

† Cary, vol. i. p. 3.

wife had two sons, Rama and Lakshman; Rama being the eldest of the four, and destined by his father to assist him in his advancing years, and succeed to the throne at his demise.*

Nothing is said of the young princes during their infancy; but when they are on the verge of manhood, a Rishi named Viswamitra appears at court, soliciting the King to allow Rama to go with him to his hermitage in the hills, and clear it from tormenting fiends, who destroyed all his attempts at a ten-night sacrifice by sprinkling the altar with blood. The King is distracted by contending feelings, his reverence for the Sage and his love for his son being equally unbounded. After trembling, fainting, and recovering, he says that his Rama, the lotus-eyed, has not yet attained his sixteenth year, and says he will himself go. He is an archer invincible; "as long as life remains will I maintain the combat with these night-wanderers, . . . the sacrifice shall be effectually protected, . . . but Rama thou must not take; he is a child, . . . unable to bear arms, . . . incapable of coping with the wily Rakshasas; . . . thou must not take my Rama; . . . by me, an old man, are these sons begotten, . . . dearer to me than life itself."

This pathetic remonstrance kindles anger in the breast of the Sage, at which the whole earth was moved, and "fear seized even the Gods." The prime minister interposes, the King gives way, and his two sons, Rama and Lakshman, are sent away with Viswamitra.† To qualify Rama for the enterprise was the first consideration: travelling along the south bank of the river, the Sage bids him touch the water whilst receiving instruction, which shall make him proof

* Cary, vol. i. p. 232

† *Ibid.*, p. 251.

against fatigue, disease, or change of form, and give him such strength of arm that no one in the three worlds shall be his equal.* The next day Viswamitra and his pupils crossed the river, and heard the mighty sound of waters caused by the confluence of the Surayu and the Jahnavi; and after defeating a female demon, who infested a forest "dark as a cloud," Rama was presented with celestial weapons. Thus prepared, the party proceeded to the hermitage, and in "dreadful combat" Rama encountered and destroyed the "night-wandering Rakshasas."†

The point to which the holy guide next conducted his young pupils was Mithila, where a certain king named Janaka resided, whose daughters and nieces would, he thought, prove desirable wives for the four young princes. The King of Mithila received the travellers with much solemnity: joining his hands together he said to the Rishi, "O thou Godlike, take a place among the great sages;" and having seated the holy man he drew near with joined palms, saying, "O thou heavenly one, today am I blessed with the water of immortality;" and then turning to his young companions, asked who were "those noble youths, of majestic gait like the elephant, courageous as the tiger and buffalo . . . with eyes like the lotus, of godlike aspect and bearing the scimitar and the quiver?" Viswamitra replies that they are the sons of the King of Ayodhya, come to Mithila to inquire after King Janaka's great bow.‡ The bow was at once sent for, and brought in an eight-wheeled carriage drawn by eight hundred men. To the man who could draw this bow the King had promised his most lovely

* Cary, vol. i. p. 259. † *Ibid.*, p. 111.

‡ Cary, vol. i. p. 548. See also Heeren, vol. ii. p. 152.

daughter, Sita. Rama alone could either lift or bend the weighty weapon, and he with one hand snapped it asunder with a crash like that of a falling mountain.

The lovely Sita was therefore to become the bride of Rama, and his brothers were to marry the three other princesses of Mithila; and as Ayodhya was only a four days' journey distant, the old King Dasaratha came with his councillors to attend the celebration of his sons' nuptials. Rare and costly presents of shawls and silks, deer-skins and precious stones, costly vehicles, were made upon the occasion, and then the whole party returned to Ayodhya, where Dasaratha's wives were eager to embrace the beautiful brides of their sons; and "all these ladies, sumptuously clad in silk, and entertaining each other with agreeable conversation, hastened to the temples of the Gods to offer incense."*

Dasaratha now made preparations for the public acknowledgment of Rama as destined to be the next king in regular succession, and as permitted during his father's lifetime to share with him the honours and fatigues of royalty; but this happiness was all destroyed by the intrigues of Dasaratha's second wife, who was jealous of Rama, and determined that her son Bharata should be the future king. Unfortunately Dasaratha had once given a promise to Bharata's mother that he would grant any two boons she pleased to ask. The promise had been made in years gone by, when he had been dangerously wounded in battle, and carefully attended by this wife, Kaikeyi; and amongst Hindus a promise was irrevocable, and therefore the wretched King felt compelled to yield, although the first boon required was to banish Rama for a period of fourteen years,

* Cary, vol. i. p. 627.

and the second to declare Bharata the heir-apparent.* No one thinks of remonstrating, and Rama and his lovely wife and his brother depart for the forests; but the exiles were no sooner gone than the aged monarch drooped in sadness. "Six days he sat and mourned, and pined for Rama all that weary time." In the middle of the seventh night a crime, inadvertently committed in his youth, rose up in his mind: he sought sympathy from Kausalya, his first wife, the mother of the banished Rama, and asked her to listen to his tale, for to this he attributed his present affliction. "Every deed," he says, "whether good or evil, brings in time its proper fruit," and men are foolish in cherishing the gay blossoms of the Palasa,† whilst they neglect the fruit-bearing Amra‡ because its flowers are insignificant. King Dasaratha then relates that when his wife was still "unwed, in virgin bloom," and he "in youth's delicious prime," and the first rains of summer were commencing, there came—

"A day of summer rain-time, filling my young soul with love;
The great sun had dried the earth-dews with his hot beams from above,
And in highest heaven turning, journey'd on his southward road,
Racing towards the gloomy region, the Departed's sad abode:
Balmy cool the air was breathing, welcome clouds were floating by,
Humming bees with joyful music swell'd the glad wild peacock's cry;
Their wing-feathers wet with bathing, birds slow flying to the trees,
Rested in the topmost branches, fann'd by the soft summer breeze;
Like the Great Deep, many twinkling, gold-shot, with gay peacock's sheen,

* Hindu Drama, vol. i. p. 281, H. H. Wilson.

† *Butea frondosa.* ‡ Mango.

Gleaming with the fallen rain-drops, sea-bright all the hills were seen;
Whilst like serpents, winding swiftly, torrents from the mountain-side
Hiss'd along, some bright and flashing, turbid some and ochre-dyed."*

The first showers of May and June were giving a reprieve from the intense heat of the previous months, and with bow in hand the youthful monarch left the city for the woods which skirt Surayu's flood, intending to try his skill as an archer upon the beasts of the forest, who come down to the river to drink in the cool of the evening. Whilst lying in ambush by the river's reedy side, he heard the gurgling sound of a water-cruse being slowly filled: this he mistook for the noise made by an elephant in drinking; it was dark, and eager to secure the game he drew forth a glittering shaft, but scarcely had the arrow flown when he heard the bitter wail of a human voice, exclaiming, "Ah me! ah me!" in dying agony;—

"Writhing on the bank in anguish, with a plaintive voice cried he,
'Ah! wherefore has this arrow smitten a poor harmless devotee?'"

The King's arrow had fatally wounded a youth who had come down to the river to draw water for his parents, who were recluses in the forest, and who is at a loss to imagine why any murderer should seek his life. "Who," he says, "should slay a hermit living upon roots and fruits? Does he want my vesture? Little will he gain from my deerskin mantle and coat of bark." But it is not for his death, he says, that he is pained, but for the destitution in which he will leave his aged parents. Horror seized the King, as in the stilly calm of evening he heard this piteous moan; and

* R. T. Griffith, Specimens of Indian Poetry, p. 11.

rushing through the reeds and bushes, perceived a young Ascetic lying transfixed by an arrow, his hair dishevelled, his pitcher cast aside, and the life-blood fast ebbing from his wound. The dying youth fixed his eyes upon Dasaratha and recognized him as the King; but still wondering what offence he can have given, he adds:

"'Ah! I am not thine only victim. Cruel King! thy heedless dart
Pierces too a father's bosom, and an aged mother's heart.
They, my parents blind and feeble, from this hand alone can drink,
When I come not, thirsting, hoping, sadly to the grave they 'll sink.'"

Fruitless now, he continues, are his Veda studies, and fruitless his father's ascetic merit; for even were his father present, he would be powerless to save, "as a tree can never rescue from the axe the doomed tree." But although his father was powerless to save, he knew that he was mighty to curse; and the gentle spirit of the sufferer recoiled from the thought that the King, the son of Raghu, would be blasted by that curse. He bids him therefore hasten to deprecate his father's consuming wrath, by being himself the bearer of the evil tidings; but begs first to have the arrow taken from his side, that he may be released from agony. Dasaratha hesitated, and the youth, rightly interpreting his hesitation, assures him that, although withdrawing the shaft will occasion death, he need not fear, for that he is not a Brahman.

"'Let not thy sad heart be troubled for thy sin if I should die;
Lessen'd be thy grief and terror, for no twice-born, King, am I;
Fear not; thou may'st do my bidding, guiltless of a Brahman's death:
Wedded to a Vaisya father, Sudra mother gave me breath.'
Thus he spake, and I down kneeling drew the arrow from his side;
Then the hermit, rich in penance, fix'd his eyes on me, and died."

The punishment which the Code of Manu awards to the slayer of a Brahman was to be branded in the forehead with the mark of a headless corpse, and entirely banished from society;* this being apparently commutable for a fine. The poem is therefore in accordance with the Code regarding the peculiar guilt of killing Brahmans; but in allowing a hermit who was not a *Dwija* (twice-born) to go to heaven, the poem is far in advance of the Code. The youth in the poem is allowed to read the Veda, and to accumulate merit by his own as well as his father's pious acts; whereas the exclusive Code reserves all such privileges to *Dwijas*, invested with the sacred cord. Many such inconsistencies are met with, showing that the Code never was in universal practice.

The King stood for a time motionless with sorrow; but as soon as he recovered himself he filled the pitcher with water from the stream, and taking the path which had been directed, he soon reached the lowly cottage of the poor old sightless couple, who were sitting like two birds with clipped wings, helpless, with none to guide them. The next scene will admit of no abridgment.

"Sadly, slowly I approach'd them, by my rash deed left forlorn;
Crush'd with terror was my spirit, and my mind with anguish torn;
At the sound of coming footsteps thus I heard the old man say,
'Dear son, bring me water quickly, thou hast been too long away,
Bathing in the stream, or playing, thou hast stay'd so long from home;
Come, thy mother longeth for thee; come in quickly, dear child, come!
Be not angry, mine own darling; keep not in thy memory
Any hard word from thy mother, any hasty speech from me;

* Code, ix. 237.

Thou art thy poor parents' succour, eyes art thou unto the blind;
Speak! on thee our lives are resting—why so silent and unkind?'
Thus I heard; yet deeper grieving, and in fresh augmented woe,
Spake to the bereavèd father, with words faltering and slow,
'Not thy child, O noble-minded; Dasaratha, Sage! am I,
By a deed of sinful rashness plunged with thee in misery.'"

The unhappy King then tells his tale, and entreats pardon; and the hermit, who can scarcely speak for weeping, tells him that had he concealed this sin its fruits would have fallen upon his head ten thousand-fold, and had it been intentional, the whole race of Raghu would have perished; and before saying more, he begs that they may be conducted to the fatal place, and be enabled once more to fold their darling in their arms. The lamentations uttered by the side of the "death-cold clay" are very touching, especially where the father urges the son, no longer living, to speak to his parents:

"'Come, dear child, embrace thy father, put thy little hand in mine;
Let me hear thee sweetly prattle some fond playful word of thine.
Ah! who'll read me now the Vedas, filling my old heart with joy?
Who, when evening rites are over, cheer me mourning for my boy?
Who will bring me fruits and water, roots and wild herbs from the wood?
Who supply the helpless hermit, like a cherish'd guest, with food?
Can I tend thine aged mother till her weary life is done?
Can I feed her, soothe her sorrow, longing for her darling son?'"

The father's thoughts then turn to the blissful mansion which his son shall attain in heaven, where he shall be welcome to those who fell nobly in battle, and dwell in Indra's Paradise with good people who loved their Acharyas, or spiritual teachers, and tended the sacred fire, and studied the Veda, and performed penance; but he denounces sorrow on the wretch by whose rash hand he fell. Whilst the parents were occupied in sorrow's last duties over the body of their son, he addressed them from a heavenly chariot in the sky, saying that his filial devotion had won for him supreme bliss, and that they must not grieve, but follow to partake his joy. The old hermit is nevertheless quite unable to forgive, and lays his curse upon the humbled King, and says to him—

> "'Thy breast shall know
> Something of the pangs I suffer—a bereavèd father's woe:
> Thus I lay my curse upon thee, for this thing that thou hast done—
> As I mourn for my belovèd, thou shalt sorrow for a son.'"

The aged pair then ascended the funeral pile of their son, and there expired. And this youthful folly, Dasaratha says, is the cause of his present distress, it is the fulfilment of the ancient hermit's curse. He bids Kausalya, his affectionate wife, farewell, and sinks in anguish for his banished Rama. He feels his eyes darkened and his memory overcast, and knows that this is the awful summons of the dark messengers of Death. His last words are for Rama, envying those who will see him return in triumph after his exile, and saying, "Ah, Rama! ah, my son!"

This beautiful episode was published in Paris in 1826, with a translation by M. Chezy, and a literal version in Latin by M. Bournouf. There is also a very pleasing translation in verse by the Rev. Dean Milman, but the quotations and abstract above are taken almost wholly from the later translation by Mr. Griffith.

Funeral ceremonies* for King Dasaratha were performed in Ayodhya with very great pomp. The body of the deceased King was wrapped in silk, placed on a bier, and committed to the flames; his wives were not burned with

* Heeren, vol. ii. p. 155.

him, although a passage occurs in which his favourite wife, Kausalya, is said to entertain the idea and wish to do so; but the practice of widows actually burning themselves on their husbands' funeral pile is believed to belong to a much later period of Hindu history. A great feast and sacrifice was made, at which animals were sacrificed and *flesh* distributed;* and then follows a lively description of the poets, panegyrists, parasites, etc., resident at an Indian Court, and details concerning Court customs and amusements, which were all abandoned out of respect for the deceased Raja. "At other times the town resounded with the noise and bustle of men and women, like the shout of contending armies; the great men ever going to and fro upon chariots, elephants, and prancing steeds." Now the pleasure-gardens were abandoned, the tables for sacrificial offerings empty, the flower-shops closed, and bankers and merchants absent.† The State was without a king; and although the poet is eloquent upon the disasters to which this exposed it, we may doubt whether Brahman poets or Brahman ministers considered in their hearts that this was any great misfortune. At any rate the principal Brahman, Vasishta, assumed the conduct of affairs, and assembled the Council, who agreed that Bharata, the son of the intriguing second wife, Kaikeyi, must be sent for and invited to occupy the vacant throne. Bharata was residing with his maternal grandfather; but although he obeyed the summons and returned immediately to Ayodhya, he refused to accept the insignia of royalty,

* See Col. Sykes, J. R. A. S. No. xii. May, 1841. At page 269 he gives a note referring to the Ramayana, book ii. sec. 61, saying that a cow and calf were sacrificed at Dasaratha's funeral, and ghee, oil, and *flesh* distributed.

† Heeren, vol. ii. p. 267; Ramayana, iii. 98.

which according to Hindu law was the heritage of his elder brother.* We are not told how his mother behaved when he thus refused to aid her wicked schemes for his advancement; but the Council resolved, that if he would not be king himself, he must go in pursuit of Rama, and persuade him to return and assume the sovereignty. Bharata accordingly set out with a splendid retinue of soldiers and attendants. His ordinary night encampments are not recorded; but in the neighbourhood of Allahabad he met a renowned Sage, bearing the Vedic name of Bharadwaja, who insisted upon making a feast, not only for Bharata himself, but for his entire army. This Sage possessed powers of enchantment, by which he compelled the forest and the rivers to bring contributions of venison, peacocks, partridges, mutton, the flesh of the wild hog, sauces, and potent spirits. The entertainment was served in a magnificent palace produced for the occasion; thousands of beautiful damsels were sent down by the God Brahmá, and celestial music floated in the air, until at the approach of daybreak Bharadwaja dissolved the spell and the whole scene disappeared. This famous dinner of venison and peacocks may be contrasted with the repast given to Viswamitra and his retainers, where the dishes were piled mountains high with honey, sugar-cane, and other dainties for licking, chewing, and drinking. The explanation is that Viswamitra and his followers were Brahmans, whilst Bharata was a Kshatriya, accompanied by warriors, to which Caste flesh-meat appears to have been habitual.

Bharata's journey was impeded by the want of roads; but able carpenters and diggers and labourers, with carts, ac-

* Heeren, vol. ii. pp. 155, 156.

companied him, breaking through rocks, building bridges, digging wells, and even making canals,* and penetrating apparently into unexplored country, crossing the Vindhya Hills in the direction of Indore, and at length discovering Rama, with his brother and his wife Sita, in the forests of the Dekkan.

The meeting between the brothers shows the utmost delicacy and generosity of feeling; Bharata lamenting his mother's ill conduct, and entreating Rama to return; Rama declining, because unless he keep his father's vow he cannot secure his father's happiness in heaven: he therefore adjures his brother to return to Ayodhya and "console the people and the twice-born. I with Sita and Lakshman will enter the forest of Dandaka. Be thou the king of men, I will be sovereign of wild beasts. Let the umbrella shade thy head, I will take refuge in the shade of the woods."† Bharata makes a pathetic remonstrance; but at length Rama embraced him, "sobbing like a staggering duck," and put an end to the discussion by saying, "Though the rising of the cool moon should cease to be pleasing; though Himavat should abandon its snow; . . . I will not relinquish my promise; . . . the sea may overflow its shore, but I will never relinquish my father's engagement." In sign of obedience to Rama's wishes, Bharata then begs him to put on the golden shoes, which he had brought. Rama does so, and returns them to his brother. Bharata then, bowing to the shoes, says, "For fourteen years I will assume the matted hair and the habit of a devotee, and feed on fruits and roots. Waiting thy return, I will reside without the city . . . committing the kingdom to thy shoes." The

* Cary, vol. iii. p. 228.

† Cary, vol. iii. p. 429.

brothers embrace, and Rama's last words are, "Cherish thy mother Kaikeyi, be not angry with her; to this thou art adjured by both me and Sita."*

After Bharata's departure, Rama came accidentally into collision with the rude people of the wild country in which he was located. A woman of their race, unfortunately, made love to him and his brother, and they, as a sign of their displeasure, cut off her nose and her ears;† but the woman had powerful relatives possessed of demoniacal power, and knew how to take vengeance on her foes. Finding other plans fail—for in open warfare Rama always gained the ascendency—she called in aid her power of sorcery, and bewitched her brother Ravana, the demon-king of Lanka (Ceylon), to be in love with Rama's wife, the lovely Sita. Ravana, finding it in vain to hope to succeed without the aid of stratagem, took with him an assistant sorcerer, disguised as a deer; and as Rama took great pleasure in the chase, it was not difficult for the deer to lure him from his cottage in pursuit. He did not leave his beloved Sita without charging Lakshman, his brother, to remain in charge; but the wily deer knew how to defeat his precaution, and when transfixed by Rama's arrow he cried out in the voice of Rama, "Oh, Lakshman, save me!" Sita heard the cry, and entreated Lakshman to fly to his brother's rescue. He was unwilling to go, but yielded to her earnestness, and she was left alone. This being the state of affairs which Ravana desired, he now left his hiding-place and came forward as an Ascetic, in a red threadbare garment, with a single tuft of hair upon his head, and three sticks and a pitcher in his hand. All creation shuddered at his approach; birds,

* Cary, pp. 472, 473.

† H. H. Wilson, Hindu Theatre, i. 281.

beasts, and flowers were motionless with dread; the summer wind ceased to breathe, and a shiver passed over the bright waves of the river. Ravana stood for awhile looking at his victim, as she sat weeping, and musing over the unknown cry; but soon he approached, saying:*

"'O thou that shinest like a tree with summer blossoms overspread.
Wearing that woven *kusa* robe, and lotus garland on thy head!
Why art thou dwelling here alone, here in this dreary forest's shade,
Where range at will all beasts of prey, and demons prowl in every glade?
Wilt thou not leave thy cottage-home, and roam the world which stretches wide,
See the fair cities which men build, and all their gardens and their pride?
Why longer, fair one, dwell'st thou here, feeding on roots and sylvan fare,
When thou might'st dwell in palaces, and earth's most costly jewels wear?
Fearest thou not the forest gloom, which darkens round on every side?
Who art thou, say! and whose and whence, and wherefore dost thou here abide?'
When first these words of Ravana broke upon sorrowing Sita's ear,
She started up, and lost herself in wonderment and doubt and fear;
But soon her gentle loving heart threw off suspicion and surmise,
And slept again in confidence, lull'd by the mendicant's disguise.
'Hail, holy Brahman!' she exclaim'd; and in her guileless purity
She gave a welcome to her guest with courteous hospitality.
Water she brought to wash his feet, and food to satisfy his need,
Full little dreaming in her heart what fearful guest she had received."

She even tells him her whole story, how Rama had won

* Westminster Review, October, 1848, p. 45.

her for his bride and taken her to his father's home, and how the jealous Kaikeyi had cast them forth to roam the woods; and after dwelling fondly on her husband's praise, she invited her guest to tell his name and lineage, and what had induced him to leave his native land for the wilds of the Dandaka forest, inviting him to await her husband's return, for "to him are holy wanderers dear." Suddenly Ravana declares himself to be the demon-monarch of the earth, "at whose name Heaven's armies flee." He has come, he says, to woo Sita for his queen, and to carry her to his palace in the island of Ceylon. Then burst forth the wrath of Rama's wife:

"'*Me* wouldst thou woo to be thy queen, or dazzle with thine empire's shine?
And didst thou dream that Rama's wife could stoop to such a prayer as thine?
I, who can look on Rama's face, and know that there my husband stands,—
My Rama, whose high chivalry is blazon'd through a hundred lands!
What! shall the jackal think to tempt the lioness to mate with him?
Or did the King of Lanka's isle build upon such an idle dream?'"

Ravana's only answer was to throw off his disguise, and with brows as dark as the storm-cloud in the sky, he carried off the shrieking Sita as an eagle bears a snake, mounting up aloft and flying with his burden through the sky. The unhappy Sita calls loudly upon Rama, and bids the flowery bowers, and trees, and river, all tell her Rama that Ravana has stolen his Sita from his home. Here our attention is again called to the beauty of a river running between groves of trees. On the former occasion, the Surayu river (or the Gogra), on which Ayodhya stands, was frequented by water-fowl, who dipped their wings into its cooling flood and then flew to the topmost branches of the trees to catch the faintest movement of the breeze, whilst the soothing hum of bees tempered the glad cry of the gay peacock. The river which the unhappy Sita loved was a tributary to the Godavery, running through the dense forests and wild districts not yet entirely explored, which lie to the north of Bombay and stretch away towards Orissa. The plash of the water-fowl bathing in the bright waters of the Godavery is the most cheerful feature of the scene; but, unlike the Gogra, it is skirted by no "sea-bright hills" with flashing torrents, but hemmed in by the weary woods of "the pathless Dandaka,"* where twining creeper-plants hanging and climbing from bough to bough, and the rich blossoms of the lofty trees, alone relieve the forest gloom.† This is the district at present inhabited by Khonds and Koles, of whose human sacrifices and other uncivilized practices Captain Macpherson has published full particulars.‡ In Rama's time the woods were not haunted by Gonds, Khonds, and Koles, but by demons and monkeys; and as he did not feel strong enough to recover Sita single-handed, he entered

* This country appears to be still "the pathless Dandaka;" for a "Friend of India" writes in the 'Times' newspaper (Thursday, October 27, 1853), "If one-half the money that has been expended in endeavouring to improve the quality of the cotton of India had been invested in improving the navigation of the Godavery," slave-labour would become a drug in America. And Colonel Cotton states, "There seems no reason why the Godavery may not become the line of a trade of a million tons a year, when once the pent-up treasures of its basin effect a breach in the barriers which have hitherto shut it up. . . . Wheat might be manufactured into flour by the abundant water-power of the Godavery, and conveyed to England by hundreds of thousands of tons."

† Westminster Review, Oct. 1848, pp. 47, 48.

‡ J.R.A.S. vol. xiii. p. 216; and also the same Journal for May, 1842.

into alliance with the monkeys. First, the monkey-king Sugriva despatched emissaries in all directions to ascertain where Sita was concealed; and when the monkey-general Hanuman ascertained that she was in a palace in Ceylon, Rama and all the allied forces marched down to the Coromandel coast, and making a bridge by casting rocks into the sea passed quickly into Lanka.* Vestiges of Rama's bridge may still be seen, occasioning much inconvenience to navigators, who are obliged to lighten heavy-burdened vessels before they can pass the rocks and sandbanks of the Straits of Manaar. After fighting a few battles, the Rakshasas (demons) were defeated, Ravana put to death by Rama, and Sita rescued from her palace-prison. Rama will however have nothing to say to his recovered wife until she shall have gone through the ordeal of fire: but as she passed through the blazing pile unhurt,† and Brahma and other Gods attested her fidelity, her husband once more received her with affection; and the term of exile over, the whole party returned in happiness to Ayodhya.

This story evidently refers to a real expedition through the Peninsula of India, and to real victories in the South; but the Hindus did not then retain conquests or make settlements in Ceylon, for at a subsequent period, about B.C. 546, the island was still, in poetic phrase, inhabited by demons, whom the Hindu Vijaya then conquered. Rama's expedition left more permanent traces amongst the "Malabars" of the neighbouring coast, where the name of Rama's

* Hindu Drama, vol. i. p. 283.

† When witnesses cannot be obtained, the Code of Manu directs the judge to cause the party accused to "hold fire, or to dive under water. He whom the blazing fire burns not, whom the water soon forces not up . . . must be held veracious."—Code, ch. viii. 114, 115.

ancestor, Ikshwaku, or Okkaaku, is still borne by ancient families.*

No certain date can be assigned to the Epic Poems, and from their length and mode of structure they may well be supposed to stretch across many centuries. The legends and facts upon which they are founded belong to the earliest periods disclosed by Sanskrit literature, but these are given with a colouring from the arts, customs, and mythologies prevailing one or two centuries before our era. We may therefore consider the Epics as affording sure types of the earliest national character, but not of the earliest national customs of ancient Brahmanical India. The reputed author of the Ramayana is Valmiki; its style and language are those of an early heroic age; and there are signs of its having been popular in India at least three centuries B.C. Recognition of the beauty of natural scenery, and readiness to attribute earthly phenomena to Divine influence, are amongst the charms of this beautiful poem. It gives free expression to the thoughts of all hearts, and adds superstitions peculiar to itself, and much probably that is wrong in every way; but genuine love for nature and genuine human affection is not suppressed, and never is counterfeit affectation substituted for hearty human emotion. The original subject of the poem is sometimes considered as mythological, and sometimes as heroic: but the mythological portions stand apart and have the air of an afterthought, intended to give a religious and philosophical tone to what was at first a tale rehearsed at festivals in praise of the ancestors of kings.

The mythological introduction states that Lanka, or

* Turnour, Epitome of Ceylon History.

Ceylon, had fallen under the dominion of a prince named Ravana, who was a demon of such power that by dint of penance he had extorted from the God Brahmá a promise that no mortal should destroy him. Such a promise was as relentless as the Greek Fates, from which Jove himself could not escape;* and Ravana, now invulnerable to man, gave up asceticism and tyrannized over the whole of southern India in a fearful manner. At length even the Gods in heaven were distressed at the destruction of holiness and oppression of virtue consequent upon Ravana's tyrannies; and they called a council in the mansion of Brahmá, to consider how the earth could be relieved from such a fiend. To this council came the "God Vishnu, riding on the eagle Vainataya, like the sun on a cloud, and his discus and his mace in hand." The other Gods entreat him to give his aid, and he promises in consequence to be born on earth, and to accomplish the destruction of the terrific Ravana. A superhuman Rishi is then found to perform a sacrifice for the King of Ayodhya, which is followed by his becoming the father of Rama and his three brothers; all his four sons being incarnations of Vishnu after a fashion, but Rama was Vishnu himself in mortal form. The same kind of tone is given to the visit the youths made to Viswamitra's hermitage; instead of their going for the ordinary purpose of learning accomplishments from learned Brahmans, it is the Brahmans who require the assistance of the divine Rama to defeat the evil spirits. The next feat was bending the great bow, which it was easy to exaggerate into a bow requiring eight hundred men to drag along: and after this Rama conducts himself very much like other mortals, until

* Westminster Review, Oct. 1848, p. 41.

his term of banishment expired, when he and his wife and brother having rapidly returned to Ayodhya, and Bharata having willingly resigned the government in his favour, he declares that the object of his being born is accomplished; and instead of reigning on earth, he and all his company return to heaven, his real abode.

CHAPTER V.

THE MAHABHARATA.

> "The verse adorn again:
> Fierce War and faithful Love,
> And Truth severe, by fairy fiction drest,
> In buskin'd measures move;
> Pale Grief and pleasing Pain,
> With Horror, tyrant of the throbbing breast."—GRAY.

THE Mahabharata is the second great Sanskrit epic, and is a work containing so many episodes, referable to various periods, that it has, with some reason, been designated a Cycle of Poems. The wars of the two rival families, known as the Pandus and the Kurus, constitute the main subject, and this portion Akbar the Great thought worthy of translation into Persian; but the appearance of the Gods upon earth, their consultations in heaven, and the episodes, are all omitted in the Persian copy.*

The Pandus and the Kurus were descendants of a king named Bharata, much respected, but apparently quite distinct from him whom we left to reign at Ayodhya. In the Mahabharata the scene of government is Hastinapura, to the north of Delhi; and for this ancestral inheritance we

* Heeren, vol. ii. p. 159; Ayin Akbari, ii. 100 *sqq.*

find the rival families contending. The right of the Pandus to priority would have been unquestioned, but that their father was a leper, and before his death obliged to resign in favour of his brother; and the sons of this brother (the Kurus) grow up in consequence ambitious of securing the kingdom to themselves, and jealous of their orphan cousins (the Pandus). There were five young Pandus, and a hundred young Kurus, all residing at Hastinapura; and having arrived at an age when the King, the Pandus' uncle and the Kurus' father,—

> "Deem'd the time arrived
> When the brave scions of each royal house
> Of Kuru and of Pandu should improve
> Their growing years in exercise of arms;
> With sage deliberation long he scann'd
> A suitable preceptor for their youth,
> Who to meet skill in war and arms should join
> Intelligence and learning, lofty aims,
> Religious earnestness, and love of truth."*

And then we are introduced to a Brahman named Drona, who occupies a prominent place throughout the story. Drona was no ascetic philosopher; and having in childhood shared the lessons and sports of the royal heir of the neighbouring kingdom of Panchala,† he felt inclined to live again at that Court, now that his old playfellow had become king. Never doubting of a hearty welcome, he presented himsef to Draupada quite unceremoniously, merely saying, "Behold in me your friend!" His reception was however totally different from what he anticipated:

* Professor Wilson, Oriental Magazine, vol. iii. p. 134.

† Panchala was between Delhi and the Punjab, and apparently descended as low as Ajmere.—H. H. W., Or. Mag. vol. ii. p. 231.

"The monarch sternly view'd
The Sage, and bent his brows, and with disdain
His eyeballs redden'd; silent awhile he sat,
Then arrogantly spoke: 'Brahman! methinks
Thou showest little wisdom, or the sense
Of what is fitting, when thou call'st me friend.
What friendship, weak of judgment, can subsist
Between a luckless pauper and a king?'"

The King of Panchala starts at the idea of friendship between a learned Brahman and one to whom the Vedas are a mystery, or between a warrior and one who cannot guide a chariot through the ranks of war, and continues:

"He to whose high mandate nations bow
Disdains to stoop to friends beneath the throne;
Hence, then, with idle dreams! dismiss the memory
Of other days and thoughts: I know thee not!"

Drona was too much astonished to speak, but he instantly withdrew from Panchala to Hastinapura, where he was most reverentially welcomed, and at once entrusted with the instruction of the five young Pandu and the hundred young Kuru princes.

The King of Panchala in the meantime was in terror to think of the awful calamities to which he had exposed himself by his contumacious conduct to a Brahman, and his first anxiety was to secure a son for his protection. He resorted to the usual Hindu plan of performing an expensive sacrifice, aided and guided by powerful Brahmans, and became in consequence the parent of one son and one daughter. Of the son very little is related, but the daughter becomes the heroine of the poem. She is of dark complexion, but of exceeding loveliness; and the only wish we have for her is, that we could change her name Draupadi, for it is almost beyond the power of art to invest a heroine having so uncouth an appellation with the poetic charm belonging to her in the Sanskrit. For the present, leaving Draupadi to grow in loveliness at Panchala, we must return to Drona and his numerous pupils at Hastinapura.

Drona had in youth been equally instructed in wisdom and in arms, and he taught the young princes "to rein the steed, to guide the elephant, to drive the chariot, launch the javelin, hurl the dart, wield the battle-axe, and whirl the mace." The Pandu or Pandava princes are the favourites of the poets, and are always represented as both more amiable and more heroic than their cousins the Kurus. Yudhishthira, the eldest Pandu, is a calm, inflexible person, who leads and supports his younger brothers; Bhima, the second, is remarkable for strength; and Arjuna, the third, is full of enthusiasm and affection, excelling in every martial exercise, and winning all hearts. Even in the boyish sports of their childhood it was always Arjuna that won the prize; nor less conspicuous were his peaceful virtues—

"Submissive ever to his teacher's will;
Contented, modest, affable, and mild."

Drona already prophesied that he would be an unequalled archer amongst the sons of men.*

When these youthful princes had all become expert in the use of arms, their great preceptor proposed to the King that a public trial of their skill should take place. A level plain was consequently chosen, on which the pious Drona reared an altar for an offering to the Gods, and a tall pavilion, in which rich seats were prepared for the King and his Queens, the courtiers and the court ladies. The archery is described

* Professor Wilson, Oriental Magazine, vol. iii. p. 138.

with great animation, and from this and other passages we learn, in Professor Wilson's words, "that the Hindus cultivated archery most assiduously, and were very Parthians in the use of the bow on horseback." The spectators were perfectly dazzled by the fearful shower of arrows which the archers let fly, sometimes whilst standing on the ground, sometimes whilst "on generous steeds in rapid circles borne." At the close of the combat Drona called for Arjuna, who modestly came forward in his radiant armour "as glorious as a cloud at set of sun," whilst the gazing crowd uprose and greeted him with "the clang of shells and trumpets, and loud shouts of admiration." The favourite hero, being thus as it were *encored*, made further exhibitions of his skill; he leapt from his chariot and vaulted into it again whilst it was whirling along at full speed. He also shot five arrows at once from his chariot into the jaws of a wild boar. A pause then ensued, during which the opposing parties sought repose; but suddenly "a clamour rending heaven" was heard behind the barrier, and Kerna, a new combatant, was announced. His ears shone with gorgeous pendants, and with bow in hand he advanced proudly like a moving mountain. This new hero was anxious to enter the lists with Arjuna, and offered to perform every feat which Arjuna had achieved; but, unknown to themselves, Kerna and Arjuna were brothers; and their mother, who was amongst the spectators, in agony at seeing them "on hostile thoughts intent," strove to prevent "the horrid strife;" but she fainted, and the combat would have commenced had not another difficulty occurred. It was necessary, according to Hindu laws of chivalry, that each warrior should declare his name and lineage; but

Kerna, having been brought up by a charioteer in ignorance of his real parents, could say nothing: he hung his head, "as when surcharged with dew the blooming lotus bows its fragrant blossom." And on this occurrence the sports were suddenly concluded.*

The jealousy and hatred of the Kurus towards the Pandus only increased as they grew to manhood; and at no long period after the trial of arms, the Kurus caused the house inhabited by the five Pandus to be set on fire. The Pandus escaped, but a woman of low caste and her five sons having been accidentally in the house and involved in the flames, the discovery of their bodies led to a general belief that the five Pandus and their mother had perished. In the meantime the brothers wandered in the woods, lived on game, dressed themselves in the skins of the animals they shot, and met with a variety of adventures, never entering courts or capitals, until news reached them that Draupadi, the daughter of Draupada the King of Panchala, was about to hold a Swayambara,—which means, that her father was inviting company to his Court, amongst whom she was to choose her future husband. Draupada still dreaded that Drona would one day resent the insult which he had offered, and he exceedingly wished to strengthen himself against this formidable foe, by procuring an alliance with the Pandus; but as the Pandus were missing, and he knew not how to find them, his only plan was to give a public entertainment and take his chance of their attending. Fortunately the five brothers were no longer in the woods, but on the road leading to Panchala; inquiring of some Brahmans the cause of the unusual throngs of people, they learned that "princes

* Oriental Magazine, vol. iii. p. 140.

with throbbing hearts" were hastening to attend Draupadi's Swayambara, and were recommended to go also and share in the gifts distributed; or, continued the Brahmans,—

> "To behold, if so your youth prefer,
> The joyous revelry that gilds the scene;
> For thither mummers, mimes, and gleemen throng,
> Athletes, who the prize of strength or skill
> Contend in wrestling or the gauntlet's strife;
> Minstrels with sounding lutes, and bards who chant
> Their lords' high lineage and heroic deeds."*

The brothers accepted the proposal, and accompanied the band of Brahmans, travelling through smiling groves and by the margin of limpid lakes, and often loitering to mark the beauties of each grateful scene. When they arrived at Panchala they took up their abode under the lowly roof of a potter, and went out daily as mendicants to gather alms.

The King of Panchala, in his anxiety to have a Pandu prince for his son-in-law, caused a ponderous bow to be framed with magic skill, requiring such strength as he believed a Pandu alone possessed, and for a mark he hung a metal plate which revolved upon an axle; and then made proclamation that he who could hit with an arrow the centre of the plate should win the princess. The site chosen was outside the city, and was enclosed by a deep ditch and lofty walls. Glittering pavilions were erected for illustrious spectators, and the crowd who pressed without the barriers found places upon scaffolds and lofty housetops. All the hundred sons of the King of Hastinapura, and Kerna, and innumerable other chiefs, attended as candidates, whilst kings sat around the throne of Draupada, on lofty seats emblazoned with gems and gold. Then the trumpets brayed,

* Oriental Magazine, vol. iv. p. 142.

and the entertainments commenced with games of skill, music, dancing, and displays of the dramatic art: thus sixteen days were passed; and then, as every chief of note was present except the Pandus, who were unknown in their disguise, Draupada felt that he had no longer any fair plea for further delaying his daughter's choice. So the lovely Draupadi was brought into the arena, ready to throw her garland upon the successful candidate.

> "Then came the Princess forth, in royal garb
> Array'd, and costly ornaments adorn'd;
> A garland interwove with gems and gold
> Her delicate hands sustain'd; from the pure bath
> With heighten'd loveliness she tardy came,
> And blushing in the princely presence stood.
> Next in the ring the reverend priest appear'd,
> And strew'd the holy grass, and pour'd the oil,
> An offering to the God of Fire, with prayer
> Appropriate."*

And now the competitors came forward, and each endeavoured to bend the bow, but all in vain. Some made such violent efforts that they fell back on the ground, exciting peals of laughter from the spectators; others freed themselves from their royal robes and diamond chains and diadems, and unfettered put forth their strength; but it was in vain, and the bow defied them all, until Kerna came, and he "the yielding bowstring drew and ponderous shafts applied," and drew forth shouts of acclamations from the multitude. But the unfortunate Kerna, being the reputed son of a charioteer, was no fitting match for the Princess of Panchala. Kerna's real father was the Sun; but this fact was unknown, and availed him nothing:

* Oriental Magazine, vol. iv. p. 143.

"The timid Draupadi in terror cried,
'I wed not with the base-born!' Kerna smiled
In bitterness, and upwards turn'd his eyes
To his great sire the Sun; then cast to earth
The bow and shafts, and sternly stalk'd away."

Amazement spread through the crowd at finding all the noble suitors foiled, but just at this moment Arjuna advanced. The Brahmans thought him a student of their tribe, and tried to hold him back from certain failure, but in vain; and some who observed his strength, like that of an elephant, and his lion port and his self-collected soul, had hopes of his success.

"Unheeding praise or censure, Arjuna*
Pass'd to the field: with reverential steps
He round the weapon circled,† next address'd
A silent prayer to Mahadeo, and last
With faith inflexible on Krishna dwelt.
One hand the bow upbore, the other drew
The sturdy cord, and placed the pointed shafts:
They flew—the mark was hit—and sudden shouts
Burst from the crowd long silent; fluttering waved
The Brahman scarfs, and drum and trumpet bray'd,
And bard and herald sang the hero's triumph."

The King and his daughter liked the appearance of the disguised Arjuna, and were very well contented at his success, but the rage of the princely suitors knew no bounds; "Behold," they cried, "the King regards us no more than straws, and deigns to wed his daughter to a Brahman boy whose craft has humbled royalty." And the lightest pu-

* Oriental Magazine, vol. iv. p. 146.

† Walking round an object of veneration is an act of worship amongst Hindus: it is not unknown to Virgil as a purificatory rite, and is frequently practised in Roman Catholic countries.—See note, H. H. Wilson, Or. Mag. vol. iv. p. 147.

nishment they can assign for such an offence is to kill the King of Panchala and all his race, and to throw the damsel herself into the flames, unless she prefer choosing a royal lord. Their gleaming swords were brandished, and Draupada turned in terror to the Brahmans. Arjuna rushed to his side; Bhima tore up a tree and stood ready for the fight; and for awhile the kings and warriors were so amazed at this novel daring of the priestly tribe that they stood still, admiring; but soon—

> "Like elephants,
> With passion maddening, headlong on they rush'd;
> Like elephants the brothers met their might."

And now Kerna and Arjuna really met in fight; but when Kerna felt the power of his youthful adversary, he was astonished, and paused to express his wonder and admiration. "No Brahman," he says, "could have displayed such skill in arms; nor breathes the man who could my strength defy, save Arjuna." Arjuna does not however declare himself, and the kings are compelled to retire, believing themselves conquered by a set of Brahmans, from whose bands shouts of triumph fill the air, whilst the trembling hand of Draupadi now ventures to fling the marriage chaplet around the neck of Arjuna.

The Pandus then make themselves known; a portion of their hereditary kingdom is given up to them, and for a period they appear to have enjoyed peace and prosperity. Yudhishthira, the eldest Pandu, exercised the sovereignty, and built for himself a beautiful city called Indraprastha, on the site of the modern Delhi, which rivalled the old capital in splendour; and nothing need have been wanting for Pandu happiness if in the pride of his heart Yudhishthira had not determined to celebrate the Rájasúya sacrifice which was an assumption of paramount authority, and of course excited jealousy and opposition amongst the contemporary kings of India.* In preparation for the grand ceremony, Yudhishthira sent his brothers in all directions to compel the different princes to acknowledge his pretensions and pay tribute; and the details of these expeditions furnish much curious information concerning the geographical and political divisions of India, at a period a little anterior to that at which Herodotus wrote very similar accounts. When the brothers returned successful, the Kurus professed their acquiescence; and Krishna, the great friend and ally of the Pandus, promised his warm and hearty concurrence, and the ministers and priests made active preparations, and invited guests from every quarter. The ceremony is described with much minuteness; the *abhisheka*, sprinkling from a sacred stream, being the essential part of it. Kings bring a variety of rich tribute, and even perform menial service upon the occasion. But whilst outwardly rendering the required homage, the jealous Kurus were secretly plotting to destroy their rivals, which they contrived by engaging the newly inaugurated King in a desperate game at draughts.† Yudhishthira seems to have been afflicted with a most unfortunate love of gambling, and was led on from stake to stake until he pledged his kingdom; and losing this

* H. H. Wilson, Notes on the Sabha Purva of the Mahabharata.—J. R. S. A., No. xiii.

† The Index prefixed to the Persian translation notes these events as follows:—"Yudishter sends his brothers into all parts to make conquests. The Kurus arrange a sacrificial feast in order to play at draughts. Preparations for the same. The Pandus, having lost at play, retire into the desert, where they continue twelve years."—Heeren, vol. ii. p. 160, *note*.

last desperate venture he was forced to agree that he and his brothers would resign the kingdom for twelve years, and spend that time in exile. Several beautiful episodes are introduced during this period of exile, and to some of these we shall refer hereafter; at present we must follow the story of the Pandu brothers, who when the twelve years had elapsed returned to Delhi, and demanded the restoration of their sovereignty. The Kuru monarch answered them with scorn, saying, they should not have so much of the soil as the point of a needle could cover, and war was the only alternative. The Pandus then made a gathering of the friends amongst whom they had spent their exile; and the Kurus also summoning their allies, there was no chief of note between the Himalaya and the ocean but was ranged on one side or the other. Drona was still the implacable enemy of the King of Panchala, with whom the Pandus had become allied by marriage; and although attached to Arjuna and his brothers when boys, this did not prevent him from acting zealously as commander-in-chief of the Kuru forces. Yudhishthira appears himself to have had the chief command over the Pandus; and Krishna, the never-failing friend of the Pandu brothers, took his place by the side of Arjuna as his charioteer, whilst at the request of Yudhishthira the ape-emblazoned banner was raised in the van of the troops.* As the hosts on either side advanced, "a sudden tumult filled the sky, . . . sands upcurled to heaven

* Oriental Magazine, vol. ii. p. 250, *note*. Arjuna's bannerb ore a figure of the monkey-general Hanuman. Having solicited the aid of this Demigod in battle, he had received permission to mount the monkey's figure on his banner, with the assurance that it would be accompanied by his protection. This is one of the few references in the Mahabharata to the earlier poem of the Ramayana.

and spread a veil before the sun, . . . shrill-screaming kites and vultures winged the darkling air, . . . angry lightnings flashed across the gloom, or blazing meteors fearful shot to earth." But all "regardless of these signs, the chiefs pressed on to mutual slaughter." Twice, "like clouds scattered before the gale," were the Pandus driven back by Drona, who appeared ever in the front, in a car by art immortal framed, although his place as Commander-in-chief was "in the rear to march secure;" whilst the gallant Kerna "led his faithful bands." But Drona was impetuous; "terror hovered over" his course, and the sanguinary plain was strewn with broken cars and elephants and steeds. Then Yudhishthira "called upon his brother Arjuna to lead his choicest squadrons to restore the day;" Arjuna obeyed, and the enemy was checked: but Drona became furious, and forgetting his years, the arrows of the veteran chief flew about with such unerring aim that the soil was sodden "with the crimson stain of the men, steeds, and elephants whom Drona's shafts to Yama's halls consigned."* Yudhishthira was dismayed; but the noble Arjuna soothed his terror, and plighted his faith to brave the arm of Drona. Many single combats are described, in one of which the brave *son* of Arjuna was distinguished; and in another, Bhima and the King of Madra† rushed at each other like two butting elephants. But Drona was still bent upon a personal victory over Yudhishthira, and, driving his chariot full upon him, struck his bow from his hand; but Arjuna stood fearless by, until the arrows flew so thick that heaven was hid and earth was darkened:—

* Oriental Magazine, vol. iv. p. 251.

† A country about Ghuzni, or Ghor, the site of the ancient Mardi.—Or. Mag. vol. ii. p. 254, *note*.

"Precursor of nocturnal shades; for now
The sun behind the western mountains sank
And gloom profound ensued; nor friend nor foe
Could longer be distinguish'd. Drona then
Commanded conflict cease, and Arjuna
Restrain'd his now re-animated troops:
Each to their tents withdrew."

This fearful battle raged for eighteen days, when, the chiefs of the Kuru party being killed, victory was declared to be in favour of the Pandus; and it became the duty of Yudhishthira to march into Hastinapura and perform funeral ceremonies for the King Duryodhana, his enemy and relative. The chivalrous tone of feeling which pervades this poem, and the similarity of some of the practices described to those of Europe in the Middle Ages, has not escaped observation.* The character of Kerna is one which seems especially to belong to days of chivalry; feeling the degradation of doubtful parentage, he indulges in no mean or cowardly ill-will, but meets mortifications with generous self-devotion and heroism. Several touching episodes relate to him; in one of which we are told, that on the eve of one of these last battles the mother of the Pandus went to him, and disclosing that he also was her son, born previous to her marriage with Pandu, she implored him to leave Duryodhana, the Kuru chief, and join his brothers in their rightful cause. But Kerna had already vowed fidelity to their opponents; and although he knew by prophecies and omens that they would perish, he firmly and sorrowfully abided by his plighted troth.†

A battle which lasted eighteen days may well be supposed

* Oriental Magazine, vol. iii. p. 134.

† Westminster Review, October, 1848, p. 53.

to have made dreadful havoc both with friends and foes; and the victorious Yudhishthira is represented as feeling unmixed sorrow and disgust. As soon therefore as the funeral obsequies were concluded, he installed younger members of the family upon the thrones of Hastinapura and Indraprastha, and determined with his brothers to set forth on a long gloomy journey to Mount Meru, to seek in Indra's heaven that rest which seemed denied to them on earth. Mr. Marshman thinks that they retired with their relative Krishna to Dwaraka, in Guzerat; and that Krishna being soon after put to death by the Bheels, they resolved to leave India, and passed through Scinde to the Himalaya mountains.* The view given by the poet is more ideal, but quite consistent with Brahmanical philosophy.

"Having heard† Yudhishthira's resolve, and seen the destruction of Krishna,
The five brothers set forth, and Draupadi; and the seventh was a dog that followed them.
Yudhishthira himself was the last that quitted Hastinapura;
And all the citizens and the court followed them on their way,
But none felt able to say unto him 'Return;'
And at length they all went back into the city.
Then the high-souled sons of Pandu and far-famed Draupadi
Pursued their way, fasting, and with their faces turned towards the east,
Resolved upon separation from earth, and longing for release from its laws;
They roamed onward over many regions, and to many a river and sea.
Yudhishthira went before, and Bhima followed next behind him,
And Arjuna came after him, and then the twin sons of Madri,
And sixth after them came Draupadi, with her fair face and lotus eyes,

* Hist. India, p. 29.

† Westminster Review, Oct. 1848, p. 57.

And last of all followed the dog, as they wandered on till they came to the ocean. . . .
And as they journeyed onwards and came unto the west,
There they beheld the old city of Krishna, now washed over by the ocean-tide.
Again they turned to the north, and still they went on in their way,
Circumambulating round the continent to find separation from earth;
Then, with their senses subdued, the heroes, having reached the north,
Beheld with their heaven-desiring eyes the lofty mountain Himavat,
And having crossed its height, they beheld the sea of sand;
And next they saw rocky Meru, the king of mountains.
And while they were thus faring onwards, in eager search for separation,
Draupadi lost hold of her hope, and fell on the face of the earth."

Bhima inquires of Yudhishthira why she fell, who had done no act of evil: he replies, "Too great was her love for Arjuna;" and thus speaking, he went onwards, not looking back, gathering up his soul into himself in his unstooping wisdom and justice. Next the fair Sahadeva fell upon the face of the earth; and when Nakula saw the fall of Draupadi and his brother, he, full of love for his kindred, fell down in his grief like them to earth. Still Yudhishthira, the stern God of Justice, went on; but when Arjuna beheld so many fallen behind, he too, the great conqueror, fell, his soul pierced through with sorrow; and lastly Bhima fell; but still the mighty King went on, nor looked behind, and now none followed but the dog, when

"Suddenly* with a sound which ran through heaven and earth,
Indra came riding on his chariot, and he cried to the King, 'Ascend!'
Then indeed did the lord of justice look back to his fallen brothers,

* Westminster Review, October, 1848, p. 60.

And thus unto Indra he spoke with a sorrowful heart :
'Let my brothers, who yonder lie fallen, go with me ;
Not even into thy heaven would I enter if they were not there ;
And yon fair-faced daughter of a king, Draupadi, the all-deserving,
Let her too enter with us ! O Indra, approve my prayer !' "

Indra says that he will find his brothers and Draupadi there before him, they having first thrown aside their mortal vestment, whilst Yudhishthira alone is permitted to enter in his body of flesh. The King next begs that the dog may be allowed to go with him, but Indra says he must be contented with having obtained his fellowship and a place in his heaven, and give up the dog ; and Yudhishthira being still unwilling to "abandon the faithful," Indra says more decidedly, "My heaven hath no place for dogs : they steal our offerings on earth." But nothing that Indra urges alters Yudhishthira's determination ; "Never," he says, "will I abandon yon poor creature, which in fear and distress hath trusted in my power to save." Indra says he has forsaken his brothers, why not then forsake the dog? to which subterfuge Yudhishthira replies with dignity :—

"Mortals, when they are dead, are dead to love or hate ; . . .
I could not bring them back to life, but while they lived I never left them.
To oppress the suppliant, to kill a wife, to spoil a Brahman, to betray one's friends,
These are the four great crimes ; and to forsake a dependant I count equal to them."

This dog* was Yama, king of death, in disguise ; and praising Yudhishthira, he now relieved him from his difficulty by showing himself in his real character. But there was still another trial to be encountered ; for upon entering

* Ward's Hindus, vol. ii. p. 448.

Indra's heaven Yudhishthira beheld his cousins the Kurus, but looked in vain for his brothers: he at once refused to remain without them, and a messenger was sent with him to the Indian hell. Here he proudly resolves to share their sorrows rather than live in heaven without them. But the whole scene was a mere illusion to prove his virtue, and the hell is quickly changed into heaven, where the brothers are left with Indra enjoying boundless bliss. And thus a tale of feud and bloodshed is closed by a melodious strain of Brahmanical philosophy.

In comparing the Mahabharata with the earlier epic, the Ramayana, we find the same freedom of character and expression; courage, generosity, and devoted affection are appreciated; faults and vices meet their natural consequences; and we are not disgusted by seeing characters screwed up or pressed down, according to some artificial standard, after a fashion exhibited by certain later Indian literature. The general customs prevailing in either poem are also similar. Brahmans instruct princes in the arts of war as well as peace; youthful heroes win their brides by feats of strength, and injuries or affronts to holy men are punished by death or loss of kingdom. But a difference is also noticeable between the poems. The Ramayana is a tale of the Solar races, the Mahabharata of the Lunar races; and we are inclined to believe that Brahmanical dominion was far more powerful with the Solar kings at Ayodhya than it ever became with Lunar dynasties. In the Ramayana, Solar kings reign in the orderly manner prescribed by the Code; Brahmans guiding political councils, and Kings commanding armies. But in the Mahabharata, on the other hand, the Lunar tribes at Hastinapura and Dwaraka carry on war at the pleasure of the kings and people with little or no reference to Brahmans. We seem in this second poem to have, in a measure, lost the Brahmanical civilization previously attained, and to be thrown back upon the Vedic period, when priests were warriors and warriors priests, and when cows and horses were actually, not typically, killed and eaten in their sacrifices. The marriage of the heroine, Draupadi, to the five Pandu brothers, is a sign of yet ruder manners adopted from the Scythic tribes of India, and is a circumstance odious to Brahmanical commentators, and quite uncountenanced by Brahmanical institutions.

CHAPTER VI.

> "For a' that, and a' that,
> Our toil's obscure, and a' that;
> The rank is but the guinea's stamp,
> The man's the gowd for a' that."—BURNS.

HAVING now disposed of the Brahmans and the Kshatriyas, our next inquiry must be into the laws which the Brahmans endeavoured to impose upon the rest of the community. All punishment is supposed to be adjudged by the King:—

"Let the King prepare a just compensation for the good, and a just punishment for the bad: the rule of strict justice let him never transgress."

"If the King were not, without indolence, to punish the guilty, the stronger would roast the weaker like fish upon the spit. . . .

"The crow would peck the consecrated offering of rice; the dog would lick the clarified butter; ownership would remain to none, the lowest would overset the highest."

"A king, desirous of inspecting judicial proceedings, must enter his court of justice composed and sedate in his demeanour, together with *Brahmans* and counsellors who know how to give him advice."*

The dignity and weight which the Code attaches to justice are worthy of the high tone of its philosophy.

* Code of Manu, ch. vii.

"When justice, having been wounded by iniquity, approaches the court, and the judges extract not the dart, they also shall be wounded by it."

"The only firm friend who follows even after death is justice, all others are extinct with the body."*

The King, or his judge, is to enter on the trial of causes "properly clothed," "his mind attentively fixed;" and he is then directed to see through the thoughts of men by external signs, by their voice, colour, countenance, limbs, signs, and actions; for from "the gesticulations, the speech, the changes of the eye and the face, are discovered the internal workings of the mind."

"As a hunter traces the lair of a wounded beast by the drops of blood, thus let a king investigate the true point of justice by deliberative arguments.

"Let him fully consider the nature of truth, the state of the case, and his own person; . . . the witnesses, the place, the mode, the time."†

So far the Code appears to speak in earnest; but when we pass on to an enumeration and description of the punishments decreed, the tone entirely changes. A witness who does not give true evidence must go "naked and shorn, tormented with hunger and thirst, and deprived of sight," to beg his food at his enemy's door. Whilst a witness, who gives an imperfect account of a transaction, is compared to a man "who eats fish with eagerness and swallows the sharp bones." Many of the punishments might indeed better be attributed to a court-buffoon than to a sedate judge, as—If a once-born man insult a twice-born, he shall have his tongue slit. If a once-born man offer instruction to a priest, hot oil shall be poured into his mouth. If a man steal

* Code, ch. viii.

† *Ibid.*, ch. viii.

gold from a Brahman, he shall have sore fingers; if he steal dressed grain, dyspepsia; if he steal holy words, or is an unauthorized reader of the Vedas, dumbness; if he steal a lamp, blindness; if a horse, lameness; and this is followed by the reflection that—

"Thus according to the diversity of actions are born men despised by the good; stupid, dumb, blind, deaf, deformed."*

The punishments awarded to murder are not less fanciful, but graduated according to the rank of the sufferer. If the person killed be a Kshatriya, the penance is a fourth,—if a Vaisya, an eighth,—if a Sudra, a sixteenth part of that which is ordained for the murder of a Brahman. But if a Brahman kill a Sudra, he only pays the fine awarded for killing a cat, dog, lizard, or crow.†

In a similar strain are the punishments referring to a future life, as—"If a man steal grain in the husk, he shall be born a rat; if a mixed yellow metal, a gander; . . . if exquisite perfumes, a musk-rat; if potherbs, a peacock; if raw grain, a hedgehog." This jesting character never could have obtained in a code of daily use, and may be viewed as strong evidence that Brahmanical arrogance assumed more than it performed, and did not positively crush the general population.

The Code reserves banking, agriculture, and all lucrative occupations for the third Caste, invested with the sacred thread, and called Vaisyas; but riches proverbially have wings, and Brahmans utterly failed in trying to chain them to their privileged orders. The laws they made for that purpose worked just in the opposite direction; for whilst minute and vexatious regulations deadened enterprise in the

* Code, ch. viii. † *Ibid.*, ch. viii.

Vaisyas, freedom from these hindrances enabled the unprivileged multitude to follow industrial callings with success.

Beneath the Vaisya caste was a Sudra caste, and a Sudra we have just seen reckoned in the Code as a sixteenth part of the value of a Brahman. Sudras, says the Code, are the offspring of Brahma's foot! From his mouth sprang Brahmans, from his arm Kshatriyas, from his thigh Vaisyas, and then from his foot came Sudras, to wait upon these superior castes: this, having been the act of Brahma, is irrevocable and not even by his master can a Sudra be "released from a state of servitude which is natural to him."* Exclusion from religious privilege follows as a necessary consequence, as a Sudra cannot wear the sacred thread. A man uninvested with the sacred thread cannot make a fire sacrifice, and one who does not sacrifice with fire cannot obtain absorption.

"The three twice-born classes are the Sacerdotal, the Military, and the Commercial; but the fourth, or Servile, is once-born, *that is, he has no second birth from* the Gayatri, and *wears no thread;* nor is there a fifth pure class."†

To read the Vêda, or even to hear the Veda read, is forbidden to Sudras; not until a man is invested with the sacred thread may he read these sacred books; and since Sudras were for ever excluded from investiture, it was a sin for a twice-born man to read the Veda even to himself if a Sudra should be present. For a Brahman to teach the Veda to Sudras was of course a greater sin, and to receive money for doing so yet more unpardonable, and to receive money from a Sudra, under any circumstances, highly unbecoming in a Brahman.

* Code, i. 81, 91.

† *Ibid.*, x. 4.

"They who receive property from a Sudra for the performance of rites to consecrated fire, are contemned as ministers of the base by all such as pronounce texts of the Vedas."

"Of those ignorant priests who serve the holy fire for the wealth of a Sudra, the giver shall always tread on the foreheads, and thus pass over miseries in the gloom of death."

Sudras are permitted to offer dressed grain, and to give praise and salutation without "any holy text;"* which means that they may perform rites procuring a *limited* amount of future bliss, but not such sacrifice as leads to absorption or unlimited beatitude. Menial service is the only occupation entirely approved of† for a Sudra; but if he fail in procuring such service, he may follow mechanical arts, with always this proviso:—

"No superfluous collection of wealth must be made by a Sudra, even though he has the power to make it; since a servile man, who has amassed riches, becomes proud, and by his insolence or neglect gives pain even to Brahmans."‡

Such is the audacious language of the Code; assuming no less than the exclusion of more than a fourth part of God's creatures from any chance of admission to the upper ranks of society, whether in this world or the next. We do not understand that Sudras were, or ever had been, in this degraded condition, but rather see a desire and design that for the future they should be suppressed. Even in the Code many passages indicate that the Sudra condition had once been different; as when a king is told that if he "stupidly look on whilst a Sudra decides causes, his kingdom will be embarrassed like a cow in deep mire:"§ and again, good men must not reside in "cities governed by

* Code, x. 126, 127.

† *Ibid.*, xi. 42, 43.

‡ *Ibid.*, x. 129.

§ *Ibid.*, viii. 21.

Sudra kings:" passages clearly showing that Sudra judges and Sudra kings were not unknown. We even find the Code tracing Sudra pedigree up to the most holy sage Vasishta. Pitris, it says, are sons of Marichi and other Pitris; and there are five classes of Pitris, amongst which are Atri, the ancestor of Daityas, Danavas, Uragas, and Rakshasas; Bhrigu, the ancestor of Brahmans; Angiras, the ancestor of Kshatriyas; and Vasishta, the ancestor of Sudras.* This passage is followed by directions, that the ground upon which oblations are offered to Pitris should slope towards the south, and the worshipper is moreover directed to turn his face towards the south or south-west whilst performing the ceremony. Obviously there had been a time in which Sudras were not viewed as slaves or serfs.† Originally, in common with other aboriginal tribes, they had faced the Hindus in war, and taught them religious superstitions in peace. Their Goddess Nirritti, in the Rig-Veda, is entreated to keep afar off with her unfriendly looks, and not to destroy Hindu worshippers; but in the Code we find Nirritti called the "Patroness of the South-west," the same quarter as that to which oblations to forefathers were to be addressed. The probable explanation is, that the Code was written in *Brahmavarta*, to the north of Delhi; and that looking to the south-west was looking to the earlier settlements down the Indus. Under certain circumstances the Code directs a sinner, even though he should be twice-born, "to walk in a direct path towards the south-west, or the region of Nirritti, until he fall dead on the ground." And for another specified offence, an orthodox Hindu is directed to "sacrifice a black or one-eyed ass, by

* Code, iii. 192, 198.

† *Ibid.*, iii. 206, 87, 91, 214, 215.

way of meat-offering, to Nirritti, patroness of the south-west, by night, in a place where four ways meet."*

These passages tell more of alliance than of antipathy between the rival races; and more recently, in the poem called Mahabharata, Professor Wilson calls attention to Sudras being mentioned with respect. When King Yudhishthira invites kings and tribes from all quarters to assist at his inauguration, Sudras are among the guests, and for them, equally as for others, food, dwellings, and entertainments are provided.† This may perhaps corroborate the opinion expressed in our last Chapter, that the Mahabharata was not written wholly under Brahmanical influence. The real state of affairs seems to have been that Hindus and Aborigines were much inclined to coalesce; and that Brahmans propounded their laws on Caste, in order to sever such alliances and preserve their race and their religion from degradation.

In an article on the Aboriginal Races of India, written in 1852, General Briggs notifies eleven distinctions between Hindus and Aborigines, and nearly all these differences have occurred subsequent to the Rig-Veda. 1. "Hindus are divided into castes;" but they were not so divided, as we have already seen, until subsequent to the Rig-Veda. 2. "Hindu widows are forbidden to marry;" this prohibition is distinctly shown by Professor Wilson to have no place in the Rig-Veda. 3. "The Hindus venerate the cow, and abstain from eating beef;" in the Rig-Veda cows were sacrificed and eaten. 4. "The Hindus abstain from the use of fermented liquors;" fermented soma-juice is drunk in the Rig-Veda. 5. "The Hindus eat of food prepared only by those of their own Caste;" on this point we have no exact

* Code, xi. 105, 119. † J. R. A. S., May, 1842; art. *Sabha Parva.*

evidence, but the regulation is not likely to have preceded the Brahmanical arrangement of Caste. 6. "The Hindus abhor the spilling of blood;" but in the Rig-Veda animals are sacrificed and enemies killed. 7. "The Hindus have a Brahmanical priesthood;" in the Rig-Veda kings perform sacrifices, and Brahmans are one amongst many classes of priests. 8. "The Hindus burn their dead;" the dead are certainly buried in the Rig-Veda, although sometimes previously burned. 9. "The Hindu civil institutions are all municipal, the aboriginal institutions all patriarchal;" the veneration of Pitris, forefathers, and the performance of sacrifice by kings and householders, looks as if the patriarchal had preceded the municipal amongst Hindus. 10. "The Hindus have their courts of justice composed of equals;" how early these courts were instituted we know not. 11. "The Hindus brought with them (more than three thousand years ago) the art of writing and science;" whilst General Briggs continues, "The indigenes are not only illiterate, but it is forbidden for the Hindus to teach them." Whether the Aborigines possessed literature in the days of Vedic song, is not to be known; but that portion of their population which retired to the Peninsula must undoubtedly have cultivated a literature for which they were not beholden to Hindus or Brahmans. Mr. Elphinstone cites the existence of this Tamul literature as evidence that society in the south of India had made considerable progress in civilization before the Hindus colonized there, and monopolized learning as the exclusive privilege of Brahmans. When at length Brahmans did settle in the south, they translated Sanskrit literature into the Tamul languages; and this again is a testimony to the cultivation of the Tamul inhabitants; for Brahmans would not have bestowed their precious literature upon indigenes or un-Brahmanical tribes, unless convinced that the newly subdued people could not be kept in subjection by mere force, and that it was politic to put public opinion under Brahmanical influence by an infusion of Sanskrit legends and philosophy.

We must therefore give up the idea that the population of India was ever divided into four distinct Castes. Rather we imagine Brahmans only to have been omnipotent in a few luxurious towns or celebrated hermitages, whilst the country at large was inhabited by people of mixed Caste, left very much at liberty to govern themselves. The Code states that the internal administration of the country is carried on by the lords of single townships, the lords of ten towns (or villages), the lords of a hundred, and the lords of a thousand towns. These officers are all appointed by the King, and are directed to report, each to his immediate superior, such robberies or tumults as he is unable to suppress. The lord of a single town receives in compensation "the food, drink, wood, and other articles" to which the King is entitled from that town; the lord of ten towns receives "the produce of two plough-lands, or as much ground as can be tilled by two ploughs, each drawn by six bulls; the lord of twenty, that of five plough-lands; the lord of a hundred, that of a village or small town; the lord of a thousand, that of a large town." These officers were to be under the superintendence of a still higher minister of the crown, "distinguished as a planet amongst stars," whose special duty was to defend the people from the rapacity of the inferior officers, who, the Code says (vii. 115), "are generally knaves, who seize what belongs to other men."

The headman* of a village is in some places called *Patél* or *Patil,* in others *Chaudhari* and *Mandal:* he is the successor of the lord, whom Manu mentions as an agent of the King; the office has now become hereditary, and in point of fact he is more the representative of the people than an officer of the King, although he is regarded still in that capacity; and the Government often exercises the power of determining which individual out of the privileged family shall succeed to the office. The headman of the village still receives a certain allowance from the King or government, but the greater part of his income is now derived from fees paid by the villagers; this system is supposed by General Briggs to have accompanied Hindus into every settlement they have made, whether in India or beyond its confines. There are three things which he considers inseparable, viz. the Sanskrit language, serfdom, and municipal institutions; and although this system is no longer found in Malwa, or in great part of the Madras Presidency, yet there is reason to believe that it did once exist throughout the country; each village having its own registrar, watchman, cartwright, washerman, barber, goldsmith, and poet, who also served as schoolmaster.† And in further evidence that the institution travelled with the language, we have the statement of Sir Stamford Raffles, that Bali, an island to the east of Java, possesses municipal institutions, the Sanskrit language, and the Brahmanical religion; and again in Java there are village associations bearing the Indian name Năgri, which Mr. Crawfurd mentions as corporations governed by

* Elphinstone, Hist. India, Appendix v. p. 249.

† These officers sign their documents with the figures of the tools which they employ. See Dr. Royle's Lecture on the Great Exhibition.

officers of their own election. This system is still characteristic of India, where "village communities" are noted "as the indestructible atoms from which empires are formed." "Village communities," says Sir Charles Metcalfe, "are little republics, having nearly everything they can want within themselves; they seem to last where nothing else lasts. Dynasty after dynasty tumbles down. Hindu, Patan, Mongol, Mahratta, Sikh, English, are all masters in turn, but the village community remains the same. In times of trouble they arm and fortify themselves, . . . collect their cattle within their walls, and let the enemy pass unprovoked. If plunder and devastation be directed against themselves, and the force employed be irresistible, they flee to friendly villages; but when the storm has passed over, they return and resume their occupations."*

Thus, instead of finding India all divided between lords and slaves, we discover a rich material of middle class, which, from the earliest ages, has maintained an amount of independence most encouraging to those benevolent reformers and hopeful governors, who from time to time spring up to bless and regenerate our perplexing Indian empire.

* Elphinstone, Hist. of India, p. 63; and Sir C. T. Metcalfe, Report of Select Committee of House of Commons, 1832, vol. iii. Appendix 84, p. 331.

CHAPTER VII.

> "Nature, a mother kind alike to all,
> Still grants her bliss at labour's earnest call;
> From Art, more various are the blessings sent,
> Wealth, commerce, honour, liberty, content."
>
> GOLDSMITH.

AGRICULTURE has flourished in India under all changes of dominion, and was practised even in the early period of the Rig-Veda, where *fields* are frequently mentioned and the produce carried home in carts. Models of ancient ploughs were exhibited at the Great Exhibition of 1851, and a species of drill-plough is attributed by Dr. Royle* to the ante-Christian centuries of which we are treating.† And not only of seed were these ancient farmers economical,

* Lecture on the Results of the Great Exhibition, p. 455.

† A plough of this description may be seen in bas-relief on Lord Aberdeen's Black Stone: it is figured in Fergusson's 'Nineveh,' p. 298; the date is supposed to be shortly before the time of Nebuchadnezzar.

but also of the soil, sowing "plants which require transplantation in the same field with rice-plants, which mature in sixty days;"* and sowing *mudga* and *masha* beneath a tall cereal, called in the Code barley, but which is in fact a millet (*Holcus Sorghum*, Linn.);† this plan is still practised. The tall grain rises quickly, and by its shade keeps the soil cool and moist for the smaller and slower-growing mudga and masha, which are known to Europeans as the *gram* with which they feed their horses. Rotation of crops is also practised by the native farmers, who alternate the pulses, which improve the land, with the cereal grasses, which exhaust it; and to India Dr. Roxburgh believes the western world to be indebted for this system. In a country so luxuriant in cocoa-nuts and other fruits, edible roots, and water-plants, it bespeaks considerable civilization to make laws in favour of agriculture; and we therefore read with interest that—

> "If the land be injured by the fault of the farmer himself, as if he fail to sow it in due time, he shall be fined ten times as much as the King's share of the crop that might otherwise have been raised."‡

And again, a Vaisya must be skilled in seeds, and in the bad or good qualities of land, and "the correct modes of measuring and weighing."§

Indigo refers itself to India by the name which it has certainly borne in Europe since the time of Pliny; in its own country it is called *Nili*, or blue. It is supposed to have been early exported to Arabia, Tyre, and Egypt, and to have been adulterated or imitated; for Pliny writes, "Cast the right indico upon live coals, it yieldeth a flame of most

* Code, ix. 38, 39.

† Roxburgh, Flora Indica, vol. iii. p. 295.

‡ Code, viii. 243.

§ *Ibid.*, ix. 330.

excellent purple."* Indigo is a common-looking little plant, with a bluish-green juice, and is only converted into a handsome colour and a permanent dye by a process of oxygenation; and Bancroft thinks it wonderful that so many thousand years ago, the natives of India should have discovered means by which the colourable matter of the plant "might be extracted, oxygenated, and precipitated from all the other matters combined with it."

In the manufacture of iron and its conversion into steel the early Hindus showed the same proficiency. Dr. Royle expresses astonishment that "a primitive people could have overcome the difficulties of smelting iron and of forging steel:"† and that these difficulties were overcome at a very remote period we have evidence; for Dan and Javan carried Indian iron to Tyre, and the Hindus of the Rig-Veda made iron tires to their wheels, as also various tools and weapons. It has lately been discovered that the far-famed Damascus blades were of Indian steel manufactured in the west of India. Mr. Wilkinson has proved that the figuring of these swords depends upon the peculiar crystallization of the *wootz,* the name by which manufactured steel is known in India. It is prepared by breaking up the ore and throwing it into a charcoal furnace, from whence it issues in a malleable state; it is then beaten with a stone hammer on a stone anvil, into what is called "an unpromising"-looking bar; and this bar being cut into small pieces is put

* The West Indies had for a time the honour of exclusively supplying Europe with indigo, for the manufacture had been neglected in the East, whilst in A.D. 1747 it was cultivated in the West; but in 1779 Mr. Prinsep, then a merchant in Calcutta, restored the trade to India.

† Lecture on the Results of the Great Exhibition, or Lecture on the Arts and Manufacture of India, p. 464.

into a crucible with dried branches of trees and the green berries of various shrubs, much importance being attached to the effect of different kinds of wood in producing different kinds of iron and steel. The crucibles are made of clay, and closed at the mouth with clay; after they have been exposed to the blast for two hours and a half, they are removed from the furnace, and the wootz, or steel, being allowed to cool in the crucible, the particles arrange themselves in the crystalline forms, which produce the peculiar watering, or *jowhar*, of the Damascus blades.* This Hindu plan of boiling iron and green leaves and wood together in a closed crucible appears to excel even the methods most approved at Glasgow and Sheffield, for Mr. Heath says that "iron is converted into cast steel by the natives of India in two hours and a half, while at Sheffield it requires at least four hours to melt blistered steel."† The iron and steel made in Mysore has, at present, equal fame with that of Cutch; but in ancient times, iron is always mentioned in connection with the Indus. King Porus presented Alexander the Great with about thirty pounds of steel, as a precious production of his country; and this steel was so much valued by the Persians, that, in their language, "to give an Indian answer," meant to give a cut with an Indian sword. From the countries on the Indus also came some of the most beautiful specimens of arms exhibited in the Crystal Palace in 1851, where "a dagger with pearls let into the centre of its blades," "a dagger containing another within it," and "a dagger opening with five blades," were all sent

* J. R. A. S., Feb. 16, 1839.

† Dr. Royle, Lecture on the Arts and Manufactures of India, pp. 466–468. Mr. Heath, managing director of the India Iron and Steel Company.

by the Rajah of Pattiala, which is a Sikh principality within the province of Delhi.*

It is interesting to turn from the steel and iron factories to the silent quarries of Bijanugur, twenty-nine miles from Bellary, above the Southern Ghats. Here the granite rocks still show distinctly marks of the chisels that hewed out the huge blocks with which the grandest of old Indian cities was constructed. The streets of Bijanugur were paved with flags of granite; its walls, pillars, arches, and even flat roofs and beams, all made of granite, some blocks being fifteen feet in breadth and some monolith statues seventeen feet in height. The tools employed were chisels, wedges, levers, and hammers: the chisels small, pencil-shaped, of steel or iron, with highly-tempered points; the wedges of iron, from two to three and a half inches long; the hammers of wood, or, if iron hammers were used, a hollow was made in the striking face, and filled with lead or soft iron, to diminish the vibration and save the edge of the chisel. In working a granite quarry, the Hindus make a series of small holes about an inch square, of different depths; whilst working these water is used, to preserve the temper of the chisels, and when finished, iron wedges are introduced into the holes, and the continued simultaneous striking of the hammer splits the granite into the required masses. The Hindus are also acquainted with the use of fire in quarrying; and by covering a convex plateau or boss of granite with dry thorny acacia-wood and setting it on fire, they cause it to split off in a flake, which is easily detached by wedges and a lever.

* Dr. Royle, Lecture on the Arts and Manufactures of India, p. 470, and Illus. Cat. part iv. p. 912. A reference to this lecture will show that tin and metallic alloys were early known in India.

For the antiquity of weaving we have evidence in the Rig-Veda, where we read of the rat gnawing the "weaver's threads;" and again in the Code, where the weaver is required to return in the woven fabric a greater weight than he received in the raw cotton;* the reason being that he is obliged to keep his threads immersed in rice-water, which necessarily increases their weight. Moist air facilitates weaving, and is indispensable for the finest qualities; it is on this account that Masulipatam and Dhacca maintained their pre-eminence, and could only be rivalled in the dry north-west by the contrivance of underground workshops. The strange appearance of an Indian spinning-wheel, made of richly carved wood and bound round by unsightly threads, was explained by the late Professor Cowper, who discovered that the clumsy-looking threads give a "tension and elasticity" not to be procured in any other way. These wheels are now silenced by the machinery of Manchester, and the time may soon arrive when it will appear incredible that a fabric of ten yards in length and one yard wide should weigh only 3 oz. 2 dwts., and pass readily through a small ring. Similar to this must have been the "woven air" of Sanskrit literature, and the robe in which a woman exhibited herself in Buddhist story and was punished for going about unclad. The muslin had been sent to Kosala as a present from the King of Kalinga.†

The products of India are traced to Greece in the time of Homer, and to Jerusalem in the days of King Solomon. The genealogy of the words for ivory and elephant is said to prove that Greece got ivory from India, through the men of Tyre, in which case the celebrated bed of Menelaus was carved from the tusks of elephants once roaming in Hindo-

* Code, viii. 356.

† Asiatic Researches, vol. xx. p. 85.

stan. There was no word in Greek for elephant, and when Herodotus first saw the animal he called it ivory, using the Sanskrit-derived word by which the tusks were known in commerce. King Solomon's apes and peacocks, in like manner, bear Sanskrit-derived names, and the algum-wood, of which he made ceilings, screens, and balconies, is supposed to be the sandal-wood of India. The precious stones of King Hiram's cargo still lie in the hills to the west of Ajmere, rich in garnets, amethysts, chrysolites, and metals; and also in the hills of Guzerat, where agates, mocha-stones, and carnelians are found about thirty feet below the surface of the soil. Nard and bdellium, calamus and cassia, were also products of India. Nard, or spikenard, grows in the Himalaya, being a plant with small hairy roots, compared by the Arabs to ermines' tails; bdellium is a fragrant gum from Kattiwar; calamus, either the delicious lemon-grass, grown in Kew Gardens, or that which yields the fragrant grass-oil; and the cassia of Scripture is the *tamala* of Sanskrit literature.* The names of these products are not the only words which Professor Lassen remarks as Sanskrit words early introduced into Hebrew by the means of trade, and the inference is, that the "Ophir" of Scripture must have been in India, and probably on the Malabar coast, the Sanskrit words in question bearing terminations characteristic of the Dekkan. Native navigators are supposed to have shipped the goods from the Indus to some port to the south of Bombay, whence they were fetched by the Arabs or Phœnicians.

The disastrous enterprise of poor Bhuja, son of Tugra,

* Pepper, although not mentioned in King Hiram's cargo, must not be omitted when speaking of the undoubted products of India.

shows that the singers of the Vedic hymns had heard of voyages in waters where no land could be seen. The Rig-Veda thus stands as a witness *within* India to the ancient Hindus having been a maritime people, whilst their settlements in Java furnish indisputable evidence from without; though commerce by land seems to have been more congenial to the general Asiatic character, and caravans of merchants may be ranked as one of those essential features of oriental scenery which equally characterize all ages.

"In the thirty-seventh chapter of Genesis," says Dr. Vincent, "the brethren of Joseph, when about to leave him to perish, saw a company of Ishmaelite or Midianite merchants approach, to whom they resolved to sell their brother as a slave. . . . Here, upon opening the oldest history in the world, we find the Ishmaelites from Gilead conducting a caravan of camels loaded with the spices of India. The date of this transaction is more than seventeen centuries prior to the Christian era; and notwithstanding its antiquity, it has all the genuine features of a caravan crossing the desert at the present hour." The Hindus probably conducted their goods as far as Persia, and were there met by the Midianites.* Queen Esther's "white and blue hangings," at Persepolis, are at any rate attributed to India, and the word *karpas,* used in the book of Esther, is the Sanskrit name of cotton.† Fairs were national amuse-

* Dr. Vincent believes the caravans to have passed through Basra to Medina, and through Petra to Egypt and Tyre, previous to the call of Abraham, and that this is the oldest line of road in the universe.—Periplus, part ii. book iii. p. 328.

† Cotton reached Europe apparently in the time of the Crusades, through the medium of Arabia, the Arab word *kutn* becoming our cotton. See

ments in India. Tribute was paid in kind, and kings were in the habit of holding great festivals, at which they collected all "the nobles and princes of the provinces." An interesting account of such a festival is given in the Mahabharata, mentioning the kings who attended and the offerings which they made. From Balkh (in Bactria) was presented a war-chariot inlaid with gold; to this another hill-rajah harnessed a pair of white horses, a third attended to the step or fender of the car, and a fourth king held the banner. From Kamboja were brought cloths of wool, and skins of animals that live in holes, also horses "partridge-spotted" and "parrot-nosed." From beyond the Oxus came vessels of iron, and swords with hilts of ivory; other mountaineers brought shawls of goats' hair, and silk of thread spun by worms; and silk garments we have already noticed as worn at Rama's marriage and at Dasaratha's funeral. From Tibet were sent the bushy tails of the yak, some white and some black, as is still the case, and valued by King Yudhishthira, as in the present day, for chowries, or fly-flappers: two of King Yudhishthira's brothers waved these chowries over the monarch, whilst two others fanned him with punkahs, and his friend Krishṇa held the sacred chank and poured upon his head the water of inauguration. Sacred chanks are shells opening to the left instead of the right; and these, with gems, coral, and "heaps of pearls," were the offering from Ceylon, whilst from the Carnatic came sandal-wood, sandal-ointment in vases of gold, and the fragrant *agallachum*,* shown by Dr. Royle

Book of Esther, ch. i. v. 6, and Dr. Royle's Lecture on the Results of the Great Exhibition, 1851, p. 487.

* Notes on the Sabha Purva of the Mahabharata, by Professor Wilson. J. R. A. S., No. xiii. May, 1842.

to be the tree *agala*, or eagle-wood,* most used when in a state of decay.

A caravan with freights of this description is described in the story of Nala and Damayanti:†—

"A caravan of merchants, elephants and steeds, and cars,
And beyond a pleasant river with its waters cool and clear;
'T was a quiet stream and waveless, girt about with spreading canes;
There the cuckoo, there the osprey, there the red geese clamouring stood;
Swarmed the turtles, fish, and serpents; there rose many a stately isle."

Damayanti is a lovely princess, wandering forlorn in search of her husband; the merchants take her for a spirit and are unwilling to speak, but she entreats assistance in her search for her lost husband. The chief says that hitherto he has encountered only "elephants, tigers, buffaloes, and bears," but he consents that Damayanti shall travel to the next city under his protection, and the caravan proceeds until—

"A lake of loveliest beauty, fragrant with the lotus flowers,
Saw those merchants, wide and pleasant, with fresh grass and shady trees;
Flowers and fruits bedecked its borders, where the birds melodious sang:
In its clear, delicious waters, soul-enchanting, icy-cool,
With their horses all o'er-wearied, thought they there to plunge and bathe."

The captain gave a signal and they encamped, but in the dead of the night down came a herd of wild elephants to the lake for water; for a moment they stood amazed at the

* Illustrated Catalogue of Great Exhibition, part iv. Colonies, p. 878.

† Poems by Dean Milman, vol. iii.

slumbering caravan, but presently, scenting the tame elephants,—

"Forward rush they, fleet and furious, . . .
Irresistible the onset of the rushing ponderous beasts. . . .
Strewn was all the way before them with the boughs and trunks of trees,
On they crashed to where the travellers slumbered by the Lotus Lake;
Trampled down without a struggle, helpless on the earth they lay:
'Woe, oh woe!' shrieked out the merchants; wildly some began to fly,
In the forest thickets plunging; some stood gasping, blind with sleep,
And the elephants down beat them with their tusks, their trunks, their feet.
Many saw their camels dying, mingling with the men on foot,
And, in frantic tumult rushing, wildly struck each other down;
Many, miserably shrieking, cast them down upon the earth;
Many climbed the trees in terror; on the rough ground stumbled some.
Thus, in various wise and fatal, by the elephants assailed,
Lay that caravan so wealthy, scattered all about or slain.
Such, so fearful was the tumult, the three worlds seemed all appalled.
'T is a fire amid the encampment,—save ye, fly ye for your lives!
Lo! your precious pearls ye trample; take them up, why fly so fast?
Save them, 't is a common venture!"

The poor Princess was suspected of being in some way the cause of the calamity, and threatened with death from clods and bamboos; but happily some "Veda-reading Brahmans" survived the scattered host, and took her in charge.

We must now conclude the subject of manufactures and commerce, by noticing the place which Commerce holds in the Law Book.

"Travelling with merchandise"* was an occupation fit only for those whom the "twice-born" despise; but "lending at interest" was a virtuous mode of subsistence, especially recommended to the third Caste (Vaisyas), although not available for Kshatriyas and Brahmans. Neither might the two first Castes *receive* interest on loans; but they might *borrow*, if for a pious use. Money-lending is carefully treated in the Code, which thus exhibits the financial system of their commerce.

The first regulation is one attributed to Vasishta, which we remember as the name of the prime minister of Dasaratha, the King of Ayodhya:—

> "A lender of money may take, in addition to his capital, . . . an eightieth part of a hundred by the month;
>
> "Or he may take two in the hundred by remembering the duty of good men; for, by taking two in the hundred, he becomes not a sinner for gain:
>
> "He may thus take, in the direct order of the classes, two in the hundred *from a Brahman*, three *from a soldier*, four *from a Vaisya*, and five *from a mechanic or Sudra*, but never more, as interest by the month."†

The subject of pledges is much considered: as, if a man use an article given in pledge without the owner's consent, he must give up his whole interest. Neither a pledge nor a deposit are lost by lapse of time; but in general if the owner sees any chattel enjoyed "by others for ten years while, though present, he says nothing, that chattel he shall not recover." "Grain, fruit, wool, hair, and beasts of burden," are named amongst the articles on which it was usual to raise money; but in all cases five per cent. is considered sufficient interest, and more than this "the wise

* Code of Manu, x. 46.

† *Ibid.*, viii. 140, 141, 142.

call usurious." Special regulations are made for the insurance of goods travelling either by land or by sea, as :—

"A lender at interest, on *the risk* of safe carriage, who has agreed on the place and time, shall not receive such interest, if *by accident* the goods are not carried to the place, or within the time.

"Whatever interest, *or price of the risk*, shall be settled *between the parties*, by men well acquainted with sea voyages or journeys by land, with times and with places, such interest shall have legal force."*

"For a long passage, the freight must be proportioned to places and times; but this must be understood of passages up and down rivers : at sea there can be no settled freight."†

The part which the Code assigns to the King in reference to commerce is too laborious, we imagine, to have been usually fulfilled by kings; but we may understand it to mean that either King, or Brahman, or Patél, as the case might be, must—

"Establish rules for the sale and purchase of all marketable things, having duly considered whence they come and whither they must be sent, how long they have been kept, what may be gained by them, and what has been expended on them.

"Once in five nights, or at the close of every half-month, *according to the nature of the commodities*, let the King make a regulation for market prices in the presence of those experienced men.

"Let all weights and measures be well ascertained by him; and once in six months let him examine them."‡

The money used was specified weights of gold, silver, and copper: one seed of *gunga*, or hemp, was the weight called *ractica*; five racticas of gold were one *masha*, sixteen such mashas one *suverna*, four suvernas one *pala*.

Two racticas of silver made one *mashaca*, and sixteen mashacas a silver *dharana* or *purana*.

* Code of Manu, viii. 156, 157. † *Ibid.*, viii. 406.

‡ *Ibid.*, viii. 401, 402, 403.

A *karsha*,* or eighty racticas, of copper were a *pana* or *karshapana;* and this piece of copper, weighing eighty hempseeds, was the lowest wages per day for a servant, he being entitled in addition to two cloths for apparel each half-year, and to a drona of grain each month: one pana was also the toll at a ferry for an empty cart; half a pana for a man with a load; but—

> "Waggons, filled with goods packed up, shall pay toll in proportion to their value; for empty vessels and bags, and for men ill-apparelled, a very small toll shall be demanded."†

The King also appears to have claimed a share in all 'treasure trove;' to old hoards deposited in the ground, which any one discovers, or to precious minerals‡ he is entitled to half; and the following passage from the Drama of 'Sacontala' would make it appear that the money of shipwrecked merchants, dying without heirs, also passed to the King.

The chief minister says, "I have carefully stated a case which has arisen in the city, and accurately committed it to writing: let the King deign to cousider it."§ The King says immediately, "Give me the leaf," and reads—"Be it presented at the footstool of the King, that a merchant . . . who had extensive commerce at sea, was lost in a late shipwreck; he had no child born, and has left a fortune of many millions, which belong, if the King commands, to the royal treasury." The King does not claim the property, but says, that "when any of his subjects lose a kinsman, he will supply the place of that kinsman."

The slight facts here collected show the commercial class bearing a relation towards the king and the learned aristo-

* Code of Manu, 134, 135, 136.
† *Ibid.*, viii. 404, 405.
‡ *Ibid.*, viii. 39.
§ Works of Sir W. Jones, vol. vi.

cracy, not altogether peculiar either to India or to centuries preceding our era. The sovereign and his court enjoyed foreign luxuries, and claimed tribute from the profits of trade. Industrial occupations were encouraged and nominally held in honour; but practically, the working of the law excluded all who engaged in arts or commerce from aristocratic rank and privilege. Amongst other restrictions it was decreed that if a Vaisya married a Sudra his children ceased to be Vaisyas, and if he married a woman of the higher caste the children became outcasts. Cumbersome enactments as to where he might go, and what he might eat, and what he might do, were also inconsistent with the enterprise and freedom necessary to commercial success; and the result was, that whilst banking and money-lending were regarded as orthodox and gentlemanly occupations, the more adventurous parts of commerce were performed by men free from hereditary rank and conventional restrictions,—often "sons of the twice-born, said to be degraded,—who are considered as low-born, and subsist by such employments as the twice-born despise."*

* Code of Manu.

CHAPTER VIII.

WOMEN.

"I thought on a' the tales, Alice,
O' woman's love and faith;
Of Truth that smiled at fear, Alice,
And Love that conquer'd death;
Affection blessing hearts and homes,
When joy was far awa',
And Fear and Hate; but Love, O Love!
Aboon and over a'!"
NICOLL.

A THOUSAND years B.C. Hindu women appear to have been as free as Trojan dames or the daughters of Judæa: hymns in the Rig-Veda mention them with respect and affection, comparing the goodness of the God Agni to that of a "brother for his sisters," and the brightness of this God to the shining of a woman in her home; women moreover go out adorned for festivals, or mingle in the midnight foray. Even in the succeeding phase of Hindu life, when Brahmans contemplated the soul beneath the shadow of Himavat, women attended their discourses and took part in their discussions. We find in one of the Upanishads a king holding a solemn sacrifice, and inviting his chief guests to state their opinions on theology, and amongst these guests "a learned female named Garga"* is conspicuous. A more pleasing instance of women's interest in holy themes is afforded by a conversation between Yajnyawalcya and his wife Maitreya :† the sage announces his intention of abandoning the world and entering upon the life of seclusion and asceticism which the Code prescribes for Brahmans in advancing years; he tells her that he will divide his property between her and his second wife, but Maitreya asks, "Should I become immortal if this whole earth full of riches were mine?" "No," replies her husband, "riches serve for the means of living, but immortality is not attained through wealth." Maitreya declares that she has then no use for riches, and entreats her husband to communicate the knowledge which leads to immortality. "Dear wert thou to me," Yajnyawalcya replies, "and a pleasing sentiment dost thou make known; come, sit down, I will expound; do thou endeavour to comprehend:" and then a discourse follows, showing that abstraction procures immortality, because affections relate to the soul, and the worshipper must learn to contemplate the soul alone, "since everything is soul;" and whatever objects are beheld, the aim must be to merge all thought and feeling into the universal Soul.

In the Code, women in the abstract are put upon a level with Sudras, children, and pupils.

"Three persons,—a wife, a son, and a slave,—are declared by law to have, in general, no wealth exclusively their own: the wealth

* Colebrooke's Essays, vol. i. p. 70. † *Ibid.*, p. 66.

which they earn is regularly acquired for the man to whom they belong."*

"A wife, a son, a servant, a pupil, and a younger whole brother may be corrected when they commit faults, with a rope, or the small shoot of a cane."†

"For women, children, persons of crazy intellect, the old, the poor, and the infirm, the king shall order punishment with a whip, a twig, or a rope."‡

"To attain the celestial world is denied to Sudras; but a woman or a Sudra may perform acts leading to temporal good."§

Women necessarily hold this subservient position because they are not "invested with the sacrificial string;" it being ordained that the "nuptial ceremony" shall be "the complete institution of women," and hold the place of the second birth received by men of rank.|| This being the case, it is a man's duty "to give his daughter in marriage" "to an excellent and handsome youth of the same class," even though she have not attained eight years of age;¶ and if the father neglect this, she may by the time she is eleven years old choose a bridegroom for herself, provided she choose one of equal rank. We have already had an instance of how this was effected in the Swayambara, at Panchala, which concluded by the lovely Draupadi throwing the marriage garland over the heroic Arjuna. We shall find that Brahmans awarded love, admiration, amusements, jewels, and ornaments, most liberally to women as wives; the only peculiarity of their system being, that a woman could have nothing of her own. "Hear now the laws concerning women," says the Code:**—

"By a girl, or by a young woman, or by a woman advanced in

* Code, viii. 16.
† *Ibid.*, 299.
‡ *Ibid.*, ix. 230.
§ *Ibid.*, ii. 223.
|| *Ibid.*, ii. 67.
¶ *Ibid.*, ix. 88.
** *Ibid.*, 146, 151, 153, 156.

years, nothing must be done, even in her own dwelling-place, according to her mere pleasure.

"In childhood must a female be dependent on her father; in youth, on her husband; her lord being dead, on her sons. . . . A woman must never seek independence:

"Never let her wish to separate herself from her father or her sons, for by a separation from them she exposes both families to contempt:

"She must always live with a cheerful temper, with good management in the affairs of the house, with great care of the household furniture, and with a frugal hand in all her expenses:

"Him to whom her father has given her, or her brother with the paternal assent, let her obsequiously honour while he lives; and when he dies, let her never neglect him.

"When the husband has performed the nuptial rites with texts of the *Veda*, he gives bliss continually to his wife here below, and he will give her happiness in the next world.

"Though unobservant of approved usages, or enamoured of another woman, or devoid of good qualities, yet a husband must be constantly revered as a god by a virtuous wife.

"No sacrifice is allowed to women apart from their husbands, no religious rite, no fasting; as far only as a wife honours her lord, so far she is exalted in heaven.

"A faithful wife who wishes to attain in heaven the mansion of her husband, must do nothing unkind to him, be he living or dead."

Obedience to her husband is the beginning and the middle and the end of female duty. If a wife neglect her husband because he drinks or gambles, she must be punished and deprived of her ornaments; but if she drinks or acts immorally, she may be superseded by another wife.* If a good wife dies before her husband, he will procure life for her in another world by sacrifice, and then "light again the nuptial fire." If the husband die first, the wife must continue till death "performing harsh duties" and "prac-

* Code, ix. 78, 84.

tising the incomparable rules of virtue, followed by women devoted to one husband." A second marriage would make her despicable, whilst death would procure certain bliss; but the Code gives no hint of its being desirable that widows should be burned with the husband's corpse: still less is this custom advocated by the Rig-Veda; in which a passage supposed to inculcate this barbarity is found by Professor Wilson to have an entirely different meaning. A woman cannot even inherit rank, that is, she cannot transmit her own inherited rank to her children: if she marry a *Dwija,* or man invested with the sacred thread, the children will have their father's rank; but if she, the daughter of a Dwija, marry a Sudra, or any uninvested person, her children fall *beneath* the rank of the father, and the son of a Sudra by a Brahman woman is the lowest of mortals. The same rule does not altogether hold regarding men, only a man of rank (a Dwija) must not make a Sudra woman his *first* wife; and the reason for this is, that his sacrifices to the Gods, and oblations to the Manes, and hospitalities to strangers, must be supplied by her, and neither Gods nor Manes would be propitiated by such offerings.* No punishment attaches to marriage between twice-born men and women of a rank below them, but the children of such a marriage do not appear to have been legally entitled to investiture with the sacred thread.†

From these extracts it is evident that "woman's rights" were wholly ignored by the Brahmanical code; but as daughters and wives are often too happy to require rights, we usually lose sight of this unpleasant truth, and find ample reason to admire Hindu representations of domestic

* Code, iii. 18. † *Ibid.*, x. 6.

bliss. "Where females are honoured, there the deities are pleased," says the Code; but if they are dishonoured and "pronounce an imprecation on a house, that house with all that belongs to it will utterly perish."*

There can scarcely be a more pleasing picture of an affectionate wife than that given of our friend Damayanti, who was discovered alone in the gloomy forest. In an earlier part of the story, she is described as very lovely, and the only daughter of Bhima, King of Vidarbha, supposed to mean Berar. Nala was the youthful monarch of Nishadha, at no great distance from Vidarbha, and although these two young people had never met, they fell in love by merely hearing of each other's beauty and merit. King Nala imparts his wishes to the sacred birds called Hansa, and a flock of these wild geese take flight in consequence for Vidarbha, and discover the lovely Damayanti in a garden attached to her father's palace and surrounded by her hundred damsels. The Hansa allure her to a little distance from her attendants, and there, by judicious discourse, succeed in making the young princess fully participate her lover's emotions. From this moment poor Damayanti is observed to pine, and her father determines that she shall hold her Swayambara, or chose her husband amongst attendant suitors.

As soon as this is announced, Nala contrives to procure a private interview, fearing lest his intended bride might not recognize him amongst the numerous chiefs and nobles whom such an invitation would assemble. When the anticipated day arrived, elephants, steeds, and chariots brought all the lords of earth as suitors; they came wearing fra-

* Code, iii. 56, 58.

grant garlands and rich earrings, and entered the court through the golden columns of the portal arch.

But amongst the earthly suitors appeared four Gods, each of whom, knowing Damayanti's inclination, assumed the form of Nala. The damsel knew that four out of the five Nalas present must be Gods, and she perfectly appreciated the honour they intended for her; but her heart was fixed on the real human Nala, and instead of rejoicing in celestial homage, she was distracted at finding it impossible to distinguish her earthly lover. In this dilemma she appealed to the Gods themselves, entreated their compassion and implored their aid. The Gods are amazed to find themselves rejected, but, in pity for the maiden's anguish, show signs of their divinity; Damayanti chooses him she loves, and Nala becomes the happy bridegroom. After the nuptial ceremony, the newly-married pair reside at Nishadha, have two children, and enjoy supreme felicity, until Nala has a spell cast over him by a certain evil spirit. The King is described as a most virtuous monarch, well-read in the four Vedas and the Puranas, gentle to all living creatures, true in word and strict in vow; but in marrying Damayanti he excited the jealousy of the demon Kali, who had himself wished for the damsel's love, and Kali in consequence was for ever haunting the palace, and watching for some unguarded moment in which to throw his evil spirit into the unhappy King. Negligence of a trifling prescribed ceremony gave, at length, the wished-for opportunity, and the virtuous Nala, now possessed by a demon, gave himself up to gambling.

For months he continued to throw the dice with ill success, his wife venturing now and then a sad remonstrance, and his wise counsellors saying that he is no longer himself;

but Nala, like other desperate gamblers, will listen to no advice. Damayanti then convenes the council in his name, and gets leave to send the children with a trusty charioteer to her father's court at Vidarbha, where alone she feels they will be safe. The infatuated King stakes his jewels, his garments, and even his kingdom, and all are lost. The demon strives hard to make him stake his wife, but does not succeed; even in madness, the King's virtue and affection were proof against that trial: but he was houseless and penniless, for his adversary decreed death to whoever should befriend him, and chased him from his palace; the dethroned monarch went forth into the woods, but not alone, for the faithful Damayanti followed. Too desperate to be soothed, her husband felt her gentle presence as an aggravation of his misery, and instead of desiring her companionship he showed where ran the road conducting to her father's home. She understood the sign, but said that with her afflicted, breaking heart and sinking limbs she could not leave him: she wished to soothe his weariness, and said all physicians owned that in sorrow there was no healing herb or balsam equal to a wife; therefore if she went to Vidarbha, he must go also. But that was an insupportable idea, for he could not endure to be seen by Bhima in his base extremity. At night they seek the refuge of a forest hut, and three times, whilst Damayanti sleeps, he resolves upon escape: he thinks that if he were aways he would go to her father, mother, and children, but that while he remains there is only misery for all.

"And departing, still departing, he returned again, again,
Dragged away by that bad demon,—ever by his love drawn back."

And after thus oscillating "like a swing," he is torn away by Kali, and flies afar.

When Damayanti wakes, she finds herself deserted, and wanders hither and thither until she meets the caravan of merchants, with whom we have already seen her. After the catastrophe of the elephants, she escaped with some Brahmans, who conducted her to a town called King Chedi's City: here she enters, disturbed, emaciate, wretched, her hair dishevelled, the boys of the place following her footsteps. The mother of the King, seated on a lofty terrace, is struck by her appearance, and sends a confidential servant, called a nurse, to bring in the sorrowful wanderer: to this high lady Damayanti tells her story, and is persuaded to remain with her at Chedi, only making the condition that she shall not eat broken victuals or "wash feet," which would have been Sudra service; and that she shall be protected from all suitors.

After a time, this poor wanderer is discovered by messengers from Vidarbha, and taken to her father's court and reunited to her children; and then her anxiety to win back her husband becomes irrepressible; but tedious was her search, and numerous her schemes, before she succeeded.

Nala had become charioteer to a King of Ayodhya, who taught him the secrets of dice in return for a knowledge of horses; for it seems as if Nala's fault had consisted in being ignorant of that science, whereas in the knowledge of horses he excelled. As soon as Rituparna, the King of Ayodhya, had fully imparted to his charioteer the science of dice, Kali was defeated, the spell broken, and the evil spirit leaving him entered a tree, which perished instantly. At this juncture a friendly Naga king (or king of snakes) offered to restore Nala to his former appearance, and he might then have returned to his kingdom and his wife, but news arrived at Ayodhya that Damayanti was about to hold another Swayambara,—which was a stratagem contrived by his deserted wife, in order to rouse up her missing lord and lead to their reunion. Damayanti's ceaseless inquiries had led her to suspect that the King of Ayodhya's skilful charioteer was no other than King Nala, and to Ayodhya therefore (but to no other place) she sent intimation that on the dawn of the succeeding day Damayanti was about to choose a second lord. Rituparna, King of Ayodhya, wishes to attend, and says *literally* to his charioteer :—

> "This woman, having bound us, attracts by her good qualities:
> Who (thus) drawn by a woman (can say) nay?
> The assembly—such the announcement—is tomorrow:
> Thus our way by measurement is one hundred yojanas."

One hundred yojanas may be five hundred miles or it may be nine hundred, and as Ayodhya stands for Oude, and Vidarbha is supposed to mean Berar, we must accept the extension, and whether four hundred or nine hundred makes small difference, the distance being in either case an anticipation of railway power and speed.

At the King's request, poor "Nala's heart was torn with anguish," but still he desired to be present himself, and promised that his master should arrive within the time; and his wonderful proficiency in the science of horses enabled him to perform the prodigious feat. Damayanti knew at once the peculiar tramp of his steeds, and mounted to the palace-roof to behold once more her "Nala, prince of men."

Damayanti's mother was the only person in her secret; her father, King Bhima, knew nothing of her stratagem, and was astonished at the arrival of a guest, whilst the guest and his charioteer were equally astonished to find no preparation for a marriage festival. All however keep their counsel with becoming dignity, and leave Damayanti to pursue her schemes without disturbance; whilst she, baffled by Nala's persevering incognito, has some difficulty in bringing about a successful *dénouement*. She at length persuades her mother to allow her to have a secret interview with the mysterious charioteer; and then she works upon his feelings, forcing him to acknowledge himself to be her husband Nala, and with great difficulty convincing him that the idea of a second marriage had never for a moment been really entertained, but that she "imagined the subtle wile" to lure him to her. The sun, moon, and winds coming forward to give testimony to her truth, her husband at length gives up his jealous doubts, resumes his proper form, and is happily reunited to his loving wife.

In this beautiful little poem we find more independence of action than the Code would willingly have accorded to women; but it occurs as an episode in the Mahabharata, which is essentially an heroic poem, describing more of the Kshatriya than of the Brahman class. Damayanti's marriage at the commencement is a similar festival to that held in Panchala for Draupadi; but it is only amongst princes and princesses that we read of such marriages, and no instance is given of a marriage in the Brahman Caste. The story of Nala is told to Yudhishthira, to console him on the occasion of his having lost his kingdom at a game of draughts; but neither the one nor the other of these gambling monarchs is blamed by the poet in accordance with the precepts of Manu, and on all occasions the tone of the Epics is so much more free than that of the Code, that they give one the impression of having had Brahman editors rather than Brahman authors. Gambling is a vice particularly reprehended in the Code, which gives the following remarkable verses referring to it :—

> "Gaming, either with inanimate or with animated things, let the King exclude wholly from his realm: both those modes of play cause destruction to princes:
>
> "Such play with dice, or by matches *between rams and cocks*, amounts to open theft: and the King must ever be vigilant in suppressing both *modes of play*.
>
> "Gaming with lifeless things is known among men by the name of *dynta;* but *samahwaya* signifies a match between living creatures.
>
> "Let the King punish corporally at discretion both the gamester and the keeper of a gaming-house, whether they play with inanimate or animated things. . . .
>
> "Gamesters, public dancers, and singers, . . . let him instantly banish from the town."*

And gambling is still further discouraged by the decree that "money lost at play" cannot be recovered from the son of a debtor or surety.†

In another episode of the Mahabharata, we find the Pandu brothers roaming in and arriving at a village; they are kindly welcomed by a family of poor Brahmans, who prove to be in great affliction, because a human victim is required from them as an offering to the local deity. We cannot but think that this deity was the earth-goddess, Tari Pennu, and that her worship resembled the systems of human sacrifice about which Captain Macpherson has furnished so much valuable information.‡ Whilst reposing in an inner apartment, the five brothers overhear the father, mother, and daughter of this simple forest family,

* Code, ix. 221–225. † *Ibid.*, viii. 159.

‡ R. A. S. I., vol. xiii. part ii. p. 216.

each urging a separate claim to be allowed to suffer for the rest.

The father commences, saying, that never would he be so base as to give a victim from his house and consent himself to live; but still he expresses great anxiety at not knowing how to provide a place of refuge for his wife, daughter, and little son after his removal. He cannot, he says, surrender his faithful wife, the sweet friend given to him by the Gods; nor his daughter, whom Brahma made to be a bride and the mother of heroes; nor yet his son; but if he offer himself, sorrow will pursue him in the world to come, and his abandoned wife and children will be unable to live without him.

The wife next speaks, and chides her husband for yielding to grief like one of lowly caste: for, "who the Vedas know, must know—

> "Fate inevitable orders, all must yield to death in turn:
> Hence the doom, the irrevocable, it beseems not thee to mourn.
> Man hath wife, and son, and daughter, for the joy of his own heart;
> Wherefore wisely check thy sorrow; it is I must hence depart:
> 'Tis the wife's most holy duty,—law on earth without repeal,—
> That her life she offer freely, when demands her husband's weal.'

She goes on to argue that he can support and guard the children when she is gone, but that she would have no power to guard and support them without him. Deprived of his protection, "rude and reckless men," she says, would come seeking their blameless daughter; and helpless and beset on every side, she would be unable to check the suit of Sudra lovers. She concludes by saying that her honoured husband will find another wife, to whom he will be as gentle and kind as he has been to her.

"Hearing thus his wife, the husband fondly clasp'd her to his breast,
And their tears they pour'd together, by their mutual grief oprest."

When the daughter overheard the troubled discourse of her parents, she put in her claim to be the offered victim; for if they died before her she would sink to bitterest misery, but if she died to preserve them, she would "then become immortal and partake of bliss divine."

Whilst they were all thus weeping, the little son opened wide his eyes, and lisped out in broken accents:—

"'Weep not, father! weep not, mother! O my sister, weep not so!'
First to one and then to the other, smiling went he to and fro;
Then a blade of spear-grass lifting, thus in bolder glee he said,
'With this spear-grass will I kill him, this man-eating giant, dead.'
Though o'erpower'd by bitterest sorrow, as they heard their prattling boy,
Stole into the parents' bosom mute and inexpressive joy."*

Happily the child's chivalry was not required, for the Pandu brothers went forth and conquered the spirit of evil, whether in the form of "man-eating giant" or "earth-goddess."

Whilst occupied with these beautiful Sanskrit tales, we feel tempted to exalt Hinduism above all other heathen institutions; but when hereafter we may have occasion to follow Hindu women into later centuries, and to consider in matter-of-fact prose to what results the legal regulations tended, we may perhaps limit our admiration to the poets, who exhibit the universal affections of human nature. Women in the poems appear as forest-trees, flowering in wild luxuriance; whilst women in real life resemble flower-

* Translated by H. Milman, Dean of St. Paul's.

ing pears and peaches nailed against the wall. In comparing ancient India with other early countries, you cannot fail to note the absence of queens or of women in any way conspicuous: you meet with no Semiramis or Cleopatra, no Miriam or Sappho, no Deborah, not even with a witch of Endor. This thoroughly domestic character of women is undoubtedly the happiest, provided it be the effect of completeness in home happiness, and as such it is represented in the beautiful episodes which we have been considering; and as at present our attention is limited to the heroic age, all moralizing may be suspended whilst we fully yield to the enjoyment of concluding this Chapter with one more tale from the Mahabharata.

A king named Aswapati sighed for offspring, and, after praying in vain for eighteen years, the gods of heaven sent him a daughter, who grew up so "bright in her surpassing beauty" that she appeared like a child of the immortals, and the princes around were so dazzled, that none sought her for a bride; this distressed her father, and he said that she must go now and make choice herself.

"Meekly bow'd the modest maiden with her eyes upon the ground,
And departed as he bade her, with attendants troop'd around:
Many a hermitage she traversed, riding in a gold-bright car,
Many a wilderness and forest, holy places near and far."

And when she came back she told her father that she had found a blind old king who had been driven from his throne by a ruthless kinsman, and who with his beloved wife had taken refuge in a hermit grove and therein passed his life; and then she says that it is his brave son, Satyavan, whom her heart has chosen,—"Satyavan has all my love." At this announcement a holy man named Narad, who happened to be present, exclaims in grief that she little knows what care and woe she chooses in choosing Satyavan; and in answer to her father's inquiries Narad allows that the young man is—

"Learned as the Gods' own teacher, glorious as the sun is he;
With the earth's untiring patience, and great Indra's bravery."

And in answer to further questions, says, he is noble,

"True, and great of soul;
Bountiful is he, and modest,—every sense does he control;
Gentle, brave, all creatures love him, keeping in the righteous way,
Number'd with the holy hermits, pure and virtuous as they."

But all these virtues lie under a cloud, which makes them profitless, for in a year, counting from this day, "Satyavan will die." "Go then, my dearest child," says the King, "and choose again;" but the daughter answers,

"Be he virtuous or worthless, many be his days or few,
Once for all I choose my husband; to that choice will I be true."

The sage and her father give way to her decided wishes, and in due time the young couple are married, and live in great happiness with the hermits in the grove. Savitri put aside her jewels, and wore the coarse raiment usually adopted by hermits, and, by her meekness and affection, won the hearts of all with whom she dwelt.

"Sadly, sadly, as she counted, day by day flew swiftly by,
And the fated time came nearer when her Satyavan must die.
Yet three days and he must perish, sadly thought the loving wife;
And she vowed to fast, unresting, for his last three days of life."

Her husband's father feared that the trial would be too great for her, but she answered, "Firm resolve has made me vow it,—firm resolve will give me strength." She kept her vow and maintained her fast; and when the third day dawned, and the fire of worship was kindled, and the morning rites performed, she reverently saluted the aged Brahmans and her husband's honoured parents, but still refused food. Presently her husband took his axe upon his shoulder to go to the wood, but she begged him to let her go also; he replies:—

"'All unknown to thee the forest, rough the path and weary thou;
How then will thy feet support thee, fainting from thy fasting vow?'
'Nay, I sink not from my fasting, and no weakness feel today;
I have set my heart on going, oh, forbid me not, I pray.'"

Savitri has always kept her sad secret from her husband, and he has therefore no idea of her real reason for wishing to accompany him; he however consents, calls her attention to the lovely woods, stately peacocks, and flowers of brilliant hue, but she can look only upon him and mourn him as one about to die. She gathers cooling fruits, and he makes the wood resound with the strokes of his hatchet; but soon a thrilling agony shoots through his temples. She sits down upon the ground, and resting his hand upon her breast he sleeps, but,—

"Sudden, lo! before Savitri stood a great and awful one,
Red as blood was his apparel, bright and glowing as the sun;
In his hand a noose was hanging: he to Satyavan stood nigh,
And upon the weary sleeper fix'd his fearful glittering eye."

This awful apparition was Yama, God of Death, come to bind and take the spirit of Satyavan: having done this he moved towards the south, Savitri closely following. Yama tries to persuade her to go back, but she says, No, wherever her husband goes there she will go also. Yama praises her sweet speech, and offers her any boon except the life of

Satyavan; and she begs that the blind king, her father-in-law, may be restored to sight, but without relinquishing her first request. Yama tries again and again to get rid of her, and says she will faint:—

> "Can I faint when near my husband? where he goes, my path shall be:
> I will follow where thou leadest: listen once again to me."

Nothing can induce her to return without Satyavan, and at length love conquers death: Yama relents; the happy wife hastens to where her husband's body lay, and, leaning upon her faithful bosom, he awakes again to sense and life. A very touching conversation follows, during which he gradually recovers his recollection; but his wife, avoiding any full explanation of what had been occurring, says:—

> "Night's dark shadows round us fall;
> When the morrow's light returneth, dearest, I will tell thee all:
> Up, then, and away, I pray thee, come unto thy parents' love!
> See! the sun long time has vanish'd, and the night grows black above."

And accordingly they return to the hermitage, where Satyavan finds his father no longer blind, and every kind of happiness awaits them.*

* 'Savitri, or the Faithful Wife,' translated from the original Sanskrit into English verse, by R. T. H. Griffith, Oxford. See also an article in the 'Westminster Review,' Oct. 1848, on Indian Epic Poetry, which most interesting paper is attributed to Mr. Cowell.

CHAPTER IX.

PHILOSOPHY.

> "Where is the sweet repose of heart's repenting,
> The deep calm sky, the sunshine of the soul?
> Now heaven and earth are to our bliss consenting,
> And all the Godhead joins to make us whole."—KEBLE.

IN all Brahmanical literature we meet with anxious questioning concerning man's soul and the universal soul, and the means by which perpetual transmigration may be escaped. This knowledge was taught in Upanishads, which professed great reverence for the old Vedas, but started discussions upon subjects quite beyond their range: of this we had some specimens in our Second Chapter, where Nachiketa went to the abode of Yama, God of Death, and entreated him to impart that "knowledge which leads to absorption." By degrees philosophers discovered that the teaching of the Upanishads was contrary to that of the Vedas, and, enrolling their new views into systems, they avowed themselves critics and opponents of the ancient books. Three systems obtained celebrity, the Sankhya, the Nyaya, and the Vedanta; and each system being divided into two parts, six schools of philosophy arose, somewhere between 700 and 600 B.C., which systems are still in force, and studied at Benares. The Sankhya system was the earliest of these, and also the most schismatic, for it starts with declaring that the Vedas have *failed* to communicate means of absolute and final liberation. Indra and other Gods, it says, declare that by drinking soma-juice they have become immortal; but in another place they say that, "Many thousands of Indras and other Gods have passed away in successive ages:" a different method is therefore necessary, "consisting in a discriminative knowledge of perceptible principles, and of the imperceptible one, and of the thinking soul."*

The Sankhya system originated with a philosopher named Kapila, who had migrated through many states of existence, and remembered the Vedas in one of his former lives. He ventured nevertheless to think that the soma-draughts, fire-worship, and the sacrifices enjoined by the Vedas, procured only happiness of limited duration, and he expounded aphorisms to secure eternal liberation.

Kapila's aphorisms are still extant; but either it was his habit to explain orally, or his written explanations have perished, for the aphorisms alone are wholly unintelligible. His pupils made and collected commentaries, and put the whole in verse, called Karika; and the Sankhya Karika, or memorial verses of the Sankhya, is the chief source from which we now derive a knowledge of this curious anticipation of modern metaphysics.† Its leading principles are, that knowledge discriminates twenty-five principles: the Soul, which is unchangeable, is one; Nature, the material of creation, another; Intellect, Buddhi, a fourth; Egotism,

* Wilson's 'Sankhya Karika,' p. 14. † *Ibid.*, pp. 17, 80, 52.

or self-consciousness, a fifth; then follow the five subtle elements which produce our senses, eleven organs, and five gross elements. Nature, or Prakriti, has three qualities, the good, the bad or perturbed, and the dark. The good quality is explained as "kindliness, restraint of the organs, correct judgment, attainment of knowledge, and supernatural power; the bad, or impetuous, as passion, anger, covetousness, sternness, discontent;" and the dark, as "madness, intoxication, atheism, sloth, and other vices." These three qualities are moreover described by their effects, as pleasure, pain, and indifference, and said to co-operate like a lamp, by union of contraries, that is, "as a lamp, which is composed of the opposites, a wick, oil, and flame, illuminates objects, so the qualities of goodness, foulness, and darkness, although contrary to one another, effect a common purpose. Buddhi (the intellect), which is produced by Nature (Prakriti), partakes of these qualities. If it be good, its properties are virtue (*dharma*), knowledge, calm self-control, and supernatural power, called *aiswarya*. The last-mentioned property enables a man to make his way into a solid rock, to sail to the sun on a sunbeam, touch the moon with the tip of his finger, expand so as to occupy all space, and swim, dive, or float upon the earth as readily as in water: through goodness, in fact, the Intellect (Buddhi) attains the "absolute subjugation of Nature," so that "whatever the will proposes, that it obtains."* The other chief product of Nature is Egotism; "but," says Dr. Ballantyne,† "egotism, thus employed, is not to carry with it the familiar import of bustling vanity," for one who would escape

* Wilson's 'Sankhya Karika.'

† Lecture on the Sankhya Philosophy, No. 52; Benares, 1850.

the charge of *ahan-kara* (egotism) is not merely to avoid talking about himself, but must not even distinguish himself from other things, or other things from himself. Self-consciousness is the organ by which the impression of individuality is conveyed to the soul; it produces the senses and all ideas conveyed by the senses, and so far resembles the *Ego*, or I, of Fichte. But here Dr. Ballantyne remarks a "striking difference between the European and the Oriental theory," for, whilst European philosophers assume self-consciousness as the certain indication of soul, Kapila declares it to be no property of soul, and to be regarded such only through delusion. Fichte calls what is outside ourselves *real* only, inasmuch as out of it arises duty and the feeling of 'Thou shalt;' whereas with Kapila the distinctness of Soul from Nature is a "radical fact." Fichte excluded a twofold nature, because it rendered unity of exposition, and consequently all philosophy, impossible;* Kapila looked upon soul as the unchangeable, ultimate reality, which can only be perceived when the transitory is destroyed. Hindu philosophers describe it by negations, and it appears therefore cold, inert, and lifeless; but from the intensity with which these idealists yearned to cast away illusory existence, we may suppose that they felt as the poet, who speaks of the marvels of night, to which sunshine makes us blind, and then sublimely indicates the greater glories hidden from us by life:†

> "Why do we then shun death with anxious strife?
> If light can thus deceive, wherefore not life?"

Kapila's doctrine however was cold and rigid; he makes the soul a passive, unimpressible spectator of joy, sorrow,

* Ballantyne, Lecture on the Sankhya Philosophy. † Blanco White.

duty, power, and knowledge, and, clothed in subtile matter, it extends "over the space of the heart the size of a finger," or, "invested in subtile matter," it hovers over a man like "the flame of a lamp over its wick."* Thus, where Yama expounds to Nachiketa the nature of the soul, he says that it "resides within that space of the human heart which is as large as a finger," and he directs him by firmness of mind to separate it from his body, "in the same manner as the pith is removed from the plant *manju*."† So also in the story of Savitri, told in the preceding Chapter, Yama comes to Satyavan with a noose in his hand, and, forcing out the vital being as it were a finger's length, bound it in his cord.‡ When the spirit, "big as the thumb,"§ has quitted the body, pain ceases, and therefore the great business of life is to acquire immunity from further lives and transmigrations. Self-consciousness and its associates must learn the nothingness of phenomena; then Soul becomes satisfied and allows Nature to repose; by which is meant, that for such a man finite existence is no longer necessary, and he is therefore permitted to shrink to the small dimensions of his "subtile body," and, departing through "the hundred and first tube," proceeding from the heart, he acquires emancipation or absorption.||

This school represents the first division of the Sankhya system; the second division is that of Kapila's pupil, Patanjali, who teaches Yoga¶ (concentration) as a *means* whereby to "cast off ignorance." The pupil is desired to

* Colebrooke, vol. i. p. 246.

† Katha Upanishad.

‡ Griffith's Indian Poetry, p. 27.

§ Wilson's 'Sankhya Karika.'

|| Katha Upanishad.

¶ From *yuj*, to keep the mind fixed in abstract meditation.

fix his attention upon that description of soul which is called *Iswara;* this word, translated *Lord,* means a person possessing power, and is a term used to any one in office; but, like our own word Lord, it also designates Divinity, and in sacred writings we shall find it usually preceded by the sacred syllable *Om.* Patanjali's Yoga school was therefore looked upon as theistic, whilst Kapila's was considered atheistic: but it is not theistic in a very satisfactory sense, for Iswara, the Lord, instead of being the *end* of devotion, is a means assisting the devotee to accomplish that intense meditation which is "without a seed" (securing the body from reproduction): then, the soul is "alone, pure, emancipated."* Yoga seems to have suited Hindus better than active virtue, for we find it adopted by all sects from the time of the Upanishads down to the present day, when Yogis are seen standing or sitting in fixed positions, wrapt in abstraction.

The second system of philosophy is the Nyaya. The first division treats upon Physics, the second upon Metaphysics: the first is called *Vaiseshika,* Particular; the second *Nyaya,* Reasoning.† The physical division claims Kánáda as its author, and teaches the doctrine of Atoms; but the theory is greatly superior to that of Democritus, because the atoms are conceived as units of matter without extent, and merely occupy a subordinate place in the research.‡ It is curious to find *ether* mentioned in this treatise as a substance which, equally with time, place, and soul, is pervading and infinite; even in the Upanishads,

* Ballantyne, p. 28; Aphorisms of the Yoga, p. 60.

† Colebrooke, vol. i. p. 261.

‡ Bibliotheca Indica, Dr. Roer, August, 1850.

which are earlier than the Schools, *ether*, together with air, fire, water, earth, is represented as an element. Elements are substance, and the schools differ in their opinion upon substance, but all agree in distinguishing substance from its qualities, and, like Bishop Berkeley, they make the reality of substance to depend upon its qualities as perceived by mind.

In the Nyaya system a man must possess *dharma*, and also knowledge of substances, qualities, etc. But although professing to embrace the universe, this system neglects in fact all that forms the subject-matter of the physical sciences, and Hindu philosophers look down in consequence with self-complacent superiority upon those who devote themselves to physical or practical science.* But whilst weak in physics, the Nyaya is strong in dialectics, leading Dr. Roer to remark, that "the philosophical researches of the Hindus are as worthy of attention as those of the Greeks." He allows that they are less easy to be understood by foreigners, owing to their neglect of analysis; but this fault, he says, they share with many other teachers of philosophy, including even Spinoza. "The Hindus are dogmatical: they commence synthetically with a statement of their principles, but do not condescend to unfold the train of thought which has led to them." Consequently "the same doctrines which might have been instrumental in enlightening thousands are now forgotten, or in the possession of a few who are hardly able to comprehend them."† But whatever the deficiencies of the Nyaya, it must have

* Synopsis of Science, Benares, 1852, advertisement ix.

† Introduction to Nyaya Philosophy, Bibliotheca Indica, Calcutta, August, 1850.

great intrinsic merit; for, in constructing a Synopsis for the Benares College, Dr. Ballantyne has made it his "standpoint." He was reflecting upon Hindu notions regarding induction, when he received a letter from Professor Wilson, suggesting that a translation of the section on inference in the Nyaya would be very acceptable to the logicians of Europe. Dr. Ballantyne examined the work in consequence, and was surprised at the resemblance which he found "between the turn of thought and expression in the writer, and in Mr. John Stuart Mill's work on Logic," which was a work Dr. Ballantyne was already using with good prospect of advantage in his college classes.*

The third system is the Vedanta: its first division, the "Purva Mimansa," is attributed to Jaimini, it is strong in praise of *dharma* (virtue); but the system is better known by the second division, the "Uttara Mimansa," taught by Badayarana (commonly called Vyasa).† This system was promulgated for the purpose of correcting the materialism of its precursors. The Sankhya says, that Nature, distinct from Soul, produced the universe: the Vedanta denies this, and declares Brahme (primordial soul) to be the only axis, centre, root, or origin of the phenomena. The Sankhya recognizes two powers,—inactive Soul and active Nature: the Vedanta calls this dualism; and asserts, that nature or matter, and all consequent phenomena, are necessary attributes of Brahme. The Veda, as *Sruti*, that which has been heard, is appealed to in confirmation of this assertion; by Veda being here meant some of the Upanishads. When the Veda says That, or the Self-existent, it

* Ballantyne, Synopsis, advt. xxvi.

† Lecture on the Vedanta, Benares, 1851.

means Brahme, and not Nature. When the Veda says that embodied souls acquire absorption, it means absorption into Brahme, not into Nature; otherwise there would be this absurd contradiction, that the intelligent would become absorbed into the unintelligent. And again, when the Veda speaks of "The One that consists of joy," it means Brahme; in support of which Panini is quoted.* "That which is within the Sun and the eye," "breath of life," and "light," also mean Brahme; and this is made evident by the holy verse called Gayatri.† So much is taught in what are called the "Vedanta Sutras," or "Brahma Sutras;" *sutra* being a word for thread, often used as synonymous with Aphorism. On one occasion the editor of a book of Aphorisms says, "Like that funambulist, the spider, which runs on a *thread*," so he relies upon the *sutras* (threads), and not upon commentaries.‡

For a further development of Vedanta doctrine we turn to a Tract called the Vedanta Sara, essence of the Vedanta. It starts from the point that Brahme is the Eternal Universal Soul, and proceeds to show man's relation towards Brahme. Human souls are a portion of the Universal Soul, "deposited in a succession of sheaths, enveloping one another like the coats of an onion;" and the aim of life must be to free the soul from these encumberments. This is to be done by knowledge, or by learning that Buddhi (intellect) and all human faculties are ignorance and delusion: Bud-

* Amongst Dr. Ballantyne's valuable works at Benares, Professor Wilson refers to his "publication of this great source of all Sanskrit grammar," the Maha Bhashya, or great Commentary on the Aphorisms of Panini.—Lecture on Oriental Literature, Jan. 1852, J. R. A. S., vol. xiii., part 2.

† Translations of this Address to Light are given in Chapter I., *ante*.

‡ The Aphorisms of the Vaiseshika, Benares, 1851.

dhi (intellect) takes the chief part in this, divesting itself of its enveloping sheaths, and then discriminating that "all is God only."* All that is not Brahme it perceives to be ignorance, and ignorance is nothing; therefore the act of the understanding, which rightly recognizes the "Indivisible" (Brahme), is itself a nonentity, and disappears in the act of recognition. The consequence is that man has no individuality; for so long as he perceives his own existence he is in "ignorance." The removal of ignorance is like the removal of a mirror in which a countenance was reflected; remove the mirror and nothing remains but the countenance, or Brahme. And thus, Dr. Ballantyne observes, when a man, with all his wits, is wide awake, he is furthest removed from the state in which he ought to be; but when he falls asleep and dreams, he shuffles off the outermost coil of his ignorance.† In proportion as he succeeds in casting this off, he becomes convinced that nothing exists besides the "Indivisible" (Brahme); and that inasmuch as he exists, he himself is the "Indivisible." Finally, he must "get rid of the habit of making even himself a habit of thought; there must be *no* object: the subject alone must remain,—a thought, a joy, an existence,—and the only one." The Tract concludes by directing the worshipper towards means for the attainment of this end. Amongst these is the meditation called *Samádhi;* the contemplation called *Dhyana;* the postures spoken of as *padma* and *svastika,* and suppressions of the breath.

We have now reviewed the three great systems,—1. The Sankhya, which recognizes soul as Purusha, but derives the universe from Nature; 2. The Nyaya, which holds similar

* Vedanta Sara, Benares.

† *Ibid.*, p. 82.

doctrine, but is chiefly noted for its logic; and lastly, the Vedanta, which denies duality, allows no independent power to Nature, and declares Brahme, the supreme Soul, to be the only true existence. The Sankhya was undoubtedly the earliest of these systems, but it is impossible to fix on a precise date for either of them. Hindu philosophers disregarded dates on principle: their idea of philosophy is observed by Dr. Roer to be something "raised above change,"* unconnected therefore with the state of society or the particular time in which it was first promulgated; and consequently we find the teachings of successive centuries hopelessly intertwined. Philosophers made their discourses orally, and if eminent, their statements were written down in Sutras, or aphorisms. These were too concise to be intelligible without explanation, and in consequence we gather our ideas of Upanishads, written it may be B.C. 800, and Sutras, written B.C. 600, from commentators of subsequent centuries. A rude outline is therefore all that can be attempted in the chronology of Hindu philosophy. In the hymns of the Rig-Veda, men are supposed to become superhuman by dint of penance and rites; and the existence of Universal Soul is alluded to. The Upanishads develope the doctrine of soul, and teach that knowledge of soul emancipates from transmigration. In the Sankhya system nature is interposed between man and soul; the Nyaya follows the Sankhya, and then, after an interval, the Vedanta system endeavours to bring back belief in soul as Brahme, to correct the tendency to materialism given by the Sankhya system. The Code of Manu seems conversant both with the Upanishads and the Aphorisms; for it frequently recom-

* Bibliotheca Indica, August, 1850.

mends suppressions of the breath, makes use of the sacred triliteral syllable *Om* (explained in the Yoga Aphorisms as *Iswara*, the Lord), and objects, like the Vedanta, to duality. To exchange the perishable for the eternal is equally the aim of all philosophers; but whilst the Sankhyas believe phenomena to be a product of nature, Vedantists look upon "the phenomenal world as the garb or vesture of God." The garb is however inseparable, and the Brahme which it invests is inactive; and this school also was in consequence wholly without belief in God as a creative, governing, almighty Will. In each system the most ambitious reasoner is obviously the worst theologian. In the first and second, belief in Brahme is extinguished by the argument that reality depends upon "perceiving intellect;" and in the third, Brahme being assumed to be the only real existence, it is argued that man's intellect is but a portion of Brahme, and that man is in a delusion so long as he perceives within himself a separate identity.

BOOK II.

INDIA AFTER THE PERIOD OF ALEXANDER.

Buddhism.

"Pour quelques personnes toutes les questions relatives au Buddhisme étaient déjà décidées quand on n'avait pas encore lu une seule ligne. . . . Pour les uns le Buddhisme était un vénérable culte, né dans l'Asie centrale, et dont l'origine se perdait dans la nuit des temps; pour les autres c'était une misérable contrefaçon du Nestorianisme; on avait fait de Buddha un Nègre, parce qu'il avait les cheveux crépus; un Mongol, parce qu'il avait les yeux obliques; un Scythe, parce qu'il se nommait Sakhya. On en avait même fait un planète, et je ne sais pas si quelques savants ne se plaisent pas encore aujourd'hui à retrouver ce sage paisible sous les traits du belliqueux Odin. Certes il est permis d'hésiter, quand à ces solutions si vastes on ne promet de substituer que des doutes ou que des explications simples et presque vulgaires."—BURNOUF, *L'Histoire du Buddhisme Indien*.

CHAPTER I.

"How beautiful was Greece!—how marvellous
In polity, and chasten'd grace severe!"—ALFORD.

HERE let us pause. The scroll of ancient India's history lies unrolled before us, partly deciphered. It bears no dates and chronicles, no dynasties; but it records generous thought and feeling, poetry, philosophy, religious aspiration, and such progress in judicature, arts, manufactures, and even sciences, that we feel almost justified in our juvenile enthusiasm for the affluent East.

The Vedic period, commencing about B.C. 1400, forms as it were an antique rustic porch leading to the fine old temple of Brahmanical grandeur. In the porch we find kings and priests standing side by side. One hymn is written by a king and another by a Brahman; and one son of a king succeeds to the throne, whilst another becomes a Brahman. But when we pass into the period of Brahmanical grandeur, we perceive Brahmans standing aloof, whilst kings, soldiers, and the multitude pay them homage. By degrees the priesthood became hereditary, and only one or two instances are there recorded in which kings, by force of penance, succeeded in obtaining Brahmanical rank. The less learned and less wealthy of the Brahman Caste perform the public offices of religion, whilst those of higher rank and superior attainments spend their lives in learned ease and literature, or else in teaching pupils, or in assisting the counsels of royalty and administering justice.

Brahmans, as a class or caste, were entitled to a provision from the public funds for their life, and to facilities for obtaining happy transmigration, or still happier emancipation in the life to come; other Castes had no power of attaining these blessings without the aid of Brahmans, and it was against the law for Brahmans to give their aid to any but those whose birth entitled them to investiture with the sacrificial thread. It was long before any disadvantage was discovered in this exclusive system. At first it seemed natural, and merely involved that those who were best qualified should guide the rest; and however great and dangerous the faults and errors, we nevertheless find the era in which Brahmans first attained supremacy to have been a period of singular richness and prosperity. The general literature probably commenced about B.C. 700; the Brahmanas, with the Upanishads and philosophic Sutras, being followed by the Laws of Manu, and these succeeded by the heroic poems. This is a literature which Ward, the missionary, exceedingly condemns, which Sir William Jones enthusiastically commends, and of which Mr. Elphinstone says, referring to the poems, "their beauties have been most felt by those whose own productions entitle their judgment to most respect."* Judging of it through translations we find faults indeed of every description, but redeemed by a light, which glows at times as if it were a reflection from primeval revelation, and which, lingering like a summer sunset, is seen athwart the rising clouds of selfish superstition and dead formalism.

The ancient Hindus excelled in all that could be attained by contemplation; and thus in grammar, logic, astronomy, and medicine, they appear to have been in advance of contemporary nations. But their language, now so celebrated, did not attain its perfection until the age of Pericles and Demosthenes had already passed. And their wonderful rock-cut temples, Dagobas, and columns belong to a later period than that which we have been studying; the Parthenon and Temple of Theseus having been for centuries enthroned upon the rocks of Athens, before the caves of Ellora and Elephanta were excavated from the rocks of Western India.

During this first Brahmanical period of Hindu history, we can detect no foreign influence; and we find but slight or doubtful recognition of India in foreign chronicles. We believe indeed that Solomon's apes and peacocks, ivory and almug-wood, came from India; and we know by the hymns of the Rig-Veda that merchants at that early period had ships "crowding the ocean;" but we do not know whether they went beyond the Malabar coast; we do not know whether Hindus ever visited the Holy Land, or whether those cunning workmen who carved in wood and overlaid pillars with gold for King Solomon, ever found their way to India. We must not indeed forget that Hindus were them-

* History of India, p. 155.

selves a foreign element in India, coming from the central nursery of Aryans, and bringing with them the Sanskrit language, and many religious ideas and customs, some of which they had held in common with the more or less civilized ancestors of the Persians, and their nomadic neighbours the Scythians. Professor Lassen calls them "Sanskrit people," after their language, whilst Benfey designates them *Aryans*, after their race; but the simpler term Hindu will serve our purpose, and will signify the people who at first drove chariots and loved horses, and worshipped Indra down the course of the Indus; who afterwards studied philosophy and improvised poetry within sight of the Himalaya; who founded cities under Brahmanical guidance through out the length and breadth of the Gangetic plains, and who lived almost wholly undisturbed and uninfluenced by foreign nations until the arrival of the Greeks. Not that a positive opinion can be pronounced upon the question; but as the commercial intercourse is supposed to have been indirect, and as the expeditions of Bacchus and Semiramis to India are reputed fabulous, and as Cyrus never went beyond the Punjab, and soon lost again what he conquered there, it is not until the time of Darius that we meet with any well authenticated foreign invasion. Darius Hystaspes produced but very slight effect on India, but his campaigns deserve attention; for he aimed at something more than conquest, and endeavoured, by studying the customs of new territories, to attach them to his government. He conquered eastern Kabul, the Punjab, and part of Sindh. It is mentioned that a great variety of Indians came to his court, and that with the fair-complexioned he could converse, but that with the dark-coloured he required an interpreter.* Darius distributed the Persian empire into twenty satrapies, one of which was India. The nineteen other satrapies paid tribute "in silver according to the Babylonian or larger talent," the sum from the whole nineteen amounting to about £2,964,000 sterling; "from the Indians, who alone paid in gold, there was received a sum equal to about £1,290,000 sterling," a sum equal to two-fifths of that received from the other nineteen. This statement is supposed to prove that northern India was at that time very rich in gold.† Darius did not himself go beyond the Punjab, but by his direction the navigation of the Indus was explored; and under his orders, Skylax, a Greek from the south coast of Asia Minor, sailed down its stream into the Indian Ocean round the peninsula of Arabia and up the Red Sea to Egypt.‡ This happened about B.C. 500, and almost immediately afterwards commenced that series of events which ended by bringing the Greeks to India.

The Ionians were a Greek colony settled in Asia, and had long paid tribute to Persia, but they still felt drawn towards their mother country; and when a quarrel arose between them and their Persian superiors, it was Greece they sued for succour. Athens at once sent twenty ships; whereupon the Ionians grew confident, and in the year B.C. 499 dared to take possession of the city of Sardis. This was in itself an act meriting punishment from the great King Darius; but the case was soon rendered more desperate by the folly

* Lassen, Indische Alterthumskunde, vol. ii. pp. 112, 114. Indians are again mentioned in the army with which Xerxes invaded Greece.

† See Grote's History of Greece, vol. iv. p. 315.

‡ Grote's History of Greece, vol. iv. p. 300.

of an Ionian soldier, who set fire to a house, and the city, being built of wood, was in consequence reduced to ashes. When Darius learned that not only Sardis was burned, but that the Athenians were assisting the revolt, he determined upon immediate vengeance against the Greeks. He collected his troops, and made preparations in his usual magnificent style; but Aristides, Themistocles, and Miltiades were then the strength of Athens; and although Darius readily reduced the islands in the Ægean Sea, his generals no sooner fought on Attic ground than the Persian warriors were defeated in the celebrated battle of Marathon, B.C. 490. Five years later Darius died, but Persia continued her attacks on Greece until B.C. 334, when, during the reign of Darius Codomannus, Alexander the Great took the initiative, and carried his troops into the heart of Asia. This great undertaking was not merely warlike, but stands on record as the first scientific expedition ever made.* Alexander was accompanied by naturalists, surveyors, historians, philosophers, artists, and poets, and was urged forward not merely by selfish ambition or an irresistible thirst for conquest, but by a desire to bring distant nations into friendly relations; and he imagined Greek influence capable of drawing the whole of Asia within a magic ring. He gave therefore Greek municipal institutions to his Macedonian colonies, and established so vigorous a system of international policy between Greece and Asia that it was only effaced by the religion and conquests of Mohammed and the Arabs.†

Enough of foreign influence is perceptible in India, after this epoch, to make it desirable that we should attend

* Lassen, vol. ii. p. 116.

† Finlay, Greece under the Romans.

closely to the movements of Alexander and his followers previous to their entering India; for even if no arts or legends can positively be ascribed to Greece, Syria, Babylonia, or Scythia, we shall be able to conjecture with more satisfaction on the Ninevite character of Buddhist architecture and a few other Buddhist mysteries, if we have touched previously upon the principal points of the great Alexander's campaigns. The Hellespont was crossed in March, B.C. 334, two years spent in successful battles and marches throughout Asia Minor, Damascus taken, several towns of Phœnicia subdued, and the celebrated siege of Tyre commenced, on the pretext of requiring to worship the Sun-god Melkart, identified with Hercules. After seven months' severe struggle, Tyre was taken and the sacrifice performed. Alexander then, accepting the submission of the Jews, marched into Egypt, where he sacrificed to the local Gods, and founded the city of Alexandria; he then crossed the Libyan Desert, to consult the oracle of Jupiter Ammon, in imitation of his reputed ancestors, Perseus and Hercules; the oracle assured him that his career would be one of uninterrupted victory.* His next campaign in Asia was distinguished by the decisive battle of Arbela, after which both Babylon and Susa surrendered.† Babylon he entered in triumph, rested during thirty-four days, conversed with Chaldæans, and made sacrifice to Belus; he then went to Susa, where he received a large reinforcement of about fifteen thousand men—Macedonians, Greeks, and Thracians,

* Grote, vol. xii. p. 190; Arrian, p. 64.

† On this occasion the distinguished historian of Greece observes:—"As far as we can follow the dispositions of Alexander, they appear the most signal example recorded in antiquity of military genius and sagacious combination" (vol. xii. p. 228).

both cavalry and infantry, and "fifty Macedonian youths of noble family, soliciting admission into Alexander's corps of pages." He then went to Persepolis, where he bears the odium of setting fire to the magnificent palace of Xerxes. But we will hope that on this and on many other occasions Alexander might justly complain of his historians,—that the Greeks were jealous, that the Macedonians could not write, and that, in the words of Mr. Prinsep, "the only justice done to him is in the affix of the title 'Great,' which his name will carry with it to all times."*

In the year B.C. 330 a traitorous conspiracy was formed against Darius, who had escaped from the Macedonians, and he fell eventually by the hands of Bessus, one of his own officers. Far from hailing this event with joy, Alexander was enraged at its baseness, and abandoned all other schemes in order to pursue the traitor: this led him a second time to Bactria, "the battle-field of every tribe and nation that has risen to dominion in the East;" and in August or September of this year, he founded the still famous city of Herat.† He then passed through a country in which his troops "suffered exceedingly from want, snow, and cold;" this being the hill-route from Herat, where the British troops were so much distressed by cold in January, 1841. The winter was passed at "Alexandria apud Caucasum," supposed to be Beghram, thirty or forty miles to the north of Kabul.‡ In the spring, B.C. 329, Alexander recrossed the mountains and pursued the traitor Bessus

* Hist. Results, H. T. Prinsep, pp. 3, 4.

† The site of Alexandria is not precisely determined. See Hist. Results, p. 15; Wilson's Ariana, p. 180.

‡ *Ibid.*, or Hist. Results, p. 15.

beyond the river Oxus: he was now in a country of Scythians, of whom Spitamenes was king or chief, and here, at Nautika, Bessus was captured. Alexander was too wise a General to advance amongst these unknown and quick-moving tribes without precautions, and whilst he sent forward exploring parties he often remained himself with his main force, establishing colonies and well-garrisoned towns fitted to secure a safe retreat. The wild chief, Spitamenes, soon justified his prudence; for although he had refused to protect Bessus, neither would he submit to be conquered, and no sooner had Alexander gone through the country and gained a battle on the northern banks of the Jaxartes, than Spitamenes fell upon his rear and endeavoured to possess himself of Samarcand; but the Greek garrison was firm, and he only succeeded in cutting off some troops sent as a reinforcement.

It was at this period that the twenty Scythian ambassadors waited upon Alexander and made the speech which may be still admired, whether we attribute it to the Scythians or to their historian, Quintus Curtius. "You," say they, "who boast of coming to exterminate robbers, are yourself the greatest robber in the world, for you have plundered all the nations you have subdued. Are not even those who live in woods to be exempted from knowing you and from feeling your violence? If you are a god, you should do good to mankind; if you are a man, you ought to hearken to the dictates of reason and humanity." Some places are mentioned in these campaigns which cannot confidently be identified; but it seems probable that, at the close of the year, he recrossed the river Oxus, and spent the winter B.C. 329–328 in cantonments at Hazarasp, and that whilst there he received a mission from the banks of the Volga.* Early in the spring, he took the field in five divisions, and overran the whole country north and east of Kabul. Spitamenes was subdued and slain; but by another mountain tribe, also called Scythians, Alexander was received with respect and magnificence, and in consequence fell in love with the King's daughter, Roxana, and made her his wife. The Greek kingdom of Bactria comprehended both divisions of Scythians, and the chiefs of mountain tribes in that quarter still claim to be descended from Iskander, meaning Alexander, "a tradition," observes Professor Wilson, "which singularly preserves the memory of a time when these countries were subject to princes sprung from the countrymen of the Macedonian conqueror."† Alexander spent altogether three years in Bactria, and the Greek power being now firmly established, he turned his attention towards India, a country he had long desired to reach and to possess; but he would have deemed a march into the Punjab unsafe, if not impracticable, had not Bactria been first subdued, "so as to prevent Bessus and the Scythians from breaking in upon the line of communication with Media and Greece."‡

In the spring of B.C. 327 the Kabul valley was reduced, and heralds sent to call upon the kings of the neighbouring districts to submit. The most important result of this proceeding was, that Mophis of Taxila (thence called Taxiles)

* Prinsep, Hist. Results, p. 17.

† Wilson's Ariana, p. 169. The assertion is made by travellers of various periods, from Marco Polo down to Mr. Elphinstone and Sir A. Burnes.

‡ Prinsep, Hist. Results, p. 12.

became an important ally, and conducted Alexander's Generals, Hephæstion and Perdiccas, along the southern bank of the river Kophen, through Jellalabad, to Attok on the Indus. Alexander himself went through the Kaiber Pass, and crossed the Indus, in April, B.C. 327, on a bridge of boats, which he found prepared for him by Hephæstion and Taxiles. The most interesting event of this year was the encounter between Alexander and Porus, a king or chief upon the river Jhilum: he appears to have held but a small territory, but his bravery, shown equally in battle and defeat, has made Porus the favourite of all historians.* Alexander at once restored his lands, only claiming certain services and tribute, and these two kings, Taxiles and Porus, continued his allies till death.

Whilst Alexander was still in the Punjab, his followers were seized with an invincible home-sickness; "they complained that they found their King always attempting one toil after another, and plunging himself and them into new hazards after he had got clear of the old ones:"† and nothing appears to have made them more impatient than the long-continued heavy rain of the periodical rainy season. When news of the discontent reached head-quarters, Alexander called a council and made a speech, but all without avail, and, ardently as he desired to press forwards to the Ganges, he was sadly compelled to yield to the clamour for returning home. Although deeply mortified, he made his preparations with characteristic energy, and his shipwrights were at once instructed to construct a fleet.

* Droysen has given details of this battle with much picturesque effect. See Lassen, vol. ii. p. 117.

† Arrian's Hist. Alex. Ex., p. 146.

But first he ordered twelve altars to be erected, equal in height to so many fortified towns, and on these he offered sacrifices to the Gods, giving thanks for his past victories, and concluding the ceremonies with a celebration of gymnastic and equestrian games.*

Whilst the ships were building, Alexander made incursions into the neighbouring states, of which many little circumstances are related. Some states were republics, in which Brahmans were not honoured, and where the women's manners were "Bacchanalian:" one nation, called Kathæans, is noted for choosing their chief or king for his personal beauty, and for destroying all weakly children: these people are supposed to spring from Kshatriya women who had married Sudras. A king named Sopeithes, in the south of Sindh, presented Alexander with hunting dogs, for which the country is famous; and another brought a precious offering of three hundred pounds of wootz, or Indian steel. One single town of Brahmans is recorded, and they are said to have been most hostile to Alexander, as a king of barbarians and heretics.

At length all things were ready for the voyage, and much is said by Strabo and Arrian of the sacrifices to the Gods and libations to the rivers with which it was commenced. Arrian describes the great order which was observed; the ships moving on a signal given by sound of trumpet, the store-ships required to keep at a certain distance from the ships which carried horses, "and these from the ships of war, lest, if they proceeded without due order, they should be dashed one against another; nor were the best sailers suffered to go out of their ranks, nor the slowest to lag

* Arrian, p. 151. † Lassen, ii. 157.

behind: it was wonderful," continues Arrian, "to hear the clashing of the oars of such a mighty number of ships at the same instant, as also the shouts of the rowers, and the commands of their officers, which the banks, often higher than the ships themselves, and the thick woods on each side of the river, so increased by compression and repercussion" that the inhabitants (politely called by Arrian "barbarians") were struck with amazement, and their wonder was increased by seeing horses embarked on board a fleet. On the fifth day they arrived at the junction of the Hydaspes and Ascesines, where, the banks being close and the channel narrow, the current is extremely rapid, causing prodigious eddies, and a loud noise heard at a vast distance. When they escaped from these straits they took refuge in a sort of bay, where the ships were all gathered together to be refitted.*

When the voyage was resumed, the King of Patala sent to offer submission and allegiance, and at Patala the Macedonians made a long and peaceful halt; but exactly where the place is situated is a question which has occasioned many learned pages of discussion. Professor Wilson gives excellent reasons why Patala was not Tatta, but more probably to the north of Haiderabad, but thinks we need not look for a perfect identification, because "the channels of the lower part of the Indus are perpetually shifting, and it may be doubted if any one of them now follows precisely the same direction that it took when the vessels of Alexander floated down the stream." The name our Professor thinks undoubtedly Indian, and probably derived from *Potálaya* or *Potálá*, a harbour, and he observes that the

* Arrian, book vi. ch. 3, 4.

name Potala, harbour, is given in Buddhist writings to a city in the delta of the Indus, in which the Sakyas are said to have lived before their migration to Kapila-vastu,* in Rohilcund.

Whilst the fleet reposed at Patala, occasional expeditions were made into the surrounding country, which is generally described as peaceful and prosperous, occupied by an agricultural population, governed by kings and Brahmans. It was in one of these expeditions that Alexander first beheld the ocean; he and his Greek and Macedonian companions had seen no sea except the Mediterranean, in which there are no tides, and their surprise at beholding this phenomenon is amusingly described by Arrian. They sailed down the Indus from Patala in light ships, and "when they arrived at the place where it is full two hundred furlongs wide, namely at its mouth, the wind blowing hard from the sea and the waves rising so high as to hinder them from managing their oars, they again put into a certain bay, which their pilots showed them, for shelter. While they continued in that situation, an accident happened which astonished them, namely the ebbing and flowing of the waters, like as in the great ocean, insomuch that the ships were left upon dry ground, which Alexander and his friends having never perceived before were so much the more surprised at: but what increased their astonishment was that the tide, returning a short while after, began to heave the ships up, so that those which stuck in the mud were raised gently and set afloat again, without receiving any damage."†

* Wilson's Ariana, p. 211, and J. A. S. B., August, 1833; Origin of Sakya Race, Csoma Korösi.

† Arrian, book vi. ch. 18, 19.

Alexander explored the mouths of the Indus, founded one or more seaports, returned to Patala, and, leaving Nearchus to command the fleet, set forth upon his homeward route. His orders were, that Nearchus should sail in the north-west monsoon, *i.e.* in November or December; but no sooner had the great conqueror departed than the inhabitants rose against the foreign force, and Nearchus deemed it prudent to wait no longer than the 9th of September, B.C. 326, although the south-west wind was still prevailing. Arrian marks the line of country through which Alexander started by describing the plants peculiar to it. In the deserts of the Gedrosi, he tells us, are myrrh-trees taller than elsewhere; also trees growing where the tide flows among them thirty cubits in height, with leaves like the laurel and white flowers sweeter than violets; and another plant, which produces strong prickles and has a thick juice more acrid than the fig.*

Whilst Alexander was in Karmania, news reached him that one of the Satraps whom he had left in the Punjab had been murdered by his paid soldiery: his commands on the occasion were, that Eudemos and Taxiles should take the management of affairs until he should send another Satrap, thus showing that Taxiles, the Hindu chief, continued to enjoy his confidence. Porus is also mentioned from time to time as receiving accessions of territory from Alexander; probably also Porus may have occasionally taken the territories of refractory chieftains upon his own responsibility, for after the lapse of four or five years we find his dominions reaching to the mouth of the Indus.

* These three plants are identified by the late Dr. Stocks as growing within twenty or thirty miles of Kurrachee. See letter from Dr. Stocks to Dr. Royle, read to the Philosophical Club of the Royal Society in 1850.

Alexander died in the spring of B.C. 323, and then commenced ceaseless wars amongst his Satraps. Eumenes, of Cappadocia, defeated and slew Craterus B.C. 322; Antigonous took the field against Eumenes B.C. 320, and whilst war was fiercely carried on amongst the rival Greeks, India shared in the general agitation. For ten years the Greeks held dominion in the Punjab; but in B.C. 317 Eudemos caused Porus to be assassinated, and then marched into Bactria, carrying with him one hundred and twenty elephants which had belonged to the Hindu king. This ignoble murder of their greatest Raja exasperated the people of the Indus, and gave a favourable opening for the schemes of a Hindu adventurer, whom the Greeks call Sandracottus. This young man was connected with the reigning royal family at Patna, but there was no place upon the throne for him, and he wandered about ready to take advantage of any tumult. The Greeks mention his having once visited the Court of Alexander, and say, that after the murder of Porus he fought his way from one territory to another until he acquired not only the lands of Porus, but also the kingdom of Patna, and acquired so much importance and stability that, when Seleucus came to restore order, he risked but one engagement with Sandracottus, and then judged it desirable to make peace, accepting elephants, and giving in return, some say, his daughter in marriage.* After this Seleucus

* This seems to be an inference from an expression in Strabo, who says that Seleucus received from Sandracottus fifty elephants and "contractâ cum eo affinitate." See Preface to the Drama of Mudra Rakshasa, by Professor Wilson, where it is observed that Seleucus relinquished territories beyond the Indus, and is said to have formed a matrimonial alliance with Sandracottus: "we have no trace of this in Hindu writers, but it is not at all improbable."—Hindu Theatre, vol. ii. p. 134.

sent a Greek named Megasthenes to reside at Patna, as his representative or *chargé d'affaires,* and chiefly through the accounts of Megasthenes do we learn what the Greeks observed and thought of India at the date of 280 years before our era. Megasthenes wrote full descriptions, but unfortunately only fragments have been preserved, and these are chiefly met with in the works of Strabo. Arrian follows Megasthenes and Nearchus, calling them "two famous well-approved authors," and in addition to these we have the general descriptions of the observing Herodotus. These writers speak of Hindu costume as just what we see it in the present day, consisting of two garments, one of which reaches to the middle of the leg and the other covering part of the head and shoulders: these dresses were sometimes of bright colours and flowered patterns; their slippers were ornamented, and various ornaments of gold and jewels were worn, earrings being particularly mentioned. Dyeing the eyebrows with henna is a practice alluded to in the Code, but the Greeks tell of beards dyed with henna and indigo, "insomuch that some of them appear white, others black, some red, some purple, and others green." This is stated on the authority of Nearchus, and is accounted for by Mr. Elphinstone on the supposition that mistakes in the mixture, or time of application, had the same effect then as in modern days.* Great people had umbrellas carried over them when they walked, but are represented as also riding in chariots which were drawn by horses in war and by oxen during a march, and on state occasions they rode on richly caparisoned elephants. Arrian's† account of the catching and training of elephants is so graphic and true to the pre-

* History of India, p. 244.

† Arrian, ch. xvi.

sent mode, that it might have been written for the 'Asiatic Researches.' The account which Herodotus gives of ferocious ants would, on the other hand, have a somewhat strange effect in a modern publication; he declares them to be such dangerous creatures, that the bravest men, mounted on the fleetest camels, are sent to seize the gold which these ants dig up. Nearchus mentions the same story, saying that he had never seen one himself, but that many of the soldiers had seen the skins of these ants brought into camp. Ctesias adds, that the Kings of Persia had the ants themselves in their menageries; and Megasthenes accounts for the fact by suggesting that the ants do not dig the gold out of the earth "for the sake of the metal, but to prepare holes wherein to shelter themselves," and ants, in India, "being bigger than foxes" in Greece, "make burrows proportioned to their bulk." All these stories are referred by Professor Wilson to the word *pippilika*, "ant-gold," being the name in common use for lumps of gold collected in the plains of Little Thibet; the name was originally given from a notion that colonies of ants, by clearing away the sand or soil, left the ore exposed, and this was the origin of all the Greek marvels.* The plant which "instead of fruit produces wool, of which the Indians make their clothes," was also striking to the Greeks: Arrian says it is "flax, or rather indeed something much whiter and finer than flax."

The village form of government did not escape Greek notice, for Strabo speaks of places in which the land was cultivated in common by all the inhabitants of a village; and he gives accounts of the measurement of fields, of irrigation, of roads, and of trades as under the superintendence

* Notes on the Sabhá Parva, J. R. A. S. No. xiii. pp. 137, 143.

of village functionaries. The police was thought excellent, and the Greeks record with admiration that not more than £3 sterling was stolen daily in the camp of Sandracottus. The revenue appears to have been collected on the principle laid down in the Code of Manu, the King's share of produce amounting to about a fourth. Supervisors, or inquisitors, are mentioned by Arrian, "who inquire into all transactions as well in the cities as in the fields," and report to the King if they live under regal government, or to the chief magistrate if in a free city, and "may not be guilty of falsehood; but indeed none of the Indians were ever accused of that crime." Arrian makes particular mention of the division of Caste, and of its being unlawful for the upper ranks "to marry a wife out of his own class;" and none, he says, "are suffered to exercise two distinct trades, or to leave off one and take up another: that is, he may not leave off husbandry and turn shepherd, nor leave off keeping sheep and become an artificer. Only a Sophist is allowed to exercise what employment he pleases; but then their lives are not easy, but vastly laborious."* By Sophists they probably meant *Yogis* and other ascetic and philosophical Brahmans, for they are described as "the most honoured class, exempt from all burdens, and only contributing their prayers to the support of the State." Some asceitcs are described as adopting ostentatious mortifications; and Alexander being curious to see these persons, requested their attendance, but they refused to come, and he then sent Onesicritus, who found fifteen men uncovered and exposed to a burning sun, "some sitting, some standing, some lying, but all remaining immovable from morn-

* Arrian, Ind. Hist., ch. xi.

ing till evening." Two Sophists are also described by Aristobulus, one young and one old, both Brahmans: he met with them at Taxila. The elder was shaved, the younger wore his hair, and both were followed by disciples. "As they passed through the streets they were received with reverence, people pouring oil of sesamum upon them, and offering them cakes of sesamum and honey. Even when they came to Alexander's table to sup in his company, they gave a lesson of resolution, withdrawing to a neighbouring spot, where the elder lay down exposed to the sun and rain, and the younger stood still all day leaning on a staff." "Other accounts describe ascetics as going about the streets helping themselves to figs and grapes, and to oil for anointing themselves, etc."* These were doubtless devotees of the various Brahmanical schools, the members of which distinguished themselves by particular fashions of tonsure. They are not likely to have been Buddhists, because although Buddhism had commenced it was not publicly honoured; and moreover Buddhists never went unclothed, and did not approve of self-torture. There are more signs of Buddhism about the Indians mentioned by Herodotus, who "put no animal to death, sow no grain, have no fixed habitations, and live solely upon vegetables;" they lived chiefly on a grain the size of millet, "protected by a calyx, the whole of which they baked and ate," by which we understand young cobs of Indian-corn. When "these Indians are sick," he says, "they retire to some solitude and there remain, no one expressing the least concern about them during their illness or after their death."† But this

* Elphinstone, History of India, pp. 236–242.

† Beloe's Herodotus, vol. ii. p. 277.

description applies equally to Brahmanical ascetics of various schools.

The Greeks mention no temples, palaces, or other large buildings; but, according to Arrian, their towns were too numerous to be reckoned, and very probably as near together as those described by Colonel Edwardes in Sindh. Arrian remarks that towns near the sea or any river were built of wood,* because no buildings of brick would last long; not merely owing to the "violence of the rains, but also of the rivers, which, overflowing their banks, cause an annual inundation over all the flat country; but the cities which are seated on an eminence are frequently built of brick and mortar." He then goes on to speak of Palibothra, the chief city of India, "in the confines of the Prasii, near the confluence of the two great rivers the Erannoboas and the Ganges," which means Patna, near the confluence of the Sone and the Ganges. On the authority of Megasthenes, Palibothra is said to be eight miles long and one and a half broad, "surrounded by a ditch which takes up six acres of ground and is thirty cubits deep; the walls are adorned with five hundred and seventy towers and sixty-four gates." They reckon the length of India "along the road called the King's Road," and they also mention milestones. Numerous conjectures are made concerning the size of India; Ctesias affirming it to be "equal in bigness to all the rest of Asia," whilst Onesicritus thinks it only one-third as large; and Nearchus asserts that the flat country extends to four months' journey. But they

* This mode of building is still adopted on the Indus, where the houses are raised on platforms twelve or thirteen feet from the ground. The houses at Rangoon, on the Irawaddy, are similarly constructed.

were aware that they knew very little about it; and Arrian says, "even Megasthenes himself seems to me not to have travelled over much of India."* They all agree in calling Palibothra, or Patna, the chief city of the Indians; and Strabo describes the magnificent processions of its festivals in terms which remind us of Alexander's entrance into Babylon:—elephants adorned with gold and silver, chariots with four horses, carriages drawn by oxen, well-appointed troops, gilded vases, tables, thrones, goblets set with emeralds and other precious stones, garments of various colours embroidered in gold, tame lions and panthers, singing birds; also birds remarkable for their plumage, sitting on trees transported on large waggons.†

* Arrian, ch. ii., iii., v.

† Elphinstone, History of India, p. 243.

CHAPTER II.

"What eye can trace thy mystic lore,
Lock'd up in characters as dark as night?"—ROGERS.

THE Macedonian invasion adds another scene to our diorama, for we now perceive the armies of Alexander traversing the whole of Asia, gathering followers in Syria, Chaldæa, Scythia, and Bactria, and pouring the heterogeneous multitude into India. From this time forward the historians of the western world may be appealed to for aid in disentangling the perplexed narratives of the East; but there was a hindrance. Hindu Kings had no dates, and the Greek version of their names was not recognizable; consequently it was impracticable to adjust the era of Alexander with that of any Indian potentate. Porus, Taxiles, and Sandracottus had no place in Sanskrit literature, although Strabo and others, who follow Megasthenes, represent the last as the most successful and powerful Raja of the period succeeding Alexander's death.

He was, they say, a military adventurer, who succeeded in fighting his way to the chief throne in India, and held his court at Palibothra, on the Ganges. But Sanskrit names translated into Greek baffled all conjecture, until about the year A.D. 1780, when it happily occurred to Sir William Jones that the Sandracottus of the Greeks might be the Chandragupta of the Hindus; and then it was observed that the Greeks often wrote the name Xandra Coptus, and that the Hindus in a similar manner wrote Chandra Gupta, —Chandra being the moon, and Gupta, protected by the family-name of several dynasties which flourished at various eras.

It was a happy day for Indian history when this discovery was made, for one date being fixed there was hope of adjusting the rest; but very much had to be done, for Sanskrit literature had opened upon scholars as a sea without landmarks. The Gods and the Kings floated free upon the waters, unfixed by dates, Vishnu and Siva side by side with Indra and Agni, Buddhism taking precedence of Brahmanism, and Buddha figuring as a Negro, B.C. 2000. But now the drifting history began to find safe anchorage, and gradually Indra and Agni, Brahme and Brahma were ranged in chronological order; whilst Vishnu and Siva were forced to give up their claims to remote antiquity. The Greek invasion and the reign of Chandragupta were as strongholds, either before or after which all names and facts were to take their places; and it was on coins, and in inscriptions, or columns, rocks, temples, and statues, that names and facts were to be sought for.

In A.D. 1787 Sir William Jones founded the Asiatic Society, in Calcutta, and particularly invited attention to inscriptions. The Society commenced its publications in quarto volumes, much occupied with questions of priority,—not only the priority of the Gods in the Vedas and Gods in the Puranas, but the priority of Pagodas in the east or of excavations in the west of the Peninsula, and many other questions now long settled. Some errors were proved, and much interesting detached information was recorded; but progress generally was slow, until the year 1828, when the late Mr. James Prinsep plunged into the subject with all the ardour of youth and genius. Professor Wilson was happily at that time still in India, and lent the essential aid of his cautious judgment and profound knowledge of Eastern languages. Thus supported, Mr. Prinsep and his enthusiastic young friends studied and collected coins until they established the fact that coins subsequent to Alexander bore inscriptions which were Hindu, but not Sanskrit. The Oriental scholars, not only of India, but of Paris and Germany, applied themselves in earnest to decipher these legends. In 1834 Dr. Mill succeeded in reading some obsolete characters on a pillar at Allahabad, and this prepared the way for the decipherment of the still older character of the coins.

To collect coins and study inscriptions became the rage; and as it was obvious that history could not be reached in any other way, it was a most justifiable occupation. In all these researches James Prinsep was the leader: he commenced with very little knowledge of Oriental languages, but his generous ardour brought him every required assistance. His was a spirit free from jealousy and vanity: he worked openly himself, and invited and welcomed every contribution from others with a genuine, hearty love for truth and progress.

A Lat, or pillar, at Delhi, was observed to bear a very long inscription in the most ancient character of the coins, that is, in the *oldest Nagari.* Presently a second inscription on the column at Allahabad was found to be precisely similar; and in October, 1834, Mr. Hodgson sent notice of three more such pillars east of the Ganges,—at Bakra, Mathiah, and Radhiah,—all inscribed in the same unreadable character. Facsimiles were attempted of some of these inscriptions, and copies sent to Europe. Professor Lassen at Bonn, and Jacquet at Paris, entered heartily into communication with James Prinsep at Calcutta, aiding him by their sympathy and their suggestions, sometimes anticipating a step in the process, and sometimes arriving simultaneously at a similar result; but it was only in India, imbued with the spirit of the people and the country, that the discovery could be completed. Those who were in Calcutta between the years 1835 and 1839, will never forget the enthusiasm prevailing in the monthly meetings of the Asiatic Society, of which James Prinsep was the secretary, or in the pages of its Journal, of which he was the editor. No fatigue or trouble was spared in procuring correct facsimiles of inscriptions, or in discovering ancient monuments and sending drawings to "Prinsep for his Journal."

In the Journals for 1835 and 1836 various notices are given of Mr. Prinsep's success in deciphering; and at length, in the Journal for June, 1837, he gives a full account in Malwa of his discovery. Captain E. Smith had sent him facsimiles of short detached sentences, cut irregularly on the pillars or rail surrounding a mound (a Tope or Dagoba) at Sanchi, in Malwa, so correct that "every word can be read, except where the stone is actually cut away."

Some of these were "apparently trivial fragments of rude handwriting," but it was precisely those short detached sentences which proved most useful; each sentence terminated with the same two letters. Now Mr. Prinsep knew that in the Buddhist temples of Ava it was the custom to place flag-staffs, and images, etc., bearing the donors' names, in the space which surrounds the chief monument, or Dagoba; this gave him the idea that these short inscriptions must be records of gifts. He modestly says therefore that "accident rather than study had the merit of solving the enigma which so long baffled the learned;" but it was an accident which could not have happened to one less well prepared, and which would have been useless unless zealously followed up. In the course of a few minutes he found himself possessed of the whole alphabet, including the letters previously gained from coins, and he now read,—

"The gift of the mother of Dharmagirika."
"The gift of Sobhagaya, the fireman or blacksmith."
"The gift of Kada, the poor man."
"The gift of Sethin's deceased daughter."

Many similar records were read, but these have been selected as most opposed to Brahmanical custom and most characteristic of Buddhism.

It would be pleasant to give further extracts from the Journals of 1836-37, but sufficient has been produced to show the character of the discoveries then made, and the great zeal with which they were pursued. It would be quite out of character with the spirit of James Prinsep anxiously to weigh the exact proportion of his work, and that of others, in these decipherments. Such anxiety would be desecration to the memory of one who simply did *all* he could, and welcomed and encouraged from others *all* they could contribute. There was no measure in his love for truth or his love for man, and in consequence his influence was genial, like the warm west wind, at whose coming the buds and flowers hastened to expand. We shall now therefore attend more to the results than to the process of the discoveries made in strange new alphabets.

All the short inscriptions recording gifts, and especially gifts from poor people or women, showed strong evidence of Buddhism as now existing in Ava and Ceylon, and their being Buddhist was confirmed when the longer inscription over the principal gateway at Sanchi was deciphered; it begins thus:—

"To the all-respected Sramanas, . . . who by deep meditation have subdued their passions."

A second inscription on the side of the gate records the name of a lady, who leaves money to devotees who shall offer up prayers for her deceased father and mother, and also money to the poor; and further,—

"In the *ratna griha*" (jewel-house, treasury,) "also are deposited three dinars. With the interest of these three dinars, . . . day by day three lamps are to be lighted . . . at the shrines of the four Buddhas."

This and another inscription on the side of the eastern gate were evidently cut after the gateways were finished; and it was therefore no disappointment to find them comparatively modern, probably about A.D. 400. But the Agathocles coin proved that these newly deciphered characters were used in the third century *before* our era; and Mr. Prinsep was most impatient to apply "the master-key" with which they furnished him, for the unlocking of the long inscription on the columns, which was already suspected of teaching the tenets of some reformer in religion. He was now acquainted with five such columns, each bearing an inscription consisting of many parts or paragraphs, and, with slight exceptions, all alike. At Delhi, in addition to those on the sides, there is one which goes round the pillar, and at Allahabad there are five lines more than are to be found elsewhere; the language is nearly the same as that of the short fragments on the rails at Sanchi, and this proved to be not Sanskrit, but a variety or derivation resembling the Pali of the Buddhist books in Ceylon. It also much resembled parts of Sanskrit dramas, where it is spoken by women or the lower classes; whilst well educated Kings, Princes, and Brahmans speak Sanskrit. From this it was conjectured that, at a time when Sanskrit was the language of the learned in Hindustan, Pali was the dialect in common use; and Mr. Prinsep inferred that the inscription was the work of Buddhists, who, "like all sects who have appealed to the common sense of the people against the learning and priestcraft of the schools, made use of the vernacular." But whilst the pillar inscriptions were still under investigation, similar engravings were found upon rocks. These were first observed upon a rock at Girnar, in Guzerat; and whilst Mr. Prinsep was endeavouring to make out a facsimile sent to him in 1837, Lieutenant Kittoe discovered a long series in a similar character on the other side of India, at Dhauli, in Cuttack. "I had just groped my way through the Girnar text and proved it," Mr. Prinsep says, "to be like that of the pillars, a series of edicts, . . . when I took up the Cuttack inscriptions, . . . and to my surprise and joy discovered that the greater part . . . was identical with the inscription at Girnar. And thus, as I had five copies of the pillar inscription to collate, chance had now thrown in my way two copies of the rock edicts."

A third rock inscription has since been found, also similar in sense, but differing in alphabet. The two first, those from Guzerat and Cuttack, were deciphered by Mr. Prinsep; but the third was not found until illness had deprived him of the power of further efforts: it is in a very peculiar character, of a Hebrew or Phœnician cast. It is called Arianian, and was first deciphered by Mr. Norris, in 1848, when he felt almost disappointed at its containing nothing more than a third edition of the proclamations of Girnar and Dhauli.

Eight copies of nearly similar proclamations have thus been deciphered, five upon columns and three upon rocks, all alike in language, with a dialect varying a little according to the province. The Punjab inscription, at Kapur di Giri, which is written in a character particularly unlike Sanskrit, has more of the Sanskrit idiom and inflections than any of the others. This may be accounted for on the principle that the English of the Highlanders in Scotland is much freer from local idioms than that of the lowland Scotch; the lowland Scotch, like the people of Cuttack and Guzerat, having a vernacular of their own; whilst the Scotch highlanders and the Punjab highlanders spoke a totally different language, whether Gaelic, Phœnician, or Babylonian, and in either case the Government proclamations would be made in the court-dialect used at the seat of Government. The purport of this proclamation proved to be mainly an exhortation from the King paramount to his people, requiring them to live according to the rules of

Dharma. We have already made acquaintance with *Dharma* as a legitimate end of existence in the philosophical writings of the Sankhyas; but there are two reasons why these Pali proclamations could not be the work of Brahmans: first, because Brahmans refused to instruct any but men invested with the sacred thread, and therefore learned in Sanskrit; and second, because a Brahmanical King would have left instruction to Brahmans, and was not likely to teach *Dharma* in his own name without even referring to Rishis (saints), or *Sruti* (what has been heard), or *Smriti* (what has been remembered). We will however first inspect the series of Edicts, and reserve further discussion until their contents have fairly occupied our minds.

CHAPTER III.

"Day broke; the morning of a mighty year
Came forth and smiled."—BARRY CORNWALL.

JAMES PRINSEP'S first joyful renderings of the inscriptions on the rocks have been revised by Wilson fully, and partially by Lassen, and more lately, Prinsep, Wilson, and Lassen's translations were revised by Burnouf. These learned men had the advantage not only of mutual assistance and of new transcripts, but also of a new original, for the inscription at Kapur di Giri was not deciphered during the lifetime of James Prinsep. Professor Wilson offered his new readings as "subject to correction in every page," and as given not in opposition, but in continuation of the work already effected. Indeed the testimony of so great a scholar to the merits of his young coadjutor is too interesting to be omitted. "With regard," he says, "to the translations which we owe to the learning and ingenuity of the late James Prinsep, we must remember that they were the first attempts to convey a knowledge of the purport of documents in a new character and unknown language; . . . copies had been published for many years, but had baffled the most eminent scholars, and remained undeciphered until James Prinsep discovered their real nature and rendered them readable; . . . whatever may be objected to particular passages . . . will not invalidate his claims to our acknowledgment and admiration for what he has accomplished with unequalled labour, incomparable ingenuity, and unrivalled success."* Not less graceful is M. Burnouf's manner of introducing his corrections. "Si je viens à mon tour, après de si savans hommes, proposer mon interprétation, c'est que comme personne ne peut se flatter d'arriver du premier coup à l'intelligence définitive de ces monumens difficiles, il n'y a personne non plus qui ne puisse se flatter d'aider à leur interprétation."

We shall first consider the fourteen Edicts on the rocks, of which Professor Wilson has collated four copies. These Edicts were issued in the twelfth and fourteenth years of the reign of a King who calls himself Piyadasi, the beloved of the Gods; and there are many reasons for believing that the person so designated is the great Buddhist King Asoka, who reigned from B.C. 260 to 220.

TABLET I.

This is the Edict of the beloved of the Gods, the Raja Piyadasi. The putting to death of animals is to be entirely discontinued, and no convivial meeting is to be held, for the beloved of the Gods, Raja Piyadasi, remarks many faults in such assemblies. There is but one assembly indeed which is approved of by the Raja, . . . which is that of the great kitchen of Raja Piyadasi; every day hundreds of thousands of animals have been slaughtered for virtuous purposes, but now although this pious Edict is proclaimed that animals may be killed for good purposes, and such is the practice; yet as the practice is not determined, these presents are proclaimed, that hereafter they shall not be killed.†

* Rock Inscriptions, Feb. 1849, J. R. A. S., xii. p. 251.

† Wilson, J. R. A. S., xii.

The literal expression is that hundreds of thousands of animals were killed daily to *make soup in the King's kitchen*, but that this was done before the King had become religious. According to the Brahmanical Code of Manu, pious people must avoid flesh-meat, and "feel tender affection for all animated bodies," occasioning "not even the smallest dread to sentient creatures."* And with the same feeling the Sankhya philosophers objected to the Vedic mode of "putting an end to pain" (obtaining absorption after death), because it involved sacrifice or was "attended by the slaughter of animals." The Brahmans had therefore already taught the virtue of respecting animal life, but a Brahmanical King would not have practised this virtue whilst he remained king; instead of proclaiming it as a rule of life for universal acceptation, he would have abdicated his throne, and have performed his fasts and asceticisms in seclusion.

TABLET II.

In all the conquered territories of the Raja Piyadasi, even unto the ends of the earth, as in Chola, in Pida (the kingdom of Satyaputra),† in Keralaputra (or Malabar), and in Tambapanni (or Ceylon), and to Antiochus the Yona Raja, and to those Princes who are allied with him, it is proclaimed that two designs have been cherished by Piyadasi,—one regarding men, and one relating to animals,—that everywhere wholesome vegetables, roots, and fruit-trees shall be cultivated, and that on the roads wells shall be dug and trees planted, to give enjoyment for both men and animals.

The above reading of Tablet II. is taken partly from Wilson and partly from Lassen; it was however Mr. Prinsep who first explored its contents and discovered the name of

* Code of Manu, vi. 14, viii. 40.

† Satyaputra means "Son of Truth." Lassen considers it the Buddhist name of the King of Pida, a place near Arcot.

Antiochus, which he had hailed with characteristic ardour. Indian antiquities excited but little attention, he observed, so long as they illustrated mere Indian history; "but the moment any name or event turns up, . . . offering a point of connection between the legends of India and the histories of Greece and Rome, . . . a spreading interest is aroused. Such was the engrossing interest which attended the identification of *Sandracottus* with *Chandragupta*, in the days of Sir William Jones; such the ardour with which the Sanskrit was studied, and is still studied, by philologists at home, after it was discovered to bear an intimate relation to the classical languages of Europe. . . . I have now to bring to the notice of the Society another link of the same chain of discovery, which will, if I do not deceive myself, create a still stronger degree of general interest in the labours, and of confidence in the deductions, of our antiquarian members, than any that has preceded it. I feel it so impossible to keep this highly singular discovery to myself, that I risk the imputation of bringing it forward in an immature shape."* This name Antiochus Mr. Prinsep had already observed in four different places, sometimes with and sometimes without the addition of *Yona* or *Yavana* Raja. Professor Lassen supposes this King to have been Antiochus II., who died B.C. 247, twelve years after the inauguration of Asoka.

TABLET III.

King Priyadasi† says:—This was ordained by me when I had

* J. A. S. B., Feb. 1838, p. 156.

† In the last discovered inscriptions at Kapur di Giri, in the Punjab, Professor Wilson observes that this name has "the more correct Sanskrit form of *Priya*, instead of the Pali *Piya*dasi." The spelling is consequently different in the different tablets.

been twelve years inaugurated in the conquered country; that amongst those united in the law, whether strangers or my own subjects, quinquennial expiation shall be held for the enforcement of moral obligations, as,—duty to parents, friends, children, relations, Brahmans, and Sramans. Liberality is good, non-injury of living creatures is good, abstinence from prodigality and slander is good. The Assembly itself will instruct the faithful in the virtues here enumerated, both by explanation and by example.*

M. Burnouf observes that this last sentence is more literally, "'D'après la cause et d'après la lettre;' à peu près comme quand on dit, *au fond et dans la forme.*"†

TABLET IV.

In past times, during many hundreds of years, there have prevailed destruction of life and the injury of living beings, want of respect for kindred, Brahmans and Sramans. But now King Priyadasi practises the Law, the drum sounds, and the Law is proclaimed by processions of cars and elephants, and displays of fireworks. That which had not been seen for centuries, is now seen, . . . in consequence of King Priyadasi's commands that the Law be practised. . . . And Priyadasi will cause the observance of the Law to increase; and the sons and grandsons and great-grandsons of Priyadasi will cause its observance to increase until the *Kalpa* of destruction.‡

A sentence here occurs which is understood by Burnouf to signify that outward conformity is not sufficient: "Cette observation même de la loi n'existe pas pour celui qui n'a pas de morale." The concluding words state that the present Edict was written in the twelfth year since the inauguration of King Priyadasi.

Burnouf reads the commencement of Tablet V. as "Virtue is difficult of performance," therefore Priyadasi

* Wilson, J. R. A. S., xii.

† Appendix to 'Le Lotus de la Bonne Loi,' x. 738.

‡ In transcribing these Tablets, words and sentences are omitted when they appear unnecessary to the sense.

and his posterity must adhere to the law. "Vice is easily committed, therefore *Dharma Mahamatra* (or great officers of morals) are appointed by me in the thirteenth year of my inauguration," whose business it will be to preside over the law and cause it to spread amongst people of all the *Pashandas,* and amongst the people of *Kamboja* (eastern Kabulistan), *Gandhara* (Candahar), and *Naristika* (Rashtika or Guzerat), and also to Pitenika, a place unknown. *Pashanda* has been shown by Professor Wilson to mean the pious of various sects. We shall give the remainder of the Tablet in the Professor's words, but he offers it as "subject to very great reservation."*

TABLET V.

They (the Mahamatra) shall also be spread among the warriors, the Brahmans, the mendicants, the destitute, and others, without any obstruction, for the happiness of the well-disposed, in order to loosen the bonds of those who are bound, and liberate those who are confined, through the means of holy wisdom disseminated by pious teachers, and they will proceed to the outer cities and fastnesses of my brother and sister, and wherever are any other of my kindred; and the ministers of morals, those who are appointed as superintendents of morals, shall, wherever the moral law is established, give encouragement to the charitable and those addicted to virtue. With this intent this Edict is written, and let my people obey it.

For Tablet VI. we shall avail ourselves of Lassen's version.†

TABLET VI.

Hitherto attention has not been given to reports and affairs incessantly, or at all times, and on this account I decree that at all times, —even when I take recreation in the apartments of the women and children, or in conversation, or in riding, or in gardens, in all places,— there shall be informers (*Prativadaka*) to make known to me the wishes of the people; and everywhere I will occupy myself with the

* Wilson, J. R. A. S., xii. p. 187.

† Lassen, ii. p. 255, *note*.

welfare of the people; and whatever I declare, or whatever the Mahamatra shall declare, shall be referred to the Council for decision. Thus shall reports be made to me. This have I everywhere and in every place commanded, for to me there is not satisfaction in the pursuit of worldly affairs; the most worthy pursuit is the prosperity of the whole world. My whole endeavour is to be blameless towards all creatures, to make them happy here below, and enable them hereafter to attain *Swarga*. With this view this moral Edict has been written: may it long endure; and may my sons and great-grandsons after me also labour for the universal good; but this is difficult without extreme exertion.

Burnouf gives the last sentence as "Mais cela est difficile à faire si ce n'est par un héroïsme supérieur."*

TABLET VII.

The beloved of the Gods, the Raja Priyadasi, desires that the ascetics of all the different beliefs (the *Pashanda*) may everywhere dwell (unmolested): they all aim at moral restraint and purity of disposition; but men have various opinions and various desires, and the ascetics obtain either all or merely a part (of what they want). However, even for him who does not obtain a large gift or alms, purity of disposition, gratitude, and steady devotion, is desirable.†

This is the general meaning attributed to Tablet VII. by Burnouf, who adopts the interpretation of *Pashanda* from Professor Wilson. Tablet VIII. is given from Wilson.‡

TABLET VIII.

In past times Kings were addicted to travelling about, to companions, to going abroad, to hunting, and similar amusements; but Piyadasi, the beloved of the Gods, having been ten years inaugurated, by him easily awakened, that moral festival is adopted (which consists) in seeing and bestowing gifts on Brahmanas and Sramanas, in seeing and giving gold to Elders, and overseeing the country and the people; the institution of moral laws and the investigation of morals. Such are the devices for the removal of apprehension, and

* Burnouf, Appendix, x. 654. † Appendix, x. 754.

‡ Wilson, J. R. A. S., xii. 202.

such are the different pursuits of the favourite of the Gods, King Piyadasi.*

In this Edict we may suppose the King to have had in his mind the Brahmanical type of excellence for Kings, as in the Code of Manu:—

"Hunting, gaming, sleeping by day, . . . singing, dancing, useless travel, a King must shun; because he only who 'has the victory over his own organs . . . can keep his people firm to their duty.'"†

TABLET IX.

The beloved of the Gods, the Raja Piyadasi, thus says:—Every man that is, celebrates various occasions of festivity, as,—on the removal of encumbrances, on invitations, on marriages, on the birth of a son, or on setting forth on a journey,—on these and other occasions a man makes various rejoicings. Such festivals are fruitless—are vain; but the festival that bears great fruit is the festival of duty (the *dharma mangala*), such as the respect of the servant to his master; reverence for holy teachers is good; liberality to Brahmans and Sramanas is good. These and other such acts constitute verily the festival of duty, and this is to be cherished as a father by a son, or a dependant by his master; . . . for the establishment of this object virtuous donations are made, for there is no donation equal to the gift of duty; . . . benevolence contracted between friends . . . is mere chaff: . . . by these means let a man seek *Swarga*.‡

TABLET X.

The beloved of the Gods, the Prince Piyadasi, does not esteem glory and fame as of great value; and besides, for a long time it has been my fame and that of my people that the observance of moral duty and the service of the virtuous should be practised, for this is to be done. This is the fame that the beloved of the Gods desires; and inasmuch as the beloved of the Gods excels, (he holds) all such repu-

* Burnouf reads, that Piyadasi, after being ten years inaugurated, "obtint la science complète de la Bôdhi, où la connaissance de ce qu'enseigne le Buddha." This he understands from a correction of the inscription made by Captain Jacobs; the word is *Bodhitena,* not *Buddhena.*

† Code of Manu, vii. 47, 45, 44.

‡ Wilson, J. R. A. S., xii. See also Burnouf, Appendix, p. 665.

tation as no real reputation, but such as may be that of the unrighteous,—pain and chaff; for it may be acquired by crafty and unworthy persons, and by whatever further effort it is acquired it is worthless and a source of pain.*

TABLET XI.

Thus says the beloved of the Gods, King Priyadasi: There is no gift like the gift of virtue, whether it be the praise of virtue, the apportionment of virtue, or relationship of virtue. This (gift) is the cherishing of slaves and dependants, pious devotion to mother and father, generous gifts to friends and kinsmen, Brahmanas and Sramanas.

Thus far is Wilson's version; the remainder is given from Burnouf.

Respect for the life of creatures is good; this is what ought to be said by a father, by a son, by a brother, by a friend, by an acquaintance, by a relation, and even by mere neighbours: this is well; this is to be done. He who acts thus is honoured in this world, and in the other world infinite merit results from this gift of the Law.

Burnouf gives "gift of the law," where in Wilson we have "gift of virtue;"† the original word being *dharma dana*, which in the Sankhya Karika means money given to pious people who promote *dharma*. The commentator of the Karika explains "*dana*, gift, as when a person assists holy men by donations of a dwelling, of herbs, of a staff, etc.," and in requital receives knowledge leading to liberation. ‡

TABLET XII.

Priyadasi, the beloved of the Gods, honours all forms of religious

* Burnouf gives the last sentence as "it is difficult to work for the *hereafter* (that is the future state), whether in high or in low station; unless by supreme heroism a man abandons all (becomes an ascetic), and that is difficult for a man in high station."—Appendix to Lotus, p. 659.

† The word *dharma* might mean 'the law;' but as it is explained in the Edict itself it is moral merit, or goodness.

‡ Sankhya Karika Bhashya, p. 156.

belief, whether professed by ascetics or by householders, both by giving alms and by other modes of showing respect. But the beloved of the Gods does not esteem alms and marks of respect so highly as the increase of that which is the essence of renown. Now the increase of that which is essential for all forms of belief is of many kinds, but nevertheless the base of it is, for each of them, praise in words. Further, a man must honour his own faith without blaming that of another, and thus will but little that is wrong occur. There are even circumstances under which the faith of others should be honoured, and in acting thus, according to circumstances, a man increases his own faith and injures that of others. He who acts differently diminishes his own faith and injures that of others; he, whoever he may be, who honours his own faith and blames that of others out of devotion to his own, and says moreover, Let us make our faith conspicuous; the man, I say, who acts thus merely injures the faith he holds: concord alone therefore is desirable. Further, let men listen to each law and follow it with submission, for such is the desire of the King, beloved of the Gods. Further, may men of all faiths abound in knowledge and prosper in virtue! And those who have faith in this or that religion should repeat this:—The King, beloved of the Gods, does not value alms or marks of respect so much as the increase of that which is the essence of renown and the multiplication of all beliefs. To this end great ministers of law, and superintendents of women, . . . and other officers are appointed, and the fruit of this institution will be the speedy increase of all religions, as well as the illumination of the law.*

The above interpretation is given wholly from Burnouf, who acknowledges the great assistance he derives from Wilson's rendering of *pashanda;* the varieties of religion included under that word being the chief subject of the Edict, which had no meaning so long as *pashanda* was understood to mean heretic.

This twelfth Edict is the most remarkable of the whole series, and it is therefore unfortunate that it is only found at Girnar, and that no second copy existsw herewith the

* Appendix, x. 761.

first might be collated. Some expressions remain, in consequence, undetermined, but the general bearing is the same as that of the seventh Tablet, which is repeated both at Dhauli and at Kapur di Giri: it awards respect to the followers of all *pashandas* (religious sects), and desires the followers of *dharma* (the law) to be respectful towards those with whom they differ. In the twelfth Tablet it is further stated that neither *dana*, gifts, nor *puja*, worship, can be compared in value with *the increase of that which is essential:* this being apparently analogous to the Brahmanical doctrine of the Code, where, so soon as a devotee has become "passion-subdued," and has learned to fix his mind upon "the spirit," he is exempt from "ceremonial acts."* A passage to the same effect occurs in the commentary on the Sankhya Karika, where, after alluding to the twenty-five principles of Kapila, as the knowledge which destroys pain, it is added, "He who knows the twenty-five principles, whatever order of life he may have entered, and whether he wear braided hair, a top-knot only, or be shaven, he is liberated: of this there is no doubt."†

The thirteenth Tablet is too imperfect to admit of a continuous translation, but it is of importance from its mention of four or five Greek Kings, who are supposed to be Antiochus II. (who died B.C. 247), Ptolemy II. (who reigned in Egypt till B.C. 246), Antigonus Gonatas (who reigned in Macedonia till B.C. 239), and Magas of Cyrene (whose date is quite unmanageable, for he died B.C. 258, previous therefore to the era awarded to the Edicts).‡ At Kapur di Giri there is also a name supposed to be that of Alexander the

* Code, vi. 49, 54, 95.

† Sankhya Karika. See *ante*, Book I. Ch. IX.

‡ Lassen, vol. ii. p. 242.

Great; the only explanation being that communication was at that time but slow between Eastern and Western Asia, and that in the careless and magnificent Eastern fashion, these names, having formerly appeared in State documents, were again inserted to add dignity to the list, although half a century had elapsed since any token had been given of their bearers still having a place among the living.*

The fourteenth Tablet is in the form of a conclusion, stating that, by command of this King, the text of the Law has been given in a short form, in a medium form, and in a developed form, and if it contains repetitions, it is owing to the importance of the thing repeated, and if it contains errors, it is owing to the mistakes of the engraver.

We have now before us the first series of those wonderful inscriptions, which, startling as volcanic irruptions, intrude abruptly into the history of Ancient India, and show no very close alliance either with the early Brahmanical systems or with the Buddhism afterwards developed. The *dharma* (law, or virtue,) which they inculcate is not at variance with the *dharma* of Brahmanical books; but to teach this in the vernacular is an innovation: for a *King* to teach or exhort his subjects is also new; and to teach all men, irrespective of caste, is a still more daring innovation. It is evident that the King, by whom these Edicts were promulgated, was no longer a slave to Brahmanical restrictions; but neither, on the other hand, had he adopted the modes of reverence peculiar to the Buddhist books. He (or the religion which he represents) was apparently in a transition state,—emancipated from old Brahmanism, but not arrived at developed Buddhism.

* Edwin Norris, J. R. A. S., vol. xii.

The King issues his Edicts in the twelfth and fourteenth years of his reign, and begins by saying, that formerly hundreds of thousands of animals were slaughtered daily for his soup-kitchen, but that he had discontinued these convivial meetings because he had observed many faults in such assemblies. Now supposing Piyadasi to be another name for Asoka, this is explained by the 'Mahawanso,' in which history we read that, during the first ten years of his reign, Asoka used to regale sixty thousand Brahmans daily in the court of his palace, but that, being disgusted "with the despicable proceedings of these persons," which he witnessed from his "upper pavilion," he desired his ministers to bestow alms with greater discrimination. He then caused "ministers of all religions separately" to be brought to him, and having seated them "he discussed their tenets,"* and then, as we infer from the Edicts, gave commands that all, according to their views, should be examples of virtue, and should dwell unmolested, and receive respect within the limits of his dominion.

The Mahawanso further informs us that at a later period, when "enjoying the breezes in his upstairs pavilion," Asoka observed a *Sramana* (Buddhist ascetic) passing the palace square; and being delighted with his sanctified deportment, he caused him to be called in, and desired him to take whichever seat best suited him: the King was startled by the *Sramana's* sitting at once upon the throne; but he nevertheless listened with reverence to his discourse, and became, in consequence, a devout convert "to the religion of the vanquisher." At this era we may suppose his good works to have commenced.

* Mahawanso, ch. v.

Tablet I. protects life. II. commands supplies of vegetable food for man and beast. III. institutes quinquennial expiations. IV. makes proclamation of *dharma* by the beat of the drum. V. institutes ministers of morality, *dharma mahamatra*. VI. institutes informers on morals, to whom the King promises audience at all hours. VII. desires the new officers not to molest pious ascetics of other persuasions. The four next Tablets touch chiefly upon the King's personal conduct. In VIII. he gives up hunting and other amusements. In IX. he gives up all festivals except *dharma*. In X. he gives up all ambition, except as touching *dharma*. In XI. he promises gifts to *dharma*, but in XII. he says, that gifts are worth less than concord, and that even religious persons who do not receive *dharma* must not be molested.

At Dhauli, in Cuttack (south of Calcutta), there are two additional Edicts, detached from the general series; they also bear the name of Piyadasi, but belong apparently to a later stage of Buddhist progress. The first is addressed to the *Mahamatra*, or great ministers, of Tosali, a town in Cuttack: it declares that the Stupa of commandment prepared for the benefit of thousands of living creatures is offered as a gift, in the same manner as a *bouquet* of flowers is presented to a person of importance. Good men, Piyadasi says, are his sons, and for his sons he desires every advantage, not only here but hereafter; therefore this Stupa has been erected to instruct the whole province submitted to his rule, and upon it the moral law is inscribed, which forbids murder, violence, and idleness; "And this Edict must be read in the month called *Nakchatra Tichya*, and thus promote the interest of the *Sangha* (Assembly) until the end of time."* The *Dharma-matra*, or ministers, and *the prince royal of Ougein* are then exhorted to hold quinquennial confessions, but during their performance the people must not abandon their customary trades and occupations.

The second of these detached Edicts is less readable than even the first, but M. Burnouf distinctly makes out the following:—"The Stupa of Dhauli will secure to me bliss hereafter till the end of time;" and, let this "Stupa of commandment be read every four months by the *Sangha;* in the interval it may be read by individuals, and thus will the good of the Assembly be secured till the end of time."

We will now turn to the corresponding series of Edicts inscribed upon the five columns at Delhi, Allahabad, Bakra, Mathiah, and Radhiah, which profess to be issued in the twenty-seventh year of Piyadasi's reign; each column has four tablets, facing the four points of the compass: in the north tablet he proclaims that his government shall be guided by the law, which is compassion, alms, truth, and purity, which he practises; but he interrupts himself with the remark, that it is easier to record one's good actions than one's sins, for "violence, cruelty, pride, envy, etc. will not raise a voice against themselves." The western tablet institutes officers called *Rajaka,* who are to soften the rigours of justice, and be as careful of the people as a nurse is of a a child: the meaning is not fully made out, but the King appears no longer to require the protection of his army, the *Rajaka* guarding him instead: the tablet concludes with granting three days' reprieve to criminals condemned to death, for the very singular reason, that by the virtue of

* Burnouf, Lotus of Good Law, Appendix x., p. 655.

fasts they may be enabled to earn bliss in a future state. The southern tablet contains an enumeration of the animals whom Piyadasi has saved from slaughter, and forbids the death of any animal during the three *four-monthly periods*, and states in conclusion: "Furthermore, in the twenty-seventh year of my reign, this present time, twenty-five prisoners are set at liberty." The eastern tablet is very doubtful; Prinsep thought it repented of the Edict issued in the twelfth year, but this reading requires confirmation.

Circling round the column at Delhi, there is another inscription, unknown to either of the other columns; it states that Piyadasi has planted banyan-trees for shade, and mango-trees for fruit, and has dug wells along the road, and that former kings had conferred similar enjoyments upon mankind; and further, he hopes that his good works, or "attachment to law," will incite those who follow him to do the same, and with this view "Let stone pillars be prepared, and let this Edict of *dharma* be engraven thereon, that it may endure unto remote ages."

Since the death of Mr. James Prinsep, yet another inscription has been discovered with the name of Piyadasi; it is not written on a pillar, but on a block of granite, not more than two and a half feet square by one and a half in depth, and this was discovered at a place called Byrath, six miles from Bhabra, and on the route to Jaypur: the dialect made use of is the ancient *Magadhi*, which was doubtless the language of the capital and the government at that period. A translation was attempted in Calcutta in 1840, by which it appeared to be another Edict issued by the King Piyadasi, but given on this occasion on the authority of Buddha; so much of this translation was however philologically improbable, that Professor Wilson waited for verifications of the original before admitting it as evidence. In 1853 a translation by M. Burnouf was published amongst his posthumous papers, which was much less strange than that made in Calcutta; but as it did not place the inscription altogether in keeping, either with the Piyadasi of the former Edicts or with the Asoka of Buddhist history, a new translation by Professor Wilson, made from a corrected transcript, is particularly welcome. These new readings differ on several points from those of Burnouf, and although based entirely upon grammatical considerations, without any reference to historical probability, they virtually remove all discrepancies.

TRANSLATION OF THE BHABRA INSCRIPTION, BY PROFESSOR WILSON.

Piyadasi, the King, to the venerable Assembly of Mâgadha, commands the infliction of little pain and indulgence to animals.

It is verily known, I proclaim, to what extent my respect and favour (are placed) in Buddha, and in the Law, and in the Assembly.

Whatsoever (words) have been spoken by the divine Buddha, they have all been well said, and in them verily I declare that capability of proof is to be discerned; so that the pure law (which they teach) will be of long duration, as far as I am worthy (of being obeyed).

For these I declare are the precepts of the Law of the principal discipline (Vinaya), having overcome the oppressions of the Aryas and future perils, (and refuted) the songs of the Munis, the Sutras of the Munis, (the practices) of inferior ascetics, the censure of a light world, and (all) false doctrines.

These things, as declared by the divine Buddha, I proclaim, and I desire them to be regarded as the precepts of the Law.

And that as many as there may be, male and female mendicants, may hear and observe them, as well also as male and female followers (of the laity).

These things I affirm, and have caused this to be written (to make known to you) that such will be my intention.

Thus corrected the Bhabra inscription becomes a consistent portion of the long series of Edicts previously inscribed by Piyadasi. At the commencement the King honours Dharma, the Law; at a later period he respects the Sangha, or Assembly; and here, in the maturity of his faith, he reverences Buddha, the Law, and the Assembly.

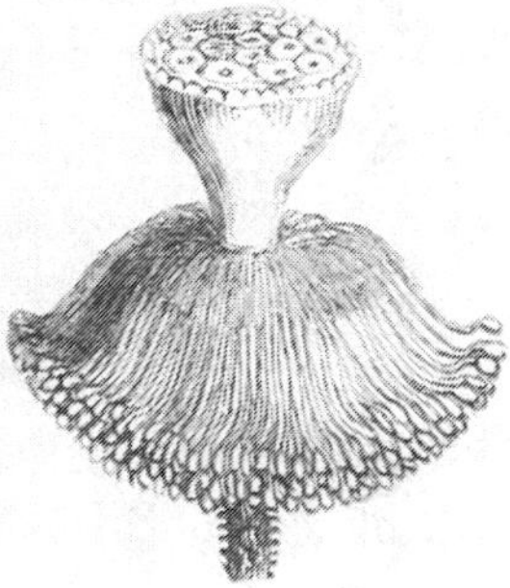

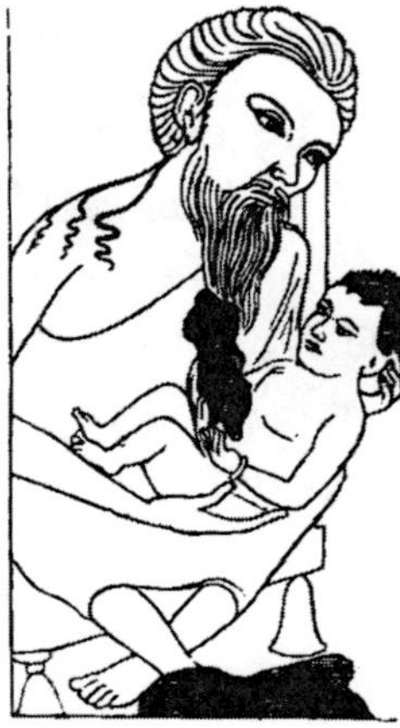

CHAPTER IV.

"What noble vanities, what moral flights, . . .
Glittering through their romantic wisdom's page,
Make us at once despise them and admire:
Fable is flat to these high-season'd sires."—YOUNG.

THE inscriptions upon rocks and pillars, being now fully established as the work of a Buddhist King, stand out before us as an exhibition of what Buddhism was subsequent to Alexander the Great, but coeval with the Greek rule of Bactria. The Allahabad pillar bears a wreath of Græco-Assyrian lotus and honeysuckle;* the form of letter used in the inscriptions is identical with that of the Greek coin legends, and the name of Antiochus, the "Yona-rajah," is given more than once distinctly written. Piyadasi's Edicts serve therefore as a fixed buttress on which to hang the long loose threads of Buddhist literature, connecting them on one side with the dim origin of Buddhism, and on the

* See vignette at the close of Book II. Chap. I.

other side with the phenomena which Buddhism exhibits in modern times. Some of the interpretations now proposed may possibly be swept away by the next critical battery, for our best authorities put forward their suggestions "subject to very great reservation:" where Wilson finds Piyadasi speaking of "Sutras and Agamas," Burnouf makes him "wish much knowledge and virtue;" where Lassen and Prinsep say, "Let the Rajaka *abide around the banyan-trees*," Burnouf gives, "Let the Rajaka (royal officers) act *without uneasiness* or *fear*;" and many similar discrepancies might be cited. But although critics differ in the rendering of particular phrases, they are all agreed as to the general import of the Inscriptions, and accept them as a record of the religion prevailing in the chief kingdom of India about the middle of the third century before Christ, or from B.C. 247 to 220. More earnest and honest than modern Buddhists, they are too independent of the Divine Spirit for contemporary Brahmans; and again, whilst too liberal and philanthropic for Brahmanism of any age, they are too free from affectation and hyperbole for Buddhists of even two centuries later. No Buddhist literature appears to have been written previous to the Inscriptions; but it is this doubtful and comparatively recent literature which alone pretends to give the history of Sakya-muni, who founded Buddhism, and of the Kings by whom he was cherished and protected. Written as it is by enthusiasts, some two or three centuries after the events recorded, we must receive it with considerable reserve, remembering that but little of it has, as yet, received that full philological criticism which was contemplated by the enlightened and lamented M. Burnouf; much however he did perform, and we thus learn that the Northern Books may be separated generally into three or four classes, as:—1. Simple Sutras, written in prose, which are imagined to give the words of Buddha, as remembered by his disciples and preserved by oral teaching, and in which he appears as a human teacher with a human audience; 2. Developed Sutras, in which Buddha claims to be heaven-descended, and tells long stories of his former births in previous ages of the universe,—his audience chiefly composed of men who had become flying Bodhisattavas through the force of Buddhism. These *vaipulya*, or developed Sutras, are written either in verse, or in prose mixed with verse, in a barbarous dialect, which confuses Sanskrit, Pali, and Prakrit forms of grammar: this, amongst other reasons, leads M. Burnouf to believe that some of them were composed or recomposed in Kashmere or the Punjab, where Buddhism flourished about the Christian era, and where Sanskrit was a foreign tongue. The third class contains the transcendental doctrines, which are Brahmanical metaphysics, carried to an extreme; and the fourth, which is not very strictly divided from the third, is made up of transcendental metaphysics mingled with Siva practices; but this corruption was ultimately rejected by respectable Buddhists in the north, and never extended to Ceylon.

The Ceylon books are also divided into Simple Sutras, Developed Sutras, and Metaphysics; but the writings now most read in Ceylon are commentaries on these earlier works, written A.D. 400, by a learned Buddhist named Buddhaghoso, from the Ganges; and a compendium also of his composition; to which books may be added a history of Ceylon, called the 'Mahawanso,' composed by a native of Ceylon named Mahanamo, out of the materials which Buddhaghoso had recently revised. The Mahawanso was finished A.D. 490. Another most popular religious work in Ceylon is the 'Milinda Prasna,' recording conversations between a King and a Buddhist sage, or hierarch, who lived in northern India during the first century A.D.; and the remainder of Singhalese literature consists of modern compendiums and compilations.

The first-named series, the books of Nipal, are written in Sanskrit, those of Ceylon in Pali: but neither collection is translated from the other; each appears independent, but taken equally from Pali oral tradition. The Burmah books are translated from the Pali of Ceylon; the Tibetan and Mongolian from the Sanskrit of Nipal, and thus we have the Nipal and Ceylon collections as joint authorities. These facts have been elicited by a long series of laborious efforts, much of which necessarily sink into the ground like piles into a quaking bog, lost to sight, but preparing a foundation for subsequent exertion. When the learned Rémusat and Schmidt thought Buddhism as old as the Deluge, they had little to guide them beyond the popular legends written in Mongolian and Chinese; for neither Sanskrit books, Pali books, nor inscriptions had been then discovered. In 1828 Mr. Hodgson announced his discovery of Buddhist libraries in the mountains of Nipal, and in 1830 sent twenty-six volumes home to London: in 1836 he forwarded copies to Paris, where the indefatigable M. Burnouf at once commenced their examination. About 1830 a learned Hungarian, Csoma Korösi, fortunately visited Tibet and acquired that difficult language; and going afterwards to Calcutta, was gladly engaged by Mr. H. H. Wilson, then

Secretary of the Asiatic Society of Bengal, on the part of the Society, to make an analysis of the Tibet Buddhist books. For this his knowledge of Tibetan eminently qualified him, and the result proved the Tibetan to be copies of the Sanskrit discovered by Mr. Hodgson. Whilst these discoveries were being effected in the north, the late Hon. George Turnour, resident at Colombo, in Ceylon, was equally successful in the south. Obtaining the confidence of influential Buddhist priests, he induced them to disclose their whole treasure of sacred literature, of which they knew very little themselves, but were willing to assist Mr. Turnour in obtaining the knowledge of Pali necessary for its investigation. Had these Singhalese Pali books been met with in the days of Colebrooke, they would probably have been cast aside, for Pali was then esteemed "a provincial jargon." When Wilson published his dramas, its character was raised, for in his preface he praises its "richness both in structure and metrical code," and shows that it must have been cultivated before the Christian era; and this prepared the public to receive James Prinsep's discovery, that Pali in different forms was the language of the Edicts and of all the early inscriptions upon rocks and temples. Books in Pali were therefore more allied to Piyadasi's edicts than books in Sanskrit, and Mr. Turnour's communications at once excited the deep interest to which they were entitled; they have not however realized all the expectations of their discoverer, for, although written in the language in which Buddhism was first taught, they are in general of less authority than the Sanskrit writings in Nipal. The explanation is, that Buddhists wrote nothing for four or five centuries, and then, writing in India, they made use of Sanskrit as the language of learned literature; but in Ceylon, where Pali was not the vernacular, but the sacred language, in which the new religion had been first taught, it was esteemed most suitable for sacred records. In a valuable memoir on Buddha and Buddhism, Professor Wilson shows that the great body of the Buddhist literature of all countries was translated from the language which the Chinese call *Fau*, and Fau he proves to be Sanskrit. A learned Chinese who travelled to India in the sixth century, to study original Buddhist documents, gives a description of its grammatical peculiarities, mentioning the dual number; and "all this," Professor Wilson says,* "is Sanskrit; and, what is more to the point, it is not Magadhi, the proper designation of the dialect termed in the south Pali. No form of Prakrit, Pali included, *has a dual number*, and the terminations of the cases of the noun are in several respects entirely distinct." The Law of Buddha was not therefore recorded in the language commonly spoken. In India, where this was Pali, the books are all in Sanskrit; and in Ceylon, where Pali was a foreign tongue, Sanskrit was translated into Pali, with commentaries in Singhalese; but whether in Sanskrit or Pali, these books are all the product of artificial conventual regulations, written under the guidance of a formal religious assembly, "après coup," as Burnouf says, "dans le loisir d'un Vihara" (or convent), and wanting therefore entirely in the fresh genuine feeling, right or wrong, and free imagination which are so charming in the early Brahmanical literature.

The most popular portions of these vast Buddhist libraries, both in the north and the south, are developed

* Lecture on Buddha and Buddhism, read at the R. A. S., April 8, 1854.

Sutras, relating the history of Buddha. His biography commences with the countless ages during which he submitted to birth and death previous to being born on earth. Not contented, like the Brahmans when narrating the history of their Sage, Kapila, with merely stating so incomprehensible a fact, the Buddhists go boldly into detail, and tell us that when Sakya (Buddha) was a king upon earth, he established peace in the universe, and had a thousand sons, all virtuous and brave; that after he was born in heaven he lived as Indra for thirty-six million five hundred thousand years, but that, desirous of saving men, he came to earth, and gave his body to a hungry tiger; and at length, having amassed the necessary amount of virtue, he approached the bosom of his mother on a white elephant. His destined mother, who was wife to the Raja Suddhodhana (in Rohilcund), dreams that this white elephant filled the universe with light; awaking frightened, she tells the King her dream, and soothsayers being consulted, predict that a child will be born to her, who shall attain either worldly or spiritual greatness. This is one amongst many sketches of Buddha's origin; sometimes histories are given of twenty-four Buddhas who preceded Sakya (the only Buddha known to history), and the three last of these imaginary Buddhas are thus mentioned:—

"The twenty-second was manifested in a pure Brahman tribe. He issued from the womb of his mother like a flame of fire from a golden furnace, and lived the life of a layman, maintaining domestic relations for four thousand years. He had three palaces, and an establishment of thirty thousand females. When he left his home to assume the religious character, he went in his state-car, drawn by six high-bred horses; and in pursuance of his example, forty thousand persons also entered the priesthood." The sacred tree of this Buddha was the Acacia. During his reign, or Buddhahood, the historical Buddha was a king who presented the twenty-second Buddha with alms, dishes, robes, sandalwood, and medical drugs. The twenty-third Buddha lived in the domestic relations of a layman for three thousand years, had three palaces, and left his home mounted on an elephant: his sacred tree was the *Ficus glomerata;* his stature was thirty cubits, and "he was invested with a golden glory, like the flames issuing from a blacksmith's forge." The twenty-fourth Buddha "bestowed largely in alms: his sacred tree was the Banyan; in stature he was twenty cubits, dazzling like the lightning in the skies, and refulgent as the full moon; and the term of his existence was twenty thousand years." The twenty-fifth Buddha was the real man with whom Buddhism originated: he had existed one hundred thousand ages, had attained the necessary attributes, and had made the earth quake seven times by the merit of his charities; and when the period arrived for his translation to earth, "the *Dewas* with loosened top-knot and dishevelled hair, wiping their tears with their hands, clad in red vestments, and assuming revolting forms," wandered through the world, to make the announcement that in one hundred thousand years the world would be destroyed. Then at length Indra, the great King of *Dewas* and other Gods, and the great Brahma assembled together, and repairing to the Buddha elect, said, "Blessed! by thee the ten probationary courses have been fulfilled, not for the purpose of realizing the beatitude of a Sakra (Indra), a Brahma, or other deity; the state of omniscience has been sought by thee for the purpose of redeeming the world, by attaining Buddhahood." They therefore request him to submit to be born; and he begins reflecting upon where and when and all the particulars, and finally determines that he must be born at Kapila-vastu, in the north of India, in a Kshattriya family; and that the Raja Suddhodhana must be his father, and the Princess Maya his mother. His future mother is then described as "exalted by the gift vouchsafed to her, enjoying perfect health and free from fainting fits." When the time for her child's birth drew near, she was seized with a longing to repair to the city of her own family; and her husband, signifying his consent, ordered the road to be smoothed and decorated with arches of plantain-trees and areca flowers, foot-cloths, etc., along which the Queen travelled in a newly-gilt palanquin. Midway she entered a forest, wherein was a hall of recreation, resorted to by the inhabitants of both cities. The trees were covered with blossoms, the woods were ringing with the melody of the sweet-toned Coïl;* and in this enchanting scene the Buddha elect was born. Extricating himself immediately from the hands of nurses, he made seven paces towards the north, and at the seventh step he stopped and "shouted forth with the voice of a lion, 'I am the most exalted in the world, I am the most excellent in the world; this is my last existence, henceforth there is no regeneration for me.'"† By which he meant he was emancipated from future transmigration. The child and his mother were then

* The Indian cuckoo; but the note is totally unlike that of our cuckoo, being a rich loud ringing strain, like the high eager tone in which nightingales occasionally sing.

† J. A. S. B., vol. vii. Sept. 1838.

conducted back to Kapila-vastu; and the mother died, as previously predicted. The child was entrusted to the care of his aunt Gotami, and carried to a temple to do homage to the God L'ha (say the Tibetans); but instead of *receiving* worship, the idol rose and showed reverence to the infant.*

At this time a Sage, or retired Brahman, living on the Mountain of Perfumes, was disturbed in the night by the quaking of the heavens and the earth: he saw a great fire, the blaze of which extended from Kapila-vastu to the mountain on which he dwelt. In the middle of the fire was a flower, and out of the flower came the lord of lions, who made seven steps and roared; and birds, beasts, and insects hid themselves in terror. Guided by this light the Sage flew through the air towards it; but when within a short distance of the palace he approached on foot, to show respect for the newly-born future Buddha.† When the Sage‡ arrived, he was reverentially welcomed by the Raja, who sent for his infant, intending it to do homage to the holy man; but this could not be accomplished with the Sage any better than with the idol. The child no sooner appears than the holy man falls down in worship, and the infant puts his feet upon his hoary head. The *tapasa* (holy man) smiled and said, "This is the wonderful mortal;" and he wept when he reflected that he should not live to see him attain Buddhahood. In consequence of these and other signs of the child's future greatness, he is named Siddhártha, the 'establisher' of faith. But whilst the wise men of the court think this his probable destiny, they also predict that if he were to lead the life of a layman he would

* Csoma Korösi, As. Res. vol. xx. p. 289. † Rémusat, *Chin-tin.*
‡ The Chinese call him a "Doctor of Reason."

become a *chakravarti*, or supreme monarch ; and this prediction so much excited the Raja's ambition that he spared no pains to fit his son for the duties of royalty, and to preserve him from the severities of a religious life.* He was instructed in sixty-four different alphabets, amongst which are mentioned the *Yavana* and the *Huna*.† When he was sixteen, "the Raja built for him three palaces, adapted to the three seasons,—one of nine, another of seven, and the third of five stories; the edifices were nevertheless of the same height, but the stories constructed on different plans." The Raja then sent leaves (despatches) to all the Sakya Princes, announcing, "My son is of age; I am causing him to be installed with me in the sovereignty. Let all send from their own homes their grown-up daughters to this house." But the Princes objected, that although the young Prince had personal beauty, he was "untaught in a single martial accomplishment, and incapable of controlling women." Hearing this, the Buddha elect offered to exhibit his proficiency in every exercise they might propose.‡ He strung the bow which requires the strength of a thousand persons, and let the arrow fly with a noise like that of thunder, and he pierced a horsehair, from which was suspended a fruit at the distance of a *yojana*. After this triumph the Sakya tribes sent their daughters superbly decorated, and the young Prince's palace was furnished with "forty thousand dancing and singing girls," amongst whom was Yasodhará, who became chief of the Zenana, and mother of his son Rahula. The Raja

* J. A. S. B., vol. vii. p. 803.
† Csoma Korösi, As. Res. vòl. xx. p. 220.
‡ J. A. S. B., vol. vii. p. 804.

is indefatigable in his efforts to divert his son from any thoughts of a religious life, but the young Prince early shows an interest in disease, decrepitude, and death; and notwithstanding all his father's earnest precautions, he encounters three predicted signs; and all the charms of his pleasure-gardens and bands of female musicians cannot withhold him from reflection. At the moment of his having encountered the third of the appointed signs, and of his having resolved in consequence to abandon domestic life, a messenger arrived to tell him that his wife Yasodhará* had become the mother of a son. He quitted his pleasure-garden, mounted his chariot, drove back to his superb, enchanting palace, and spent the night in contemplation. His most beautiful women crowded round and endeavoured to delight him with their singing and musical instruments, but when they perceived his indifference, they said, "Why should we fatigue ourselves?" and went to sleep. When the Buddha elect, sitting cross-legged on his couch, perceived "these sleeping females, some in ungraceful attitudes, some with dishevelled hair, some gnashing thoir teeth, some muttering," he "became the more thoroughly confirmed in his abhorrence" of his lay life. "Unto him the splendid and charming palace, like unto the mansion of Indra, became, as it were, a disgusting object, filled with loathsome corpses," and he resolved that on that very day his final separation from lay connections should take place. Rising at once, he went to the door of the apartment and called, "Who is there?" Channa, who had been born the same day with the Buddha elect, was sleeping on the threshold, and replied, "Prince, it is I, Channa." The Buddha elect

* J. A. S. B., vol. vii. p. 805.

then said, "This very day am I resolved to effect my great final deliverance: without uttering a word bring me a swift *sindhawa* (steed)." Channa replied, "*Sadhu* (well), Lord;" and seeing the superb charger *Kanthaka* standing under a canopy decorated with jessamine flowers, he said, "It is proper that this charger should be caparisoned today for the final deliverance of my master." Unwilling to go without seeing his new-born infant, the young father, the Buddha elect, proceeded "to the chamber of the mother of Rahula, and gently opened the door. At that moment a silver lamp, lit with fragrant oil, was shedding its light on the interior of the chamber, and the mother of Rahula was slumbering, with her hand resting on the head of her infant, who was reposing under a superb canopy. The elect, his foot still resting on the threshold, and intently gazing, thus meditated: 'If I remove the hand of the Princess, to take up my child (and embrace him), she will be awakened, and thus an impediment will be produced to my departure. Let me then, after I have attained Buddhahood, return and see my son.' He then descended from the upper apartments of the palace and sprang upon his steed, saying, 'Do thou, my cherished Kanthaka, in one night translate me.' He would have had some difficulty in getting through the guarded gates of the town, but his tutelary *Dewata* came to his aid. In the course of the night he traversed three kingdoms, and performed a march of thirty *yojanas*,* and reached a river, over which his horse leaped and landed him in a bed of sand on the opposite bank. The Buddha elect then said, 'Channa, my friend, take thou my regal orna-

* A *yojana* is sometimes four miles and a half, sometimes five, but it seems to be most frequently reckoned as a distance of nine miles.

ments and my charger, and depart; I am about to enter into the religious life.' Channa entreated permission to do the same, but was not allowed. Kanthaka, the charger, took the parting still more to heart, and, after proceeding a certain distance and finding the Buddha elect no longer visible, unable to endure his grief, expired, and was reproduced in the form of a *Dewa* in the Tatwatinsa heavens." The Buddha elect then passed seven days in a mango-grove, "in the enjoyment of sacerdotal happiness, dazzling in his yellow raiment, like the sun under the blazing clouds of a glaring sunset," etc. After a time he crossed the Ganges, and entered the city of Rajagriha, celebrated for its superb palace, resplendent with gems, and here he at once commenced the Buddhist practice of begging alms from house to house. The inhabitants were awe-struck by his remarkable and godlike appearance, and when, having collected scraps sufficient, he went outside the gate to eat his uninviting repast, King Bimbisara himself repaired to the spot, and held "intercourse with him as refreshing as the intercourse of relations;" but although the Buddha elect enjoyed the King's conversation, he resisted his entreaties to remain and accept wealth and luxuries. "Maharaja," replied he, "to me there is no longer need either of the enjoyment of wealth or the gratification of the passions; severed from the domestic and lay ties, my aspirations are directed to the attainment of supreme omniscience."*

The Buddha elect next sought the Brahmanical schools which were held on the hills near Gaya: he first became the pupil of Arada Kalama, and afterwards of Rudraka; but after acquiring all the knowledge these teachers could com-

* J.A.S.B., vol. vii. p. 809.

municate, he appears to have been convinced that Upanishads and aphorisms, whether of Kapila or Kanada, etc., were insufficient to produce the state of exaltation at which he aimed; he therefore left Rudraka and took with him five pupils, who, being of the Sakya tribe, had attached themselves to him.* For six years he gave himself up to ascetic seclusion, meditation, and hardship, and carried fasting to such an extreme that he reduced himself to a skeleton, and his complexion, which had been of a fine golden hue, became black. But this emaciated condition of body he found weakening to the mental powers, and, convinced that this could not be the means by which to attain Buddhahood, he left his retreat, and making alms-pilgrimages through the neighbouring villages, obtained a full supply of food. By this means he regained his health and his complexion, but he lost his pupils, who gave him up as a person whose resolution had failed, and went to live by themselves at a hermitage near Benares.

After this the Buddha elect went alone into a forest, and contended with powers of darkness. Mara, called God of Death, is represented as jealous lest Prince Siddhártha (the Buddha elect) should overthrow his dominion. A strange scene is described, in which Mara advances against him with all his legions, making an uproar as if bursting the earth, which was heard from a distance of a thousand *yojanas*. Mara, mounted on his tusked elephant, and accompanied by his army, equipped with swords, axes, javelins, bows, arrows, spikes, clubs, rings, wheels, and assuming the faces of deer, lions, bears, monkeys, serpents, cats, owls, buffaloes, etc., and with terrific unnatural forms of men,

* Lassen, vol. ii. p. 69.

demons, and spirits, continued rushing towards the spot on which the Buddha elect was seated at the foot of the *Bodhi* tree (*Pipal*). Indra, Brahma, and other celestials who had been in attendance upon the Buddha elect, all fled at the terrific approach of Mara, "the great mortal, as if he were Maha Brahma himself, alone retaining his position." Crashing storms and awful earthquakes, and every other imaginable device, were alike resistless, and by the power of his merits the great mortal overcame the efforts of Mara, and during the course of the night attained omniscience and realized sanctification; and having thus acquired in perfection the virtues (inherent in) all the Buddhá, he chanted forth the Hymn, which is the established thanksgiving of a Buddha (on the achievement of Buddhahood).

"Performing my pilgrimage through the (*sansara*) eternity of countless existences, in sorrow have I unremittingly sought in vain the artificer of the abode (of the passions), *i. e.* the human frame. Now, O artificer! thou art found. Henceforth no receptacle of sin shalt thou form; thy frames (literally, ribs) broken, thy ridge-pole shattered: the soul (or mind) emancipated from liability to regeneration (by transmigration) has annihilated the dominion of the passions."*

After this victorious consummation of his trials, he remained for seven weeks in a sort of trance, during which time he was supported entirely by his miraculous attributes; on the forty-ninth day he washed his face and cleansed his teeth with the twigs of the Nagalata creeper, and accepted parched rice and honey from two travelling traders; but still he lingered in the forest, reluctant to commence his great undertaking, and doubtful apparently whether he was sufficiently qualified. "Alas," he exclaimed, "that *dharma*

* J. A. S. B., vol. vii. p. 813.

should devolve on me to be established!" Brahma and other divinities are then represented as saying, "The world is assuredly about to perish; Bhagavan (lord), vouchsafe to propound the *dharma.*" From this moment his resolution never failed him; and considering where he should commence, he remembered the services formerly rendered to him by his five pupils, and determined that to them, in the deer-forest near Benares, he would first proclaim the supremacy of *dharma.* The time is supposed to have been April or May, B.C. 588. He approached the *Isapatana,* or holy residence,* and his former pupils recognized him in the distance; but they said one to another, "Here is the *Sramana* Gotama (or Sakya), who having indulged in good things and recovered his stoutness of person, acuteness of senses, and brilliancy of complexion, comes hither; but we will not bow down to him, we will only prepare a seat." Bhagavan, divining their design, manifested toward them such an amount of benevolence that they were wholly unable to carry their intention into effect; and bowing down, they rendered him every mark of reverence. Thereupon announcing to them his attainment of Buddhahood, and taking a suitable seat, he expounded to them a discourse upon *dharma.*

There is beauty and truth, as well as absurdity, to be detected in these tales; and the superficial resemblance which they bear to parts of Christian Scripture is such as to make one thoughtful. In truth, Buddhism still lies entangled in a net; and the time has not yet arrived when, like the lion in the fable, the nibble of a mouse can set it free. We do not know whether these resemblances should

* Literally the city of Siva, which Benares has been always designated.

be attributed wholly to the similarity of human vanity and human hopes in all ages of the world; but we could almost imagine that, before God planted Christianity upon earth, he took a branch from the luxuriant tree and threw it down to India. It was from the Tree of Truth, and therefore it taught true morality and belief in future life; but it was never planted, therefore it never took root and never grew into full proportions; and it was *thrown* upon earth, not *brought*, and though man perceived it heaven-born, he knew not how to keep it alive. When its green leaves drooped, he stiffened them and stifled them with varnish; and soon, although bedizened with tinsel, it shrank into formal atheism or dead idolatry. It is difficult wholly to suppress discussion of this kind, even when convinced that it is but little to the purpose, because the subject to be discussed has so little distinctness. Sometimes the artificial character of the tales is sufficiently conspicuous, as when we find a number of Buddhas all made according to one pattern, and the three last born like flame, or resplendent like fire or gems; occasionally we may also detect a legend at various stages of its growth, as in the story of the holy man who visited the infant Buddha. The Ceylon books represent him as going out of respect to the Raja to wish him joy on the birth of a son; but the Chinese version adds miraculous signs, and a bright light which guided the Sage from his home on the mountain to the King's palace in the city. So also in reference to Buddha's birth, the Ceylon books relate that his mother dreamed that an elephant from Chadanta rubbed her side whilst she was pregnant, and state that Chadanta was a lake in the Himalaya celebrated for its breed of elephants; and since elephants were much esteemed, there was nothing unnatural in supposing that the Queen received this mark of affection from her elephant as a sign of future greatness in her child. The Tibet translation gives a very different aspect to the tale, saying that the Buddha elect entered the womb of his mother as a six-tusked elephant. Mr. Turnour accounts for this by supposing that the Tibetans translated *chadanta* literally as six-tusked, instead of giving it as the name of a place.* In Pegu the story took a different turn. Such are the legends now current amongst northern Buddhists, and yet Csoma Korösi says their sacred books contain no mention of the virginity of Buddha's mother.† The individual threads of Buddhist literature are indeed of doubtful character, many-coloured, tangled, and confused; but nevertheless we may conclude as we began, that, whether more or less fictitious, they are an indispensable link between the edicts of Piyadasi and existing Buddhism.

* Turnour, J. A. S. B., vol. vii.

† Csoma Korösi, Analysis of the Dulwa; As. Soc. xx. p. 299.

CHAPTER V.

"Dim echoings,
Not of the truth, but witnessing the truth."
SYDNEY YENDYS.

PROFESSOR LASSEN speaks of Buddhist tales as shells of fiction enclosing kernels of truth; and what we gather as truth from the shell of fiction just exhibited is, that Buddha was a man, and not a myth, as the Chinese Tien-ti of the nineteenth century is said to be. Buddha's personal beauty, and the portraits and images given as likenesses of him, were myths, or rather mere abstracts of Hindu conventional ideas of beauty; and the names given to his father and mother, himself and his native city, are all shown by Professor Wilson* to be allegorical, and thus the semi-fictitious character of the *literature* is confirmed; but as smoke betokens fire, so the floating gaseous wreaths of Buddhist story may be believed to spring from a fact, the

* Buddha, Buddhism, p. 19.

existence of a man of individual and decided character who lived between the years 640 and 560 before our era. He was, as we have seen, the son of a *King*, who chose to pass through the severe noviciate of study and hardship required only of the highest order amongst Brahmans, and so soon as his probation was concluded he announced himself a Teacher, as was the custom with learned Brahmans; but, unlike the Brahmans, he gathered his pupils as freely from the unprivileged races as from the high-born. In the Brahmanical Sutras we must seek an explanation of the doctrine which he announced, and we there find that the full attainment of *Buddhi* (intelligence) endows its possessor with *aiswara* (supernatural power).* But Buddhi was not mere intellectual superiority, it was to be acquired through *dharma*, duty, goodness; therefore when the princely ascetic believed that by the force of *dharma* he had attained *Buddhi*, and become possessed of *aiswara*, he believed no more than was deducible from his Brahmanical education: he believed, in other words, that his long-continued ascetic privations and his strenuous course of study had so expanded his intellect that he had become omniscient. So far he was not unbrahmanical; his peculiarity was not in his metaphysical apprehensions, but in the enlarged, definite, practical conclusions which he drew from philosophic data: he overlooked dis-

* The Brahmans derived the word *aiswara* from Iswara, the Supreme Spirit, and called those who attained it Isis, or Rishis. Speaking of supernatural power conferred by science and holiness, M. de St. Hilaire says, "Les légendes sont pleines de ces superstitions et de ces extravagances, qui sont à l'usage des Brahmanes longtemps avant que le Bouddhisme ne les adopte et les sanctionne à son tour.—Voir mon *Premier Mémoire sur le Sankhya*, dans les Mémoires de l'Académie des Sciences Morales et Politiques," p. 208, *note*.

tinctions of caste, and believed that what was truth for one man was truth for all, and taught that self-denial and unworldliness were not good merely for boys and elderly *dwijas* (persons invested with the sacred thread), but that men of all ages and races, and also women, might attain blessedness after death, by mercy, charity, mendicity, and hardship whilst on earth.

This liberal doctrine met with opposition from the Brahmans, whose monopoly it invaded, but with encouragement from the cultivators, merchants, and other classes, whose rights it advocated, and was generally favoured by the contemporary Kings, who were glad of its indirect support against Brahmanical domination. The new teacher seems to have abandoned his name Siddhártha as soon as he became a religious character, and to have been thenceforth called either Buddha (the enlightened), Gotama, or Sakya; Gotama being the favourite name in the south and Sakya in the north—wherefore is not stated, but if the northern books were compiled under Scythian patronage, as seems probable, this name will have been a compliment to the rulers, implying that the Buddha sprang from a family related to their race: in the Ceylon books the name Gotama is almost always preferred, but as this is also the name of a distinguished Brahmanical philosopher (author of the Nyaya school of philosophy), it will be less perplexing to call Buddha usually by some of his other names. *Muni*, saint or holy man, is often added to Sakya, making Sakyamuni, and this the Tartars read as Chingemuni, who figures as chief object of worship amongst the Buraets on the Selinga river;* Sakya and Gotama are therefore equally

* Erman, Travels in Siberia.

names of the Buddha, "he by whom truth is known"*; and in the books he bears likewise a variety of epithets, as Bhagavat, Sugata, and Tathagata. We will now note some incidents in the life of this remarkable individual, as given by Buddhist writers, always keeping in mind that, although the events narrated occurred about B.C. 600, the narrative usually communicates opinions and a tone of thought not earlier than B.C. 200, and sometimes of a considerably later date.

The rainy season commenced soon after Sakya's arrival at Benares, and, as this puts a stop to travelling, he remained with his former pupils in the deer-forest, in the edifice "near which no living creature could be deprived of life;"† and he then began to teach *dharma*, or "turn the wheel of the Law,"‡ and gained many converts, especially amongst the *Vriji* of *Vesali*. One of his first friends was Bimbisara, King of Magadha, and this was an hereditary friendship, their fathers having also been great allies. Rajagriha being at this time Bimbisara's capital and usual place of residence, he presented Sakya, "the great ascetic," with a residence, or *Vihara*, in a bamboo-grove adjoining,§ and here, during the first year of his teaching, he was joined by his two chief disciples, Shariputra and Mogalana; Shariputra being the disciple of his right hand and Mogalana of his left hand,|| whilst his cousin Ananda became his per-

* Professor Wilson observes that "much erroneous speculation has originated in confounding 'Buddha' with *Budha*, the son of Soma and regent of the planet Mercury."—Vishnu Purana, *note*, p. 393.

† Turnour, J. A. S. B., vol. viii. p. 815. ‡ Lassen, vol. i. p. 810.

§ This Vihara was called Kalandaka, after the name of a bird.

|| Csoma Korösi, Anal. Dulwa: Trans. As. Soc., vol. xx. p. 51, and J.A.S.B., vol. vii. pp. 816, 817.

sonal and constant attendant. He is described as moving about attended by these and numerous other disciples, "as the moon amongst planets," or "the elephant amongst beasts," etc., just as a Brahman or a Raja in the epic poems moves amongst his followers. He seems to have held public discussions in various places, and is said to have been visited by a King near Ougein, who was dissatisfied with the teaching of "a Gymnosophist Brahman." The King came with a pompous train of attendants, and found Sakya-muni in a grove; the conversation was chiefly carried on between Buddha's disciples and the Brahman, and turned upon the usual subjects of emancipation and deliverance.*

On another occasion a Brahman disputant came from the Dekkan, where he had been studying: he found Sakya sitting in the centre of his disciples, who formed a curve on each side of him, like the horns of the moon, while Shariputra stood behind with a *chowrie,* or cow-tail, flapping away flies. The Brahman starts his objections to Buddha's doctrine, but is told that his state of feeling is the consequence of "attachment," and he is directed to strive to acquire a state free from "attachment," and further instructed as follows:—

> "This gross and material body is formed by the union of five great elements. A disciple should dwell upon the idea that the body is constantly subject to birth and death; he must dwell on the idea of freedom from attachment, on annihilation and abandonment. If a respectable disciple has reflected on these things, then love, attachment, affection, etc. are conquered, and no longer exist."

This is the old Sankhya doctrine of five elements, and of

* Csoma Korösi, Anal. Dulwa, p. 446.

man's liberation (from transmigration) being effected by his perception of the "nothingness" of everything! But Buddha's discourse does not even refer to Prakriti (eternal nature) or Purusha (universal soul), it merely urges the acquisition of *indifference*, because all sensations, whether pleasant or unpleasant, will cease at death.*

The converts most frequently mentioned are Kings and merchants, as in the following little story of the King of Roruka, which, whether partly true or wholly fictitious, gives a distinct picture of the manner in which Buddhism is supposed to have been promulgated.

Rudrayana, who was King of Roruka, sent to Bimbisara, the King of Magadha, a coat of armour endowed with wonderful properties and covered with jewels. Bimbisara was at a loss for a present of sufficient value to send in acknowledgment, so taking the armour he bowed down his head to the feet of Buddha and begged advice. Buddha told him to get a piece of cloth, and have represented on it the image of a Tathagata, meaning himself; the artist began his task, but every time he looked at Buddha he felt fascinated and unable to continue his work. Buddha then threw his shadow on the cloth, and desired the painter to fill up the outline and write beneath it the Buddhist formula of refuge. The following version is in verse, and translated by M. Burnouf:—

> "Commence, depart (from your home); apply yourself to the Law of Buddha;
> Annihilate the army of death, as an elephant upsets a cottage of reeds.
> He who walks without distraction under the discipline of this Law,

* Burnouf, p. 457.

Escaping from birth and the revolution of worlds, puts an end to sorrow."

"If any one asks what are these sentences, the reply is: the first is the introduction; the second, the instruction; the third, the revolution of the world; the fourth, the effort."

The artist having written this from the dictation of Buddha, he then desired Bimbisara to address the following letter to King Rudrayana:—

"Dear friend,—I send you as a present the most precious thing in all the three worlds: you must have the road decorated for two *yojanas* and a half, and go out yourself to receive it at the head of your army, composed of four descriptions of troops: you must place it in a wide open place, and not uncover it until you have paid it worship and every kind of honour. Attention to what I recommend will secure to you a great amount of merit."

When Rudrayana read this letter he felt angry impatience, and assembling his council proposed calling out his army to lay waste the dominions of the King who sent it; but his counsellors persuaded him that Bimbisara, being a magnanimous King, would not trifle with him, and that the better course would be to obey his instructions to the letter, and then, if dissatisfied, means of vengeance would not be wanting. The road was therefore made, and honours rendered as prescribed, and then the covering publicly removed. Now it so happened that some merchants from Madhyadesa (including Magadha) were at this time in the town of Roruka, and the moment they beheld the portrait they exclaimed, "Adoration to Buddha!" When the King heard the name Buddha, of whom no one had spoken to him before, he felt his hair to stand on end, and turning to the merchants said, "Who is it that you call Buddha?" To which the merchants replied, "Great King, it is the Prince of the Sakya race, born on the banks of the River Bhagirathi, near the Hermitage of the Rishi Kapila, of whom it was predicted that if he remained at home he would become a Chakravarti Raja (supreme monarch); but that if he shaved his hair, put on yellow garments, and abandoned home for a religious life, he would be a Tathagata (complete and perfect Buddha)." After this explanation, King Rudrayana readily comprehended the precepts and causes of existence, etc., and "laying aside all worldly affairs, seated himself with his legs crossed, his body erect, his mind collected, to meditate on the causes of successive existence; and, cleaving with the thunderbolt of science the mountain of ignorance, he saw before him the state *Srota-apatti*;" and when he had learned the four truths he repeated the following stanza:—

> "My perception of knowledge has been purified by Buddha, who is the jewel of the world: adoration to that good physician, to whom my cure must undoubtedly be due."*

This story bears the marks of an ancient legend with later additions. It is old, because the scene is on earth and Sakya-muni is a man amongst men; but the intermixture of verse is a sure sign of later addition, and the introduction of Tathagata and Bhagavat as appellations of Sakya-muni are also suspicious. Tathagata means, He who has come (or has gone) in like manner;† meaning that Sakya-muni was one of a succession of Buddhas: but whilst there is no

* Burnouf, pp. 340–4, from the 'Divya Avadana.'

† Turnour, Mahawanso, Introd., pp. 106–8, and Klaproth, note to Fahian, p. 191.

proof that this doctrine was a part of original Buddhism, there are many reasons for supposing it to have been an afterthought. So also with the epithet Bhagavat, which means the divider, the distributor, or ruler; it is an old Sanskrit word, but not used in the sense of Deity until after the Christian era. A third sign of comparatively late date may be suspected in the fixed attitude assumed by the new convert, the Vedanta mode of "conquering ignorance" by the aid of posture being more recent than Kapila's doctrine of Buddhi and five elements.

Sakya-muni is represented as living all the earlier part of his career in Magadha, the kingdom of Bimbisara; but, with the consent of this Raja, he accepted an invitation from Prasenajit, the King of Kosala, whose chief city was Sravasti.* This kingdom was, like the Panchala of the Pandus, a part of the country since known as Oude. Sravasti and the Viharas, or convents, in the neighbourhood are the scene of many of the Buddhist tales. Great dissatisfaction is said to have been caused by the King of Kosala's adoption of Buddhism, all his offerings of lamps, incense, garlands, and perfumes going now to Bhagavat. A set of devotees called Tirthyas showed open hostility, complaining that before the "great ascetic" came, they were honoured by kings, ministers, Brahmans, and housekeepers, and received from them clothing, food, seats, medicines, and other things, but that now none but Sramana Gotama and his assembly received these things. The

* Professor Lassen calls Bimbasara King of Kosala, and Prasenajit King of Sravasti, which is apparently an oversight, Bimbisara being King of Magadha, with Rajagriha for his capital, and Prasenajit being King of Kosala, with Sravasti his capital. Indische Alterthumskunde, vol. ii. p. 17.

Tirthyas are described as men "who did not know all, but who thought they knew everything." The original meaning of the word was "one who makes the round of the sacred tanks;" but they made themselves so conspicuous by their hostility to Buddhism, that in Buddhist literature a Tirthya usually means a factious opponent.*

A story is told of six Tirthyas persuading King Prasenajit to allow them to try their strength in public against Sakyamuni. The great ascetic was then at Rajagriha, but he accepted the challenge, bid his followers "wash and mend their vestments," and started with them for Sravasti. A long hall is said to have been erected for the occasion, with a throne for Bhagavat and a *mantapa* (tower or spire). After sending a messenger flying through the air, Bhagavat entered into a meditation so intense that a flame issued from the lock of the door and set the whole edifice on fire, but before water could be procured the fire had extinguished itself without injuring the building. At length Indra and Brahma and many hundred thousands of gods came to assist, and amongst them two Naga Kings, who presented a thousand-leaved lotus, the size of a cart-wheel, all of gold, with a stalk of diamond. Bhagavat placed himself upon the lotus, his legs crossed, his body erect, and his mind concentrated, and then created an endless mass of similar Buddhas, reaching up to the heaven Akanichtas, some of whom were repeating, "Commence, depart," etc. The effect was so triumphant that the chief Tirthya drowned himself in the next pond.† The remaining Tirthyas fled in dismay to

* Burnouf, pp. 200 and 163; p. 158, *note*.

† Burnouf, p. 190, Legend of Mendhaka. In a note to the 'Lotus of Good Law,' Burnouf supposes this city to be Pandukara, a town of Berar. Lotus, p. 689.

a distant city, where they persuaded the inhabitants to refuse admission to Bhagavat. There happened however to be in this town the daughter of a Brahman from Sakya-muni's native place, and this woman, getting a lamp, descended the city wall at night, and went to render homage to the great ascetic; he, perceiving her favourable disposition, taught her the four truths, so that she acquired faith in the formula of refuge; he then bade her go to a man in the town named Mendhaka, and tell him that Bhagavat had come to that place upon his account, and that the fine which the town awarded to all who should visit him should be paid out of the purse carried by Mendhaka's son, and that however many fines were paid it would still continue full. As soon as Mendhaka received the message, he paid the fine, went to Bhagavat, learned the *four truths,* and saw before him the state which leads to *nirvana.*

The "four truths,"* so frequently mentioned in the Sutras, are worthy of particular attention, as incorporating some of the most ancient Buddhist doctrine. The first states that all existence is grief; the second, that existence is caused by the passions; the third, that the passions may be extinguished; and the fourth gives the means of accomplishing this extinction; the whole together constituting Sakya-muni's answer to the inquiries of ascetic Brahmans as to his mode of dealing with the evils of birth, old-age, sickness, and death. The same idea is expressed in the popular stanza commencing, "*Ye dharma hêtuprabhavâs;*" the translation of which is,—

> "Those duties which originate in cause;
> Their causes the Tathâgata has declared:

* Burnouf, 'Lotus of Good Law,' Appendix, v., p. 517.

What is the counteraction of those (causes),
The great Sramana has equally explained."

A summary of this occurs in the Life of Buddha (Lalita Vistara).

"Birth being no more, old-age and death are not; therefore by annihilation of birth, old-age and death are annihilated; and as ignorance is the ultimate cause of existence, then by the removal of ignorance all its consequences are arrested, and existence ceases; by which means old-age, death, wretchedness, sorrow, pain, anxiety, and trouble, the whole mass of suffering becomes for ever extinct."*

This stanza was first observed upon the pedestal of a mutilated statue of Buddha, dug up amongst some ruins near Bakra; but it has since been discovered upon endless statuettes at Sarnath, and also in the books both of Ceylon and the north. In some of the Sutras it is followed by the Buddhist exhortation or invitation given above:—

"Arise! depart (from your house), apply yourself to the law of Buddha. Annihilate the army of death, as an elephant upsets a cottage of reeds. He who walks without distraction under the discipline of the law, escaping from birth and the revolution of worlds, puts an end to sorrow."

Unfortunately this discipline of the Law was supposed to require quiescence in a disciple; and another verse expresses that ignorance (or vice) causes action, that transmigration is the consequence of action, and that he only who abstains from action escapes from its effect.

M. Burnouf has taken much pains to ascertain whether the Pali or the Sanskrit version is the original, and his conclusion is, that the Pali form of the Ceylon books is older than the Sanskrit of the north; but that neither the

* H. H. Wilson, Memoir on Buddha, Buddhism, p. 17.

one nor the other can be identified as precisely the original formula of the first Buddhists. He only determines that, metrically and grammatically, it shows itself to have been current in a popular dialect before being fashioned into a classical form.

CHAPTER VI.

"Horizon there was none,
But vast infinitude
Spread over and below."—ALFORD.

To follow Sakya-muni through all the tales which have been recorded, would only be to mystify the subject; but we shall do well to note how he is said to have passed his life under the protection of contemporary kings, and then to rehearse shortly the closing scenes of his life, as related in the legends and poetry of Buddhist religious romance.

Sakya-muni's friend and patron, Bimbisara of Rajagriha, was murdered by his son Ajatasatra, and the new King commencing his reign in hostility to Buddhists, the "great ascetic" left his dominions and lived almost entirely at Sravasti, in Kosala. Prasenajit, the King of Kosala, was a friend, and probably connection, of Sakya-muni's father, and through his friendly mediation Sakya was induced once more to visit his native place. A large Vihara was erected in a banyan grove for the occasion, and each family of the Sakya tribe sent one member as a disciple or follower. This is only related as a passing visit; and Sakya-muni appears to have lived again at Kosala, until King Prasenajit was dethroned by his son, and the new King made war upon Sakya's native city, Kapila-vastu. He returned to Magadha, in which country Prasenajit had taken refuge; but this King died soon afterwards, from eating immoderately of turnips, and then indulging too freely in draughts of spring water.* Ajatasatra, the King of Magadha, had now relaxed his hostility to Buddhism; and it seems suddenly to have occurred to him that the sagacious Sakya-muni might assist in manœuvring him into possession of the neighbouring town of Vesali. To effect this object he sent his prime minister to visit Sakya, and the conversation which ensued is given in detail. Vesali was a city famed for the beauty of its gardens, its baths, jewels, horse-furniture and sports.† The government was carried on by a confederation called Lichhawi Rulers (or Vriji Princes), and its constitution was something peculiar to itself. Marriage was forbidden, and high rank attached to the lady who held office as Chief of Courtesans. The affairs of government were discussed in Assemblies of Elders, governed by traditional laws and books, as in other Hindu republics; but the criminal proceedings differed. If the Council convicted any one of crime, they sent him to the *Mahamatra,* or chief officer of justice; and if this second authority thought him innocent, he was acquitted; but if the Mahamatra confirmed the decision of the Council, he

* Csoma Korösi, As. Res., vol. xx., p. 87.

† J. A. S. B., vol. vii., p. 992.

was given over to the Professor of Law and four other officers in succession, the final verdict resting with the King.* By this we may understand that, like all republics in India, they paid taxes to the King who "protected them;" and to this King appeal was made in cases of emergency. Ajatasatra wished however to obtain more complete dominion over Vesali, and concocted a plan with Sakya-muni for producing internal dissension, which led ultimately to the accomplishment of his wishes.

The great ascetic felt now that his life was drawing to a close; and soon after his interview with the King's minister he assembled the members of the Vihara in which he was living, on the Vulture Mountain, near Rajagriha, and made them farewell discourses in preparation of his moving to the place in which it was destined he should die, or, in Buddhist language, obtain *nirvana*. At Patna, then no more than a village, he was lodged in the new Rest-house, built by Ajatasatra for the accommodation of his messengers.† When he arrived at Vesali he was lodged in a garden belonging to the Chief of Courtesans, and received a visit from this grand lady, who drove out to see him, attended by her suite in stately carriages. Having approached and bowed down, she took her seat on one side of him and listened to a discourse on *dharma*. She then requested him to accept a repast which she would prepare the next day for him and his disciples; and having obtained his consent, signified by silence, she rose from her seat, bowed down, walked three times round him, and departed. On entering the town she met the Rulers of Vesali, gorgeously

* J. A. S. B., vol. vii. p. 993, *note*; Lassen, vol. ii. p. 80.

† Such Rest-houses are still in use in the Bihar districts.

apparelled; but their equipages made way for hers. They asked her to resign to them the honour of entertaining Sakya-muni; but she refused, and the great man himself, when solicited by the Rulers in person, also refused to break his engagement with the lady.

It was now the season of Varsha, or rains; and telling his followers to accept invitations from the neighbouring inhabitants, Sakya-muni retired with Ananda to the Cocks-foot Vihara, not far from Vesali. Whilst there he was seized with illness, and although he in a great measure recovered, he felt that at his advanced age and with his infirmities he could not long survive. He called the members of the Vihara together, and told them that within three months he should realize *nirvana;* and then exhorted them to renounce passion, keep their thoughts under subjection, adhere to *dharma,* and, "escaping the eternity of transmigration, achieve the extinction of misery." A little to the north of Vesali, he visited a place called Pawa, where Chundo, a goldsmith, lodged him in a mango-grove; and, according to the Ceylon narrative, he there ate pork at his own particular request, and, according to his own prediction and expectation, was taken ill, and felt it necessary to hasten his journey to Kusinara, a town on the Bhagirathi, near which he wished to breathe his last. When he reached the forests of Tirhut (to this day famous for their timber), "the Saul-trees shed flowers, although it was not the season for them to be in blossom, the air rang with heavenly music, and perfumes were showered from the sky. The aged teacher laid himself on his left side, and desired the disciple who stood in front fanning him to stand aside, because the *Devatas* of ten thousand worlds, who hovered in the air to watch and lament, should not have their view of him intercepted."* Crowds of men as well as *Devatas* were in attendance, some disciples of his old master, Arada Kalama, amongst the rest; and he breathed his last (or achieved *nirvana*), whilst discoursing upon *dharma* and discussing the relative merits of different religious systems.

Bhagavat is represented as himself giving minute directions that the ceremonies attending his funeral should be conducted in a manner precisely similar to those performed for a Chakravarti Raja; these appear to have been such as are described in the Mahabharata, at the funeral of Dasaratha, but whether really performed for Sakya-muni, or invented afterwards, may be doubted. At length, whilst lying beneath the Saul-trees, he says to his followers, "I am exhorting you for the last time; transitory things are perishable: without procrastination qualify yourselves for *nirvana*." These were the last words of Tathagata. "At this moment the earth quaked, the music of the gods rang in the air, and gods and men sang hymns." Brahma said:†

"All things gathered in this world must be relinquished. The man who had no equal, Tathagata, who had great powers and clear eyes, at last has died!"

Indra sang:

"A compound thing is not lasting, all things subject to reproduction must assuredly perish: it is a happiness for such to be at rest (or arrive at extinction)."

The disciple Anaraddha said:

"He who with a firm mind was a protector, he who had found steadiness and tranquillity, no longer indicates inspiration and respi-

* J. A. S. B., vol. vii., p. 1005.

† Csoma Korösi, Anal. Dulwa, As. Res., vol. xx. p. 309.

ration. The immaculate Muni, whose aim was *nirvana*, has expired. He endured the agonies of death in the full possession of his faculties. His mental faculties expired like the extinction of a lamp."

The disciple Ananda had not yet attained that state of conviction or of knowledge which was called becoming an *Arhat*, and to him the death of Bhagavat was in consequence very appalling; he said:

"When the all-perfect Buddha Supreme expired, then was there great terror; then stood the hair on end."

So also the other disciples who had not attained *arahathood* wept aloud, with uplifted arms, or rolled upon the ground, exclaiming, "Too soon has Bhagavat expired; too soon has the Eye (*chakka*) closed upon the world." But the *Arhats* sat tranquil and composed, saying, "Transitory things are perishable; how in this world shall we gain permanency," etc.

Anuradha, being the chief disciple present, then took the direction of the rest, and, after spending the remainder of the night in discoursing with Ananda upon *dharma*, he desired Ananda to go early in the morning, with his begging-dish in hand, to announce the death of Bhagavat to the Mallians, who inhabited Kusinara. Ceremonies for the funeral are then arranged, and the corpse of Buddha carried into the city in a grand procession: not only the Kusinara Mallians, but also *Devatas* assisted, and so much of the divine Mandara, or Coral-flower, fell from heaven on the occasion that the whole town was covered with it. Many other details are given of the offerings made and the honours paid, but these are recited in a very extravagant and artificial tone, and need not be particularized. The concluding ceremony of setting fire to the corpse was delayed until Kasyapa could arrive. He had become chief disciple since the death of Mogala, and Shariputra had remained at Rajagriha, endeavouring to confirm the faith of Ajatasatru, who had but recently begun to listen to Buddhist doctrine. The quaking of the earth gave Kasyapa notice of the moment at which Bhagavat expired; he also perceived meteors, and heard the sound of drums beaten by the *Devas;* he knew therefore that Bhagavat was delivered entirely from pain, and said calmly, "This is the case with every compound thing."* But Ajatastara, having "a faith without roots," would, he knew, be in consternation at the melancholy news, and he feared that the effect would be to cause the King to vomit blood and die; he therefore directed Yarchat, one of the chief ministers at Rajagriha, to go into the King's garden, and cause a series of pictures to be painted, representing how Sakya-muni descended from the heaven called Tushita into the womb of his mother, being in the shape of an elephant; how at the foot of the pipal-tree he attained Buddhahood; how at Varanasi (Benares) he turned the wheel of the Law of twelve kinds; how at Sravasti he displayed great miracles; how at some other town he descended from the heaven to which he had gone to instruct his mother; and how, after having tamed and instructed men, he went to his last resting-place in Kusinara.

After this Kasyapa directed Yarchat to take seven long basins, or troughs, filled with fresh butter, and one filled with the powder of sandal-wood, and place them in the garden. The King was then to be induced to come into the garden and observe the pictures, and when he fainted, as he

* As. Res., vol. xx. p. 309.

would on discovering Buddha's death, Yarchat was to place him in a trough of butter, and as soon as the first melted he was to be removed to the second, until he had passed through the seven troughs of butter, and lastly, he was to be laid in the powdered sandal-wood, which would complete his restoration.*

Having made these arrangements, Kasyapa set out for Kusinara, and at Pawa met a man carrying some of the celestial coral-flowers which had fallen from heaven at Bhagavat's death. As soon as he arrived at the Mallian Coronation Hall, he walked three times round the funeral pile, and then, making an opening at the bottom, bowed down his head at the feet of Bhagavat, and immediately the funeral pile spontaneously ignited. For some days the Kusinara Mallians sprinkled scented water on the ashes, and then Ajatasatra, and the Vriji Princes of Vesali, and the Sakyas of Kapila-vastu, and others, sent to beg for the corporeal remains, as relics. The different claimants seeming likely to go to war on the occasion, a Brahman, with a measure called a *drona* in his hand, reminded them that Buddha had been *patient,* and had praised the virtue of patience, and that it would be highly unbecoming to raise a contest over his remains. "Rather let us," he said, "divide the relics into eight portions." The relics were therefore measured in the *drona,* and lastly, the *drona* served as a ninth relic. The nine *dagopas* cannot however be traced, and none of those yet existing can be dated earlier than the age of Asoka.†

* The effect of sandal-wood as a refrigerator occurs also in the Legend of Purna, where a man trembles and shivers in consequence of carrying a log of this wood upon his shoulders. Burnouf, vol. i. p. 235.

† As. Res., vol. xx. p. 312.

And here we pause to draw a long breath, or heave a sigh. We believe that Sakya-muni lived and died true to his type of excellence, and it is impossible to dwell earnestly upon his career without feeling a deep interest and a strong wish to reconcile the contradiction presented by the sublimity of the man and the poverty of the religion. Speculations upon this subject are not perhaps quite prudent, but they can scarcely be avoided, and are therefore given, although with an apology.

Sakya-muni felt, as earnest men in every age have felt, dissatisfied with all that is finite, and he believed, as was the custom of his age and country, that years of meditation in seclusion could raise him even above the condition of the demi-divine Bhrigus and Ribhus of Sanskrit literature. Sakya sought for God, although he knew not that it was for God he sought, and, with all the power and energy of which man is capable, he devoted his whole being to the pursuit; and he found God in a degree far exceeding that usually vouchsafed to man, but it was unconsciously. He knew that there was something better than earth could give; he knew that benevolence and duty were better than human reward, whether in this world or in a future state; and he knew that he was aspiring above all the Gods and the Demigods of the popular creed; but he knew not the voice that taught him; he knew not that "God drew him," therefore he did not teach his disciples to watch and seek as he had done; therefore he used no prayer, and taught no prayer, and bade his disciples look no higher than himself; and therefore, no sooner was his influence removed, than the whole system began to degenerate into self-glorification and lying, hypocritical cant.

Had Sakya-muni known that duty was the law of God, and that the *nirvana* for which he yearned was going home to God, he might have saved millions of men from idolatry; but such knowledge was utterly beyond his reach. We may believe that his unconditional surrender of *himself* to duty gave him a clear perception of right and wrong: he never thought of reward for himself, and abandoned every lighter wish for that which he believed to be *right*, and, as we believe, he trusted implicitly that this would lead to eternal union with the Eternal Essence of the Universe: but this was not what he taught. True to the conceit and self-sufficiency of his age and country, he believed that he had wrested a secret from the Eternal: his clear and fresh perception of right and wrong he looked upon as a spell, which he could communicate to others, and thus enable his followers to attain the advantages he had gained, without enduring the painful, tedious, self-denying probation which he had endured.

CHAPTER VII.

"Meanwhile the winged heralds, by command
And trumpet's sound, throughout the host proclaim
A solemn council forthwith to be held."—MILTON.

THE progress of Buddhism after Sakya-muni's death has been agreeably recorded in the Ceylon Chronicles, translated by Mr. Turnour; and from these we gather that Kasyapa claimed to be Leader of the Assembly, because Buddha had said to him, "Kasyapa, thou shalt wear my hempen robes."* And it was soon apparent to the new chief, or hierarch, that decided measures were required for

* Turnour, J. A. S. B., vol. vii. pp. 1007, 1011.

holding the community together; an old dotard was working insubordination, saying, "Weep not, bewail not; we are happily rid of that ascetic, . . . who kept us in subjection, saying, this is permissible and that is not permissible; . . . now whatever we may desire that we can do."* And Kasyapa, fearing that the teachings of the divine teacher might become extinct, determined to convene a general assembly for the purpose of preserving the words of Buddha. He wished to have five hundred members, and he wished particularly to have Ananda amongst them, because he had been more constantly with Buddha than any other disciple; but it so happened that Ananda had not yet attained that state of conversion called by Buddhists Arhathood; whereas the four hundred and ninty-nine other members were Arhats. Nevertheless Ananda was elected. It was next determined that the five hundred should meet at Rajagriha for the rainy season, and that no other *Bhikshus*, that is, no other Buddhist mendicants, should be admitted to the city during that period. These arrangements being made, Kasyapa said to them, "Beloved! ye have leisure now for forty days, after which time no excuses will be admitted, neither in reference to father or mother, or getting a refection-dish or robe made; . . . do therefore what requires to be done."†

The disciples then dispersed all over India, and at the commencement of the rains the five hundred met at Rajagriha. Their first anxiety was to get the Viharas repaired, which had been neglected and untenanted for more than a twelvemonth. With this object, a deputation placed itself

* Turnour, J. A. S. B., vol. vi. p. 512; 2 Kings, ii. 13.

† *Ibid.*, vol. vi. p. 515.

at the palace-gate, petitioned the King, and obtained a promise of artificers. When the Viharas were finished, they again sought the King, and begged for his aid in appropriating a cave in the neighbourhood as a Hall of Assembly. The King was again propitious, and a suitable hall was prepared and "adorned, as if by Viswakarma, the divine artificer himself." And now when all was ready, and the assembly on the eve of being convened, Ananda was in great distress at being still "deficient in sanctification. He spent the whole night in peripatetic meditation, and reflected that Buddha had told him that by perseverance he would be shortly sanctified. Since then, he thought, a declaration of Buddha admits no qualification, my own exertion must be over-anxious." Endeavouring therefore to feel more trust he sought repose, and "whilst in the act of reclining . . . his mind extricated itself from the dominion of sin," and he attained Arhathood; and "with a countenance full of sanctity, purity, brilliancy, and splendour," he attended the meeting with the other Bhikhus.* At this meeting, whilst Kasyapa presided, Upali rehearsed the discourses relating to discipline; and Ananda those which referred to morals and general conduct. Different portions of these discourses were consigned to the disciples of different eminent Elders as their especial charge; a certain number, for instance, "to the disciples of the deceased Shariputra," and others to the pupils of Anuraddha. This is recorded as the first Buddhist convocation held at Rajagriha, at the close of the rainy season, in the autumn of the year B.C. 543.

After this period the principal Rajas for several centuries

* J. A. S. B., vol. vi. p. 518.

were unfavourable to the new religion, and it made but little progress in wealth or power. Morals were apparently more than usually corrupt in India; for not only Ajatasatru but three succeeding kings of Magadha obtained the throne by murdering their fathers, and then at length the populace cried out and said they would have no more of the "parricidal race;" and deposing the reigning Raja, they installed the eminently wise minister named Susanaga, who reigned eighteen years.* Susanaga had the reputation of being the child of the unmarried lady who held office at Vesali, where the Vriji determined "that it would be prejudicial to the prosperity of their capital if they did not keep up the office of 'Chief of Courtesans.'" Susanaga was a most accomplished person, and was succeeded by his son Kalasoka, or Kâkavarnin,† who removed his capital from Rajagriha to Patna, called Pushpapura (city of flowers), and first called Pâtali-pura and later Pâtaliputra.‡ This is the town in which Ajatasatru was building forts a century previous, when Buddha passed through it shortly before his death, and at that time it was a mere village.

During the reign of Kalasoka, or Kâkavarnin, insubordination was observed in a Vihara at Vesali, into which ill-disposed people had insinuated themselves for the sake of a subsistence. "These shameless ministers of religion," says the Ceylon Chronicle, "pronounced the following ten indulgences allowable:"§—

* Mahawanso, iv. 16.

† *Kakavarna* means "black as a raven," and was the name or epithet usually applied to Kalasoka by Brahmanical historians.—Lassen, vol. ii. p. 83.

‡ Wilson, quoted by Lassen, vol. ii. p. 82, *note*.

§ 'Mahawanso,' translated from the Pali by Mr. Turnour. The 'Mahawanso' is a history of Ceylon, written by a Buddhist resident at a Vihara in Ceylon, about A.D. 400.

1. The preservation of salt in horn.*

The rule being, that salt could only be kept seven days; and the innovation, that *in horn* it might be kept longer.

2. The allowance of two inches.

Buddhists are forbidden to take food after midday; the innovation allows two inches' shadow of the declining sun.

3. Indulgence in the country.

Which means, taking in the country what is denied in the Vihara.

4. Ceremonies in sacerdotal residences.

Performing ceremonies in private houses, which should be observed in the appointed Hall.

5. Obtaining subsequent consent.

Whereas consent of Elders ought to precede religious acts.

6. Conformity to example.

No example is an excuse for a forbidden act.

7. Acceptance of whey.

But whey, equally with milk and other food, is forbidden after twelve o'clock.

8. Acceptance of *toddy* resembling water.

Whereas no fermented beverage is admissible.

9. The use of seats covered with cloths without fringes.

No costly covers, whether with or without fringes, are allowed.

10. The acceptance of silver and gold.

All precious metals are prohibited.

* Turnour, J. A. S. B., vol. vi. p. 728, from Buddhagosa's Commentary, written about A.D. 400.

An eminent Buddhist, named Yasas, hearing in the course of his pilgrimage that these ten indulgences were being propagated at Vesali, felt it necessary for the preservation of *dharma* that he should endeavour to suppress them. He went therefore and took up his abode at the Vihara indicated; but finding it impossible to suppress the schism without assistance, he went into the hills beyond the Ganges to consult other eminent elders. These all agreed that an aged Buddhist named Revata was the person to whom they should refer as chief authority, or hierarch, of the community. To the Sthavira (elder) Revata of Soreya, therefore they applied, and he expressed his willingness to accompany them to Vesali; but being infirm, he travelled slowly and by water. At one of their evening halting-places an embassy from the schismatics appeared, with presents for Revata; but the offerings were declined, and the "messengers of the sinful fraternity" being dismissed by the holy Revata, made their way to Patna, and gaining admission to the presence of the Raja Kalasoka, they entreated his protection against the designs and aggressions of certain priests resident in the provinces, who were hastening to take possession of their Vihara. Kalasoka, supposing them really oppressed, promised them redress, and sent messengers to remonstrate with Revata; but in the night he had a dream, and thought he was thrown into a place of torture after death. The King's sister was a gifted Buddhist, and possessing the usual Buddhist accomplishment of flying through the air, she came instantly to the aid of her brother, told him that he had offered to assist the wrong party, and that he must unite himself with Revata and uphold true *dharma*; and, "by adopting this course," she concluded, "peace of mind will be restored to thee." As soon therefore as day dawned, the King proceeded to the Vihara; and having assembled and examined all the disputants, he perceived that Revata and Yasas were upholding true *dharma*, and to them he promised his royal protection. Revata then advanced into the middle of the assembly, and caused the rules to be read, and by these rules selected eight persons, himself being one, for the purpose of examining into these controverted indulgences. The eight persons selected then withdrew to a Vihara, "free from the strife of men," and so secluded that not even the note of a bird could be heard in it. Having determined that all the indulgences were inadmissible, they returned to the chief Vihara; and selecting seven hundred out of the twelve hundred who had been collected by Yasas, a second convocation was held, under the guidance of Revata and the protection of the King Kalasoka.* The system of discipline was purified, and the whole of *dharma* and Vinaya, or morals and discipline, were revised, and the sitting was brought to a close in eight months. This second convocation was held at Vesali, at the close of the first century after Buddha's death, B.C. 443.

After Kalasoka, the Magadha dynasty becomes exceedingly confused: he was in fact succeeded by Kings who were approved of neither by Brahmans nor Buddhists, and in consequence their history is nowhere told intelligibly; but the general version is, that the "nine Nandas" reigned about this time, and that one or more of these brothers was the sovereign of Patna, when Alexander the Great made his way across the Indus, and that when, after Alexander's

* Mahawanso, ch. iv.; Lassen, vol. ii. p. 85.

retreat, the west of India was agitated by the murder of Porus, the weak government of the Nandas was usurped by the adventurous Chandragupta and his clever companion Chanakya. Chandragupta reigned thirty-four years; his son Bindusara twenty-eight years; Bindusara leaving one hundred and one sons, "the issue of sixteen different mothers." Amongst these sons was the celebrated Asoka, who was so wild and turbulent in his youth that his father thought him safest at a distance, and sent him to reign as viceroy at Ougein. Whilst administering that government he formed an attachment to the lovely and youthful daughter of a *setthi*, or president of corporation, at Ougein.* This lady was the mother of Asoka's two celebrated children, the Prince Mahendra and the Princess Sanghamitta; and with them and his wife he continued at Ougein, or Avanti, until messengers arrived with "a leaf," announcing that his father was upon his death-bed. Asoka started instantly, leaving his children behind: their mother sent them afterwards to Pátna, but remained herself with her father. When Asoka arrived, the ministers rubbed him with saffron and lac, boiled in an iron pot, for what purpose is not explained;† but we are elsewhere told that Asoka had a remarkably rough skin, so that we may suspect the ministers of wishing to make it appear smooth;‡ at any rate, when the dying King was in such a state that scarcely any life was left, Asoka, "decorated with all sorts of ornaments," was presented to his father, although Susima was the son

* Mahawanso, v., xiii. † Asoka Avadana, Burnouf, p. 363.

‡ "And Rebekah . . . put the skins of . . . goats upon his hands, and upon the smooth of his neck; . . . and Isaac said unto Jacob, Come near, I pray thee, that I may feel thee, whether thou be my very son Esau or not."—Book of Genesis, xxvii.

for whom he had asked and whom he had wished to nominate as his successor.

As soon as Bindusara died, Asoka raised the *chatta* (umbrella) of universal dominion; and, by way of extirpating "all disaffected persons," put ninety-nine of his father's sons to death, only reserving Tissa, who was born of the same mother as himself. No record is given of the first years of his reign; but as his dominion extended much further than that of previous sovereigns, we may suppose that he was engaged in war or diplomacy. "In the fourth year of his accession to his sole sovereignty" he caused his inauguration to be solemnized, on which occasion the Ceylon historian records that *Dewatas*, as well as men, combined to do him honour. Mangos, saffron, medicinal substances, and tooth-cleaners were brought from the Himalaya; yellow cloths, woven without seams, were brought by the Nagas; but more extraordinary offerings were "the elk, wild hog, and winged game, which went to the royal kitchen of their own accord and then expired; herds of cattle led forth by tigers, and loads of paddy brought by parrots. Mice husked the paddy, and boars worked in the royal arsenal with hammers." So much for the historical simplicity of the Mahawanso,* never backward in the invention of marvels in the honour of pious Buddhists! Asoka's eldest brother, Susima, whom he had deprived of life, left a widow and infant son; and thinking her child unsafe near the court, this poor woman went out to live in a neighbouring village of outcasts called Chandalas. Whilst in this retreat the child was noticed by a Buddhist as worthy of Buddhist training, or, in Buddhist language, as "possessing the requisites for

* Mahawanso, ch. v.

Arhathood." The little Nigrodha was consequently brought up in a Vihara in Patna, and happened just to have attained *Arhathood* at a time when King Asoka was feeling disgusted with the greediness of Brahmans. Following the example of previous reigns, sixty thousand Brahmans were regaled daily at his palace; "but noticing from his upper pavilion the despicable proceedings of these persons, . . . the King enjoined his ministers to bestow alms with greater discrimination, . . . and caused to be brought to him ministers of all religions separately" (meaning, probably, of the various Brahmanical schools), "and having seated them and discussed their tenets and given them alms, allowed them to depart." Whilst reflecting upon their conduct and doctrine as he enjoyed the air in his lofty apartment, he observed an ascetic crossing the palace-square, whose sanctified deportment was most edifying to him. This stranger, although unknown to Asoka, was his nephew, by name Nigrodha. The King desired that he should be brought into his presence; and although his visitor seated himself upon the throne and exacted homage from the King, his discourse was so impressive that Asoka undertook from that day to provide rice daily for Buddhist priests; and no long time elapsed before both the King and the people generally were established in the tenets of Buddhism.

From this period the affairs of Ceylon are so interwoven with those of India, that it becomes necessary to know something of that island's history. According to the old Sanskrit poem, the Ramayana, Ceylon or Lanka was originally inhabited by an evil-disposed demoniacal race; and although conquered by Rama, they retained possession of their island, and appear again in history about B.C. 500, when Vijaya and a little band of Hindus set foot upon Ceylon. The story is told in the Mahawanso "under the veil of fables;" and the veil being removed, we find that a lady of royal birth, in the north of India, brought shame upon her family by marrying a man of low birth named *Sinha* (lion); and the lady and the lion, being banished from court circles, took refuge on the southern coast. Their son Vijaya scorned the obscure life which he was forced to lead with his parents, and made his way to Ceylon, where his adventures so much resemble those of Ulysses with Circe, that had the works of Homer been accessible in Ceylon, the author of the Mahawanso must have been convicted of plagiarism, says Mr. Turnour. Vijaya and his companions had no sooner landed, than the Queen, or chief of the female demons, sent her servant to them in the form of a dog. The stratagem succeeded,—"dogs are only found where there are inhabited villages," say the men,—and following the dog, seven hundred of them fell into the power of the sorceress. Vijaya, alarmed at the prolonged absence of his companions, followed them, seized the demon, and threatened to put her to death; but she restored the missing men, transformed herself into a beautiful bride, and assisted him to kill the King and seize the government. Two years afterwards Vijaya's Hindu followers were anxious to have him regularly installed as sovereign; and as that could not be done unless he married a princess of rank equal to his own, they sent a deputation to Southern Madura, to request King Panduwo to send his daughter. The King consented, and his daughter embarked, accompanied by seven hundred daughters of the nobility. When she arrived, Vijaya dismissed his native wife, promising her a maintenance of *bali* (offerings).

This story is told with some variation by the Chinese traveller Fa-Hian. A merchant, named Sinhala, went with five hundred companions to an island inhabited by demons, for the purpose of procuring pearls and precious stones; the demons inhabiting the island assumed the form of beautiful women, and allured them into their town, which was called the Iron Town. In the night Sinhala had a dream, showing him into what danger he had fallen. Rousing his companions, they all escaped to the sea-shore, where a wonderful horse stood ready to transport them across the sea. When the demons found themselves abandoned, they complained to the King; and although Sinhala warned him of the true nature of the beautiful Ogress, he and all his family fell victims to her snares. The morning after the sorceress had been admitted to the palace, the ministers went to obtain audience, and found nothing left but bones. No one could explain the calamity, until enlightened by Sinhala; and the relation of his sagacity and courage so struck the people that they forthwith made him their King. Sinhala then collected troops, and embarking them in boats, fought the female demons until they either sank in the sea or sought refuge in another island. Sinhala destroyed the Iron City, and settlers quickly coming from various quarters, he soon established a kingdom, called after himself, Sinhala.*

This is evidently a northern adaptation of the story in the Mahawanso, and is related in nearly the same manner in a Nipal book, '*Karunda Vyuha*,' or "Construction of the Basket of Qualities," of Avalokiteswara, it being ex-

* Note by Landresse; Fa-Hian, p. 338, from a Chinese work, called '*Pian-i-tian*.'

plained that Sinhala was Buddha in one of his former births, and that Avalokiteswara was the horse which saved him. With this saint of lengthy name we shall have to make further acquaintance hereafter, and he is only mentioned here in order to explain the accompanying outline of a painting from the Caves of Ajunta, in which Sinhala and his companions arrive in boats to fight the female demons; and, victory being accomplished, worship is offered to the Saint in the form of a horse, and the King receives consecration.

Sinhala, or rather Vijaya, was succeeded on the throne by his descendants; and contemporary with Asoka we find a King Mutasiva, whom Asoka vainly endeavoured to convert to Buddhism.*

We must now return to the affairs of the Buddhist convents, or Viharas, at Patna, on the Ganges, which were thrown into disorder by some of the old *Tirthyas*, who contrived to get admission and to introduce heretical doctrine. This so much distressed the aged Mogalaputra, who then presided, that he gave up his charge to a younger man, and went to a mountain beyond the Ganges, to reflect in solitude on measures for averting the dangers which threatened his religion. When the Hierarch was gone, the disorder increased, and the Assembly felt it impossible to perform the *Upasathas*. The suspension of this rite was reported to the King, who, ignorant of the reason for its suspension, sent over his officers to command its performance: the presiding priest still refused, and the officer cut off his head;

* Mutasiva sent to Asoka gems, chank-shells, eight descriptions of pearls, etc. Àsoka sent various things in return, amongst which were costly hand-towels, which are cleaned by being passed through the fire, and a message announcing his conversion to Buddhism.—Mahawanso, xi.

Escape and Coronation of Sinhala. (Painting from the Caves of Ajunta.)

this occurred several times, until the King's brother rushed to the presidential chair and prevented further carnage. The King was appalled when the circumstances were made known to him, and in great distress of mind sent a deputation to the aged Mogalaputra. After repeated solicitations, the venerable man at length consented; as he was infirm, a boat with a state canopy was sent for his accommodation. The King received him with the greatest reverence, gave him a pavilion in his own garden, and held frequent conversations with him. After expelling the sixty thousand *Tirthyas*, Mogalaputra selected one thousand of the right-believing as members of an Assembly, which sat in convocation for nine months, and restored *dharma* to purity in the eighteenth year of Asoka's reign, B.C. 241 or 245.

CHAPTER VIII.

"Where now the haughty empire that was spread
With such fond hope? Her very speech is dead."
WORDSWORTH.

MOGALAPUTRA exerted great influence over King Asoka, and this circumstance probably accounts for the difference which we have already observed between the two series of the stone-cut Edicts. In the first series the King speaks with equal respect of Brahmans and Sramanas, and makes no reference to Buddhist institutions; in the second series he commands the observance of the three sacred days and of the *upasatha* ceremonies, and shows other symptoms of progress in Buddhist doctrine.* The Books affirm that he had become the obedient and enthusiastic disciple of his venerable guest, and although we cannot entirely unriddle the puzzle of the King's two names of Piyadasi and Asoka, or explain all the dates satisfactorily, there is a general and undeniable coincidence in his history as developed in the

* In the recently-published work of M. Barthélemy St. Hilaire he makes nearly the same observation: "On peut remarquer que Piyadasi met dans ses édits les Brahmanes avant les Sramanes; mais dans ceux qui ont été promulgués après le concile il met toujours les Sramanes avant les Brahmanes."—Du Bouddhisme, p. 169, *note*.

Edicts and related in the Books: not indeed that any close resemblance could be established, or need even be expected, between short inscriptions and lengthy poems. The first are a record of the very words in which an actual proclamation has been made, whilst the second are amplifications worked up at leisure, according to the fancy or genius of the artist. Possibly, if some future Rawlinson should decipher stone records of the Siege of Troy, we should find that the original Hector or Agamemnon bore about the same relation to his prototype in Homer as the Piyadasi of the Edicts does to the Asoka of Buddhist literature. Nevertheless Buddhist books must not be neglected, for these Sutras and legends and poems are the basis upon which all modern Buddhism has been erected; and it is only by acquaintance with the foundation, that we can hope rightly to understand the superstructure. Taking therefore that most tedious and extravagant of legends, the 'Asoka Avadana,'* and sifting the facts, we find that the King accompanied Mogalaputra on a pilgrimage to all the places rendered holy or remarkable by the events of Buddha's life. At the tree under which he had attained Buddhahood, a monument, or *chaitya,* was to be erected, and persons engaged to live on the spot and preserve the tree. A monument, or *dagoba,* was also to be erected on the spot where Buddha died; and after all the places connected with Buddha had been reverently worshipped, the King expressed a wish to do honour to Buddha's first disciples, and to raise dagobas to the memory of Shariputra and Mogalana. The legend says, the

* Legend of Asoka in the 'Divya Avadana.' M. Burnouf explains *Avadana* as legends which explain present actions by events in previous states of existence, p. 11.

King raised these dagobas at Jetavana (meaning Kosala, near Fyzabad), where old bricks and rubbish show that much masonry has perished. At Sanchi dagobas to Shariputra and Mogalana actually exist;* and when once it was established as an act of merit to erect monuments to deceased Buddhist saints, the most distinguished saints would inevitably have many dagobas in various places and of various ages. The King was next persuaded by his venerable guide to allow his eldest son, Mahendra, to become a Sthavira (elder) in the Buddhist hierarchy. Mogalaputra persuaded him that a son and daughter were the best offerings he could make to Buddha; and as Agnibrahma, his daughter's husband, had already become a Buddhist and abandoned his wife, the King consented that the Prince Mahendra and his sister Saughamitta should enter the Buddhist community, making the usual vows of celibacy and going through all appropriate ceremonies with the utmost pomp.† Mogalaputra then, "reflecting on futurity, perceived that the time had arrived for the establishing of the religion of Buddha in foreign countries, and despatched Sthaviras into foreign parts."‡ Perhaps this is a second edition of the despatching of *dharma mahamatras* to the dominion of Antiochus, etc., recorded in the Edicts; or perhaps Mogalaputra looked upon Asoka's *dharma mahamatra* as mere lay teachers, in nowise lessening the necessity that well-instructed *Sthaviras* should give instruction in those benighted regions. It is at any rate well authenticated that Buddhist missions were

* J. R. A. S., vol. xiii. p. 110. 'Topes of Central India,' by Major A. Cunningham.

† Mahawanso, ch. v. p. 39 (small edition).

‡ Mahawanso, ch. xii.

at this time made, and that Asoka's son, Mahendra, was appointed to Ceylon. "The profoundly sapient great Mahendra was enjoined by his preceptor, the son of Moggali, to convert the land of Lanka;"* but thinking it would be best to wait until after the death of the old King Mutasiva, Mahendra went in the meantime to visit his mother, near Ougein: this lady's name was Chetiya; she is described as living in a city called Chetiyagiri, and the remains of her city are supposed to be still visible in the extensive and interesting ruins of Sanchi.† She was overjoyed at the arrival of her son, and established him in the Chetiya Vihara, built by herself; and whilst he spent six months preaching to his maternal relations, and converting Bhandu, the son of his mother's "younger sister's daughter," we must follow the proceedings of the Buddhist missionaries in other quarters. To Kashmere and Kandahar Mogalaputra sent *Majjhantiko*. To Maharashtra and to the Yona country and to Aparantaka he sent Sthaviras named *Rakkito*. But to the Himalaya he sent Majhima and Kassapa, which are most welcome names, for the reason that in the dagobas at Sanchi Major Cunningham has discovered a relic "of the emancipated Majhima;" also relics of the emancipated Kassapa, son of Koti, and of *Haritiputra*, the son of Hariti; a certain Yakho in the Himavanta, "together with his wife Harita," being commemorated in the Mahawanso as having attained the first stage of sanctification, etc. At Sanchi also there are relics and inscriptions to Mogalaputra, thus showing that the Books and the Dagobas are agreed as to who were the eminent people contemporary with and subsequent to Asoka, and also in some cases as to the precise

* Mahawanso, ch. xiii.

† J. R. A. S., vol. xiii. p. 114.

place in which their celebrity was acquired. Kasiyapa is said, in the Mahawanso, to have accompanied Majhima, and Majhima is twice mentioned in the Sanchi inscriptions as having been an *acharya* to Himavat. Kashmere and Candahar, and the neighbouring regions are mentioned in the Mahawanso as afflicted by thunderstorms, which destroyed their crops, and which they attributed to the power of *nagas* (snakes), whom they worshipped. In the time of Alexander the Great, two snakes were kept at Taxila for worship, and the Mahabharata also makes allusion to the snake-worshippers of the north-west of India; but there is still a mystery about the Nagas, to which we shall have further occasion to allude. On this occasion the Nagas became most willing converts to Buddhism; the Sthavira said, "Do not, as formerly, give way . . . to anger; . . . but, evincing your solicitude for the happiness of living creatures, abstain from the destruction of crops, . . . live, protecting mankind." And the Naga king being convinced by this discourse, "placing the Sthavira on a gem-set throne, respectfully stood by fanning him." And after recording how many discourses were preached, and how many thousands of persons were converted, the historian adds, that "from that period to the present day the people of Kasmira and Gandhara have been fervently devoted to the three branches of faith, and the land has glittered with yellow robes."*

The mission to Ceylon was still more important and lasting in its effects; for, even to our "present day," in the nineteenth century, the "yellow robes" glitter, and the religion of Buddha prevails, but very little altered from what it was when carried there by Mahendra, about B.C. 246.

* Mahawanso, ch. xii.

Devanipiatisso had become sole sovereign in Ceylon, and Mahendra meditated, "The period has arrived for undertaking the mission enjoined by my father." Accompanied by other devotees, he then made the journey, "rising aloft into the air, . . . and instantaneously alighting on the superb Missa Mountain,"* which means Mehentele, a hill rising abruptly from the wooded plains about eight miles to the north of Anuradhapura, where the remains of Buddhist temples, steps, walls, and cells may still be seen. These flying saints happened to arrive during the celebration of a "Salila" festival for the amusement of the inhabitants of the capital, when the King, with a retinue of forty thousand men, engaged in an elk hunt, and in the course of the pursuit came to Mehentele, or the Missa Mountain, upon which Mahendra had alighted.

"A certain *Deva* of that mountain," says the Mahawanso, "being desirous of exhibiting the *theros*,† having assumed the form of an elk, stationed himself there in that neighbourhood, grazing. The sovereign descrying him, and saying, 'It is not fair to shoot him standing,' sounded his bowstring; the elk fled, . . . the King gave chase," and came upon the Buddhist priests. Mahendra rendered himself alone visible, considering that the King might be alarmed if too many persons presented themselves. The King's name was Devanampiatisso (*tisso*, "well-pleasing to the Gods"), but Mahendra addresses him simply as Tisso, and says, that he has come from Jambudwipa (India) to teach him the faith of Buddha. The King remembered

* Mahawanso, ch. xiii.

† *Thero* is the Pali form of *Sthavira*, and means *elder*, or a Buddhist priest of experience.

the communication which Asoka had made upon this subject (during the reign of his father), and "laying aside his bow and arrow," and approaching this "Rishi," and conversing graciously, he seated himself near him. These appear to be the scenes depicted in the picture from the Caves of Ajunta, of which a tracing is given on the page opposite: the only difference being, that the northern artist represents the friendly *Deva* in the form of a lion, which stands proudly near the saints, one of whom is concealing himself beneath the trees.

On the right hand we see the next scene, in which the King sits conversing with the pious Mahendra; and above are depicted men, women, and children, sitting in the stables. This also accords with the Ceylon history, which speaks of the Princess Annula and her five hundred women as very early converts; and after saying that "these females attained the first stage of sanctification," it continues, "The inhabitants of the town hearing of the pre-eminent piety of the *thero* from those who had seen him the day previous, and becoming impatient to see him, assembled and clamoured at the palace-gate. Their sovereign hearing this commotion, inquired respecting it; and, learning the cause thereof, desirous of gratifying them, thus addressed them:— 'For all of you (to assemble in) this palace is insufficient; prepare the great stables of the state-elephants, there the inhabitants of the capital may see these *theros*.' Having purified the elephant stables, and quickly ornamented the same with cloths and other decorations, they prepared seats in due order."*

Here again the northern artist makes a slight alteration,

* Mahawanso, ch. xv.

Buddhism carried to Ceylon. (Painting from the Caves of Ajunta.)

substituting horses for elephants. At the bottom of the picture, to the right, a man appears to be suffering punishment, a circumstance to which no allusion is made in the Mahawanso.

After the Princess and her ladies had attained the second stage of sanctification, they were anxious to enter the order of priesthood; and, as Mahendra explained that men could not ordain women, the Ceylon monarch took his advice and sent messengers to India, requesting King Asoka to send his daughter, the renowned Priestess Sanghamitta, and to send also in her charge the right-hand branch of the sacred Bo-tree. During the voyage Nagas came and endeavoured to obtain possession of this treasure; and Sanghamitta, yielding to their importunity, permitted them to take it to their Naga King, and retain possession of it for seven days.

The next great event in Ceylon was the erection of relic-shrines, called Dagobas, and as these required relics, another deputation was sent to King Asoka begging for Buddha's right canine-tooth and right collar-bone. This request was granted, and the bones arrived in safety; but at a later period, when a King of Ceylon, celebrated by the name of Dushtagamini, sent for relics, they were waylaid by Nagas; and this piratical reverence and worship of the Nagas is probably the subject of the bas-relief at Sanchi.†

Mahendra's latest works appear to have been the institution of Viharas or convents at Anuradhapura, and on the neighbouring hill of Mehentele, upon which he usually resided. We read of "sixty-eight rock cells" and "thirty-two sacred edifices."*

* Mahawanso, ch. xvi.

† See woodcut at the close of this Chapter.

The pious King Devanampiatisso was succeeded by his equally pious brother Uttiyo, in the eighth year of whose reign Mahendra died, and in the tenth year he died himself, on which occasion the Buddhist historian makes the following characteristic observations, with which we must conclude our notice of Ceylon Rajas:—"This monarch, Uttiyo, reigned ten years; thus this mortality subjects all mankind to death. If mortal man would but comprehend the relentless, the all-powerful, irresistible principle of mortality, relinquishing (the hopeless pursuit of) *Sansara** (eternity), he would, thus secured, neither adhere to a sinful course of life nor abstain from leading a pious one. This (principle of mortality), finding he had "attained this (state of sanctity), would be paralyzed, and its power (over him) utterly extinguished."†

Previous to these events the poor old King Asoka, in India, had fallen into many afflictions. His good wife, who gave mango-trees to the Buddhists, died,‡ and he unfortunately "raised to the dignity of queen-consort a malicious and vain creature," who was jealous of the presents he made to the sacred tree, and tried to poison it with the fang of a toad.§ Still worse was her jealousy of Asoka's son, Kumala, whose eyes she caused to be put out, but was herself burnt to death in consequence. Asoka is represented as growing childish in his later days, weakly giving all he possessed to the Kukkuti Vihara, until restrained by his grandson, Sampadi, who acted as Vice-King at Patna;||

* Professor Wilson explains this word as not eternity, but perpetual succession or revolving of births.

† Mahawanso, ch. xx.

‡ J. A. S. B., vol. vi. p. 967.

§ Mahawanso, ch. xx.

|| Burnouf, 426.

at length, three years after his disastrous marriage, he died, B.C. 226, after a reign of thirty-seven years.*

The reign of Asoka appears to have been the noonday of Buddhist prosperity, during which the devotees became a powerful body, with well-organized Viharas, or convents, in which luxury was prohibited and the sacred records studied and preserved. The holy men were not allowed seats of costly cloth, nor umbrellas made of rich material, with handles adorned with gems and pearls; nor might they use fragrant substances, or fish-gills and bricks for rubbers in the bath, except indeed for their feet. Garlic, toddy, and all fermented liquors were forbidden, and no food permitted after midday. Music, dancing, and attendance upon such amusements were forbidden. Nor were they allowed seal-rings or stamps of gold; but stamps of a baser metal they might have, provided the design were "a circle, with two deer on opposite sides, and below the name of the Vihara."† This regulation was probably made in reference to mythological emblems employed by the Bactrian Greeks, and it is only in the northern books that we meet with it. In Ceylon it was an act of merit to enrich the Vihara in every way possible. A pious King (Dushtagamini) consoled himself on his dying bed by rehearsing his good deeds, and amongst others mentions the woollen carpets which he gave to the Vihara, and the golden ladle which he substituted for the cocoa-nut commonly in use.‡

Some inscriptions, discovered on the walls of the ruined Viharas at Mehentele, give us further insight into the wealth and importance to which these wonderful institu-

* Lassen, vol. ii. p. 271. † Csoma Korösi, As. Res. vol. xx. pp. 86, 87.
‡ Mahawanso, ch. xxvii., p. 164.

tions occasionally attained;* the date being A.D. 262, and the language what Mr. Turnour calls "the abstruse idiom and phraseology employed in regal and sacred documents."†

The devotees are to rise at dawn, to meditate on the four preservative principles, to perform ablutions, to attire themselves in yellow robes, to resort to a neighbouring convent to perform religious offices, to partake of *conjee* (rice-water) and rice, and duly to serve such members as are prevented attending through sickness. Twelve cells are assigned to those who expound the Abhidharma, seven to those who preach the Sutras, and five to the students of the Vinaya. The regulations regarding property provide that donations made to devotees shall not be appropriated otherwise, but that all lands and products shall be enjoyed in common and not possessed individually. The regulations regarding servants require that no retainer shall be dismissed without the concurrence of the whole community; and amongst these retainers we find, overseers of villages, cooks, writers of accounts, and receivers of income. If the servants attached to *daageys, bogeys,* and *pilemageys* embezzle the offerings, they are to be punished by hard work: *daageys* being houses or sheds in which offerings to a neighbouring Dagoba are placed; *bogeys* being similar houses, placed under a Bo-tree, to receive the offerings to the tree; and *pilemagey* being a similar house with the addition of an idol or idols.‡ Some regulations have in view the protection of tenants upon temple-lands, from whom

* Eastern Monachism, p. 156.

† Epitome History in Ceylon Almanac, 1832.

‡ These are the words used in Mr. Armour's translation, and belong probably to the local vernacular.

fees must not be exacted, nor their cattle compelled to labour for the Vihara: hereditary service fields shall not be resumed, and palm-trees, mee-trees, and other fruit-bearing trees shall not be felled without consent of the tenant. All temple-lands pay certain fees; but some lands are wholly set aside for the benefit of the Vihara, and the revenues of these lands, after paying the allotted wages, shall be entered in books, so that the whole may be under inspection. The items in these accounts were, expenditure on account of the Maha Patera (great bowl), hired servants, repairs.

Those who acted inconsistently with their yellow garments, by destroying life in the chase or otherwise, were to be expelled.

A second inscription of the same date, but upon a separate rock, specifies the exact sums to be given to Vihara servants, and is interesting from showing the services required; priests reading *bana* (sacred books) during the rainy season; priests reading *bana* at the conclusion of the rains; cook, florist, plasterer, scavenger, maker of sandals, one that spreads cloths on the ceiling, ditto on the floor, one who furnishes a water-strainer monthly, one who furnishes incense, oil, flowers for offerings; painters, carpenters, braziers, stone-cutters, goldsmiths, blacksmiths, lime-burners, washers of vestments and bed linen.

More than one hundred persons* are enumerated as servants to this monastery, and amongst these are a physician and a surgeon. In the time of Asoka, we are told that a devotee suffered dreadfully from a thorn in his foot, and that Asoka, hearing of this, reflected that a timely applica-

* Eastern Monachism, p. 156.

tion of a palmful of butter might have saved a dangerous ulcer, and decreed that in future, medicines should be dispensed daily at the four gates of the town of Patna. Whether or not this was the commencement of medical practice in Viharas need not be decided, but it is at any rate well ascertained that Buddhist devotees early studied the art of healing, and that the chief merit of the still-existing Viharas, or Lamasarais, in Tibet, is their knowledge of herbs, drugs, and surgery.

Relics carried from India to Ceylon intercepted by Nagas.

Demetrius.

CHAPTER IX.

"So roll, thou ancient Chronicle,
The ages' mist away."—ALFORD.

THE best Chroniclers of the ages succeeding King Asoka in Northern India are coins, and from these, and from such scant facts as are incidentally supplied by native and foreign histories, we learn that after the death of Asoka his large dominions fell into three divisions, each son or grandson becoming King of the province of which he was previously the viceroy. Sampadi, at Patna, and Kumala, at Taxila, were Buddhists, but Jaloka,* in Kashmere, adopted Saiva worship. Buddhists he persecuted, and Viharas he pulled down, until arrested by the apparition of a threatening Goddess, at whose suggestion he restored the ruined edifices; but so soon as he gained a victory over Euthydemus, then invading India, he instituted a festival of thanksgiving† to

* Lassen suggests that Jaloka, written probably for Jayaloka, means "Conqueror of the world," and is another name for the Northern King whom the Greeks call Sophagasenas.—Lassen, vol. ii. p. 273.

† Lassen, vol. ii. p. 274.

his favourite God Siva. Thenceforward we find but little mention of Hindu monarchs, and must take what facts we can from the coins and notices of Græco-Bactrians. Antiochus the Great advanced to take vengeance upon Euthydemus, who had declared himself an independent King in Bactria; but the great King was conciliated by Demetrius, the handsome son of Euthydemus, and a marriage took place between this youth and a daughter of Antiochus. The great King then pushed forward into India, and "renewed with Sophagasenas the treaty made with his predecessor;" which is understood to mean, that Antiochus renewed with *Jaloka* the treaty previously made with Asoka (or Piyadasi), to which allusion is made in the Edicts.* This treaty did not however deter Demetrius from subsequently invading India, and it is in token of successes in that country that he wears the elephant's head upon his helmet.

Whilst Demetrius was absent, Bactria was conquered by Eucratides, the Greek governor of Sogdiana. Castor and Pollux mounted, beautifully executed, are the prevailing device on the reverse of his coins. Those which are square have a bilingual inscription, Arianian on one face, Greek barbarized on the other. About fifty years later, Agathocles, who reigned where the grape-vine flourishes in the valleys of the Hindu Kush, wreathes vine-leaves round his head, fastens his fillet with a thyrsus, and has a vine and panther on the reverse of coins which bear a bilingual legend, the equivalent of the Greek being an alphabet of genuine Indian family. On a second series of Agathocles coins the legend is Greek only; on the reverse Jupiter holds in his outstretched hand a little three-headed Moon-

* Lassen, vol. ii. p. 273.

Goddess,* whilst the clumsy square copper coins of this same King bear on the reverse a woman dressed like an Indian dancing-girl, with a legend in old Indian (Pali) characters, "Nania," showing that she is the Anaites, Nanania, Ashtoreth, or Astarte, of Assyria. The coins of Menander give similar indications; but we must tarry no longer amongst the Greek Kings, whose numerous coins have all to find a place within little more than one hundred years, for B.C. 120 they are dethroned by a Scythian named Mayes,† calling himself King of Bactria, and imitating with his best endeavours the beautiful Greek coinage. This King and his successors are supposed to have held long contests with Menander and others, on whose coins are inscribed Soter (Saviour), in record of occasional success against the new intruders. About this same period, and contemporary both with Greeks and Scythians, another series of Kings or rulers has been discovered, through the medium of coins and rock inscriptions: these are the Sahs of Surashtra, or Guzerat, who flourished from B.C. 157 down to B.C. 57. Their coins are not without traces of fine workmanship, but one set of features is made to serve for the whole series, and although the face is in profile the eye is full-fronted: the features, mustachios, and earrings are of Indian character, whilst the reverse exhibits the heavenly bodies, a three-coned pyramid, and a waving line.‡ The pyramid has been supposed to be Mount Meru, and a waving line symbolizes water, so that the whole might typify "Mitra, Varuna, Aditi; Ocean, Earth, Heaven," the invocation with which the Vedic bard

* Wilson's Ariana, pp. 209, 297, 299. † Lassen, vol. ii. p. 371.
‡ Wilson's Ariana, p. 411.

Kutsa invariably concludes his hymns. But it is more probable that the Sahs combined the symbols of several diverse faiths, according to the prevailing spirit of the age.

Suddenly Greeks, Sahs, and Scythians vanish, and Vikramaditya, of Sanskrit celebrity, occupies the whole stage of Western India. This King's reign belongs to our Third Book, when Brahmanism gains the ascendency over Buddhism; the interruption it makes is very short, for about the year B.C. 24 the whole territory was once more under foreign sway. Scythians again descended from the table-lands of Asia, but Scythians of a different stamp from the barbarous hordes of King Azes. The Chinese call them Yu-chi, and they are supposed to be one with the White Huns of history and the Jats of modern India: evidently they were people of intellect, and worthy of descent from the original Zoroaster. All their coins exhibit objects of worship; the earlier ones indicate Persian fire-worship,—flames issue from the shoulders both of busts and standing figures, and the legend is *Ardethro*, God of Light; the word *Korano* follows the name of the King, a word supposed to indicate an elected King, it having been Scythian custom to choose from amongst the late King's sons the one most worthy to succeed him.* On later coins, the King's name and titles are written in ill-executed Greek characters, without any second legend in Arianian; and on the reverse appears Siva leaning upon his bull Nandi, his trident in hand, and his hair drawn up to a point like a flame; or instead of the flame he wears a cap surmounted by a crescent moon. On the reverses are inscribed,—*Helios*, the Sun-god, *Mao*, the Moon-god, *Nanaia*, the Moon-goddess, and

* Lassen, vol. ii. p. 827.

Athro, or *Ardethro*, the god of Fire. Nanaia we have already noticed upon the coins of Agathocles; she is the goddess mentioned in the Apocrypha, in whose temple Antiochus was slain.* Her worship seems to have taken strong hold of the people of the Kashmerian provinces with which we are at present occupied: her memory is still cherished in Afghanistan, Hindus and Mohammedans both invoking her as *Bibi Nani*, Lady Nani. Amongst other devices upon these coins, there is a running figure holding a large transparent veil, in which he seems about to envelope himself, whilst from his head radiate sunbeams; *Oado* is the legend, by some interpreted as Wind, but the appearance is much more in favour of his being the Sun† running through his daily course until enveloped in the veil of night. A figure holding a lance and having a nimbus with the legend *Pharo* is identified as an Iranian God of Rain.‡ Many others show Saiva attributes; the figure, sometimes a man, sometimes a woman, the dress Indian, the form occasionally classic, but oftener disfigured by four arms, or even six arms and three heads.

Thus far we find these Yu-chi Scythians adopting Greek coinage, and occasionally a Greek God or device, but leaning religiously toward the worship of fire and the heavenly bodies. But as their rule upon the confines of India became more established, we reach the fact on which our present interest in them is grounded. Upon the coins of a King Kanerki appears the image of Sakya Sinha, or

* "For when the leader was come into Persia, and the army with him, that seemed invincible, they were slain in the Temple of Nania, by the deceit of Nania's priests."—2 Maccabees iv. 13. Wilson's Ariana, p. 362.

† Wilson, p. 362.

‡ Lassen, vol. ii. pp. 827, 842.

Buddha, this name being apparently a variety of the name Kanishka, who was a King well known both to Brahmanical and Buddhist literature as a zealous protector and promoter of Buddhism. On a copper cylinder found in an adjacent tope, the name is Kanishka, and also in the inscription on a great stone covering the relic-cell in this tope.* The coins bearing the name of Kanerki are very numerous, the same probably belonging to several successive kings, and the whole series is known consequently as the Kanerki coins. Upon those of Oerki the words Adi Buddha† have been detected, and at this epoch Buddha's

Gold Cup.‡

image is often represented with flames at the shoulder, in imitation of Magian symbolism; an image of this kind, found in Tirhut, is figured in the fourth volume of the

* Lassen, vol. ii. p. 1177.

† Adi Buddha simply means First Buddha, the doctrine Adhi Buddha, the Supreme, belongs to a later period.—Lassen, vol. ii. p. 1176.

‡ Wilson's Ariana, plate iv.

'Bengal Journal.' A large head of Buddha with snakes* on his head may be seen in the same Journal, and on a gold cup found in the Manikyala Tope we see Buddha's head surmounted by flames. At this stage of symbolism, lions and snakes are used as couches and footstools, either for Sivas or Buddhas, and Siva doctrine and formulas of magic are intruded amongst the Buddhist sacred books. This demoralizing confusion was not however permitted to prevail entirely unchecked, and although the coinage of the Kanerki princes gives evidence of wide latitudinarianism, Buddhist hierarchs at length obtained an ascendency; this is admitted even in a Brahmanical Sanskrit history called the 'Raja Tarangini,' where it is said that three kings of Turushka descent reigned in Kashmere, each of whom founded a town which bore his name; they were protectors of virtues, and built *viharas*, schools, and *chaityas* (topes or dagobas); during the long period of their rule the whole of Kashmere was the enjoyment of Buddhists, and Nagarjuna was the spiritual lord. From the Chinese we learn that these *Turushka* Princes were so formidable that young Princes from China were sent to them as hostages; the Court residing in winter in India, in the spring and autumn at Candahar, and during the heat of summer up in the mountains to the north of Kabul. "And now," says the Ceylon history, "the yellow robes glittered (again) in Kashmere, and Hushka, Jushka, and Kanishka . . . founded colleges and *chaityas*." The *Nagas* of this country were converted, it will be remembered, in the reign of Asoka,† but the numerous topes and architectural remains with which it abounds appear to be referable to

* Lassen, vol. v. p. 484.

† Mahawanso, ch. xii.

the rule of the Kanerkis. They consist of tumuli common to many ancient nomadic tribes, under the protection of a mound or dagoba characteristic of Buddhism, and accompanied by fragments of the architecture and sculpture of Viharas, exhibiting beauty unaccountable unless explained in the same way as we account for the good workmanship of the coins, by supposing that when the Greeks were forced to abandon the country they left workmen who had profited by their instruction. Judging by their coins, these Scythic kings wavered for a time between Mithraic worship, Saiva worship, and Buddhism, but finally united the three, taking Mithraic symbols of flame and the heavenly bodies and belief in Swayambhava, joined with the general forms and doctrines of the Buddhists. During the reign of Kanishka, a great Buddhist assembly or convocation was held in Kashmere, which repudiated many Sivaite compositions; some objectionable Tantras were however retained, unwillingly as Burnouf thinks, even hierarchs not having power to exclude compositions which had become so popular. The leader of this fourth Buddhist assembly was Nagarjuna, or Nagasena, the name being spelt in both ways: he was born in Berar (Vidharba), and is supposed to have been sixty years old when he put forth his celebrated philosophical system, known as the Madhyamika.* His delight was in transcendentalism,—"Wisdom arrived at the other shore," and his works are still popular in Ceylon, although his doctrine is called by Burnouf "scholastic nihilism," for he doubts everything, and to this circumstance his school is supposed to owe its name, *Madhyamika*, intermediate. The following are examples of his negative

* Lassen, vol. ii. p. 1163, *note*.

mode of argument:—"Thought does not see thought: it is like the blade of a sword, which cannot cut that blade; it is as the extremity of a finger which cannot touch that finger. . . . Thought or mind is the object to be examined: that which is not apprehended (by the senses) is not perceived; that which is not perceived is neither past, future, nor present; that which is neither past, future, nor present has no proper nature; that which has no proper nature has no origin; that which has no origin has no distinction." And again it is asserted that Buddha himself is nothing,—a word, an illusion, a dream."* Herein Nagarjuna differs essentially from the Brahman philosophers, who, as we have seen, assert "the perpetuity of the subject." The book containing this, and much more to the same effect, claims to have been written by Nagarjuna, and Nagarjuna claims to have been the friend and spiritual adviser of Kanishka. Possibly Nagarjuna taught, like the Greek philosophers, one doctrine for the initiated and another for the public; for his name is appended to a Tantra work on magic circles, which is described as "miserable in doctrine, odious and degrading in principle."† Or perhaps the Kanerkis allowed him to direct Viharas and colleges, but reserved to themselves the privilege of worshipping universally. We might even imagine that they worshipped Nagarjuna himself; for on some of the later coins of the series the obverse (where a figure of the King usually appears) is occupied by a holy personage, who sits upon snakes, with one hand elevated, in the act of teaching.‡ This looks very much as though

* Burnouf, Introduction, pp. 561, 562.

† *Ibid.*, p. 558.

‡ Wilson's Ariana, Plate xiii., 8, 10.

Lama worship had then begun, Nagarjuna being the Lama, or Teacher, and the snakes an allusion to his name. Manjusri of Nipal is another saint, who acts a similar part. He was born twice for the benefit of mankind: on the first occasion B.C. 200, when he peopled Nipal; the second time in the first century of our era, when he taught the celebrated formula "Om mani padma hum." *Om* being the mysterious tri-literal monosyllable sacred to Brahmans before Buddhism existed; *Mani* meaning jewel, *padme*, lotus, and *hōm* or *hum*, something analogous to Amen. In Nipal Manjusri is still worshipped; but in Tibet the invocation "Om mani" is addressed to Padmasri, a saint or deity who has no human history or name. He is represented as a graceful youth, bearing in his hands a jewel and a lotus; but in the sacred books his name is Avalokiteswara, and his history is given in a legend called 'The Basket of the Good Qualities of the Saint Avalokiteswara.' In this work he is shown to be the same with Padma-pani, and declared to be *the* Buddha of this era; which is in itself the Lama doctrine of successive divine hierarchs. A second version of this legend in verse is much more in detail, and contains the important addition of "Adi-buddha." "At the commencement," it says, "Adibuddha, the Self-Existent, called Swayambhu, appeared in the form of a flame. From the spirit of Adibuddha . . . emanated Avalokiteswara," and also five Dhyani Buddhas, white, yellow, red, blue, green. The whole vault of heaven is filled with Buddhas, Dhyani Buddhas, Pratyeka Buddhas, Bodhisatwas, Arhats, Aryas, and Sramanas, Adibuddha being seated on the summit. The date assigned to the poem is about A.D. 1200. Dhyani Buddhas may have sprung into notice some centuries earlier, but they were peculiar to Nipal, and never recognized in the mythologies of other Buddhist countries.*

We have now traced the outline of the course which Buddhism took in northern India, when checked in the more central provinces, our object being to watch the variations adopted when it encountered foreign faiths. In Ceylon, where it was insulated, it has retained the Indian stamp; but even there a periodical succession of Buddhas is believed in, and statues are raised to Maitreya, as the Buddha who will next be born on earth. This is a very slight sketch of a very complicated subject; but to fill it up would be always tedious and often impossible, and it must suffice if it but indicate the relation which Sakya Sinha's original movement bears to the cumbrous Buddhism of later ages.

* Wilson, Buddha and Buddhism, p. 27.

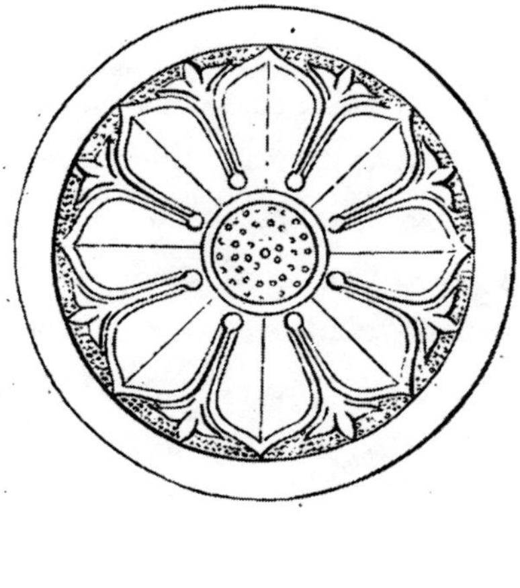

CHAPTER X.

"The evidence of others is not comparable to personal experience; nor is 'I heard' so good as 'I saw.'"—*Chinese Maxims*, J. F. DAVIS.

DURING seven or eight centuries after the Christian era, Buddhists were in turn patronized, neglected, and persecuted by the Kings of India. At one period a long series of coins exhibits Buddhist symbols; at another time we find Buddhist Viharas and Ascetics tolerated in a Sanskrit Brahmanical drama; and, in other ways, we learn that Buddhists chased from the Ganges took refuge in Nipal, or we discover them amongst the volcanic hills of the Dekkan, where we shall have occasion to notice their wonderful excavations. But before taking up the subject of Buddhist architecture, it will be interesting to learn in what condition the religion appeared to Chinese Buddhists visiting India during the early centuries of our era. Fortunately the Chinese had not only the enterprise to come and see, but intelligence sufficient for recording their observations. "Depuis le quatrième siècle de notre ère jusqu'au dixième," says M. Stanislas Julien, "les pélerins Chinois qui sont allés dans les contrées situées à l'ouest de la Chine, et particulièrement dans l'Inde, pour étudier la doctrine du *Boud-*

dha et rapporter les livres qui la renferment, ont publié un grand nombre de relations, d'itinéraires, et de descriptions plus ou moins étendues des pays qu'ils ont visités." Generals and magistrates sent on Government missions were also in the habit of recording what they observed, for the interests of war, politics, and commerce; one of these works being in sixty volumes, with forty books of drawings and maps; but unfortunately this valuable collection, and most of the other works, are lost or hidden, and only known through the mention made of them in Chinese Encyclopædias.* The earliest book of Chinese Travels extant is what Rémusat calls "Fo-koue-ki, ou Relation des Royaumes Bouddhiques." It is the work of a Chinese Buddhist, named Fa-Hian, who left the western capital of China A.D. 399. He writes in the third person, and commences, "Formerly Fa-Hian was afflicted to see the precepts and the theological works on the verge of destruction, and already injured by omissions. For this reason he departed, accompanied by several companions, to seek in India the laws and precepts of the religion."† He gives a striking description of the "river of sand," which is the desert where our contemporaries, MM. Huc and Gabet, suffered so much from burning winds, they having started precisely in the same direction; but as in the time of Fa-Hian Lhassa had not attained Buddhist celebrity, he and his companions crossed the "Montagne de Grandpère Blanc" further to the west, and visited Khotan, where they witnessed the ceremonies performed on the first day of the fourth moon. The streets were swept, watered, and decorated. Curtains were

* Stanislas Julien, Preface to Trans. Hiouen-Thsang, p. 111.

† Rémusat's translation.

hung before the gates. The King and the Queen and a company of beautiful women were seated on a pavilion above the principal gate. Presently a great procession of images approached, the images being placed within pavilions drawn upon cars: when the procession was within a hundred paces of the gate, the King descended to give it welcome. He took off his tiara, put on new clothes, and with naked feet prostrated himself before the chief image, and paid homage by scattering flowers and burning incense. As the images passed through the gate, the ladies on the pavilion above threw down so great a profusion of flowers as to cover the car. Festivals of this description were numerous, each having appropriate cars, and each Temple making its own distinct procession. The travellers were lodged in a Vihara (or convent) built in a square, where all the occupants took their repast in common; no noise was heard from basins or platters, and no word was uttered during meals. The religious buildings of this town are described as peculiarly magnificent: one temple was eighty-four years in building, occupying three kings' reigns. Sculptures are particularized, and gold and silver images decorated with precious stones, also gilded windows and doorposts of gold.

Whilst amongst these mountains, probably at Ladak, the five-yearly Assembly took place, to which Buddhists from all quarters came and assembled like clouds, with pomp and gravity. The Hall of Assembly was decorated with banners and hangings, a throne of rich silk adorned with gold and silver lotus-flowers, and below the throne elegant seats. The King and his ministers were in attendance, and performed their devotions according to the law. This ceremony is usually held in spring, and lasts one, two, or three months; and when it is over, Fa-Hian remarks that the King, his ministers, and other persons of distinction, give their horses, shawls, and whatever they have of value to the Sramanas (priests) or Assembly, and afterwards purchase them all back again. This country is so cold that grain is ripened with difficulty; but as it was observed that the snow never came on until the Sramanas were provided for, the King forbade them to receive their annual supplies until the whole harvest was gathered in. The devotees of this region are remarked by Fa-Hian as using praying-wheels or cylinders. He also observes that, in travelling towards the west, each kingdom has a different language, all barbarous; but that, although a barbarous vernacular is the spoken language, the sacred books are written in the language of India, which is studied in the numerous convents, where strangers are warmly welcomed, entertained for three days, and then dismissed. He sees the gigantic statue of Maitrya, which on certain occasions glistens with light, and he visits the scenes of all the extravagant legends of Buddha's sacrifices, and sees the Pillars set up in commemoration. Proceeding further east, he comes to the town where the begging-dish of Sakya Sinha refused to be stolen by the King of the Yu-chi: he put it on an elephant, but the elephant would not move; he put it in a car, but the car could not be stirred; so the King turned devotee, raised a dagoba to hold the dish, and built a Vihara for seven hundred holy men. A little before midday these holy men, all dressed in white, take the precious dish from its enclosure, pay homage, burn perfumes, and in the evening put it back into its shrine.* That *white* should be the dress adopted in this

* Fa-Hian, ch. xii. p. 77.

convent is worthy of remark, because the holy men represented in the paintings from the Caves of Ajunta* are mostly in white; whereas Buddhist literature gives white as the dress of laymen, and yellow as the distinguishing colour of religious robes.

In another town, probably Jellalabad, he speaks of the bones of Buddha's skull, guarded by eight royal ministers, each of whom daily affixes his seal to the door of the dagoba in which they are enshrined. Every morning this relic is placed upon a throne, the King and Court come to offer flowers and perfumes, and priests mounted on an elevated pavilion sound drums, conch-shells, and copper cymbals. In India, the places of Buddha's birth and of all the remarkable events of his life, are visited, and legends of the utmost extravagance or *development* are recounted; snakes or *nagas* are also mentioned with reverence; and a story is told of elephants who did temple-service in an abandoned Vihara, where "the elephants are seen to come taking water in their trunks to water the ground;" this may possibly explain the device on the pillars at Kennary, where elephants sprinkle water upon dagobas.† The woods, he says, are filled with monuments, but he could not visit them from their being so much infested by tigers and white elephants; from which we may infer that the present formidable Tarai, or jungle, was even then beginning to encroach upon human habitations.

At another place, apparently in Oude, a little snake, or

* See pictures now in the Crystal Palace, Sydenham.

† Fergusson, Rock-cut Temples, p. 36. It is also the subject of a bas-relief on the eastern gate of the Bhilsa Topes.—Major A. Cunningham, p. 212.

naga, whose ears were edged with white, was fed and worshipped daily. In this neighbourhood also Fa-Hian visited the "Grove of Restored Sight." The legend is, that five hundred blind men had taken up their abode here; that Buddha preached the law in their favour; that they recovered their sight; that each man stuck his staff in the ground and turned in adoration towards the temple, and that when they looked round again their staves had all taken root and were growing into trees. Fa-Hian found the devout inhabitants of the neighbouring Vihara in the habit of resorting to this grove for contemplation after dinner.

When Fa-Hian reached the kingdom of Magadha he found Buddhism held in great respect. Kings and nobles had given fields, houses, gardens, orchards, farms, and cattle to the Viharas, and recorded their donations upon plates of iron; and the Buddhist communities being thus provided with houses, lands, food, and clothing, constantly occupied themselves with good works and the study of their sacred books. Some of the Viharas adhered to the simple Sutras; but generally Fa-Hian found what he calls *la grande translation* very much preferred. The colleges, he says, are built in a grave majestic style, and *Sramanas* from all quarters of the globe make them their resort. Hospitals were also established, at which the poor, the lame, and the sick of the surrounding country received food and medical relief. No wine was drunk in these Buddhist countries, and neither wine-houses nor shambles were found within their towns. Garlic and onions, pork and poultry were forbidden; and the only people allowed to hunt or sell meat were Chandalas, whose very name

Fa-Hian explains as "odious;" "their dwellings," he says, "are separate from those of other men; and when they enter a town or market they are obliged to strike on a piece of wood to announce their presence." This custom is still in force in southern India; the more favoured races requiring the unhappy outcasts to give sufficient warning to enable them to escape all contact.

The Kings of these prosperous districts took off their tiaras to do homage to the priests; and both Kings and nobles gave food with their own hands to the *Sramanas*, and then sat near them on a carpet, but never occupied a raised seat if a priest were present. Capital punishments were not allowed, but fines resorted to instead, or, in extreme cases, the right hand was amputated. The only money mentioned by the Chinese journalist is cowrie-shells. "In the kingdom of Magadha," says Fa-Hian, "the towns and villages are large; the people rich, fond of discussion, but compassionate and just in action; and the paintings and sculptures such as this age could not produce." He then proceeds to describe a grand annual festival, when a tower of lances is erected upon cars, which are covered with hangings representing images of all the celestial divinities. These hangings are so arranged that each corner is attached to a little image of Buddha surrounded by Bodhisatwas. On these occasions the streets are crowded, and the people entertained with theatrical representations and gymnastic exhibitions; flowers and perfumes are scattered in profusion, and when night falls the whole scene is illuminated by lanterns. Fa-Hian mentions a pillar on which is inscribed, "The great Asoka gave . . . to the religious of the four quarters: he ransomed it from them for money, and this he did three times." At a town called Nili he saw another pillar surmounted by a lion, with an inscription recording the foundation of the town. Fa-Hian was altogether so much delighted with Magadha, and with the grave sedate deportment of the Sramanas, that he remained three years in the kingdom; and hoped if in future he should become Buddha he might be born in Magadha, and not on the eastern frontier, where the Sramanas "neglected the precepts and transgressed in their *devoirs*."*

Fa-Hian's companions returned from Magadha to China; but his first desire being that the precepts should penetrate the Land of Han, he embarked on the Ganges, arrived in sadness at Tamlouk, and proceeded to Ceylon, which he calls the "Island of Lions." He there finds *bana* (the Law, or sacred books) being read publicly three times every month, halls being erected at every four crossway for the purpose. But image-worship was also fully established; and an image of blue jasper, holding in its hand a pearl of inestimable value, was to our traveller "dazzling and majestic beyond expression." Many years had now elapsed since Fa-Hian had quitted his native country; and always speaking in the third person he says, "The people with whom he had had intercourse had all been people of strange countries. The mountains, the rivers, the herbage, the trees, all that met his eyes was new to him. And of those with whom he had first started, some had separated from him, others had remained behind, and others were dead. In reflecting on the past his heart was filled with thought and sadness. Suddenly, by the side of the jasper figure he saw a merchant making an offering to the statue of a Fan of

* Ch. xxxvi.

white silk from the country of Tsin (China); although unperceived, this caused him so much emotion that tears ran down his cheeks."

Fa-Hian also found the tooth-relic enjoying a full measure of popular esteem, and thus describes a festival held in its honour:—"Ten days previously, the King having carefully chosen a large elephant, a preacher arrayed in royal robes mounts, and, striking the drum, proclaims Buddha's chief merits as,—'He abandoned the Queen his wife; he tore out his eyes to give them to another man; he cut his flesh to ransom a pigeon; he threw his body to a hungry tiger; he spared neither his marrow nor his bones: . . . it is thus by practising austerities and macerations for all living beings that he succeeded in becoming Buddha.'" Ten days afterwards the tooth is carried to Mehenteli, pictures of the five hundred manifestations of Buddha being placed upon the sides of the road. Amongst these manifestations are mentioned his transformation into "Lightning," into "the King of the Elephants," and into the "Wonderful Horse." During its whole progress the tooth is surrounded by successive crowds of worshippers, and when it arrives at the mountain of Mehenteli it is carried up to the hall of Buddha, where thick clouds arise from burning perfumes, and where lamps are kept lighted, and religious acts are practised uninterruptedly for ninety days and nights.*

* The tooth-relic is scarcely less honoured now than it was in the days of Fa-Hian, only it follows the Court, and has migrated with the Royal family from Anaradhapura to Kandy. Images are also universal in Ceylon, and often of gigantic size, and a building erected for the occupation of an image is usually well built, and covered with tiles; in Burmah these are gilded, but even in Ceylon the house of the image is made more costly than the houses for priests.

About two centuries later, another eminent Chinese undertook this difficult pilgrimage, safely returned to his native land, and handed down to posterity a record of his impressions. Hwan Tsang was the son of a much-esteemed man of letters, who lived a life of study in retirement. Hwan Tsang describes his father as tall, with kindly eyebrows and brilliant eyes, wearing ample vestments and a broad girdle, which gave him the air of one of the *literati*. Hwan Tsang was the youngest of four sons, grave from childhood, and showing wonderful intelligence; one of his elder brothers took him with him to his convent, thinking him well suited to become a teacher of the doctrine of Buddha. The Emperor published a decree that twenty-seven members of this convent should be ordained, and although Hwan Tsang was too young to be a candidate, he was selected on account of his distinguished ability. He was at this time only thirteen years of age, but he studied with ardour, comprehended quickly, and never forgot what he had once acquired. Political disturbances interrupting study in the capital, the brothers retired to the country where they shed tears of joy at meeting two renowned teachers from the west.

As soon as he has attained his twentieth year, Hwan Tsang is fully admitted as a monastic member, and during the following summer he studies the books called the Vinaya, the Sutras, and the Shastras. He sometimes meets with passages which he cannot understand, and seeks help from the studious at other convents. He is however constantly called upon to take a part in religious discussions, from which he uniformly retires victorious: he nevertheless perseveres in trying to get his own difficulties solved, and as the sacred books themselves are proved to contain many contradictory texts, he resolves to travel to the West, in imitation of Fa-Hian: he is told that the route is difficult and full of peril, but he sounds his heart and satisfies himself that his courage is equal to the undertaking. The Government forbids his journey, and he is obliged to depart secretly and alone. He prays to the statue of Maitreya for a guide, and a guide appears: his guide afterwards fails him and he meets with various adventures, until he reaches the sandy desert; he is perishing for want of water, and does not know his way, but he prays without ceasing to Avalokiteswara, saying: "Hwan Tsang seeks neither riches nor profit, praise nor reputation, his only aim is the acquirement of superior intelligence and of the correct law. I feel, O Bodhisattwa! that your affectionate heart is constantly occupied with delivering creatures from the pains of life, and never were there more cruel pains than those I suffer. Canst thou be ignorant of them?" He thus prayed until the middle of the fifth night, when suddenly he was refreshed by a cooling breeze; a voice spoke, a vision appeared, his horse took a different direction, and he arrived in fertile pastures and beside sweet waters.* Hwan Tsang took a more northerly course than Fa-Hian, and visited I-gou, a place identified as Hami, or Khamil: here the King strives to attach him to his service, and his anxiety to retain a learned Buddhist at his Court is so great that when Hwan Tsang declines he uses compulsion, absolutely forbidding his departure. The Sage is firm, and steadily refuses food, until on the fourth day the King gives way, but makes two requests; first, that on his return he will live

* These deserts were still haunted by spirits in the days of Marco Polo. See Preface Stan. Julien, p. xli.

at his Court three years; and secondly, that when he is born again as Buddha, he, the King of I-gou, shall be his patron, as Bimbisara and Praesnajit were of Sakya Sinha. Hwan Tsang spent a month with this zealous King, holding conferences and teaching and receiving profound homage. When the conferences are concluded, the King presents the Chinese travellers with warm dresses, masks, gloves, and boots to defend them from the cold they were about to encounter: he also gave Hwan Tsang satin, silk, horses, and servants, and twenty-four letters of recommendation to the Khans, or Kings, whose territories he wished to traverse, each letter being accompanied by a piece of rich satin. Hwan Tsang feeling overcome by such great liberality, addressed a letter of gratitude to the King, which commences: "Hwan Tsang has heard that whoever desires to traverse a great river or a deep ocean has need of a boat and oars," and he proceeds to show at great length that Buddha has furnished such a boat, and that his doctrine had reached China more than six hundred years ago, but that, owing to the great distance from the country of Buddha, the translations and interpretations of texts had become incorrect and contradictory, and that on this account he had undertaken to visit the scenes in which Buddha first promulgated the Law. He concludes with compliments to the King, on the blessings which he secures to his kingdom of I-gou, and also to the countries of Leou-lau and Yu-chi. Once returned to China, he says, "I will translate the Books, I will promulgate the unknown truths, I will hew down the forest of error, I will destroy false doctrine, I will restore omissions in the doctrine of the Elephant; perhaps by these poor merits I may respond to your immense benefits. Tomorrow

I must take leave of your Majesty, and my heart is torn by the idea of the separation."

From Khamil our traveller still pursued a western route, going to the north of Lake Lob and crossing the mountain now called Mussur Durban, the snowy scenery of which he describes with great effect. After much suffering from cold and hunger he descends upon the borders of the vast Lake Issikul, or Temourtou; and here they find a Khan, rich in horses, occupied in hunting, and wearing a green satin mantle and a bandeau of ribbon with long ends fastened at the back of his head, like the Tartar and Parthian kings in Wilson's 'Ariana.' He was surrounded by officers dressed in brocade mantles, with their hair twisted or plaited, and a troop of men mounted on camels or horses, with garments of fine wool or fur, and bearing long lances, bows and arrows, and banners. The royal residence was a tent ornamented with flowers of gold and protected in front by mats. But although this Khan was a barbarian, living in a tent of felt, it was impossible, says our traveller, not to regard him with admiration and respect. These people adored fire, and would not sit upon wood because wood contained fire: they were very convivial, enjoyed noisy music, and regaled themselves with wine, mutton, veal, rice, cream, sugar, etc. After the repast was over, Hwan Tsang was requested to explain the Law: he taught them the ten virtues, love for living creatures, and the means of arriving at the other shore, or final deliverance. The Khan lifted his hands, threw himself on the ground, and declared that he received this instruction with faith. He then endeavoured to persuade his guest not to go further. "India," he said, "is very hot, their tenth moon resembling our fifth moon, and to judge by your appearance you would be dissolved. The inhabitants are nearly naked, have no respect for propriety, and do not deserve your presence." Hwan Tsang again expresses his ardent desire to seek the Law of Buddha and trace his steps amongst the monuments of antiquity; and the Khan then made search in his army for a good linguist and with his help prepared letters of recommendation, and on parting presented Hwan Tsang with a red satin religious dress and fifty pieces of silk. After passing through a desert where heaps of bones are the only sign-posts, the travellers arrive in Samarkand, where the inhabitants worship fire, do not believe in Buddha, and are inhuman savages, until Hwan Tsang teaches them the Law and induces them to abandon all their barbarous customs. From Samarkand he goes through a Pass called the Gates of Iron, the precipitous rocks of which contain iron and are surmounted by bells of wrought-iron and cast-iron.

He now crosses the Oxus and arrives at Balk, where he is charmed with its magnificent site, commanding a view of universally fertile plains and villages. He mentions one hundred convents within the town, and many other monuments connected with Buddhism. Here he resided above a month, receiving much honour from Kings and priests; and again crossing snowy mountains he arrives at Bamian, where the King invites him to his palace. The objects of interest in this town are numerous, and he remains a fortnight; then loses his way, blinded by a snow-storm, in the hills, and meets with hunters who guide him to Kabul. All the members of the one hundred Viharas, with the King at their head, come out to receive and invite him; and he is perplexed to know which to prefer, until one

Convent urges the irresistible claim of having been originally built for the accommodation of a Chinese Prince (sent as a hostage). The memory of this Prince was held in great honour, and his image represented upon all the walls of the building. He had enriched the convent in many ways; and in anticipation of its requiring repairs, had deposited gold under the right foot of a statue of Buddha. This money was now required, the cupola of a stupa or dagoba having fallen into ruins, but the money could not be got, the earth groaning and trembling terrifically whenever any one approached the spot. Hwan Tsang is entreated to lend his influence: he burns perfumes before the statue and makes a petition, promising himself to weigh the treasure and prevent unnecessary expenditure. He then commands the workmen to dig, and at a depth of about seven or eight feet a copper vase is found containing several hundred pounds' weight of gold, and a quantity of carbuncles.*

On all occasions Hwan Tsang shows great reverence for relics, giving at one time fifty pieces of gold, one thousand pieces of silver, four banners of silk, two pieces of brocade, and two religious dresses, after which he scattered a profusion of flowers.† He alludes to all the legends mentioned by Fa-Hian and others in addition, but these it is unnecessary to repeat. To dwell upon his accurate geographical descriptions would be more interesting, but inconsistent with our present purpose. We will therefore merely notice that in Kashmere he studies the works of a disciple of Nagarjuna, refers to the conversion of the Nagas (or inhabitants of the country), and to the great

* Hwan Tsang, p. 74.

† *Ibid.*, 78.

council called by King Kanishka for the revision of the Buddhist books.* On this occasion he says sacred texts were engraved on sheets of copper, enclosed in a cell of stone, sealed, ornamented with an inscription, and surrounded and surmounted by a stupa.† In Kashmere our traveller remained two years, and then proceeded to the Ganges: he sees great numbers of Viharas and Buddhist monuments; sometimes the Vihara is sixty feet high, and the monument a cupola of stone over a statue of wood. In Shravasti (in Oude) the buildings were in ruins; and in Kapila-vastu, the kingdom of Sakya Sinha's father, ten deserted towns are noted. At Raja-griha, in Magadha,‡ or Behar, he saw many memorials of the King Asoka, and esteemed himself fortunate in being received into a convent where an aged man resided who had been favoured by a personal interview with the celestial beings known as Avalokiteswara, Mandjusri, and Maitreya.

He speaks of the religious edifices of Nalanda, a neighbouring village, as surpassing those in other parts of India. The dwelling-houses, or Viharas, have four stories; and the pavilions (Chaityas, or temples) are adorned with pillars, paintings, sculptures, and precious stones. The sectarians of the eighteen schools, he says, are collected in the *Samgharamas* of Nalanda,§ where they study every kind of work, from "les livres vulgaires, les Védas," up to works on medicine, the occult sciences, and arithmetic.

After an absence of seventeen years Hwan Tsang returned

* Hwan Tsang, 95. † *Ibid.*, 96.

‡ Magadha is that portion of Behar which lies to the south of the Ganges.—Hwan Tsang, Preface, p. lx.

§ Hwan Tsang, 151.

across the mountains to China, where he is received with great honour by the Emperor, who wished to make him his prime minister; but the sagacious Traveller objects, that he is unqualified, having never studied Confucius, the soul of administration, and that a religious life is his desire. The Emperor wishes he would accompany his army; but Hwan Tsang says that his principles forbid combats and bloodshed, and at length obtains leave to retire to a convent amongst the hills far away from the sounds of markets and villages, where he may translate in peace the six hundred sacred books brought with him from India.

CHAPTER XI.

ARCHITECTURE.

"And some in marble mould
Have toil'd with form and mien
That unportrayed image to unfold,
And named some fabled thing unseen—
Something they know not, yet would love,
Apollo, Pallas, Jove,—
Then turn away; 't is in the bosom pent,
And all that art can do is vain and impotent."

WILLIAMS.

HEATHENS, no less than Christians, feel a yearning of the heart for something beyond the gratification of worldly wants and vanities. This yearning Buddhists mainly sought to express by memorial monuments. They were philosophers; they did not ascend hill-tops like the Persian, and prostrate themselves before the infinity of God's horizon; they did not, like their fathers, watch for the rising sun as the emblem of "all that has been or will be," nor, like their Vedic ancestors, did they kindle sacred fire, sending flames up as messengers to Deity. They were philosophers, and neither sun-worship, nor fire-worship, nor Indra-worship satisfied their wants: they felt all these ceremonies as superficial tinsel, or cumbersome coverings to the inner core of truth. But, like Thomas in the Tale of the Tub, in trying to tear off the gold-lace they also tore away the coat; or, to change the metaphor, they rejected every component of the religious atmosphere until, under the painful pressure of a vacuum, they welcomed a mirage and adored their Teacher's Relic-shrine.

We have already had occasion to observe that Buddhism was an attempt to make general, doctrines hitherto restricted to learned and privileged classes. But the public cannot accept abstractions, and the more vague and negative the doctrine, the more absolute its demand for visible types and images; and consequently in every country the foot-prints of Buddhism are gigantic monuments, pillars, towers, caves, and temples. This architecture is divided into four classes:—

1. Funeral Mounds and Relic-shrines.
2. Pillars and Towers to commemorate events.
3. Convents or Viharas.
4. Chaitya, Caves, or Temples.

Of these by far the most conspicuous class is that first-named, and monuments of this description, have so constantly accompanied Buddhism that an inclination has arisen to treat all traces of analogous mounds or monuments as indications of Buddhism. But this assumes too much; for although we know that Buddhists made memorial mounds and monuments, we are far from knowing that all memorial mounds and monuments were made by Buddhists. The fact is, that our earliest evidence of such monuments in

India dates about two hundred years B.C.; whereas Tumuli are found all over the world, giving traces of the first wanderers on the face of the earth, or recording names the earliest known to history. In the high plains of Asia, and in the Peninsula of India, in ancient Lydia and Greece, in Etruria and Sardinia, and in Scandinavia and Great Britain may such remains be seen. The tomb is usually circular, with inner chambers and an entrance, the outside occasionally ornamented with steles, like the tomb of Alyattes in Sardis; and the inner tomb being sometimes concealed and closed by another built outside it, as the Regulini Galassi tomb in Etruria.

The original cell is usually square, composed of six flat stones, with earth heaped up around in the form of a circular mound; and on certain occasions the whole is raised upon a hill or artificial platform, and surrounded by one or more circles of upright stones or pillars. Sometimes however hundreds of uncovered stone sepulchres are found in secluded valleys and groves. Captain Newbold describes such tombs as scattered throughout southern India,—left in secluded spots by races of whom tradition is silent. "It is certain," he says, "that they are not the sepulchres of any of the sects of Buddha, Jineswara, or Brahma, or of the snake-worshippers who preceded them. Whose bones then do these huge blocks of granite cover? Throw down one of the side slabs, with its circular aperture, and we have the cromlech or dolmen. Clear away the Cyclopean superstructure, and we behold the Druidical circles and the cairn. If we turn our eyes northerly to the mountains of Circassia, we there start with surprise on seeing an absolute facsimile of the mysterious tombs of southern India, with the circular aperture:"* which tomb is thus figured in Bell's work.†

It is hidden in a forest, and nothing is known of its history. The dimensions of its prototypes in India are about five feet by nine for the side-slabs, with a roof measuring thirteen feet by twelve. The ancient tombs described by Pallas, south of the Yenisec, in Siberia, "of enormous size, usually surrounded by flat or upright stones," are also left by unknown people who have vanished. Similar to these are the monuments of our own native Isles, formerly called Druidical, as, The Ring of Stennis in the Island of Orkney, a prostrate cromlech, lying "beside the gigantic ruins of the circle which once enclosed it;" and the cromlech or circle in Lamlash Bay. The antiquity of these northern remains is in many cases attested by their lying beneath an accumulation of slowly-formed peat-moss.‡ Sometimes the encircling stones are connected by flat stones, as at Stonehenge; but this appears to have been a modification of the older custom of single pillars, or monoliths. And almost universally the ancient cairns, cromlechs, tumuli, and tombs

* J. R. A. S., vol. xiii. pp. 90-94. † Bell's Circassia, p. 282.

‡ Archæology and Pre-Historic Annals of Scotland.—D. Wilson.

are traced to people who were not of the Sanskrit-speaking races, from whom we derive our origin, but of the mysterious people which preceded Hindus in India, Greeks in Greece, Romans in Italy, and Celts in Scandinavia and Great Britain. The subject deserves and requires much more research, but it seems evident that cromlechs, cairns, and effigies of serpents travelled westward with Turanian tribes who were often metal-workers; and that people of allied race in India (often called *Nagas*) made similar tombs independent of Buddhism, and previous to the rise of that religion. The people inhabiting the hills to the north of Sylhet make monuments of this description at the present time, and they appear to be a people allied in race with the Gonds, Koles, and other Aborigines of India; and, like the tomb-makers in Arcot and Scandinavia, the inhabitants of the Khasiya hills are metal-workers. Mr. Walters speaks of "two or three thousand monuments, great and small."* And, further to the north-east, Dr. Hooker sees at Nurtiung "several acres covered with gigantic, generally circular, slabs of stone, from ten to twenty-five feet broad, supported five feet above the ground upon other blocks." These monuments he mentions as a curious feature in the scenery of the mountains and in the habits of their savage population.

It seems therefore not unreasonable to conjecture that Buddhism adopted funeral mounds and monuments from the Turanian people, who were at all times its most numerous and enthusiastic supporters.

A most confusing variety of names has been given to these Buddhist monuments:—Tope and Stupa, meaning

* As. Res., vol. xvii. p. 500.

that they are lofty pyramidical structures; Dagoba, referring to their office as relic-shrines; and Chaitya, a word for sacred monuments of any kind, whether funereal or otherwise. The large Tope at Sanchi (Central India), described in Major Cunningham's valuable work, is probably one of

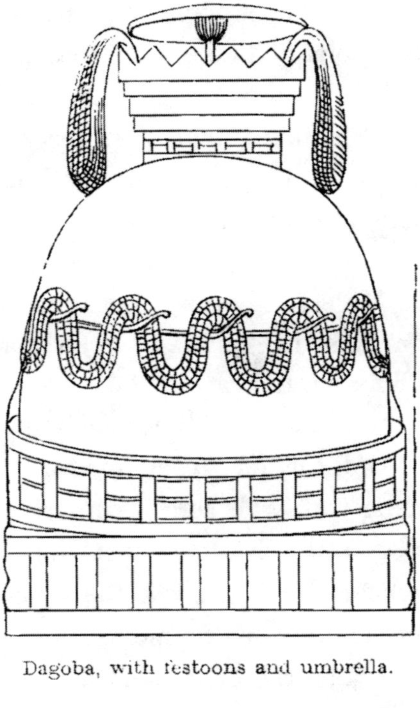

Dagoba, with festoons and umbrella.

the oldest yet remaining. It stands on the western edge of a hill, enclosed by a court one hundred and fifty yards by one hundred, which is entered by lofty gates facing north, south, east, and west. At three of the corners were small Topes, and at the fourth a small temple. The large Tope is a solid dome of brick and masonry, one hundred and six feet in diameter and forty-two feet in height, rising from a plinth of fourteen feet, which served as a terrace for

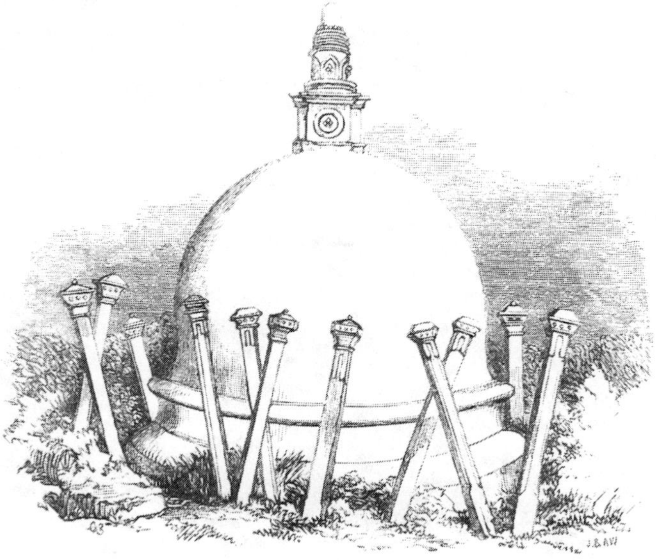

View of the Lanka Rama, a Dagoba to the north of Anuradhapura, in Ceylon, from a Sketch by Captain I. J. Chapman, F.R.S., of the Royal Artillery.

"Lanká-Rámo is situated to the north-west of the Maháwihára. It was erected by King Abha Sen, or Tisso, whose reign commenced A.D. 231. In 1829 it was in excellent preservation, having been repaired within the last century. The Dágoba was then coated with *chunam*, a most excellent kind of white cement, which has a resemblance to marble; and the pillars on the raised platform which sustains the dome had generally retained their places. The whole suggested how magnificent the others must have been in the days of their glory."—*Captain I. J. Chapman, Remarks on the City of Anurádhapura*, (Journn. R. As. Soc. xiii.)

the convenience of worshippers. The tallest of the Topes in the Punjab is nearly double this height, and is also solid, with the exception of chambers for relics at different heights. Of the same description are the celebrated ruins, called temples, in Ceylon: the Jeṭawana and the Thupa-Rama at Anuradhapura, and the beautiful ruin which crowns Mehenteli, are all alike mere relic-shrines, the Jetawana being a mass of brick-work sufficient for building a wall ninety-seven miles long, twelve feet high, and two feet broad. In Tibet, where first a conception of Adibuddha, the Supreme, and then of living Buddhas, has been added to original Buddhism, dagobas are unimportant; but in Burmah, where (as in Ceylon) Buddhism retains its first low level, we are startled to find that the grand edifice called the Shwe-dagon, three hundred feet in height, is not a temple in which to worship, but a solid pyramid, and itself the object to be worshipped.

The second form of Buddhist architecture consists of Towers and Pillars set up to commemorate an event or do honour to a building. When Jacob took a stone and set it up as a pillar, in token that the place wherein he had dreamed was "the Gate of Heaven," he adopted this primitive mode. Such pillars, carved or uncarved, are common all over the world, but we do not meet with them in India earlier than the Buddhist King Asoka. And always supposing that Asoka is one and the same with Piyadasi, he set up six or seven of these Laths, or columns, whereon to inscribe his Edicts. The capitals of these pillars are of the usual lotus-form,* and are encircled either

* Suggested, we imagine, from the appearance of a Lotus pericarp and stamens, after the fall of the petals. See Vignette, *ante*, p. 247.

with the reed and ball, or with the honeysuckle and lotus, which are the architectural ornaments of Greece and Assyria, whilst they are surmounted by lions or griffins, also significant of Assyria. These pillars are supposed to have stood, like the Jachin and Boaz of King Solomon, in front of some holy edifice, and one such pillar yet remains, watching like a sentinel at the entrance of the Viswakarma, Karli, and other celebrated Cave-Temples of western India.

Of towers erected with the same intent, the Tower of Babel was probably the earliest instance; but, although not uncommon at very early periods in western Asia, Buddhists appear first to have introduced them into India. Few of these erections now remain; but happily the custom survived when Buddhism became extinct, and two beautiful Towers of Victory may be seen in Central India, the one erected in the eighth and the other in the eleventh century.*

Viharas, or convents, constitute our next division; and these may be regarded as more radically Buddhist than any other form of Buddhist architecture. Sakya-muni himself

* See Fergusson's Illustrations of Architecture in Hindostan, pl. xi. 8.

required conventual residences, with numerous cells for his followers, and a central hall wherein to address them. Religious Brahmans had long been accustomed to dwell in hermitages apart from the bustle of life, and the *Brahmavarti,* of the Code of Manu, was a district celebrated for such *asramas.* But the genius of Buddhism required dwellings on a larger scale, and, as we have already remarked, it soon began to seek relief in the magnificence of architecture for the deadness of its worship.

The structural Viharas have all perished in India, but the Caves, which were fashioned in imitation of those wooden prototypes, yet remain to exhibit the stages by which their ultimate perfection was attained. The outline given above is from a Cuttack Cave of the simplest form,—a mere verandah added to a natural cavern. In such cases, the preaching-hall was a wooden building erected, when required, for periodical readings of the sacred books. By degrees the Verandahs became more decorated, and the sleeping-cells were arranged around a central hall; and at last we find twenty beautiful pillars supporting this hall, and its walls adorned by paintings,—copies of which adorn the Indian Court at Sydenham.

At Anuradhapura, in Ceylon, may be seen the remains of a grand Vihara, erected B.C. 161 by King Dushtagamini, called the Loha prasada, or, Loha maha paya, from *loha*, iron, its roof having been of metal. It had nine stories, each containing one hundred apartments; the whole was supported upon pillars of stone, and Baldæus honours it by marking Anuradhapura on his map as "the place of the thousand pillars."* It is fully described in the Maha-

* Mahawanso, ch. xxvii. p. 164.

wanso, and Lassen dwells upon this description with great interest, because he considers it the most ancient authentic description of an Indian building extant.* The embellishments may be those of a later period, but we need not hesitate to admit that the dimensions are given correctly, and that the middle of the building was occupied by a hall supported on pillars. The upper stories of this nine-storied building were of timber, and required frequent renewal, and sometimes the nine stories were reduced to five stories; but the thousand pillars lived through all vicissitudes, and were still in wonderful preservation when seen by Captain Chapman in 1820.†

The third class of Buddhist architecture is the Chaitya Cave. "These," Mr. Fergusson observes, "are the temples or (if I may use the expression) churches of the series, and one or more of them is attached to every set of caves in the west of India, though none exist in the eastern side." "Unlike the Viharas," he continues, "the plan and arrangement of all these caves is exactly the same, and though the details and sculpture vary with the age in which they were executed, some strong religious feeling seems to have attached the Buddhists to one particular form for their places of worship. In the Viharas we can trace the progress from the simple cavern to the perfect monastery, but these seem at once to have sprung to perfection, and the Karli Cave, the most perfect, is, I believe, also the oldest in India." Mr. Fergusson looks upon them as copies of the interior of structural buildings, and adds, that "it is not one of the least singular circumstances attached to their

* Lassen, vol. ii. p. 420.

† Transactions R. A. S. vol. iii.; also J. R. A. S. vol. xiii. p. 170.

Interior of Vihara at Ajunta. (Fergusson, No. 17.)

A Chaitya Cave.

Interior of the Karli Cave.

history that no trace of such buildings exists in India, nor I believe in Ceylon, nor in the Buddhist countries beyond the Ganges."*

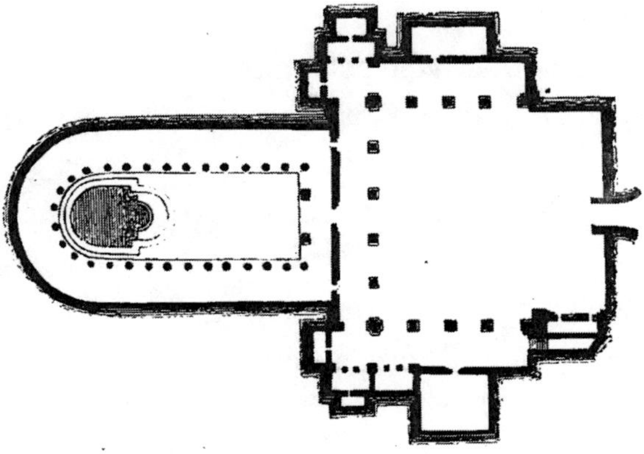

The Chaitya Caves are very imposing, and are described with enthusiasm by Lady Calcott, Captain Seely, Lord Munster, and every one who visits them, whether learned or unlearned. "They consist of an external porch, or music-gallery, an internal gallery over the entrance, and a centre aisle, . . . twice the length of its breadth, roofed by a plain waggon-vault; to this is added a semi-dome terminating the nave, under the centre of which always stands a Dagoba or Chaitya." A narrow aisle surrounds the interior, separated from the centre aisle by a range of massive columns, and this smaller aisle or passage is usually flat-roofed. A very interesting part of the arrangement was the manner in which the Cave was lighted: across the front there is a screen, in which there are three doors,—the largest, in the centre, opening to the nave, the others to

* Rock-cut Temples, p. 6.

the side aisles; over the screen the whole front is a great window, usually in the horseshoe form, as seen in the exterior of the Viswakarma; the whole light thus falls upon the Chaitya or Dagoba, and the effect from the dark colonnade is described as most remarkable.

Architecture thus confirms our previous observations, that although Buddhism originated in India, and was based upon Hindu philosophy, it was mainly fostered and developed by people who were not Hindus. Its architectural forms are those of other countries, and it owes its success, not to Hindus, but to the underlying Turanian population who became enthusiastic converts both in India, Ceylon, and in Northern Asia. These people had a natural love for raising mounds; and from the foreign artists and architects who came in the wake of Alexander they learned to elevate mounds into monuments, verandahs into Viharas, and image-cells into temples.

CHAPTER XII.

"Earnest sympathizing meditations upon the actual efforts of men to discover the secret of their life, and the ends for which they live, contain equal encouragements to humility and to hope."—F. D. MAURICE.

LET us now look down the long vista up which we have been toiling, and try to gather up a connected outline of the shifting phantom known as Buddhism. We have studied it in royal Edicts, in Literature, in Coins, Sculptures, and Symbols, in the Journals of the Chinese, and in Architecture. The Edicts of Piyadasi we look upon as its earliest reliable manifestation, and we feel that the teacher under whose influence they originated was, in Buddhist language, "a man both wise and great;" one who preached grandly on the sin of destroying life, the excellence of kindness, the instability of riches, and the blessedness of abstraction from the pleasures of sense. This doctrine the King, in the Edicts, rehearses: he comes forth, as it were, in sackcloth; he repents of indulgence in travelling and hunting, and rejoicings at births and marriages, and in the destructive hospitality of his soup-kitchen; and he causes the drums to beat, and fireworks to be displayed, and a great procession to be made, for the public proclamation of *dharma*, which is virtue as inculcated by Buddha. These Edicts do not touch upon religion; they are moral enactments, good in themselves, but far less beautiful if viewed as abstract truth than portions of the Brahmanical Code. Their peculiarity is, that they are addressed to all mankind without restriction,—a liberality unknown to Brahmans; and that they breathe an earnest purpose of imposing Moral Law upon the Universe,—an exertion wholly inconsistent with Brahmanical pride and indolence.

But if Buddhism was a sincere effort to advance man's general welfare, and if, even in its degenerate form, it encourages less vice than other idolatry, why, it may be asked, was it so distasteful to Aryan (or Sanskrit-speaking) races, and so little elevating to its Scythic-derived converts? Because, we answer, Buddhist morals are like gathered blossoms,—flowers cut away from the root of morals. A Buddhist teacher acknowledges no superior; and if the Edicts are too liberal for Brahmans, they are also too independent of Almighty power. Brahmans taught in the name of Brahma, and looked reverently on the Sun and the Dawn, on the Fire and the Flood, as tokens of Supreme and universal Soul. But the Edicts claim no higher authority than that of the King who proclaims them: he has cast aside the gods of the Vedas, and has not yet deified the memory of Buddha. All previous worship had been swept away, and teaching alone offered in its place. No Agni, no Indra, no Iswara, under any name was worshipped; for Buddhism, not content with proclaiming the equality of men, imagined the same equality to pervade the Universe. This scheme makes infinite space one vast republic, peopled by gods and men, who alike enjoy infinite equality and are alike subject to endless successions of perishable life. From time to time a chief arises who, by his personal qualities, attains omniscienc and a modified supremacy, and such a chiefship was claimed by Sakya-Muni. Buddhists believe that whilst on earth he held spiritual dominion, and that when he died he passed away into unknown and inaccessible regions, where for some he exists merely as a memory, for others as a being with power to enforce his precepts, but for none as a power ruling beyond the influence of Buddhism.

Sakya-Muni, striving to be independent of divinity, reminds one of the air-plants of his native jungles. Like the Dendrobium, which disdains to cast its roots into the soil, Buddhism strives to owe nothing to extrinsic power, and, like the graceful Dendrobium, it becomes an epiphyte. The first support of Buddhism was the philosophy of the Brahmans, but when cut adrift from Brahmanical learning and spirituality, this would have proved insufficient, but for alliance with foreign faiths, and the adoption of foreign arts and customs. The first feeling of popular Buddhism seems to have implied a cry of "Down with the Brahmans! all beings are equal! let gods and men start fair!" And next we find Buddhists learning from the unknown makers of cairns and cromlechs to erect mounds in memory of Buddha; and these mounds not being sepulchres, relics were placed within, and the structure called a Dagoba,* shrine of a relic. In further imitation of their nomadic converts, they placed circles of stones around their monuments, standing like worshippers, who do homage to a sacred object by walking round it. Foreigners, from Assyria apparently, taught them to erect single pillars to commemorate events, and to make halls supported by central columns, and to raise many-storied buildings upon a thousand-

* Mr. Fergusson derives this word from *dhatu*, relic, and *gabba* or *garba*, shrine or womb. Illust. Handbook of Architecture, vol. i., p. 8.

pillared base. Who gave the model for their beautiful Chaitya Caves, where the Dagoba disfigures the pillared aisles and vaulted roof, is not *decided;* but on the one hand it is shown that the Temple of Solomon had much in common with Assyrian architecture, and on the other hand, a close connection is discovered between Buddhist architecture and that of Assyria.*

And contemporary with, or rather earlier than, the dates assigned to, the splendid Buddhist excavations, we meet with what may be called touches and snatches of Hebrew recollections incorporated in the Buddhist Sutras. As, for instance, in the Asoka legend, where the old King wants to make his eldest son his heir; but his ministers prefer Asoka, and softening his rough skin with saffron and lac, take him to his dying father and deceive him as effectually as Rachel deceived old Israel. In another story, giving a last morsel of food to a holy person during a drought is followed by clouds and showers of food. A money-bag used for the promotion of Buddhism is as unfailing as the widow's cruise; and like Elijah, Buddha transfers his authority to his successor by bidding him wear his ascetic mantle. The stories of Buddha's birth belong exclusively to the second and later periods of Buddhist literature, and thus it is quite possible that their authors should have had an indirect and remote knowledge, not only of Jewish prophecy but of the Christian Gospels; but a reference to Christian teaching is most decided in the later Buddhism of Tibet.

And now if we retire a little from the easel, what is the outline we find traced upon our canvas?

1st. We have the Edicts so liberal and pure that we are

* Fergusson, Nineveh and Persepolis, pp. 113, 349, and Rock-cut Temples, p. 17.

ready to exclaim, "This is God's writing on the wall!" but the Daniel was wanting to interpret, and they degenerated into egotistical formalism.

2nd. We have the Buildings, Columns, Excavations, and Coins, showing that art—glorious art from Assyria and Greece!—gave to hidden Buddhism the torch which has made her conspicuous to the Universe and attractive to the populace.

3rd. We have Buddhist Literature,—and this is positively repulsive: a formal, conceited, extravagant tone pervades the whole. No sentiment comes from the heart or goes to the heart. Good moral maxims are at times rehearsed, but there is no freshness of feeling and no simplicity of character. Eternal rest, or *nirvana*, is to be obtained by the extinction of natural emotions. We entirely lose therefore the generous love and devotion of the Brahmanical tales; here there is no love conquering death, or brethren emulous of suffering for each other. One incident follows another with inexhaustible invention, but arranged according to a preconceived rule; something in the fashion of musical airs with variations, fugues, acrostics, or anagrams. There is in fact no freedom, no swelling thought too big for utterance. A Buddhist Teacher is never himself a learner,—his sole object is to prove and explain. A vigorous modern thinker writing of art as the answer which the human spirit makes to the Supreme, says, "Some nations have called their poets Finders. The countenance of the true poet, while at work, is that of one listening or receiving."* To the Sanskrit bards this attitude is not unknown; but Buddhists never listen and never "look up." The first act of their infant Buddha, according to their ad-

* A. J. Scott, Discourse on the Range of Christianity, p. 42.

miring Chronicle, was to take seven steps upon the earth and shout forth, "I am the most exalted on the earth."* And it was in the same spirit that the Singhalese priest answered Bishop Heber's question of "Do you worship the Gods?" by "No, the Gods worship me."† In Buddhism, temples for universal worship, and precepts for general acceptance, dazzle you for an instant like a heavenly vision; but when you look again the gleam of glory has passed, and the stars of heaven can no longer be distinguished from the false lights of the morass.

And yet, tricked out in borrowed trappings, Buddhism has been imagined capable of accounting for Christianity. It is painful to find any honest mind giving such undue value to superficial resemblances, and only one such instance shall be noted. The writer to whom we allude assumes that Buddhism is "Christianity without Christ." As well might he call it "Judaism without God." The argument runs thus‡:—"To a mind already impressed with Buddhistic belief and Buddhistic doctrines, Christianity was no abjuration of an old faith, . . . but a mere qualification of an existing belief, by the incorporation into it of the Mosaic account of the creation, and original sin, and the fall of man." This means, that a Jew in adopting Buddhism produced Christianity; therefore that the Gospels of the New Testament are fictions, more groundless than Buddhist Sutras; for the Buddha of the Buddhist writings was a real historical person; whereas if Christianity be derived from Buddhism there has been no Christ, and the Gospels are

* Pali Annals, J. A. S. B., Sept., 1838, p. 801.

† 'Ceylon Friend,' for 1838, vol. ii.; Printed Report of Schools, p. 5.

‡ 'Liverpool Journal,' 1852. The article is reprinted from the 'Reasoner,' No. 293, and is based upon an abstract of Huc's Travels in Tibet and Tartary.

tales invented in imitation of those which relate the birth, life, and death of Sakya-Muni, whom we call Buddha.

Such an idea cannot be dragged too fully into daylight. It can only be harmful when whispered in carelessness or ignorance, and listened to by ignorance. So far from Buddhism accounting for Christianity, it seems to me that a careful consideration of its merits and defects leads strongly to an opposite result. Buddha lived when morals were extremely corrupt, and with honest energy and self-denial he induced men to give up luxuries and live in communities apart from worldly aims, occupying themselves in acts of kindness and ascetic self-denial. Were it possible for a man to produce a Divine religion, here was the man. He did not countenance the fanaticism of contemporary ascetics who went about half-starved, unclothed, and with unwashed, matted hair, but he required his followers to provide simply for the wants of this life, and look for eternal rest beyond. Thus far we may believe that he made himself servant to what his soul recognized as right and true. But he was too weak to be able to separate his intuitions from himself, and he bade his converts follow *him* and become a part of the machinery which he had constructed; and thus he closed for them the access by which himself had risen. He was not to blame for sharing in the intellectual errors of his day, but for seeking to stereotype them upon the minds of his disciples. To Sakya-Muni the body and the material world were corrupt illusions, and "escape" was in consequence his watchword. No expression of joy in the beauty of creation, no delight in human affection, no anticipation of universal love, whether on earth or in heaven, is ever attributed to him. Buddhist precepts and hopes are all confined to negatives:—Not to injure living creatures: Not to indulge in luxury: Not to drink fermented liquors: Not to marry or live in families: Not to enjoy the sights and sounds of nature: Not to encounter future birth or life.

Such are the duties and the hopes of Buddhists; and therefore he who does least harm and feels least joy realizes the highest type of excellence, and he who escapes from perishable illusion realizes the highest type of happiness. Buddhist transcendentalism is indeed a dreary waste through which you wander, feeling as though you had fallen into Jean Paul's dream, where the Bell of the Universe tolls, mankind awakes in consternation, and Christ declares that he has been in Heaven and in Hell, but cannot find the Father: there is no God! there is no God!

BOOK III.

INDIA SUBSEQUENT TO BUDDHISM.

"The great body of the present religious practices of the Hindus are subsequent in time and foreign in tenor to those that were enjoined by the authorities which they profess to regard as the foundations of their system."—H. H. Wilson, *Oxford Lectures.*

CHAPTER I.

"In every country where there are national legends they are always deeply and vividly impressed with a feeling of the magnificence or loneliness in the midst of which they have arisen."—*Guesses at Truth.*

In the Mahabharata, Siva is the god of the Himalaya mountains, its summits his brow, its lofty crags and forests his hair. The Ganges could not descend to earth until he consented to receive its waters on his head. When he was propitiated, and Ganga heard the word "descend!"

"Full of wrath, the mandate heard Himavan's majestic daughter,
To a giant's stature soaring, and intolerable speed,
From heaven's height down rushed she, pouring upon Siva's sacred
head."

But with such pride and impetuosity she came, that the

God grew angry, and locked up her struggling floods amid his labyrinthine hair, until, being again propitiated, he permitted the waters to burst forth and find their way to the plains of India by seven separate streams.

We first hear of Siva worship about B.C. 300, some centuries after the first promulgation of Buddhism, but before Buddhism had become the Court religion. At that time Alexander the Great was dead: Seleucus held Bactria and Babylon, and his ambassador Megasthenes dwelt with Hindu Rajas at Patna, on the Ganges. Brahmanical philosophy had before this time made war upon the Vedas; Rain and Fire-worship had become obsolete, and Sacrifice typical; the Greeks were not therefore likely to see Soma-festivals, or to hear of offerings to Indra and Agni; and as the philosophic Brahmans reserved their religious doctrine for the privileged few, the only obvious religions were those of the populace, which Megasthenes describes as Siva worship on the hills and Vaishnaiva worship in the plains. The first was, he says, celebrated in tumultuous festivals, the worshippers anointing their bodies, wearing crowns of flowers and sounding bells and cymbals. From this the Greeks conjecture that Siva worship must be derived from Bacchus or Dionysus, and have been carried to the East in the traditionary expedition which Bacchus made in company with Hercules. This view was confirmed by finding that the wild vine grew in some of the very districts where this worship flourished. But these conjectures are treated by Professor Lassen as pure invention, and all that he accepts from the observations of Megasthenes is, that Siva worship was prevalent in the hills of India previous to the reign of Chandragupta.

For a time the Brahmans resisted this innovation, and refused their patronage both to Siva and his worshippers; but the popular current was too strong for their virtue, it swept away their breakwaters, and left them in danger of unimportance and neglect. Then perceiving their selfish errors, and looking for a selfish remedy, the old Brahmans resolved to consecrate the people's harbours, or, in other words, to adopt the people's gods. Unable to stand like Moses, firmly promulgating a law which they declared Divine, they took the part of Aaron and presided over worship to the Golden Calf. From this era the morality and grandeur of ancient Brahmanism degenerated. Brahmans still wrote beautiful poems, but with an obvious motive of connecting the newer gods with the older mythology. One of these, on Siva, is the work of Kalidasa, who is supposed to have lived B.C. 56.

At that period Vikramaditya reigned at Ougein, in Malwa, and invested his country with such brilliancy that he and his Court have never ceased to be a favourite theme with Sanskrit bards and dramatists. Nine poets are described as nine jewels sparkling around his throne, and amongst these jewels Kalidasa was pre-eminent. It is indeed possible that Vikramaditya's poets may, like King Arthur's knights, partake of a traditionary character, and have lived not all contemporary, but in successive centuries. But this does not disturb the main fact that, nearly coeval with the Christian era, Buddhism was subdued and its asceticism interrupted by the victorious career of a Hindu King who honoured Brahmanical literature and Brahmanical religion.

The poem alluded to above is entitled 'The Birth of the War-God.' It is incomplete, for it gives the history of the War-God's father and mother, and their espousals, but finishes before his birth. The scene is in the mountains always spoken of as Siva's dwelling-place, and the poem opens with an allegorical description of Himalaya as a proud mountain-king with his diadem of snow, who—

> "Lifting high
> His towery summits till they cleave the sky,
> Spans the wide land from east to western sea,
> Lord of the Hills, instinct with Deity."

Gems and gold and sparkling ores are described as the inherent riches of the realm, amongst whose wilds "the eager hunters roam, tracking the lion to his dreary home." Around its zone are dark shadows which the sylphs love :—

> "Till the big rain-drops fright them from the plains
> To those high peaks where sunshine ever reigns;
> There birch-trees wave, that lend their friendly aid
> To tell the passion of the love-born maid,
> So quick to learn with metal tints to mark
> Her hopes and fears upon the tender bark."*

In the caves and valleys winds resound, which are described as a glorious hymn led by Himalaya; and within the mossy caverns magic herbs pour forth a streaming light; whilst through the forests the wild kine roam with "tails out-spread and bushy streaming hair."

Himalaya, thus rich and powerful, was the father of one lovely damsel whom he married to Siva, but Siva had not then apparently acquired importance; for Himalaya treated his son-in-law with scorn, and the "tender soul" of his daughter was so torn with anguish at seeing her

* Specimens of Old Indian Poetry, by Ralph T. Griffiths,—'Birth of the War-God Kalidasa.'

husband contemned, that "her angered spirit left its mortal cell:" in other words, she died; and from that moment Siva knew no love. Clad in a rude coat of skin, he lived for nought but prayer and solitary thought. His followers inhabited the clefts of the hills, their bodies tinted with mineral dyes, with mantles formed of the bark of trees, and red garlands twined around their hair. High up on the mountains, with only these companions, the mournful Siva dwelt.

> "The holy Bull before his master's feet
> Shook the hard-frozen earth with echoing beat;
> And as he heard the lion's roaring swell
> In distant anger from the rocky dell,
> In angry pride he raised his voice of fear,
> And from the mountain drove the startled deer.
> Bright fire—a shape the God would sometimes wear,
> Who takes eight various forms—was glowing there:
> Then the great Deity who gives the prize
> Of penance, prayer, and holy exercise,
> As though to earn the meed he grants to man,
> Himself the penance and the pain began."

Whilst Siva thus lived in stern seclusion, his lovely and lamented wife was born again, and was as before the daughter of Himalaya. She was more beautiful than ever, and her father could never "satisfy the thirsty glances of a parent's eye." She was decidedly a new existence with an individuality of her own, but—

> "As herbs beneath the darksome shades of night
> Collect again their scattered rays of light;
> So dawned upon the maiden's waking mind
> The far-off memory of her life resigned,
> And all her former learning in its train,
> Feelings and thoughts and knowledge came again."

And therefore the one fixed desire of her life was to win the love of Siva. Her beauty was so remarkable that no enterprise could appear too great for her achievement.

"There was a glory beaming from her face,
With love's own light, and every youthful grace . . .
Bright as a Lotus, springing where she trod,
Her glowing feet shed radiance o'er the sod:
That arching neck, the step, the glance aside,
The proud swans taught her as they stemmed the tide;
Whilst of the maiden they would fondly learn
Her anklets pleasant music in return. . . .
What thing of beauty may the poet dare
With the smooth wonder of those limbs compare?
The young tree springing by the brooklet's side,
The wounded trunk, the forest-monarch's pride?
Oh no! too cold, too chilling cold the tree, . . .
This too unyielding for such rivalry."

Her voice was sweeter than the voice of the Koïl, the glance of her "soft liquid eye, tremulous, like lilies when the breezes sigh.

"Which learnt it first—so winning and so mild—
The gentle fawn, or Mena's gentler child?"

Fortunately it suited the schemes of all the Brahmanical Gods that this beautiful and love-lorn damsel should become Siva's wife, for they were jealous of Siva's continued penance, which tended to give him supreme dominion in the mythological realms; and moreover a mighty fiend was abroad who deprived them of their offerings, and this enemy, named Tarak, was destined to be conquered by no other than a son of Siva. It was therefore decreed that the lovely Uma should be taken to the retreat of Siva. She presented herself, and—

"The Hermit welcomed with a courteous brow
That gentle enemy of hermit vow;
The still pure breast, where Contemplation dwells,
Defies the charmer and the charmer's spells:
Calm and unmoved he viewed the wondrous maid,
And bade her all his pious duties aid.
She culled fresh blossoms at the God's command,
Sweeping the altar with a careful hand:
The holy grass for sacred rites she sought."

But she made no progress until Kama, God of Love, was sent to her aid. A beautiful picture is thus drawn of the coming of Love, accompanied by his comrade Spring:—

"How fair was Spring! to fill the heart with love,
And lure the Hermit from his thoughts above.
In that pure grove he grew so heavenly bright
That Kama's envy wakened at the sight. . . .
Then from its stem the red Asoka threw
Full buds and flowerets of celestial hue,
Nor waited for the maiden's touch, the sweet
Beloved pressure of her tinkling feet. . . .
How sighed the spirit o'er that loveliest flower
That boasts no fragrance to enrich its dower!
For Nature, wisest mother, oft prefers
To part more fairly those good gifts of hers:
There from the tree Palasa blossoms spread,
Curved like the crescent moon, their rosiest red,
With opening buds that looked as if young Spring
Had pressed his nails there in his dallying. . . .
"The cool gale speeding o'er the shady lawns
Shook down the sounding leaves, while startled fawns
Ran wildly at the viewless foe, all blind
With pollen wafted by the fragrant wind.
Sweet was the Koïl's voice—his neck still red
With mango-buds on which he just had fed—
'Twas as the voice of Love to bid the dame
Spurn her cold pride, nor quench the gentle flame. . . .
E'en the pure Hermit owned the secret power

Of warm Spring coming in unwonted hour;
While Love's delightful witchery gently stole
With strong sweet influence o'er the saintly soul."

The bees, the elephants, the goats, the flowers, the trees, the birds,—all feel the "glowing touch," save Siva, for

"No charmer's spell may check the firm control,
Won by the Holy, o'er the impassioned soul."

Therefore when Love and Spring arrived at the mighty Hermit's door, his servant went to them with his finger on his lip, saying:

"Peace! be still!
Nor mar the quiet of this holy hill.
He spake, no dweller of the forest stirred,
No wild bee murmured, hushed was every bird,—
Still and unmoved, as in a picture, stood
All life that breathed within the waving wood."

Siva, with his three eyes, looked very awful, sitting on a tiger's skin beneath a pine-tree upon a mound. He was absorbed in thought, his shoulders bent, his feet beneath him, and his hands pressed upon his breast. In each ear was a double rosary, serpents were wreathed in his hair, his neck was a bright blue, and his dark eyebrows bent sternly with a terrible frown. His eyes glared fiercely, but were fixed in devotion's meditating gaze.

"Calm as a full cloud resting on a hill,—
A waveless lake when every breeze is still;
Like a torch burning in a sheltered spot—
So still was he, unmoving, breathing not. . . .
At all the body's ninefold gates of sense
He had barred in the pure intelligence,
To ponder on the Soul which Sages call
Eternal Spirit, highest, over all."

Kama was perfectly frightened at the awful sight, and hid himself amongst the tangled flowers and clustering trailers, and even dropped his sweet arrows in despair, until the lovely damsel Uma came, adorned with all the brightest flowers of spring. As she approaches, led by Love, Siva

> "Breathes, he moves, the earth begins to rock;
> The snake, her bearer, trembling at the shock."

The beautiful Uma bent so low that the flowers in her ears fell to the ground, whilst with brow relaxed,

> "'Sweet maid,' cried Siva, 'surely thou shalt be
> Blessed with a husband who loves none but thee!' . . .
> Like the moon's influence on the sea at rest
> Came Passion, stealing o'er the Hermit's breast,
> While on the maiden's lip that mocked the dye
> Of ripe red fruit, he bent his melting eye;
> And oh! how showed the lady's love for him,
> The heaving bosom, and each quivering limb!
> Like young Kadambas, when the leaf-buds swell,
> At the warm touch of Spring they love so well:
> But still with downcast eyes she sought the ground,
> And durst not turn their burning glances round."

Kama thought the moment had arrived when he might surely aim a successful shaft, but instantly Siva recovers his self-possession: he is unwilling to lose the benefit of his accumulated amount of penance; and quelling the storm of passion in his troubled breast, he looks round to seek the cause of this unusual tempest in his soul; and discovering the bold young archer, Love, he bends upon him a look so fiery that poor Kama is instantly burnt to ashes; and having thus blasted the hinderer of his vow, Siva and all his train withdraw to solitudes in which woman's face is never seen.

"Now woe to Uma! for young Love is slain,
Her Lord hath left her, and her hope is vain:
Woe, woe to Uma! how the mountain-maid
Cursed her bright beauty for its feeble aid! . . .
Penance must aid her now, or how can she
Win the cold heart of that stern Deity?
Penance, long penance,—for that power alone
Can make such love, so high a Lord, her own."

But the idea of penance was most distressing to Uma's mother, who kissed her child, wept, sighed, and prayed; but the daughter's will is stronger than the mother's prayers, and the resolute maiden sends to her father to beg him to grant her some solitude, in which she might give her whole soul to penance and to prayer; and the great Himalaya gives her in consequence that hill which the peacocks love, and which is known to all ages by her name.

"Still to her purpose resolutely true
Her string of noble pearls aside she threw, . . .
And clad her in a hermit coat of bark . . .
With zone of grass the Votaress was bound,
Which reddened the fair form it girdled round. . . .
Alas! her weary vow has caused to fade
The lovely colours that adorned the maid;
Pale is her hand, and her long finger-tips
Steal no more splendour from her paler lips. . . .
"The maid put off, but only for awhile,
Her passioned glances and her witching smile;
She lent the fawn her morning melting gaze,
And the fond creeper all her winning ways. . . .
Her gentleness had made the fawns so tame,
To her kind hand for fresh sweet grain they came;
And let the maid before her friends compare
Her own with eyes that shone as softly there."

Many hermits came to see her, and found the fires of worship kindled, no rite forgot, and the grove so pure that even savage monsters lived together in love and peace; but Uma feared that her penance was too mild to yield the need she sought, and now,

> "Full in the centre of four blazing piles
> Sate the fair lady of the winning smiles,
> While on her head the mighty God of Day
> Shot all the fury of his summer ray:
> Yet her first gaze she turned upon the skies
> And quenched his splendour with her brighter eyes.
> To that sweet face, though scorched by rays from heaven,
> Still was the beauty of the Lotus given;
> Yet, worn by watching, round those orbs of light
> A blackness gathered like the shades of night."

After spending the summer scorched by the heat of fire, she was drenched in autumn by the annual rains, and in winter she lay upon

> "the cold damp ground,
> Though blasts of winter hurled their snows around."

At length her penance exceeded that of the most renowned anchorites, and she earned the glorious title of Apáraná—Lady of the unbroken fast! Then came to her a hermit of the first rank in sanctity,—

> "With coat of skin, with staff and matted hair,
> His face was radiant and he spake her fair.
> Up rose the maid the holy man to greet,
> And humbly bowed before the Hermit's feet:
> Though meditation fill the pious breast,
> It finds a welcome for a glorious guest.
> The sage received the honour duly paid,
> And fixed his earnest gaze upon the maid,
> While through her frame unwonted vigour ran;
> Thus in his silver speech the blameless saint began."

He asked how her tender frame could perform her firm

spirit's task, and bring the grass and fuel and water required for the daily offerings. He then noticed her careful tending of the flowers, "Till like thy lip," he says, "each ruddy tendril glows;" he observes also how—

"With loving glance the timid fawns draw nigh;
Say, dost thou still with joy their wants supply?
For thee, O Lotus-eyed! their glances shine,
Mocking the brightness of each look of thine.
O Mountain-Lady! it is truly said
That heavenly charms to sin have never led;
For even Penitents may learn of thee
How pure, how gentle, Beauty's self may be. . . .
Purest of motives, Duty leads thy heart,
Interest and pleasure there may claim no part.
O noble maiden! holy sages tell,
Friendship may soon in gentle bosoms dwell,
Seven steps together bind the lasting tie;
Then bend on me, dear saint, a gracious eye!
Fain, lovely Uma, would a Brahman learn
What noble guerdon would thy Penance earn."

The Hermit urges this question in various ways, asking what can move one so faultless "to dwell in solitude and prayer apart." Can it be, he suggests at last, that she desires a husband?—

"Oh forbear the thought!
A priceless jewel seeks not, but is sought:
Maiden, thy deep sighs tell it is so."

And then the gallant anchoret expresses great surprise that any one could have looked upon her with indifference. "Surely," he continues,

"Thy loved one, vain in beauty's pride,
Dreamed of himself when wandering at thy side,
Or he would count him blest to be the mark
Of that dear eye, so soft, so lustrous dark!"

He however consoles her by saying that he has himself a rich store of merits won by a year of penance, and that she shall have the half, name her secret purpose, and give up stern hardships.

A beautiful passage follows, in which the fair Uma makes her attendant tell the story of her love, and the attendant then explains that, as the Lotus disdained all gods except the God of Day, so Uma had disdained all love except the love of Siva :—

> "For him alone, the trident-wielding God,
> The thorny paths of Penance hath she trod ;
> But since that mighty one hath Kama slain,
> Vain every hope, and every effort vain. . . .
> Alas, poor maid ! she knows no comfort now,
> Her soul 's on fire, her wild locks hide her brow. . . .
> Oft as the maidens of the minstrel throng
> To hymn great Siva's praises raised the song,
> The love-lorn lady's sobs and deep-drawn sighs
> Drew tears of pity from their gentle eyes."

At length in despair she came to this holy grove, but alas ! although since then "The fruit hath ripened on the spreading bough, no fruit hath crowned her holy vow." When the maiden ceased, the Brahman turned in secret joy to Uma, and asked if this was indeed the darling secret of her breast. "She clasped the rosary in her quivering hand," and replied,—

> "'O holy sage, learned in the Vedas' lore,
> 'T is even thus Great Siva I adore ;
> Thus would my steadfast heart his love obtain,
> For this I gladly bear the toil and pain ;
> Surely the strong desire, the earnest will,
> May win some favour from his mercy still.'

'Lady,' cried he, 'that mighty Lord I know,
Ever his presence bringeth care and woe,
And wouldst thou still a second time prepare
The sorrows of his fearful life to share?
Deluded maid, how shall thy tender hand,
Decked with the nuptial bracelet's jewelled band,
Be clasped in his, when fearful serpents twine
In scaly horror round that arm divine? . . .
On Siva's heart the funeral ashes rest,
Say, gentle lady, shall they stain thy breast,
Where the rich tribute of the Sandal-trees
Sheds a pure odour on the amorous breeze?'"

She, he says further, should ride upon the king of elephants, and could she bear the scorn of being borne by Siva's bull? Siva is of unknown ancestry, poor, dressed in the vilest garb,—

"'No charms hath he to win a maiden's eye:
Cease from thy Penance, hush the fruitless sigh.
Not 'mid the gloomy tombs do sages raise
The holy altar of their prayer and praise.'
Impatient, Uma listened; the quick blood
Rushed to her temples in an angry flood;
Her quivering lip, her darkly-flashing eye,
Told that the tempest of her wrath was nigh.
Proudly she spoke: 'How couldst *thou* tell aright
Of one like Siva,—perfect, infinite!
'Tis ever thus, the Mighty and the Just
Are scorned by souls that grovel in the dust.
Their lofty goodness and their motives wise
Shine all in vain before such blinded eyes.
Say, who is greater, he who strives for power,
Or he who succours in misfortune's hour?
Refuge of Worlds, oh how should Siva deign
To look on men enslaved to paltry gain?
The spring of wealth himself, he careth nought
For the vile treasures that mankind have sought;
His dwelling-place amid the tombs may be,

Yet monarch of the three great worlds is he.
What though no love his outward form may claim,
The stout heart trembles at his awful name!
Who can declare the wonders of his might,
The Trident-wielding God, who knows aright?
Whether around him deadly serpents twine,
Or if his jewelled wreaths more brightly shine?
Whether in rough and wrinkled hide arrayed,
Or silken robe in glittering folds displayed;
If on his brow the crescent moon he bear,
Or if a shrunken skull be withering there?' "

The conclusion of Uma's eloquent defence of Siva is remarkable, for she says, that in calling him of ancestry *unknown,* there had been *one* word of truth amid the slanderous speech, for—

"How should mortal man
Count when the days of Brahma's Lord began?
But cease these idle words; though all be true,
His failings many and his virtues few,
Still clings my heart to him, its chosen lord,
Nor fails nor falters at thy treacherous word."

And forthwith she desires her attendant to send away the evil-speaking Hermit; for although he is most guilty who begins such faithless speech, yet he who stays to listen also sins.

"She turned away, with wrath her bosom swelling,
Its vest of bark in angry pride repelling,—
But sudden, lo! before her wandering eyes
In altered form she sees the sage arise;
'Tis Siva's self before the astonished maid,
In all his gentlest majesty displayed.
She saw, she trembled, like a river's course
Checked for a moment in its onward force
By some huge rock amid the torrent hurled,
Where erst the foaming waters madly curled;

One foot uplifted—shall she turn away?
Unmoved the other—shall the maiden stay?
The silver moon on Siva's forehead shone,
While softly spake the God in gracious tone:—
'O gentle maiden, wise and true of soul!
Lo! now I bend beneath thy sweet control!
Won by thy penance, and thy holy vows,
Thy willing slave, Siva, before thee bows!'"

The remainder of this poem is painfully incongruous. Taken as a narrative of earthly love it presents beautiful pictures of father, mother, daughter, husband, and bride; but details of domestic bliss, which are in themselves most pleasing, and even holy, become irreverent and shocking when related of a being proclaimed to be a manifestation of the Supreme and Triune God. This irreverent mingling of the divine and human is far less felt in Greek mythology; for not only are the Greek gods less human, and less occupied on earth with all the affections and interests of men; but, on the other hand, the Greeks never reached the sublimity which the Brahmans of all ages have occasionally attained in their conceptions of Supreme Deity. The passages of this poem, which inculcate *faith* and attribute supremacy to Siva, may possibly be additions belonging to a subsequent development of religious doctrine; and for the present setting these aside, the poem may be enjoyed as a charming and fanciful tale in which the gloomy, awful Siva is won to love and happiness by the bright daughter of the snow-crowned Himalaya. Continuing the history, then, Siva had no sooner avowed his love than the gentle Uma entreated him to ask her father's sanction. An august deputation of heavenly powers waits in consequence upon Himalaya, who receives them in the presence of his wife and daughter; she, whilst the messengers were speaking,

> "Bent her head
> To hide her cheek, now blushing rosy red,
> And numbered o'er with seeming care the while
> Her Lotus-petals, in sweet maiden guile.
> With pride and joy Himalaya's heart beat high,
> Yet ere he spake he looked to Mena's eye;
> Full well he knew a mother's gentle care
> Learns her child's heart and love's deep secret there:
> And this the hour, he felt, when fathers seek
> Her eye for answer, or her changing cheek.
> His eager look Himalaya scarce had bent
> When Mena's eye beamed back her glad assent:—
> O gentle wives, your fondest wish is still
> To have with him you love one heart, one will!"

A gorgeous description is given of the royal city on the day of the wedding, when crowds of noble dames were seated under canopies upheld by pillars decked with gems and gold. The bride's hair was graced with feathery grass and wild flowers, amid which a glittering arrow was introduced, and behind each ear was placed an ear of barley. We must forbear to touch upon her beauty, or on that of Siva, whose head-ornament, the "withering skull," became as a "bright coronal;" whilst his "mid-eye" beamed softly, as a mark of glory, and his "twining serpents" changed into ornaments set with blazing gems. At the moment when he is permitted by his chamberlains to behold his bride arrayed in all her loveliness,—

> "His lotus-eyes
> Flashed out the rapture of his proud surprise;
> Then calm the current of his spirit lay
> Like the world basking in an autumn day.
> They met, and true love's momentary shame

O'er the blest bridegroom and his darling came;
Eye looked to eye,—but quivering as they met,
Scarce dared to trust the rapturous gazing yet. . . .
Thrice, at the bidding of the priest, they came
With swimming eyes around the holy flame;
Then, at his word, the bride in order due
Into the blazing fire the parched grain threw,
And toward her face the scented smoke she drew;
While softly wreathing o'er her cheek it hung,
And round her ears in flower-like beauty clung.
'This flame be witness of your wedded life;
Be just, thou husband, and be true, thou wife!'
Such was the priestly blessing on the bride.
Eager she listened, as the earth, when dried
By parching summer suns, drinks deeply in
The first soft droppings when the rains begin:—
'Look, gentle Uma!' cried her lord, 'afar
Seest thou the brightness of yon polar star?
Like that unchanging ray thy faith must shine!'
Sobbing she whisper'd, 'Yes, for ever thine!'"

CHAPTER II.

"For spirits, when they please,
Can either sex assume, or both."—MILTON.

WHEN Kanerki and the Indo-Scythians became settled in India they inscribed Okro on their coins, thereby indicating Siva by one of his Sanskrit epithets, Ugro, "The Fierce;" and later in the series Okro becomes Ordokro, and this it is conjectured means *half*-Okro, or half-man, half-woman, and accounts for the female form so frequently invested with Siva attributes. The coin etched at the head of the present Chapter bears on its obverse the head of King Kadphises;* but on other coins of the same series Siva appears as an elegant male figure, his hair drawn up to a point ending in flame, but still leaning on a humped bull. The later coins frequently give four arms to the god or goddess, each hand holding a weapon of war; but the barbarism of a third eye is not introduced on coins. Professor Lassen† alludes to some with three heads. Siva being thus represented as the highest God of a *Trimurti*,—as also to be

* Wilson's Ariana, p. 356, plate 10, fig. 17; and Lassen, vol. ii. pp. 844, 1089.

† Vol. ii. pp. 847, 1092.

seen in the sculptures at Elephanta, Ellora, and other temples,—it is supposed that different sects adopted different forms; some Siva as threefold, others, Siva as symbolized

by flame. In Kashmere vestiges yet remain of temples in which Siva was worshipped as flame or Swayambhu.

In the poem which we have just been considering, Siva is the supreme deity, and fire one of his eight shapes. In the Introduction it is Brahma, "whose face turns every way," and who "bodies forth the mystic three," and "fills three persons;" but when toward the conclusion Siva presents himself to the other Gods and announces his wish to wed the daughter of Himalaya, the ancient sages above the moon address him as the "World's Great Father," and entreat him to tell his wondrous nature; for, although they see his outward form, they have no means of knowing him as he should be known, and are at a loss whether to consider him as a creator, preserver, or destroyer. No very definite answer is given to this inquiry; but on occasion of the wedding the three Gods are thus described:—

"Brahma came on—Creator, Lord of Might,—
And Vishnu glowing from the realms of light. . . .
In those three persons the one God was shown;
Each first in place, each last,—not one alone:
Of Siva, Vishnu, Brahma, each may be
First, second, third, among the Blessed Three."*

And this is, in few words, nearly all that need be said about the religion of India in the early centuries of the Christian era. A threefold Almighty power became more distinctly recognized; in some localities and at certain epochs Siva was this Power. Often gloomy and ungainly, riding an awkward bull and delighting in sad symbols, but free from the odious attributes assigned to him in later times, Kalidasa's dramas all begin with an invocation to Siva; and in his celebrated poem, called the 'Cloud Messenger,' the town of Ougein is especially mentioned as the head-quarters of Siva worship. The story is as follows:—Amongst the hills of the Himalaya reigned Kuvera, a demigod, celebrated for his wealth: his Court was held at the rich city of Alaka; and here an unfortunate demigod (called a Yaksha) had suffered Indra's elephant to trespass upon a garden placed under his charge. His sentence of punishment was banishment for a twelvemonth to the Dekkan, the peninsula of India; and there the poem finds him, grievously lamenting his separation from the beloved wife who was pining for him in his home at Alaka. Eight weary months had he been suffering exile, and he was now so worn and shrunk that his golden bracelets slipped from off his arm. It was the month of July, when the rainy season commences, and all travellers start in haste for their homes, eager to take advantage of the first cool showers, and equally

* Page 73.

anxious to escape the coming floods which render travelling impossible. Sadly the exile looks at the lowering sky, which all other men's wives will hail with joy as the sign of the absent husband's return; but suddenly it occurs to him that a cloud, "the friend of Indra," going to his home in Alaka would take a message to the partner of his woes. Gathering flowers he makes an offering and invokes sympathy. Leading a painful life, counting the moments of the lingering year, "she still lives," he says; "for female hearts, though fragile as the flower, are firm when hope supports them." The blessings attendant on the prayers of the Cloud are then noticed, as, the languid jessamine lifts its head, nature revives, the buds open, and at last

> "Earth's blazing woods in incense shall arise,
> And warbling birds with music fill the skies."*

Ougein was not in the direct northern route; but it is proposed that the Cloud shall make a slight deviation, and pay homage there to Siva, "the God whom earth and Heaven and Hell obey." This beautiful city was greatly in want of so refreshing a visitor; for its river was wasted to a thread not bigger than a braid of hair, and was bleached with the withered foliage rudely showered from the overhanging trees. The Cloud's next resting-place was to be the poor exile's home, the mountain-city of Alaka, where he describes his house as a bower, made conspicuous by the beauty of its flowers; whilst a

> "Golden column on a crystal base,
> Begirt with jewels, rises o'er the place."

But the messenger is entreated not to present himself to the beloved occupant until he has disguised his awful

* **Meghaduta**, by Kalidasa, translated by Professor H. H. Wilson.

size. His poor wife, he says, is nipped by chill sorrow, her dear lips dried by parching sighs, and her pallid cheek resting sadly on her hand. Her favourite bird, the "tuneful Sarika," is with her, and she strives to soothe her own grief by mourning over her feathered prisoner's kindred fate. Her lute, or *vina,* lies idle, for she cannot sing for tears, and tears also have corroded its silver strings. She sits in her beauty and loveliness—

> "Not wholly waking nor resigned to sleep;
> Her heavy eyelids languidly unclose,
> To where the moon its silvery radiance throws
> Mild through the chamber; once a welcome light,
> Avoided now and hateful to her sight."

Having thus excited the sympathy of his aerial messenger, the exiled husband sends this message to his wife,—that she must bow to fate, and learn courage from her husband's firmness, remembering that "very few are always wretched or always blessed."

> "Life, like a wheel's revolving orb, turns round,
> Now whirled in air, now dragged along the ground."

And he concludes by expressing confidence in the benevolence of the Cloud, who will answer his wishes not in deeds, but words. "To thee," he says, "the thirsty Chataca* looks up, and thy answer is a falling shower." And in the present case the Cloud so well performed its embassy, that the Gods in Alaka relented, the husband was quickly restored to his beloved wife, and both were thenceforth blest with ceaseless joy.

* The Chataca is a poetical bird, supposed to live wholly upon rain-water.

Whatever may have been the condition of women, as women, in Ancient India, it is quite evident that the matrimonial relation was often one of great honour and deep affection. In both these poems the wife is as necessary to the husband as the husband to the wife. When Siva is widowed he turns ascetic; when the Yaksha is banished, the sole cause of his "wild despair" is his separation from his wife; and, on the other hand, when poor Kama, the God of Love, is blasted by the lightning of Siva's angry eye, it is his darling wife that sings a lament for him; at first she swooned away, but

> "Too soon her gentle soul returned to know
> The pangs of widowhood,—that word of woe! . . .
> 'Speak to me, Kama! why so silent? give
> One word in answer,—doth my Kama live?
> There on the turf his dumb cold ashes lay,—
> That fiery flash has scorched the soul away. . . .
> Sure woman's heart is strong, for can it be
> That I still live while *this* is all of thee?'"

And she consoles herself, in Indian fashion, by thinking that she will throw herself on his burning funeral pile, and be again united with him in a future world, before Heaven's maids have been able to throw their winning glances over him. A slight difficulty however occurs; for Kama having been annihilated by a glance, both soul and body vanished in the viewless air, and it is difficult to know how to prepare the funeral rites. Her lament on this occasion is too beautiful to be omitted:—

> "'As dies a torch when winds sweep roughly by,
> So is my light for ever fled, and I,
> The lamp his cheering rays no more illume,
> Am wrapt in darkness, misery, and gloom.

Fate took my love and spared the widow's breath,
Yet fate is guilty of a double death;
When the wild monster tramples on the ground
The tree, some creeper garlands closely round,
Reft of the guardian which it thought so true,
Forlorn and withered, it must perish too.
Then come, dear friend! the true one's pile prepare,
And send me quickly to my husband there;
Call it not vain; the mourning lotus dies
When the bright moon, her lover, quits the skies. . . .
Set water near us in a single urn,
We'll sip in Heaven from the same in turn,
And to his spirit let thine offering be
Sprays, fresh and lovely from the mango-tree,
Culled when the round young buds begin to swell,
For Kama loved those fragrant blossoms well.'"

This melancholy consummation is happily averted by a heavenly voice, which breathes around the mourning widow, and tells her that Kama will come again so soon as Siva has been won by Uma; and the raging of her wild despair being thus soothed,

"She watched away the hours, so sad and slow,
That brought the limit of her weary woe,
As the pale moon, quenched by the conquering light
Of garish day, longs for its own dear night."

In the dramas which belong to this period, a little more of domestic life is revealed, and we shall find that the Hindu arrangements in matrimony were not exactly satisfactory to all parties, even in the palmy days of Indian chivalry. The Drama extends over many centuries; but the finest Plays belong to our present era, in which Siva was chief divinity and Kalidasa chief poet. Fortunately Professor Wilson has enabled English readers to enjoy much of the literary thought and poetic merit by which these productions are characterized. Translations of a few dramas have also appeared from other hands, and all are welcome, not merely for their intrinsic freshness and uncommon imagery, but as pictures of life, "Life in India," and especially Life in Ougein, when native princes reigned in peace, and when prosperous Brahmans were tolerant of powerful Buddhist institutions. The Hindu drama claims to be entirely of native growth; neither Persia, Arabia, nor Egypt appear to have possessed a theatre; and although Greece and China both delighted in the stage, the Hindus must be allowed the merit of originality, for their Plays "exhibit," says Professor Wilson, "characteristic varieties of conduct and construction which strongly evidence both original design and national development."* The greater part of each Play is written in Sanskrit, although Sanskrit had ceased to be a living language; and thus, like the Latin Plays annually represented at Westminster in the present day, they were but imperfectly understood by the audience and were wanting in dramatic effect. All the droll parts however were given in the language of common life, and the puns and jokes will have been universally appreciated. The general rule is to make only the great people talk Sanskrit, and to allow buffoons and women to discourse in the vernacular. Kalidasa's Play of the 'Hero and the Nymph' commences by the Manager's coming forward to make an invocation to Siva:—

> "May that Siva who is attainable by devotion and faith, . . . to whom alone the name of Iswara is applicable, and who is sought with suppressed breath by those who court final emancipation, bestow upon you final felicity!"

* Hindu Theatre, H. H. Wilson. vol. i. preface, p. 12.

Suddenly a cry of "Help! help!" is heard behind the scenes: a troop of heavenly nymphs enter in the air, the King Pururavas meets them, driving an aerial car from the opposite side. The nymphs entreat him to rescue their friend, the graceful Urvasi, who has been torn from them by a haughty Danava. The King waits but an instant to ask "Which path pursued the wretch?" and, urging the rapid steeds to swiftest flight, before the car divides the scattering clouds like dust, whilst the whirling wheel deceives the eye and seems to circle double round the axle: the waving chowrie* which ornaments the horses' heads points backward, and backward streams the banner from the breeze. This rapid driving soon overtakes the foe, and presently the "deer-emblazoned banner" of the King is again seen advancing; but he now drives slowly, the fair nymph Urvasi having fainted in his car. This does not prevent the King from falling violently in love; and the damsel was already in the same predicament, for she no sooner recovers her power of speech than she says apart, "What thanks I owe the Danava" (for making this hero my deliverer, being understood); but whilst the whole party is indulging in sweet emotions, a rushing sound of chariots is heard from the east, and a messenger appears to recall the nymphs to Swarga, their heavenly home, and thus the lovers for a time are parted.

In Act II. the scene is the Palace Garden, the King's confidential buffo friend Mánava enters and says,—

"It is mighty inconvenient for a Brahman like myself, one so much sought after and subject to such frequent invitations, to be burdened with the King's secret! Going so much into company

* The white bushy tail of the Yak, or Tibet cow, fixed on a gold shaft.

as I do, I shall never be able to set a guard upon my tongue. I must be prudent, and will stay here by myself in this retired temple until my royal friend comes forth from the council-chamber."

Whilst he is sitting in a corner with his face hid in his hands, the Queen's confidential attendant comes in, saying to herself, that her mistress is sure that since the King's return from the regions of the Sun he is changed, and must have left his heart behind him. So she determines to get the truth out of Mánava, sure that "a secret can rest no longer in his breast than morning dew upon the grass."

And accordingly the woman gets the better of the man, and it is confessed that if the King has, in an absent fit, been calling his Queen by the name of Urvasi, why then Urvasi must be the name of the King's new love. Whilst this scene is going on, the Warder proclaims the sixth watch, which answers to the hour of two, a period set apart for royal recreation, and immediately the King leaves his council-chamber and comes to the garden-bower to indulge in thoughts of Urvasi. Whilst thus occupied, he feels his eyes twinkle, and hails it as a token that his moon-faced nymph is hovering near; and at last the heavenly damsel, no longer able to restrain herself, drops a leaf inscribed with words of love. The King is in an ecstasy of happiness, until his Queen, coming into the garden, happens to get a sight of this leaf, and her grief and indignation throw perplexity upon his bliss. Mánava (the buffo) proposes that her Majesty should order dinner, and so put an end to all discomfort; but the Queen's feelings are too deep either to be diverted by a joke, or soothed by the idle protestations with which the King endeavours to secure peace. The Queen withdraws in silent dignity, and in the evening sends her chamberlain with a message, which he delivers as follows:—

"Glory to the King! So please your Grace, her Majesty expresses a wish to be honoured with your presence on the terrace of the pavilion of gems, to witness from it the entrance of the moon into the asterism Rohini."

The King obeys, expecting to find her repenting her petulance and seeking a renewal of his love. The scene must have been one of considerable dramatic effect. The Queen has laid aside all her ornaments, and looks very lovely in the simple white dress of a devotee. She presents trays of sweetmeats and perfumes and flowers to Mánava and the chamberlain, and then, after making similar offerings to the King, she throws herself at his feet, and calls upon the "Moon and his favourite Rohini" to hear and attest the promise which she makes her husband,—

"Whatever nymph attract my lord's regard,
And share with him the mutual bonds of love,
I henceforth treat with kindness and complacency."

Before leaving, she states that her object has been to promote his happiness by sacrificing her own, and she then withdraws to lead a life of secluded devotion, and is no more seen upon the stage.

The discarded Queen looked so divine in her adversity, that Urvasi, who was hovering near invisible, felt slightly jealous; but no sooner did the King venture to invoke her presence than she playfully came behind him, covering his eyes with her hands. All is then resigned to love, the King abandons his capital, throws up the reins of government, and spends his whole time with Urvasi in loneliest groves. One day however he cast a momentary glance upon another nymph; Urvasi was jealous on the instant, pushed him from her, and, forgetting in her ill-humour that women were forbidden access to a neighbouring grove, she fled across the prescribed boundary and was changed into a vine for her temerity. Her distracted lover followed, and day and night searched all the woods in vain.

Act IV. has much the character of a melodrama. It opens with a chorus of nymphs, lamenting the loss of their beloved companion Urvasi:—

> "The swans along the stream that sail
> A fond companion's loss bewail;
> With murmuring songs they soothe their grief,
> Or find from tender tears relief."

Presently the scene changes to another part of the forest, where invisible voices sing,—

> "The lord of the elephant train
> Now wanders afar from his mate,
> And franticly comes to complain
> To the woods of his desolate state.
> Distraction his vigour consumes,
> As he plunges amid the dark bowers;
> Whilst o'er his vast bulk sweetly blooms
> The garland of wild forest-flowers."

This song is interrupted by the hasty appearance of the King, in dress disordered and with mind unhinged by grief. At one moment he believes some fiend to have carried off his bride, and he calls upon him to suspend his flight. Hail and rain fall, and he finds it is no fiend that he is addressing, but a friendly Cloud:—

> "The cooling rain-drops fall, not barbed shafts,
> And I mistake the lightning for my love.
>
> [*Faints, and reviving sings,—*

"I madly thought a fiend conveyed
Away from me my fawn-eyed maid:
'T was but a Cloud that rained above,
With the young lightning for its love."

He then wanders on, making poetical and moral reflections, and asking all the birds and beasts if they have seen his love. The peacock gives him no reply, but beats a merry measure, pleased to show his glories unrivalled by the floating tresses of the lovely Urvasi. He next observes the Koïl cowering amid the shady branches of the Jambu. "She, of the birds, is wisest famed," he says, and he thus addresses her:—

"Say, nursling of a stranger nest,
  Say, hast thou chanced my love to see
Amidst these gardens of the blest,
  Wandering at liberty,
Or warbling with a voice divine
  Melodious strains more sweet than thine? . . .
Why did she leave
One so devoted to her will?
[*And then, as if in reply, he continues, turning to his left:*
In wrath
She left me; but the cause of anger lives not
In my imagination: the fond tyranny
That women exercise o'er those who love them
Brooks not the slightest show of disregard.
How now! the bird has flown. 'T is ever thus
All coldly listen to another's sorrows."

He wanders past the elephants beneath the Kadamba-tree and the lake upon which swans and the lotus-plants were floating, and reaches a mountain-cliff, adown the rocky sides of which rush glistening springs. He calls "Urvasi," and hears a reply,—it was but the echo of his words.

Overcome by fatigue, he sits exhausted by the bank of the stream, saying,—

> "Fatigue has overcome me. I will rest
> Upon the borders of this mountain-torrent. . . .
> Whilst gazing on the stream, whose new-swoln waters
> Yet turbid flow, what strange imaginings
> Possess my soul, and fill it with delight;
> The rippling wave is like her arching brow,
> The fluttering line of storks her timid tongue."

Yet further he wanders, singing verses of considerable beauty, until at length his steps are arrested by the sight of a ruby; but what could he do with the gem, now that she is gone whose brow it would have best adorned? "Why distain the ruby with my tears?" Whilst thus considering, a voice in the air tells him, that by virtue of that gem he shall recover his lost bride. He then takes it, saying, he will wear it on his diadem, and hold it dear to him as to *Iswara,* his crescent-moon. Immediately a mysterious emotion on the sight of a vine induces him to caress the clinging plant, and at his touch it changes into Urvasi.

CHAPTER III.

> "The audience are motionless as statues, . . .
> What subject shall we select for representation
> That we may ensure a continuance of their favour?"
>
> *Prologue to Sakoontala.*

SAKOONTALA, another work by Kalidasa, is a drama long since introduced to European Orientalists by their distinguished leader Sir William Jones. But his translation, although valuable not only as the first Sanskrit drama that appeared in English, but also for its intrinsic merit, was made before correct Sanskrit manuscripts were accessible. The corrupt and modern text weakens "the bold and nervous phraseology of Kalidasa," clothes "his delicate expressions of refined love in a meretricious dress," and dilutes by repetition "ideas grand in their simplicity." For these reasons a new translation* is a most welcome addi-

* Sakoontala, translated from the Sanskrit of Kalidasa by Monier Williams, Professor of Sanskrit at Haileybury.

tion to our literature, and the more so because Professor Williams gives in metre those portions which are poetry in the original. Like the beautiful verses already quoted, here again is poetry fit to tempt an English reader to study Sanskrit; but as Kalidasa has already engaged much attention, only a few short passages can be admitted.

Sakoontala, about to leave her childhood's home, grieves at parting from the little fawn which she had nurtured: her revered and beloved guardian says,—

> "Weep not, my daughter, check the gathering tear
> That lurks beneath thine eyelid, ere it flow
> And weaken thy resolve; be firm and true—
> True to thyself and me; the path of life
> Will lead o'er hill and plain, o'er rough and smooth,
> And all must feel the steepness of the way;
> Though rugged be thy course, press boldly on."

Different in character, but not less beautiful, are the reflections of a King who has "attained the objects of his aspirations," and finds that his troubles then *begin.*

> "'Tis a fond thought, that to attain the end
> And object of ambition is to rest;
> Success doth only mitigate the fever
> Of anxious expectation; soon the fear
> Of losing what we have, the constant care
> Of guarding it, doth weary. Ceaseless toil
> Must be the lot of him who, with his hands,
> Supports the canopy that shields his subjects."

Heralds behind the scenes cry, "May the King be victorious!" and one comes forward, saying,—

> "Honour to him who labours day by day
> For the world's weal, forgetful of his own;
> Like some tall tree that, with its stately head,

Endures the solar beam, while underneath
It yields refreshing shelter to the weary."*

The effect of pathetic music on a sensitive person is thus described :—

King. "Strange ! that song has filled me with a most peculiar sensation. I seem to yearn after some long-forgotten object of affection.

"Not seldom in our hours of ease,
When thought is still, the sight of some fair form,
Or mournful fall of music, breathing low,
Will stir strange fancies, thrilling all the soul
With a mysterious sadness, and a sense
Of vague, yet earnest, longing. Can it be
That the dim memory of events long past,
Or friendships formed in other states of being,
Flits like a passing shadow o'er the spirit ?"†

It is with regret one leaves so attractive a poet as Kalidasa, but we must now turn our attention to the "Toy-Cart," a lively drama, giving pictures of daily family-life in India, probably before the Christian era.‡ It commences with an invocation to Sambhu, or Siva, "as he sits ruminating with suspended breath, whilst his serpents coil around his knees."

The scene of this drama is the famous city of Ougein, in Malwa, and the state of society it represents "sufficiently§ advanced," says Professor Wilson, "to be luxurious and corrupt." The heroine, Vasanta, belongs indeed to the

* Page 124. † Page 121.

‡ Hindu Theatre, H.H. Wilson, vol. i. p. 9.

§ By some this Play is attributed to the second century B.C., a century previous therefore to the reign of Vikramaditya. Professor Lassen, on the other hand, assigns the two first centuries after Christ as the earliest era of the drama. See Introduction to Sakoontala, M. Williams, p. 6, and Lassen's Alterthumskunde, vol. ii. pp. 1113, 1147.

class of courtesans countenanced by existing Brahmanical governments. She is a lady of spirit and generosity, and evidently holds a station not esteemed degrading. The hero, Charudatta, is a Brahman, reduced to poverty by his munificence: he has an affectionate wife and darling son; but, according to Vasanta's notions, this presents no reason against her falling in love with him. Nor, on his part, does he regard the possession of a virtuous wife as an impediment to the indulgence of a new affection. His friend, the simple-hearted shrewd Maitreya, has more misgivings on the subject; but his doubts relate to the possible character of the new love, not to the rights or comfort of the wife. On our first introduction to Charudatta, we find him lamenting that, instead of those rich offerings which he formerly presented to the Gods, he is now reduced to a "scant tribute to the insect tribe." "To die," he says, "is transient suffering; to be poor, interminable anguish," because "the guest no longer seeks the dwelling," "the love of friends hangs all unstrung; and from poverty comes disrespect, and from disrespect does self-dependence fail." He says, he would have given up the world and become an ascetic, but that he had not liked to impose such hardship upon his wife. Suddenly a tumult is heard in the street, to which Charudatta's house has a side or back entrance (the approach to the main entrance being through a court), and flying down the street appears Vasanta pursued by a dissolute Prince and his companions. "Stop, lady, stop!" cries the Prince's servant; "she runs along like a peahen in summer with a tail in full feather, whilst my master follows her like the young hound that chases the bird through the thicket." Luckily at this moment Charudatta happened to open the side door of his mansion, and in rushed the fugitive, cleverly making her scarf brush out the light of the lamp as she passed; and the night being pitch dark, the whole party were then at fault. After much blustering and threatening the Prince and his suite depart.

Charudatta relights his lamp and discovers Vasanta, and he and she forthwith salute each other with apologies, until Maitreya says, "Whilst you two stand there nodding your heads to each other like a field of long grass, permit me to bend mine, although in the style of a young camel's stiff knees, and request that you will be pleased to hold yourselves upright again." As a pretext for further intercourse Vasanta begs permission to leave a casket of jewels in Charudatta's house, saying, that it was for the jewels that the villains were pursuing her.

In the next scene of interest a robber is "creeping along the ground, like a snake crawling out of his old skin." He feels the wall until he discovers a rat-hole, which he hails as an omen of success, and then considers how to proceed, saying, "The god of the golden spear teaches four modes of breaking into a house,—picking out burnt bricks, cutting through unbaked ones, throwing water on a mud wall, and boring through one of wood;" and, as Charudatta's wall was of baked bricks, he picked them out, doubting whether to make the aperture in the shape of the *Svastika* or a water-jar; and, feeling at a loss for a measuring-line, he makes use of his Brahmanical thread, which, he observes, is a most useful appendage to a Brahman of *his complexion*, for it serves to measure the depth and height of walls, to withdraw ornaments, to open a latch, or to make a ligature for the bite of a snake.

Having entered through the breach, he contrives to abstract the casket from beneath the head of Maitreya, then lets fly what he calls the "fire-flapping insect," which hovers round the light and puts it out with his wings, and finally he escapes. The household wake up just as he departs, and are in a terrible consternation at the loss of the jewels. Charudatta feels that a foul blight will now for ever rest upon his fame; but his wife, in the inner apartments, whilst expressing joy that he is himself unhurt, takes a string of jewels "given to her in her maternal mansion," and over which she alone had control; and, fearing that her husband's "lofty spirit" would not accept them from her, sends for Maitreya, pretends that she gives them to him because he is a Brahman, and feels sure that they will be used for the relief of her husband. Her confidence is not abused: Maitreya presents the jewels to Charudatta, and, after some reluctance and hesitation, Charudatta bids Maitreya take them to Vasanta, tell her that he had unhappily lost her casket at play, and intreat her to accept this offering in its place. When Maitreya reaches the dwelling of Vasanta, he gives graphic descriptions of the place:—

"The threshold is very neatly coloured, well swept, and watered; the floor is beautified with strings of sweet flowers; the top of the gate is lofty, and gives one the pleasure of looking up to the clouds; whilst the jessamine festoon hangs tremblingly down, as if it were now tossing on the trunk of Indra's elephant. Over the doorway is a lofty arch of ivory; above it wave flags of saffron colour, their edges curling in the wind like fingers, saying, 'Come hither.' Young mango-trees in crystal pots support the doorposts; the door-panels are of gold studded with adamant. . . . The whole cries 'Away!' to a man who is poor." Entering the first court, he sees a line of palaces as white as the moon; golden steps set with coloured stones lead to the upper chambers, whence crystal windows, festooned with pearls, look down upon Ougein. The porter dozes in his seat as stately as a Brahman deep in the Vedas; and the very crows, crammed with rice and curds, disdain the fragments of the sacrifice. In the second court are the stables,—the carriage-oxen, the rams kept for fighting, a monkey "tied as fast as a thief," and the *mahouts* feeding elephants with balls of rice and *ghee*. In the third court young men are gambling. The fourth court is used for music and dancing, and the recitation of plays and poems. The fifth court is redolent of oil and assafœtida: the kitchen sighs softly forth its fragrant and abundant smoke; the butcher's boy is washing the skin of an animal; the cook is surrounded with dishes; the sweetmeats are mixing, and the cakes are baking. The sixth court is entered by an arched gateway of gold and gems: it is the jewellers' court, where jewellers are examining pearls, topazes, sapphires, emeralds, rubies, the lapis-lazuli, coral, and other jewels; some set rubies in gold, some work gold ornaments on coloured thread, some string pearls, some grind the lapis-lazuli, some pierce shells, and some cut coral: here we have perfumers drying the saffron-bags, shaking the musk-bags, expressing the sandal-juice, and compounding essences. The seventh court is an aviary, where the doves bill and coo in comfort, where the pampered parrot croaks, like a Brahman Pundit chaunting hymns when stuffed with curds and rice, and where the *maina* chatters as glibly as a lady's-maid issuing her mistresses commands to her fellow-servants, while the *koïl*, crammed with juicy fruit, whines like a water-carrier." It must be remembered that Maitreya was hungry himself, and viewed all these overfed *gourmands* with a little envy. In the eighth court he sees Vasanta's brother, "dressed in silk raiment, glittering with rich ornaments, and rolling about as if his limbs were out of joint;" and next he observes that lady's mother "dressed in flowered muslin, her feet, shining with oil, thrust into a pair of slippers;" a very portly old dame he thinks, but cannot imagine how she got into her seat, unless, like an unwieldy image of Siva, she was set up first and then the walls built round her. At length he enters a lovely garden, where the yellow jessamine, and the *grandiflorum,* and the *Zambac,* and the blue *Clitoria* float in festoons between trees of delicious fruit; here in an arbour he receives a kind welcome from Vasanta, the owner of all this splendour. Maitreya tells his story, and presents the string of diamonds; Vasanta smiles, takes the diamonds, puts them to her heart, and playfully bids Maitreya tell that sad gambler, Charudatta, that she will call upon him. Now it so happened that Vasanta already knew the truth of the case, and was again in possession of her casket, for the thief was in love with a servant-girl of hers, to whom he brought his prize. The girl immediately recognized the casket, and succeeded in persuading her lover to restore it to Vasanta, and, by saying that he was commissioned so to do by Charudatta, escape the reputation of being a thief.

Act V. opens with a fine description of a storm :—

"The gathering gloom
Delights the peafowl and distracts the swan,
Not yet prepared for periodic flight. . . .

Through the air. . . . The purple cloud
Rolls stately on, girt by the golden lightning . . .
As by a yellow garb and bearing high,
The long white line of storks. . . .
From the dark womb in rapid fall descend
The silvery drops, and, glittering in the gleam
Shot from the lightning, bright and fitful, sparkle
Like a rich fringe rent from the robe of heaven.
The firmament is filled with scattered clouds;
And, as they fly before the wind, their forms,
As in a picture, image various shapes,
The semblances of storks and soaring swans,
Of dolphins, and the monsters of the deep,
Of dragons vast and pinnacles and towers."

In the midst of this deluge Maitreya returns, and complains to Charudatta that Vasanta and her damsels smiled and laughed and made signs, but kept the jewels: "A pretty job," he says, "to lose a necklace worth the four seas for a thing of little value, and one we neither ate nor drank, and which a thief carried off." Whilst yet talking, Vasanta arrives, under cover of an umbrella, but nevertheless "her locks are drenched with rain, her gentle nerves shaken by angry tempests, and her delicate feet by cumbering mire and massy anklets wearied." The lady enters, approaches Charudatta, throws flowers at him, and says, "Gambler, good evening to you." Playfully she makes her attendant restore the casket, tells him he should not have sent the jewels, and presently he and she confess mutual affection.

In Act VI. Vasanta sends the necklace to Charudatta's wife, saying, "I am Charudatta's handmaid and your slave; then be this necklace again the ornament of that neck to which it of right belongs." But it is returned with these words, "Madam, you are favoured by the son of my lord;

it is not proper for me to accept this necklace: know that the only ornament I value is my husband." Presently the child comes in, complaining of its little cart because it is only made of clay, whilst the child of a neighbour has one of gold. Vasanta caresses the child, laments her poverty, takes off her ornaments, fills his cart with her jewels, tells him she is his mother, and bids him buy a toy-cart of gold, and it is from this incident that the drama obtains its name.

Charudatta's arrangement was that the next day he should meet Vasanta at the Old Flower Garden, and going forward himself he left orders that Vasanta should follow in his curtained carriage drawn by oxen. But whilst Vasanta was preparing, the carriage of her persecutor, the dissolute Prince, was stopped at Charudatta's door, owing to the road being blocked up by country-carts, and in the confusion Vasanta jumped in by mistake. Soon after the Prince meets his carriage, and is well enough pleased to discover Vasanta within, until, finding her as obdurate as ever, he tries to strangle her, and leaves her for dead beneath a heap of dry leaves. Just then a Buddhist devotee appears upon the stage; he had formerly been a bathman and rubber of joints, but, inveigled by gamblers, he was reduced to the extreme of misery, and about to be sold as a slave, when Vasanta, with her usual generosity, gave him protection and redeemed his debt. Determined never again to touch the dice, he had joined the Buddhists, and now, in virtue of his daily duty of begging his food, he was wandering about; he had just been washing his outer garment and was about to spread it out to dry upon the heap of dry leaves beneath which Vasanta lay, when he perceived a hand and heard a sigh, and anon discovered his beloved protectress. His expression is, "It is the lady Vasanta, the devoted worshipper of Buddha." Vasanta makes signs for water: no water is near, but the Sramana applies his wet garment to her face and she revives.

The plot of this Play is further complicated by the adventures of Aryaka, a cowherd, who conspires against the unpopular and weak King then upon the throne: he is described as a man with "arms like the elephant's vast tusks, his breast and shoulders brawny as the lion's, his eyes a coppery-red." The Government succeeded once in capturing this insurgent, but he escaped from his prison and had taken refuge in Charudatta's carriage at the time it was waiting at his door for Vasanta. The driver mistook the clank of his chain for the jingle of the lady's bangles, drove on and brought him to the garden. The unhappy Charudatta, grieved though he be at his disappointment, is too generous not to help a fugitive in his distress, and desires Aryaka to go forward in the carriage until safe beyond the frontier. In Act IX. we are introduced to a Hall of Justice, where the Prince accuses Charudatta of being the murderer of Vasanta, and where Charudatta is tried according to the Code of Manu. The end of the whole is, that Vasanta reappears just as Charudatta, adorned with a funeral wreath of oleander, is about to be executed; and Aryaka having at the same moment defeated the King and obtained possession of the throne, Charudatta is not only released, restored to life and honour, but receives high office and dominion from the new sovereign. Charudatta is now anxious to show his gratitude to the Buddhist Sramana who saved Vasanta; and, as the devotee says it is his wish "to follow still the path he has selected, because all else is full of care and change," he procures for him the honourable appointment of "Chief of the Viharas." The Prince's servant, who had also assisted and who was a slave, is made a free man, and the Chandalas, who had purposely delayed the execution, are made heads of their tribe; even the wicked Prince is set free by the benevolence of Charudatta, whose wife embraces Vasanta, calling her "happy sister;" and the Tenth Act closes on a scene of perfect unanimity and bliss.

In the eighth century arose another dramatist, whose works still enjoy a popularity second only to those of Kalidasa. Bhavabhuti flourished at the Court of Kanouj, A.D. 720: he was a native of Berar, and delights in descriptions of its gloomy forests. His style is vigorous and harmonious; but, "although classical, it is highly laboured," —the author being fond of an unseasonable display of learning." His Play of 'Malati and Madhava' is interesting, not only on account of its plot and poetry, but for the hints it gives of the prevailing religious Siva worship, then beginning to assume a terrific character, and Buddhist convents being tolerated under Brahmanical governments. To the superiors of these convents indeed we find Kings and Prime Ministers entrusting the education of their children. Madhava, the hero, is son to a King of Behar, and is sent to Ougein to be instructed in logic under the auspices of a female Buddhist devotee, a friend of his father's, and the Superior of the Buddhist Institutions in Ougein. This same woman has been nurse, and is still the confidential friend, of our heroine Malati, who is daughter to the Prime Minister of Malwa. The scene is laid in Ougein, and a pleasing description given of the town and its surrounding scenery as seen from a neighbouring height.*

> "How wide the prospect spreads—mountain and rock,
> Towns, villages, and woods, and glittering streams.
> There, where the *Para* and the *Sindhu* wind,
> The towers, and pinnacles, and gates,
> And spires of *Padmavati*, like a city
> Precipitated from the skies, appear
> Inverted in the pure translucent wave.
> There flows *Lavana's* frolic stream, whose groves,
> By early rains refreshed, afford the youth
> Of *Padmavati* pleasant haunts, and where,
> Upon the herbage brightening in the shower,
> The heavy-uddered kine contented browse."

The character who gives the above description is another female Buddhist who has attained the rank which confers the power of flying through the air: and consequently through the air she came from a hill in Berar, sacred to a Sivaite goddess. The whole Play shows that occasional union of Buddhism and Sivaism which we have already remarked on coins, and in the Tantra portions of the northern Buddhist books. The devotee pauses in her flight to render homage at a Sivaite temple, "fane of the Lord of *Bhavani*, whose illustrious image is not of mortal fabric." "Hail! all hail!" she cries, "Creator of the universe! source of the sacred *Vedas!* God of the crescent-crested diadem! destroyer of love's presumptuous power!"

Professor Wilson says "there is more passion in the thoughts of Bhavabhuti than in those of Kalidasa, but less fancy:" he makes no attempt at wit, but, "on the other hand, he expatiates more largely in the description of pic-

* H. H. Wilson, Hindu Theatre, vol. ii.; Introduction to 'Malati and Madhava.'

turesque scenery and in the representation of human emotions, and is perhaps entitled to even a higher place than his rival as a poet."*

The Mudra Rakshasa† is again different from either of its predecessors, and with this we must conclude our notices of Hindu dramas. The plot is a series of political intrigues without a single love-scene, and almost without the introduction of a woman. Much variety is nevertheless contrived: one of the spies goes about with a scroll inscribed with figures of Yama, about whom he sings verses, and calls his performance a Yama show, in virtue of which he gains admission to the houses of rich men, and exhibits in the courts where the women and children reside. Another spy, or secret messenger, disguises himself as a snake-catcher, holds the following conversation with the passengers in the street, fronting the house of the man with whom he wants to communicate:—

"*Scene before Rakshasa's house.*

Enter VIRADHA, *an agent of Rakshasa, disguised as a snake-catcher.*

Viradha. Those who are skilled in charms and potent signs may handle fearlessly the fiercest snakes.

Passenger. Hola! what and who are you?

Viradha. A snake-catcher, your Honour; my name is *Jirnavisha.* What say you, you would touch my snakes? What may your profession be, pray? Oh, I see, a servant of the Prince,—you had better not meddle with snakes. A snake-catcher unskilled in charms and antidotes, a man mounted on a furious elephant without a goad, and a servant of the King appointed to a high station and proud of his success, these three are on the eve of destruction. Oh! he is off.

Second Passenger. What have you got in your basket, fellow?

Viradha. Tame snakes, your Honour, by which I get my living.

* Hindu Theatre, vol. ii. p. 122.

† *Ibid.*, vol. ii. p. 127.

Would you wish to see them? I will exhibit them here, in the court of this house, as this is not a convenient spot.

Second Passenger. This, you blockhead, is the house of Rakshasa, the Prince's minister; there is no admittance for us here.

Viradha. Then go your way, Sir: by the authority of my occupation I shall make bold to enter. So,—I have got rid of him."

Viradha then changes his language from the Prakrit vernacular to Sanskrit, and makes a long soliloquy.

When Rakshasa is informed that a snake-catcher is anxious to see him, he feels his left eye throb, which is an unlucky omen, and he desires that the man may receive a donation and be sent away. A servant goes therefore to the snake-catcher and says,—

" *Servant.* Here is for your pains; for not seeing,—not for seeing.

Viradha. Inform the minister that besides exhibiting snakes I am a poet, . . . and give him this."

The verses show that he is the bearer of news, and procure him an immediate audience.

We will allude but to one more drama,—Retnavali, or the Necklace. It is considerably later than any of those yet mentioned, and shows a more complicated mythology. The Benediction alludes to Siva thus:—"May that presentation of the flowery offering, made by the mountain-goddess to her mighty lord, preserve you! May Siva ever be your trust! Prosperity attend illustrious Brahmans!"

In the conduct of the plot, and also in the style of the language, there is a marked imitation of the celebrated Kalidasa, but more extravagance. At the commencement the Queen and her damsels celebrate the festival of Kamadeva, "the flower-armed God," "the lord of Reti." He is supposed to be abiding in an Asoka-tree, and the Queen, standing near this tree, presents to his image gifts of sandal, saffron, and flowers; and as soon as the worship of the divinity is concluded, she, according to prescribed usage, offers similar adoration to her husband. Amongst other incidents a great sage is mentioned as having arrived from a hill-temple consecrated to Siva in Berar: his sanctity has conferred upon him gifts of magic, and he teaches the King the craft of making flowers blossom at any season; but the most striking scene is one in which a magician from Ougein exhibits his art in the presence of the King, Queen, and Court. He comes forward laughing and waving a bunch of peacock's feathers, saying,—

> "Reverence to Indra, who lends our art his name! . . . What are your Majesty's commands? would you see the moon brought down upon earth, a mountain in mid-air, a fire in the ocean, or night at noon? . . . What need of many words? By the force of my master's spells I will place before your eyes the person whom in your heart you are most anxious to behold."

After the King has said, "Now, Sir, display your power," he waves his plume and cries,—

> "Hari, Hara, Brahmá, chiefs of the Gods! and thou their mighty monarch, Indra, with the host of heavenly spirits . . . appear rejoicing and dancing in the heavens!
>
> [*The King and Queen look up and rise from their seats.*
>
> *King.* Most wonderful!
>
> *Queen.* Extraordinary indeed!
>
> *King.* See, love! that is Brahmá throned upon the lotus; that *Sankara,* with the crescent moon, his glittering crest; that, *Hari,* the destroyer of the demon race, in whose four hands the bow, the sword, the mace, and the shell are borne. There, mounted on his stately elephant, appears the King of *Swerga;* around them countless spirits dance merrily in mid-air, sporting with the lovely nymphs of heaven, whose anklets ring responsive to the measure."

The spectacle is interrupted by the arrival of ministers

from Ceylon, and the magician is dismissed; but whilst the King is giving audience to his newly-arrived guests, a cry arises that

> "The inner apartments are on fire. The flames spread over the roof of gold; they wind around with clouds of smoke . . . and fill the female train with fear."

The King rushes into the flames to rescue a maiden whom he loves; but he no sooner releases her from her imprisonment than the flames disappear, and the palace stands unharmed, and the semblance of fire is found to have been the work of the magician, who possessed similar skill to that displayed in the presence of the King of Prasenajit, at Kosala.

CHAPTER IV.

"When at length four weary months have fled,
Vishnu rises from his Serpent-bed."*—*Old Indian Poetry.*

When historical data are notoriously slight and scattered, students can do little more than rehearse and make summaries. A muster-roll of the kings, whose unpronounceable names appear on coins, could teach but little, for it would be too hard a lesson for the memory; but a slight outline of the facts beaten out from Archæology may be traced and retraced with advantage, so often as fresh facts appear.

* The Serpent-couch is the mythological snake Ananta, whose thousand heads formed a canopy over Vishnu during his four months' sleep,—supposed to allude to the four months of the periodical rains. (See Wilson.)

Commencing* therefore about B.C. 160, we find Menander, Apollodotus, and other Greeks, holding dominion on the Indus. Guzerat and the lower part of Scinde is governed either by Hindu viceroys, under Greek sovereigns, or by public assemblies, choosing a chief who acknowledged fealty to the Greek superior. In B.C. 157, this condition of affairs was changed by a dynasty of Hindus called the Sahs; they were independent kings in Guzerat, issued their own coins, and carried on extensive public works successfully for about one hundred years. In B.C. 57 the Hindu hero Vikramaditya conquered Greeks, Indo-Scythians, and Sahs, extending his sovereignty from the Nerbudda to the Himalaya, making Ougein, in Malwa, his capital city, but holding Kashmere also under his dominion. In B.C. 26 the Yu-chi Scythians, under Kadphises, Kanerki, and their followers, made conquests in India, and for a time got possession of Scinde and Malwa. In A.D. 91 died Salihavana, a Brahmanical Hindu Raja, celebrated for having delivered Malwa from the Kanerkis and their Indo-Scythian or Turanian followers. The next important event is the death of Meghavahana, whose name signifies "Great Rider upon the clouds." He was a zealous Buddhist; his death occurred A.D. 144, and from this time forth Brahmanism appears to have kept the ascendency in all the important towns of India. After this period we find Buddhists of note and learning going to China, or settling themselves in Nipal, Kashmere, or in Southern India; and it is reasonable to conjecture that persecution or neglect in earlier sites drove Buddhist colonies to establish themselves among the western

* The above sketch is made from the careful deductions of Mr. Thomas, in the 'Journal of the Asiatic Society,' vol. xiii.

hills of the Peninsula, where their wonderful excavations at Ellora and Ajunta are so notorious.

The next important Hindu dynasty is the Guptas; and, judging by the coinage, it appears that the Mint of Minnagara on the Indus, established by the Greeks, was used first by the Sahs, then by the Kanerkis, and lastly by the Guptas. The series of Gupta is very long, and the symbols undergo considerable variation. They commence with Siva and the Bull,* and the Peacock of Siva's son, or his wife, seated on a lion, holding in her hand a lotus. At length we come to a stout man on horseback called Mahendra Gupta, dressed in loose trousers, a buttoned coat, and a full-bottomed wig,—the counterpart of wigs worn both in Buddhist and Sivaite paintings at Ajunta and Arungabad. In A.D. 319 the Guptas were driven out of Guzerat by the Sena family, who had acted as their viceroys, and, taking the name of Vallabhi, this became one of the most celebrated of Hindu dynasties; their capital was on the eastern coast of Guzerat, but now lies buried beneath overwhelming sands. From the Chinese we know that Buddhism was still patronized in some parts of Central India even so late as A. D. 645; but during the seventh century it gradually declined and disappeared; whilst Sivaism adopted gloomy and terrible forms, and then both Poetry and Architecture point to the rising superiority of the old God Vishnu. This deity appears in the earliest books, even in the Rig-Veda hymns, but merely as one amongst many

* Skanda Gupta has his fame recorded on a pillar at Gorakpur, as resembling Indra in his rule, possessed of the chiefest of riches, and born of the royal race of Guptas, whose earthly throne was shaken by the wind of the bowing heads of a hundred kings. J. A. S. B., vol. viii., p. 37.

inferior divinities. In the epic poems he is also mentioned, but rather as an after-thought, to give dignity to the popular heroes Rama and Krishna. In the Bhagavat Gita, the poem which we have now to consider, he is, on the contrary, an integral part of the composition. With Krishna as a friendly warrior we have already made acquaintance; but in the Bhagavat Gita, Krishna is identified with the God Vishnu, and the God Vishnu is declared to be the Supreme Deity from whom all things have issued, and into whom all will be absorbed. This poem is attributed to the seventh or eighth century of our era, and it acknowledges the two divisions of the Sankhya philosophy; but, avoiding the Buddhist error of driving abstract argument into nothingness, it rests mind, virtue, and phenomena upon God. It does not deny inferior Gods, and it devoutly believes in transmigration, and in a material form of Supreme Deity; but to a Christian who has waded through the arid wastes of Buddhist Sutras it sounds almost as a far-off echo of home to a Siberian exile. It pretends to a place as episode in the Mahabharata, an epic poem which must have been eight hundred years old before the Bhagavat Gita can have been written, but its being so placed is consistent with the Brahmanical aim of investing old literature with a new religious character. The story of the Mahabharata serves therefore as a framework, giving us again the generous Arjuna and his friend the powerful Krishna. The last tremendous battle between the Kurus and the Pandus is about to begin. The forces on either side are marshalled face to face; Krishna stands by Arjuna in his splendid chariot drawn by white horses, whilst on the opposite side the chief of the Kurus, shouting like a lion, blows his shell to raise the spirits of his followers; immediately other shells reply, and the clangour is excessive. Arjuna is overcome with distress at the idea that the enemies opposed to him are all of his own kindred,—grandsires, cousins, tutors, bosom-friends; he would rather die, he says, than be the murderer of his race. "I wish not for victory; I want not dominion; . . . although they would kill me, I wish not to fight them; no, not even for the dominion of the three regions of the universe, much less for this little earth." And at length he puts his bow and arrows aside, and sits down, "his heart overwhelmed with affliction." Krishna combats his arguments, telling him, that to stand still in the field of battle is contrary to duty. Arjuna replies respectfully, "I am thy disciple, instruct me, my understanding is confounded; I see nothing that could assuage the grief which drieth up my faculties, even were I to obtain a kingdom unrivalled upon earth, or dominion over the hosts in heaven." Krishna then applies a different argument, saying, it is folly to grieve either for the dead or for the living, "because the soul neither killeth nor is killed, it is without birth, and cannot be destroyed in this its mortal frame." Arjuna must therefore fight without trembling; for to fight is his duty as a Kshattriya, and duty requires men to work bravely and without concern for the result. Krishna's argument will be yet more favourably explained if we once more borrow from the beautiful translations of 'Old Indian Poetry,' for which we are indebted to Mr. Griffith:—

"Know that What Is can never cease to Be,
What Is Not can Be never: they who see
The mystic Truth, the Wise, alone can tell

The nature of the things they study well.
And be thou sure the mighty boundless Soul,
The Eternal Essence, that pervades this Whole,
Can never perish, never waste away;
The Indestructible knows not decay. . . .
Up, then, and conquer! in thy might arise!
Fear not to slay It, for It never dies. . . .
As men throw off their garments worn and old,
And newer raiment round their bodies fold,
The ethereal spirit leaves its mortal shell,
And finds another form wherein to dwell.
Essence of Life! It lives, undimm'd its ray,
Though fiercest fire or keen dart seek to slay. . . .
Incomprehensible! It knows not change,
Boundless in being, limitless in range.
This is the Nature of the Soul, great Chief!
It lives for ever, therefore spare thy grief. . . .
All that is born must die,—that dies, be born again."

Krishna further warns his disciple not to be guided exclusively by the speculative portion of the Sankhya philosophy, but to attend also to the practical; and not to delight "in the controversies of the Veds," which ordain innumerable ceremonies and lead to mere transient enjoyment, but to be "free from duplicity, to stand firm in the path of duty, free from care and trouble." "Let the motive," he continues, "be in the deed, and not in the event. Be not one whose motive for action is the hope of reward. Let not thy life be spent in inaction. Depend upon application, perform thy duty, abandon all thought of the consequence, and make the event equal, whether it terminate in good or evil; for such an equality is called *Yog*. The action stands at a distance inferior to the application of wisdom. Seek an asylum then in wisdom alone . . . When thy reason shall get the better of the gloomy weakness of thy heart, then shalt thou have attained all knowledge which hath been, or is worthy to be taught. When thy understanding, by study brought to maturity, shall be fixed immovably in contemplation, then shall it obtain true wisdom."

Such a wise man is called a Muni. His wisdom is established when in all things he is without affection, and neither rejoiceth at good nor is cast down by evil; when, like the tortoise, he can draw in all his members and restrain them from their wonted purposes. What happiness can he enjoy who hath no rest? The heart, which followeth the dictates of the moving passions, carrieth away his reason as the storm the bark in the raging ocean. But he obtaineth happiness whose passions enter his soul (or heart) as the multitudinous rivers flow into the unswelling passive ocean.

In Lecture III. Arjuna begs Krishna to explain how it is that, if the use of the understanding be superior to the practice of deeds, he should be urged to so dreadful an undertaking as war with relatives. Krishna replies, that exemption from action is only to be obtained by a previous wise performance of action for unselfish motives. Warnings are then given against self-sufficiency, and against illiberality towards others. A man who has much knowledge and might dispense with outward works, must not drive those from works who are slow of comprehension and less experienced than himself; rather should he still perform works, in order to induce the vulgar to attend to them. But whilst a wise man performs works, he must not be led astray by the pride of self-sufficiency to suppose that he himself is the executor of those actions which are performed by the principles of his constitution. And then, speaking in his character of *Iswara*, God, or the Lord, Krishna says,—

"Throw every deed on me, and, with a heart over which the soul presideth, be free from hope, be unpresuming, be free from trouble, and resolve to fight."

In the following Lecture Arjuna ventures to question Krishna concerning his nature and the length of time which he has existed; Krishna replies,—

"Both thou and I have passed many births: mine are known unto me, but thou knowest not of thine.

"Although I am not in my nature subject to birth or decay, and am the Lord of all created beings; yet, having command over my own nature, I am made evident by my own power; and as often as there is a decline of virtue and an insurrection of vice and injustice in the world, I make myself evident; and thus I appear from age to age for the preservation of the just, the destruction of the wicked, and the establishment of virtue."

Some interesting observations follow, upon the great varieties of men's actions and the various modes in which they worship or sacrifice. Some sacrificing their "breathing spirit," others their organs and faculties; all worship is acknowledged to be beneficial, but that worship alone is wise which recognizes God, or Iswara, in everything:—

"God is the gift of charity, God is the offering, God is in the fire of the altar, by God is the sacrifice performed; and God is to be obtained by him who maketh God alone the object of his works."

In Lecture V. we learn, that to abandon works means to abandon the hope of reward, and to act wholly in a spirit of faith. Krishna says:—"Children only, and not the learned, speak of the speculative and the practical doctrines as two; they are but one, for both obtain the same end;" and whilst to be a recluse without a spiritual state of mind is to obtain pain and trouble, he who is employed in the practice of his duty presently obtaineth *Brahme.* To these difficulties Krishna replies, that the discipline called *Yog* only requires practice and temperance, and, although difficult, may be attained by one who hath his soul in his subjection; but supposing death to occur before this happy consummation, the man endued with faith will not be destroyed.

"No man who hath done good goeth unto an evil place. A man whose devotions have been broken off by death, having enjoyed for an immensity of years the rewards of his virtues in the regions above at length is born again in some holy and respectable family, or perhaps in the house of some learned *Yogi.* The Yogi is more exalted than *Tapasas,*—those zealots who harass themselves in performing penances,—he is more respected than the learned in science, and superior to those who are attached to moral works; wherefore, O Arjuna! resolve thou to become a Yogi. Of all Yogas I respect him as the most devout who hath faith in me, and who serveth me with a soul possessed of my spirit."

It will be unnecessary to follow this poem or treatise through its laboured exposition of the Vedanta system, with its eight distinctions and its three qualities and the three mystic words, this, and the Sankhya systems, etc. we studied sufficiently in the Chapter on Philosophy at the close of Book I. But we must dwell upon the views of Faith and Deity which are here displayed, for they deviate considerably from any which we meet with at an earlier epoch.

"The man who performing the duties of life, and quitting all interest in them, placeth them upon *Brahme,* floats like a lotus on the lake unruffled by the tide."

"The man who keepeth the outward accidents from entering his mind, and his eyes fixed in contemplation between his brows; who

maketh the breath to pass through both his nostrils alike in expiration and inspiration; the man who is happy in his heart, at rest in his mind, and enlightened within, is a *Yogi*, and obtaineth the immaterial nature of *Brahme*, the Supreme."

In Lecture VI. we find the following sketch of a *Yogi* :—

"He is a recluse of a subdued mind and spirit, free from hope and free from perception. He planteth his own feet firmly on a spot that is undefiled, neither too high nor too low, and sitteth upon the sacred grass which is called *Kusa*, covered with a skin and a cloth. There he, whose business is the restraining of his passions, should sit with his mind fixed on one object alone, in the exercise of his devotion for the purification of his soul; keeping his head, his neck, his body steady without motion, his eyes fixed on the point of his nose, looking at no other place around."

This condition cannot be attained by him who eats more than enough or less than enough; neither by him who hath a habit of sleeping much, nor by him who sleepeth not at all. A man is called devout when his mind remaineth thus regulated within himself; and the Yogi thus employed is like a lamp, standing in a place without wind, which waveth not.

Arjuna ventures to express that, considering the restlessness of human nature, he cannot conceive the permanent duration of such a doctrine. "The mind, O Krishna!" he continues, "is naturally unsteady, turbulent, strong, and stubborn; I esteem it as difficult to restrain as the wind." He also intimates a wish to behold Krishna as the Universal Spirit, or "Mighty Lord." Krishna says, that as his natural eye would be unequal to the sight, he will give him a heavenly eye for the purpose; and having thus spoken,—

"The mighty compound and divine being Hări made evident

unto Arjuna his supreme and heavenly form; of many a mouth and eye; many a wondrous sight; many a heavenly ornament; many an up-raised weapon; adorned with celestial robes and chaplets; anointed with heavenly essence; covered with every marvellous thing; the Eternal God, whose countenance is on every side! The glory and amazing splendour of this mighty Being may be likened to the sun rising at once into the heavens with a thousand times more than usual brightness. The son of Pandu then beheld within the body of the God of Gods, standing together, the whole universe divided forth into its vast variety. He was overwhelmed with wonder, and every hair was raised an end. He bowed down his head before the God, and thus addressed him with joined hands:—

"'I behold, O God! within thy breast the *dewas* assembled, and every specific tribe of beings. I see Brahma sitting on his lotus throne; . . . I see thyself of infinite shape, . . . with abundant arms, mouths, eyes, . . . etc.; but I can neither discover thy beginning, thy middle, nor thy end. . . . Again I see thee with a crown, and armed with club and *Chakra*, a mass of glory darting refulgent beams around. . . .

"'Of the celestial bands I see some flying to thee for refuge; whilst some, afraid, with joined hands sing forth thy praise. . . . The world, like me, are terrified to behold thy wondrous form gigantic, . . . with many mouths and eyes, . . . and with rows of dreadful teeth. Thus I see thee touching the heavens, and shining with such glory; of such various hues, with widely opened mouths, and bright expanded eyes. . . . Having beholden thy dreadful teeth and gazed on thy countenance, Time's last fire, I know not which way I turn! I find no peace. . . . The sons of Kuru, and even the fronts of our army, seem to be precipitating themselves hastily into thy mouths, discovering such frightful rows of teeth! whilst some appear to stick between thy teeth with their bodies sorely mangled. . . . As flowing rivers roll on to the ocean, so these heroes rush on towards thy flaming mouths. As troops of insects seek destruction in the flaming fire, even so these people, swelling with fury, seek their own destruction. Thou involvest and swallowest them, whilst the whole world is filled with thy glory. Deign to make known to me, thou most exalted! who is this God of awful figure.'"

The concluding chapters are chiefly occupied with explanations of Brahmc or essential essence, substance, nature, and qualities, taken apparently from the Upanishads; but the application is different, for the worshipper is not directed to fix his mind upon Brahme, the indefinite essence of deity, but upon the personal God Vishnu, of whom Krishna was a visible form. The following lines are taken from Mr. Griffith's poetical translation of these passages :—

> "Life of all life! prop of this earthly frame!
> Whither all creatures go, from whence they came,
> I am the Best; from Me all beings spring,
> And rest on me, like pearls upon their string.
> I am the Father, and the fostering Nurse,
> Grandsire, and Mother of the Universe;
> I am the Vedas, and the Mystic Word,
> The Way, Support, the Witness, and the Lord.
> They who with pious care have studied o'er,
> And made their own the triple Veda's lore,
> Whose fires have glow'd . . . . . .
> . . . hie to Indra's holy sphere, and share
> The joy of Gods, ...
> And gain their longing bliss, but for a day.
> But those a nobler, higher blessing find,
> Who worship me with all their heart and mind:
> Me, only Me, their wrapt devotion knows,
> With Me alone their tranced spirit glows. . . .
> Do all thine acts to Me through all thy days,
> Thy food, thy gifts, thy sacrifice, thy praise;
> Then will the bonds of actions done by thee,
> Worthy or evil, leave thy spirit free;
> And thy pure soul, renouncing earthly care,
> Will come unshackled, and My Essence share.
> Though equal looks on all things I bestow,
> Nor enmity nor partial fondness know;
> Yet happy they who love Me faithfully,
> I dwell within them ever,—they in Me."

This is the same principle of *bhakti*, or faith, which we found faintly appearing in the north-west Provinces, where, shortly after the Christian era, Siva was worshipped as *Swayambhu*, and Sakya-Sinha as Adi-Buddha. Minor deities were in neither case altogether banished; and it was becoming possible to the worshipper to conceive the Eternal Essence, as a Unity, holding personal relations towards mankind. Professor Wilson notices the resemblance of the doctrines of the Bhagavat Gita to those of some divisions of the early Christian schools, and hints that the remodelling of the ancient Hindu systems into popular forms, and "in particular the vital importance of faith, were directly influenced by the diffusion of the Christian religion."* We hail also with satisfaction a similar opinion from Professor Lassen. Brahmans he believes to have met with Christianity in the countries bordering upon Kashmere. St. Thomas he believes really to have visited Parthia; and although he denies the possibility of St. Thomas himself having reached Madras or any part of India, he sees no reason to doubt that Christian churches were introduced into southern India within the first four or five centuries of our era.†

* Oriental Magazine, vol. iii.

† Indische Alterth. vol. ii. p. 1103; see also Wilson, Introd. Vishnu Purana, p. 8.

CHAPTER V.

> "'Tis the old-age of day, methinks, or haply
> The infancy of night." BARRY CORNWALL.

IT cannot be determined when the heroes Rama and Krishna became elevated to the dignity of divinities; but legends of Vishnu thus personified are given at length in the Puranas, and are evidently derived from the same religious system as the Ramayana and the Mahabharata. A gradual change may be traced from the domestic elemental worship of the Vedas, "addressed to unreal presences," down to "the sectarial fervour and exclusiveness" of modern Hindu idolatry. Of these modern modes the Puranas are the chief exponents: they are voluminous works written at different periods, and compiled under various circumstances; none of them, probably, in all respects the same works as were current under this name in the century previous to Christianity,* and in their present forms "the oldest of them not" estimated as "anterior to the eighth or ninth cen-

* Oxford Lectures, H. H. Wilson, pp. 25, 27, 31.

tury," whilst some are not above three or four centuries old.* They appear to have been composed chiefly during the religious ferment, which had for its object the extermination of the Buddhists, beginning in the third or fourth century of our era. The doctrine of the sufficiency of faith alone is "carried to the very utmost of that abuse of which it is susceptible. Entire dependence upon Krishna, or any other favourite deity," not only obviating the necessity of virtue, but sanctifying vice.† Krishna as the boy Cowherd, or Krishna as the lover of Radha, are the characters in which he is most popular. These legends we shall find in the Vishnu Purana, translated by Professor Wilson; and some acquaintance with them is necessary if we would understand the mythology exhibited in literature, religion, paintings, and architecture, since the disappearance of Buddhism from India.

Vishnu is announced as born on earth, in the family of Yadu, and consequently "whoever hears the account of the race of Yadu shall be released from all sin." The Yadus were settled at Dwaraka, on the west coast of Guzerat: their government was chiefly carried on by means of public assemblies, at which even women were present; and although they had a king, no great importance seems to have attached to his office. At the period of the following story Krishna lived amongst the Yadus as a powerful and successful warrior. At times he is alluded to as a form of the God Vishnu, but never in the character of an earthly sovereign. The following is abridged from Wilson's 'Vishnu Purana:'—

* Vishnu Purana, Introd., H. H. Wilson, pp. 3, 6, 9.

† Oxford Lectures, H. H. Wilson, pp. 25, 27, 31.

STORY OF THE SYAMANTAKA GEM.

A king named Satrajit enjoyed the privilege of a personal acquaintance with the Sun. As he walked along the seashore at Dwaraka he addressed hymns and praises to him, and presently the divinity appeared and stood before him; but the shape was indistinct, and the King said, "I have beheld thee, Lord, in the heavens as a globe of fire; now do thou show favour to me, that I may see thee in thy proper form." On this, taking the jewel called Syamantaka from his neck, he placed it apart, and Satrajit then beheld him of a dwarfish stature, with a body like burnished copper, and with slightly reddish eyes. Having offered his adorations, the Sun desired him to demand a boon, and he requested to have the jewel. The Sun immediately presented it to him, and then resumed his place in the sky. Satrajit placed the spotless gem of gems upon his neck and returned to Dwaraka; but the inhabitants, startled at the approach of such effulgence, fled in consternation to the warrior Krishna, saying, "Lord, assuredly the Divine Sun is coming to visit you." Krishna smiled at their fears, and assured them that they had not seen the Sun, but merely their own king Satrajit, to whom the Sun had presented the Syamantaka gem. Satrajit in the meantime reached his house, and there deposited the jewel, which, by virtue of its presence, yielded eight loads of gold a day, and averted fearful portents, wild beasts, fire, robbers, and famine.

Krishna was privately of opinion that this wonderful gem should have been given to Ugrasena, another Yadu chief and his own near relative, but he said nothing, in order to avoid quarrels. Satrajit nevertheless lived in terror lest Krishna should demand the jewel, and in order to preserve it he transferred it to his brother. Now it was the peculiar property of this jewel, that although it was an inexhaustible source of good to a virtuous man, it caused death to the wicked. The King's brother was not virtuous; but he took the gem, hung it round his neck, concealed it from view, mounted his horse, and went into the woods to hunt.

In the chase a lion killed him, and, taking the jewel in his mouth, was trotting off, when he was observed and killed by the King of the Bears, who, securing the gem, retired to his cave and gave it to his little son to play with. When a length of time had elapsed and the King's brother did not reappear, whispers began to circulate that this must be Krishna's doing, who, desirous of possessing the jewel, had killed the wearer.

These rumours no sooner reached the indignant Krishna than, collecting a number of Yadavas around him, he tracked the course of the hunter; and the impressions of the horse's hoofs giving full evidence that both horse and man had been killed by a lion, Krishna was at once acquitted. Wishing however to recover the gem he followed the steps of the lion, and arrived at the spot where the lion had been killed by the bear; and then tracking the footsteps of the bear he arrived at the foot of a mountain, where he desired his followers to wait for him whilst he ascended to the cavern residence of the King of the Bears.

He had scarcely entered when he saw the nurse holding up the jewel to the child in her arms. Seeing Krishna with his eyes fixed upon the gem, the nurse screamed, and the King of the Bears came at her cry. A conflict then took place between Krishna and the bear, which lasted one and twenty days. After seven or eight days Krishna's followers gave him up, returned to the town, and reported he was dead. This was a most fortunate circumstance for Krishna, for his relations immediately performed funeral rites, and the food and water thus offered supported him in his combat; whilst the bear, bruised in every limb and exhausted for want of food, cast himself upon the ground and declared that his mighty antagonist must be invincible, and "a portion of Narayana, the defender of the Universe."* Krishna acknowledged this to be the case, explained the purpose of his being on earth, and relieved the pain which the bear suffered from his wounds; and he and the bear then became such good friends that the former accepted the bear's daughter in marriage, and taking the jewel accompanied his bride to Dwaraka.

When the people beheld him returning to them alive, they were seized with such delight that old people recovered youthful vigour, and men and women assembled around the father of the hero offering congratulations. Krishna related to the assembly everything exactly as it had happened, and, restoring the jewel to the King, was exonerated from the crime of which he had been accused.

The King alone remained uneasy, reflecting that he had been the cause of the aspersions cast upon the character of the hero; and, with a view to reconciliation and safety, he presented his daughter to Krishna as a wife. This proceeding had precisely the reverse effect to that intended; for three of the most distinguished Yadu chiefs had already been in treaty with the King for the possession of this

* Narayana is one of Vishnu's names.

daughter; and when he disgraced them by conferring her upon another, they made a league amongst themselves to kill the King, seize the jewel, and support each other if attacked in consequence by the mighty Krishna.

At this conjuncture news arrived at Dwaraka that Krishna's friends, Arjuna and his four Pandu brothers, had been burned in their house by order of the Kurus. Krishna knew that they had escaped, but they were in danger, and he started instantly to their assistance. His absence gave the offended lovers a safe opportunity for killing the King and seizing the gem; but the King's daughter was Krishna's wife, and seized with fury she mounted her chariot, travelled to her husband, and implored him to avenge the heinous wrong. Although Krishna is ever internally tranquil, his eyes flashed whilst she told her tale; but when he spoke it was to beg his wife to dismiss excessive sorrow, for it required not her lamentations, he said, to excite his wrath. Krishna quickly returned to Dwaraka, and the chief who had struck the blow took alarm, and his two associates refused help: he left the jewel with the one named Akrura, mounted a very swift mare that could travel a hundred leagues in a day, and fled towards Upper India. Krishna forthwith harnessed his four horses to his car, and, accompanied by his brother, set off in quick pursuit. The mare of the fugitive was true to her hundred *yojanas;* but on reaching Mithila, in Tirhut, she dropped down dead. When Krishna reached the spot he left Balarama in the car, and running over a few miles of rough ground, which no carriage could have traversed, he discharged his discus and struck off his adversary's head whilst yet at a considerable distance. He then searched the man for the jewel, but unable to find it he returned, and told Balarama what had occurred. Balarama flew into a rage, believing that Krishna had secreted the precious gem; and in consequence he refused to return to Dwaraka, and for three years remained in cities on the Ganges. Akrura in the meantime obtained the throne of Dwaraka, and kept the gem in secret. For fifty-two years he lived in affluence, the virtue of the gem averting death and pestilence; but at the end of that period he abandoned his throne and his duty, taking flight with some allies in a neighbouring political disturbance; then came portents, snakes, dearth, and plague. So strange a coincidence induced Krishna to call a public assembly, at which it was agreed that Akrura must be recalled; and no sooner did he return than the plague and famine ceased. Krishna was now confirmed in his belief that Akrura had possession of the Syamantaka gem; and on the pretext of a festive celebration, he called a meeting of Yadavas at his own house. After other business was dismissed, he laughed and joked and said to Akrura, "Kinsman, you are a very prince in your liberality; but we know very well that you have the precious wealth-supplying jewel in your possession. Your holding it has been to the great benefit of this kingdom, so with you let it remain; but my brother Balarama suspects that I have it, therefore out of kindness to me show it to this assembly. Akrura hesitated, but said at length, "It is true that the jewel of the Sun was entrusted to me: it has caused me much anxiety; and fearing that you might not consent to my being the holder of a jewel so essential to the welfare of the kingdom, I forbore to divulge that it was in my hands; but take it now yourself, and give the care of it to whomsoever you please." Akrura then drew forth a small gold box, and took from it the jewel, and the whole chamber was illuminated by its radiance. "Here," said Akrura, "is the gem, let him to whom it belongs now take it." At the sight of this wonderful jewel the assembly was clamorous with delight. Balarama claimed it as the joint property of himself and Krishna; and Krishna's wife claimed it as having been given to her father; and Krishna himself said that he stood between the two like "an ox between the two wheels of a cart." He addressed himself however to Akrura as follows:—"This jewel has been exhibited in order to clear my reputation: it is the joint right of Balarama and myself, and is the patrimonial inheritance of my wife; but to be of advantage to the kingdom it must be in the charge of a person leading a life of perfect purity. Now as I have sixteen thousand wives, and Balarama is addicted to wine, we are out of the question; and I and my brother and my wife unite with all the Yadavas in requesting that you, most bountiful Akrura, will retain the jewel as heretofore for the general good." Thus urged Akrura accepted the jewel, and thenceforth wore it publicly round his neck, where it shone with dazzling brightness. The story concludes with the following remark:—

> "He who calls to mind the vindication of Krishna from false aspersions, shall never become the subject of unfounded accusation in the least degree, and living in the full exercise of his senses shall be cleansed from every sin."

In a subsequent story, Vishnu's supremacy is distinctly declared, and the frolics of his childhood, when born upon earth as Krishna, are related with much dramatic effect. The first scene is at Mathura (or Muttra), on the Jumna, then inhabited by the Bhojas, a division of the Yadavas. Vasudeva has just married a maiden of celestial beauty; he sits in a car beside his bride, and Kansa, the king of the tribe, acts as his charioteer. Suddenly a voice deep as thunder comes from the sky, telling Kansa that he is a fool, for that the eighth child of the damsel in the car will take away his life. Kansa immediately draws his sword and is about to destroy the prophecy by slaying the damsel, but her husband interposes, saying, "Kill her not, great warrior! and I will deliver to you every child that she may bring forth." Appeased by which promise, and relying on the character of Vasudeva, Kansa desists.

The scene here changes: Earth, groaning under her load of sin and trouble, seeks relief from the gods assembled upon Mount Meru. "Vishnu," she commences, "is the mighty inscrutable being of whom other gods are but a part. This assemblage is but a part of him. The sun, the wind, the saints, the Rudras, . . . the Aswins, fire, . . . all are but forms of the mighty and inscrutable Vishnu. . . . The heavens painted with planets, etc., fire, water, wind, and myself; . . . the whole universe consists of Vishnu." She then proceeds to relate, that at present many demons overrun and harass the region of mortals, and that the chief demon, formerly killed by Vishnu, had revived in the person of the cruel King Kansa, at Mathura. When the gods had heard the complaints of Earth, Brahma, at their request, explained how Earth's burden might be lightened; and since even himself and the other celestials were but impersonations of Vishnu (or Narayana), "Let us," he says, "repair to the northern shore of the Milky Sea, and, having glorified Hari (Vishnu), report to him what we have heard. He who is the spirit of all, and of whom the universe consists, constantly, for the sake of Earth, descends in a small portion of his essence to establish righteousness below." The Gods accordingly repair to Vishnu, and address him, partly in the language of the Vedas,* as "without name or colour, hands or feet, one and multiform, the eye of all, and wearer of many shapes; as fire, though one is variously kindled, and though unchangeable in essence is modified in many ways. To thee, Spirit Supreme! be adoration; Thou assumest a shape, not as a consequence of virtue or of vice, but for the sole object of maintaining piety." The unborn, universal Hari (Vishnu), being pleased with these eulogiums, asked what they desired, and when Brahma explained that the Earth was oppressed by demons, he bade the gods go down to the earth, each in his own portion, and wage war with the mighty Asuras, and for himself he promises to become impersonated as the eighth child of Vasudeva, and in that character to destroy the evil Kansa.

In the meanwhile Vasudeva was true to his promises, he had delivered up all his children to the King, and six had been put to death as soon as born. The seventh child was a portion of Sesha, who was a portion of Vishnu, and this child, named Balarama, was miraculously transferred to Rohini, another wife of Vasudeva. The eighth child was born in prison, and was Vishnu, as Krishna. The guards of the prison were on this occasion charmed by a spell, and the father enabled to fly with his infant to the further side of the river Jumna,

* Vishnu Purana, *note*, p. 495.

where he safely reached an encampment of Gopis, or cowherds, who had come to Mathura in order to pay tribute to Kansa. Whilst the Gopis were yet sleeping, Vasudeva contrived to exchange his child with that of Nanda, the chief of the Gopis; and consequently when Nanda's wife awoke, she found the little Krishna, and rejoiced at having a boy as black as the dark leaves of the lotus. Vasudeva's wife, Rohini, was one of this tribe, and the brothers were consequently brought up together, and became constant companions, although ignorant of their real birth and close relationship.

Vasudeva was however very uneasy so long as the Gopis remained living in their waggons on the banks of the Jumna, and going once more to Nanda, he urged that after the yearly tribute had been paid it was not safe for men of property to tarry near the Court. "Up, Nanda! quickly, and set off to your pastures!" and accordingly, their goods being placed in their waggons, the cowherds returned to their village, called Gokula.

Krishna occasionally startled the community by amazing feats of strength;* as on one occasion when put to sleep in a little bed beneath a waggon, he kicked up his feet, upset the vehicle, and broke in consequence a whole set of pots and pans. He and his brother were in fact most troublesome children, creeping everywhere amongst dust and ashes and getting into the cow-pens amongst the calves to pull their tails; and when tied to a large mortar to keep him quiet, Krishna ran off with it and pulled down a couple of trees, laughing and showing his little white teeth at those who came to see what had caused the crackling noise. When

* Vishnu Purana, *note*, p. 509.

Krishna became a lad, he had a long and arduous contest with a serpent, which, ending successfully, is a favourite subject with Hindu artists. On another occasion his bro-

ther Balarama fought a demon who had mingled in their boyish sports: the game consists of jumping with both feet at once, two boys together, and the one who holds out longest, or comes first to a given point, is victor, and the vanquished then carries him on his shoulders.*

At the conclusion of the rainy season, when the skies were bright with stars, the herdsmen were busily engaged in preparing a sacrifice for Indra; but Krishna, resolving to put the king of the celestials into a passion, persuaded Nanda to worship mountains and cattle, and have nothing to do with Indra. "Kine," he said, "are our support; we have neither fields nor houses; we wander about hap-

* Vishnu Purana, *note*, p. 518.

pily where we list, travelling in our waggons; we are then bound to worship the mountains and offer sacrifices to cattle. What have we to do with Indra?" Offerings of curd, milk, and flesh were in consequence presented to the mountain, and then the worshippers circumambulated the cows and bulls, who bellowed as loud as roaring clouds. Indra's anger broke forth in a furious tempest, which lasted seven days and seven nights, but Krishna protected the distressed community by plucking up the mountain and holding it aloft as an umbrella until the tempest ceased, when he planted it again upon the earth.* Upon witnessing these marvels, the herdsmen wished to render worship to Krishna, but he desired them not to inquire into his nature, but to be contented that he lived among them as a friendly relative. He next amuses himself amongst the *Gopis*, or young damsels of the tribe: he begins by singing sweet low strains, such as women love, and the girls all quit their homes, approach, and are entranced.

At about this period the cruel King Kansa gets information that Krishna is the eighth child of Vasudeva, whom he believed he had killed when an infant, and from whom it was predicted he would meet his death. He sent therefore for one of his nobles, and told him confidently that two vile boys, portions of Vishnu, had been born amongst the Gopis for the express purpose of destroying him, and he bade the Yadu chief go to the settlement and bring them to Mathura, on the pretext of their being present at the festival of arms to be celebrated at the lunation. During the trial of arms, he intended to oppose the youths to his most experienced

* A remarkable representation of this occurs upon the sculptured rocks of Mahabalipur.—Wilson's Vishnu Purana, *note*, p. 527.

boxers, and if not thus destroyed to send his elephant against them; and lastly, his design was to seize upon the flocks and herds of their supposed fathers, for the Gopis, he says, have always been his foes. The Yadu chief accepts the commission, but secretly rejoices in having thus an opportunity of beholding a form of Vishnu. "I shall," he says, "see *Kesava,* who is without beginning or end; by worshipping whom with a hundred sacrifices Indra obtained the sovereignty over the Gods. *Hari,* whose nature is unknown to Brahma, Indra, etc., he who is all and is present to all, he, the unborn, who has preserved this world in the various forms of a fish, a tortoise, a boar, a horse, a lion, glory to that being whose deceptive adoption of father, son, brother, friend, mother, relative, the world is unable to penetrate! Glory to him who is one with true knowledge, who is inscrutable, and through whom, seated in his heart, the Yogi crosses the wide expanse of worldly ignorance and illusion! I put my trust in that unborn, eternal *Hari,* by meditation on whom man becomes the repository of all good things." On another occasion, the same person makes an address to Vishnu, from which the following are extracts :—

"'Salutation to thee who art uniform and manifold! . . . Salutation to thee who art truth and the essence of oblations! Salutation to thee whose nature is unknown, who art beyond primeval matter, who existed in five forms, as one with the faculties, with matter, with the living soul, with supreme spirit! Show favour to me, whether addressed as Brahma, Vishnu, Siva, or the like. I adore thee whose nature is indescribable, whose purposes are inscrutable, whose name even is unknown; for the attributes of kind or appellation are not applicable to thee, who art THAT. . . . But as the accomplishment of our objects cannot be obtained except through some specific form, thou art termed by us Krishna, Achyuta, Ananta, or Vishnu. . . . To him who is one with true knowledge, who is and is not perceptible, I bow. Glory be to him, the lord Vasudeva!'"

Three other names are added, it being customary for worshippers of Vishnu to address him as identical with his brother, his son, and his grandson, and the names usually given are Krishna, Balarama, Pradyumna, and Anirudha.*

Krishna's visit to Mathura ended of course in the death of Kansa; but it is unnecessary to follow all the strange jumble which it makes, of Krishna as Vishnu, and Krishna sporting with men and maidens. On one occasion he offended the King of Benares, who worshipped Siva, and Siva sent in consequence a vast and formidable female, like flame out of fire, blazing with ruddy light, and with fiery radiance streaming amidst her hair. Angrily she called to Krishna and departed to Dwaraka. Krishna was playing at dice, and, seeing the apparition, said to his discus, "Kill this fierce creature whose tresses are of plaited fire." The fiend terrified fled to Benares, but the discus pursued, and, consuming the King and all his forces by its radiance, afterwards set fire to the city, in which the magic power of Siva had concealed herself.

Many stories are told also of his marriage with Rukmimi, daughter of a king of Behar, and of his wild music and dancing with Radha and the Gopis. These are favourite subjects of poems, from one of which Mr. Griffith gives us the following pleasing verses. Nanda, Krishna's foster-father, is the first speaker:—

"Go, gentle Radha! seek thy fearful love;
Dusk are the woodlands, black the sky above;

* Vishnu Purana, *note*, p. 530.

Bring thy dear wanderer home, and bid him rest
His weary head upon thy faithful breast."

A pitying maiden then reveals that Krishna is near at hand, and says,—

"In this love-tide of spring, when the spirit is glad,
And the parted—yes, only the parted—are sad,
Thy lover, thy Krishna, is dancing in glee
With troops of young maidens, forgetful of thee.

"The season is come when the desolate bride
Would woo with laments her dear lord to her side,
When the rich-laden stems of the Vakul bend low
'Neath the clustering flowers in the pride of their glow:
In this love-tide of spring when the spirit is glad, . . .
Thine own, thy dear Krishna, is dancing in glee,
He loves his fair partners and thinks not of thee."

Radha's image however lingered in his breast, and dissatisfied amid his dancing, "he sought his faithful love, and mourned his darling in the shady grove." But she was no longer there, and he sings,—

"She is fled, she is gone! Oh, how angry was she
When she saw the gay shepherd-girls dancing with me!
Oh! how could I speak to her? how could I dare
Entreat her to stay and to pardon me *there?*
Oh, Hari! vile Hari! lament thee and mourn,
Thy lady has left thee, has left thee in scorn!

"How bright in her anger she seems to me now,
With her scorn-flashing glance and her passion-arch'd brow!
And her proud trembling eye in my fancy I see,
Like the lotus that throbs 'neath the wing of the bee.
Oh, Hari! vile Hari! lament thee and mourn,
Thy fair one has left thee, has left thee in scorn!"

Krishna's life appears to have closed amid civil feuds;

for he is said to have assisted in destroying his native city of Dwaraka, and to have migrated with the remnant of the Yadava tribe to the Punjab, and finally to have received his death from a hunter, who shot him whilst absorbed in contemplation under the trees of a lonely forest.

CHAPTER VI.

"Far, like the comet's way through infinite space,
Stretches the long, untravell'd path of light
Into the depth of ages."—BRYANT.

OUR way has now been threaded hastily, but methodically, through the three marked periods of Ancient India; and in concluding this sketch of those great periods, it only remains for us to indicate the onward progress of the schemes which then originated. Three privileged castes and one subordinate we have seen as the intention, but now we read, "In the present day the only one of the original castes extant is the Brahman; the Kshatriya, Vaisya, and Sudra are extinct; and the innumerable castes which are now met with are in part the representations of the ancient mixed castes, but in a still greater degree are the progeny of later times, and distinctions unauthorizedly assumed by the people themselves."* Even Brahmans are very different to what was intended; for whilst men of this caste are often poor and illiterate, and obliged to support themselves by the work of their hands, men of low caste are frequently the influential religious guides of society.†

And also, "the Kshatriya caste is extinct;" that is, Kshatriyas no longer exist as a division of society. The whole country of Rajputana claims to be inhabited by Kshatriyas; but if such claims were admitted, Kshatriyas would be changed from a caste into a tribe; and the fact still remain, that soldiers, and even Rajas, may be and usually are without the sacrificial thread with which Kshatriyas were originally invested. The third privileged caste, the Vaisyas, are no longer heard of; and Sudras are more changed than even Brahmans. Instead of being serfs, as was intended, they are a small independent race or family, proud of their lineage. Kings of Magadha have been Sudras, the whole nation of Mahratta is Sudra, and in many parts of India writers and artists are exclusively Sudras. The Brahmanical system of caste has therefore proved a failure; failing to maintain nobility, but fixing fast the fetters of hereditary self-importance.

* H. H. Wilson, Oxford Lectures, p. 59.

† *Ibid.*, p. 29.

The effect of Brahmanical regulations upon women may be considered more at length, for the position of women has ever been one of the most remarkable features of social life in India. The Code of Manu gives woman no independence; she *belongs* to father, brother, or husband, "and neither by sale nor desertion can she be released."* So long as the husband lived and loved, the wife's happiness required no more; but under any circumstances she had no resource, and if he died she was required to live in a state of ascetic penance for the benefit of his disembodied soul, and in the hope of securing to herself a place in his mansion of eternal bliss. And behold the consequence: "many Koolin Brahmans marry ten or fifteen wives for the sake of money, and never see the greater number of them after the day of marriage." They wash, scour, and cook by night and by day, and "are treated worse than the inferior animals;" and when the husband dies, the chief wife is bound down with bamboos and burned upon his funeral pile. Here is the moral! The law makes woman the property of man, and her fate is slavish drudgery whilst he lives, and death upon his funeral pyre when he dies! But nature has not entirely succumbed to law, and the fine free woman's character of the Sanskrit epics has not been universally suppressed in India. Colonel Sleeman gives a most touching account of a Hindu woman whom he had known upon the banks of the Nerbudda: she was the widow of a Brahman of a numerous and highly respectable family, and begged permission to burn herself with the body of her husband. This being refused, and a guard placed to ensure obedience, she sat down by the edge of the water and refused food.

* Code of Manu, ch. ix., pp. 198, 85, 86, 87.

The family were urgent that she should return home if she could not get permission to be burned, for whilst she remained fasting on the bare rock the law required that they should likewise fast; but neither children nor grandchildren could induce her to relent, although she was certain of respect and kindness from them if she lived. From Tuesday the 24th November, 1829, when her husband died, until the Saturday following, did she sit immovable, and then Colonel Sleeman believed it his duty to withdraw the prohibition. He rode to the spot and spoke to her; her mind was firm and collected, and she said that her determination was to mix her ashes with those of her departed husband, and she should wait until he gave permission, assured that God would in the meanwhile sustain her life, although she dared not eat or drink. Looking at the sun then rising over a beautiful reach of the Nerbudda river, she said calmly, "My soul has been for five days with my husband's near that sun; nothing but my earthly frame is left, and this I know you will in time suffer to be mixed with the ashes of his in yonder pit, because it is not in your nature or your usage wantonly to prolong the miseries of a poor old woman." After much conversation, she convinced Colonel Sleeman that religion alone impelled her. "My soul," she repeated, "is with Omed, and my ashes must here mix with his." Colonel Sleeman could make no impression on her, either by promising wealth and honour if she lived, or suggesting the displeasure of Government towards her children if she were burned. She held out her arm, saying, "My pulse has long ceased to beat, my spirit has departed, and I have nothing left but a little earth, which I desire to mingle with the ashes of my husband. I shall suffer nothing in burning, and if you would have proof, order some fire, and you shall see this arm consumed without my feeling pain." Colonel Sleeman asked her when she had first resolved upon being a Suttee, and she said it was thirteen years ago, when bathing in the river near the spot on which she then sat; and the idea fixed itself in her mind as she looked at the splendid temples before her, erected by the different branches of her family over the ashes of their relatives who had from time to time been burned as Suttees. The Colonel thought it unjustifiable any longer to resist her determination; but he required from her chief relations a formal written agreement that no other member of their family should ever attempt the same. He also prohibited the building of any temple on the spot; but unfortunately, during his absence, his post was held by a Resident unacquainted with the circumstances, and a commemorative temple was erected.*

One of the most illustrious characters in native Indian history is Alia (or more correctly, Ahalyá) Bhye, a woman—pious, compassionate, clever, and energetic—who governed the country with so much wisdom and firmness that her supremacy was acknowledged by all the surrounding states: but she was a Mahratta, and owed her independence of character to the free though turbulent character of her nation. When the daughter of Alia Bhye lost her husband, she desired to burn herself upon his funeral pile. Unlike an orthodox Hindu, Alia Bhye remonstrated and endeavoured to dissuade her daughter; but the touching reply of the young widow was, "You are old, mother, and a few years will end your pious life. My husband and my only child

* 'Rambles,' by Colonel Sleeman, ch. iv.

are gone, and then you follow; life will be insupportable to me; but the opportunity of terminating it with honour will then have passed."*

But whilst Hindu women of the present day are chiefly remarkable for helpless submission and frivolity, the women of the free Bheels, who inhabit hills and forests, are mentioned with much interest by Sir John Malcolm and others labouring successfully for their advancement. The following short anecdote shows a generous courage and self-reliance wholly wanting under Brahmanical institutions.† During the examination into the guilt of Nadir Singh, a girl fourteen years of age was examined, whose father and husband had been instruments in committing the murder of which he was accused. She was asked if they put the deceased to death: "Certainly they did," was her firm reply; "but they acted by the Dhumnee's (or lord's) order." She was told this did not clear them; for that it was not an affray, but a deed committed in cold blood. "Still," she remonstrated, "they had the Dhumnee's order." The person conducting the examination shook his head, whereupon the girl rose from the ground on which she was sitting, and, pointing to the two sentries who guarded the door, exclaimed with strong feeling, "These are your soldiers; you are their Dhumnee; your words are their laws; if you order them this moment to advance and put me, my mother, and my cousin, who are now before you, to death, would they hesitate in slaying three female Bheels? If we were innocent, would you be guilty of our blood, or those

* Oriental Magazine, vol. i. p. 117.

† Sir John Malcolm's 'Central India:' Captain T. D. Stuart assisted at the trial, and noted down the expressions at the time.

faithful men?" She then sat down, saying, "My father and husband are Nadir's soldiers."

The religions of India have fared no better than the political institutions. The Brahmans tried to debar the people from spiritual light, and the people dragged the Brahmans down into idolatrous darkness. Popular heroes and wild fancies became exalted into divinities, and Siva and Vishnu were but the forerunners of an ever-increasing mythological assemblage. Durga is wife to Siva; Kartikeya, riding a peacock, son to Siva; Ganesa, a fat man with an elephant's head, removes difficulties, presides over the entrance of edifices, and is invoked at the commencement of all undertakings.* But one feels very little encouraged to pursue the subject of India's idolatries, for in general they are lamentably debasing, as may be seen in the ceremonies daily enacted, or as may be learned from the pages of the missionary Ward, or the fearful revelations of Thuggism.

Turning from religion to architecture, we find splendid temples arising after the religion had ceased to be sublime. The age of the Vedas has left no buildings; and even the Greeks, who write of India B.C. 300, and who tell us of cities, gates, towers, and wells, mention no large or public building. All the known architecture of India dates later than the periods of foreign occupation; and the splendid ruins, consecrated to Vishnu or Siva, which are figured in the works of Tod and Fergusson, are supposed to range from the fifth or sixth, down to the ninth century, A.D. The ornamentation of these temples is singularly beautiful, as may be seen in the elaborate drawings made under

* Elphinstone, Hist. Ind., 89.

the direction of Colonel Tod, and bequeathed by him to the Royal Asiatic Society.

The semicircular panel ornament figured above, the leaf-scroll at the conclusion of Book I., the vases which conclude this Chapter and Chapter IV., and the peacock panel heading Chapter V., are all from pillars in a temple at Cheetore,* which Mr. Fergusson thinks cannot be earlier than A.D. 727; whilst the beautiful ceilings in Tod's Rajasthan are from temples at Chandravarti, about A.D. 692. It is worth while to make close acquaintance with these fine buildings, and with those at Barolli and in the Mokundara Pass, for they belong strictly to Hindu history; whilst nearly all architecture of later date in India "is so mixed up with Mohammedan details as to be scarcely recognizable at first sight from that style."† It is not perhaps sufficiently remembered in England that some of the most celebrated cities in Western India, as Aurungabad and

* Tod's Rajasthan, vol. ii. p. 734.

† Fergusson's Ancient Architecture of Hindostan, Preface, p. iv. and pp. 33, 34, 36, plates v. vi. vii. and others.

Dowlatabad, are "in all their buildings and forms as purely Mohammedan as Bagdad or Damascus."* But putting aside Mohammedan buildings, with which we are not at present concerned, we shall find almost universally that the finest temples in India are the oldest. For in that country, Mr. Fergusson says, "all the styles of architecture have their history written in decay: of any two buildings or specimens of art of any sort, if one is more perfect or of a higher class than the other, we may at once feel certain that it is also the more ancient of the two."† As national monuments of a different character, we may point to the

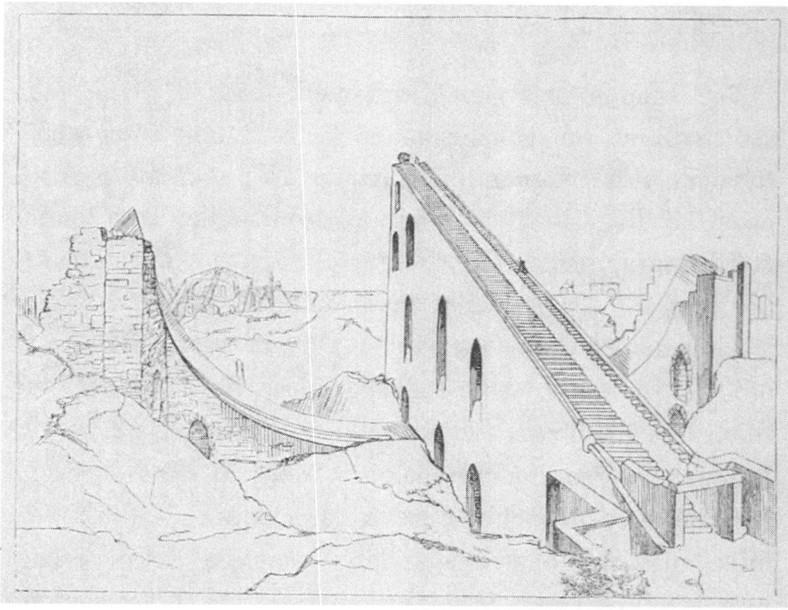

lofty Dial and extraordinary "mural instruments for astronomical purposes"‡ near Delhi, which immortalize the

* Fergusson's Ancient Architecture of Hindostan, Introduction, p. 2.

† *Ibid.*, p. 11.

‡ Daniell's Antiquities of India, plates xix. and xx. A full account of

memory of the Raja Jey or Jaya Sing,* who reigned from A.D. 1699 to 1743. The beautiful vignette heading to this Chapter is the balcony of Jey Sing's Observatory at Benares, which affords another memorial of the delight which this Emperor took in scientific observations.

Astronomy is one of those sciences which has resisted the deadening influences of the last nine centuries, and even in these degenerate days can boast of votaries capable of mastering ancient Hindu learning, and of comprehending European science, if it be exhibited from a Hindu point of view. At a meeting of the Asiatic Society, in Calcutta, June 17, 1837, two works were presented written in the Mahratta and Hindi languages, by two natives, for the purpose of explaining the correct system of astronomy to their countrymen. After arguing in vain for eight years, Mr. Lancelot Wilkinson had an opportunity of making them acquainted with Hindu astronomical books; and immediately the real size and shape of the earth, and other important physical facts, were understood, and conviction carried to their minds.* Subhaji Bapu had the master mind which exercised its influence over all the other Pundits. "He was lost in admiration when he came fully to comprehend all the facts resulting from the spherical form of the earth; and when the retrogressions of the planets were shown to be so naturally accounted for on the theory of the earth's annual motion, and when he reflected on the vastly superior simplicity and credibility of the supposition

these Astronomical Buildings is given by Dr. Hunter in the fifth volume of the 'Asiatic Researches.'

* This is supposed by Dr. Kitto to be the form of the dial seen by King Hezekiah, described as the "Steps of Ahaz." Buddhists reckoned time by *inches* (see *ante*, p. 294), but the form of their dial is not indicated.

that the earth had a diurnal motion, than that the sun and all the stars daily revolve round the earth, he became a zealous defender of the system of Copernicus. He lamented that his life had been spent in maintaining foolish fancies, and spoke with a bitter indignation against all those of his predecessors who had contributed to the wilful concealment of the truths that had once been acknowledged in the land."*

In Metaphysics we have already had occasion to notice the ingenuity and perseverance of Hindu speculation.† Of Hindu attainment in medicine much also might be said, as attested by the flourishing schools in Calcutta and other parts of India. And that India has not lost her ancient skill in arts and manufactures, we have had ample evidence in the exquisite muslins, embroideries, shawls, and kincobs, the dyes and scents, the magnificent carved furniture, the gold and silver filagree, the trophies of jewelled arms, and other attractions of the Indian Department of our Great Exhibition in 1851, and that of Paris in 1855. And when thinking of India's actual attainments and resources, it is difficult to refrain from a digression upon the magic of railway communication; upon the good which one hopefully anticipates, although evil effects be first apparent: we see indeed that it first unearths and exasperates wild Santhals, but one hopes that it may bring many groups of retired Pundits within the influence of European civilization, although denied the rare blessing of a Lancelot Wilkinson as resident amongst them. And religiously, how wide the question!—but we

* Letter from Mr. Wilkinson, the Governor-General's Agent at Bhilsa, Journal of the Asiatic Society of Bengal, vol. vi. p. 401.

† *Ante*, p. 292.

must forbear. Ancient India is our subject, and of Ancient India we must take leave, casting one lingering glance upon its best-loved features.

Wherever man has thought much, we find that he has by necessity thought much upon religion, for the mind of man seeks for God as surely as the sunflower seeks the sun. Ancient Hindus were men of intellect; their institutions devoted a large portion of their society to contemplation, and the result is, that religion was ever the strongest point of interest in their history. But India's holy books, instead of being a record of God's commands or a narrative of man's confiding trust, are a mass of heterogeneous tales and wild conjectures, in which practical views of duty, chiefly negative, alternate with intuitions sublime but evanescent and theoretical. First, we have seen Brahmans capable of sublime thought striving to fetter their fellow-creatures with hereditary rank and hereditary occupations. Secondly, we have seen the democracy of Buddhism sweeping away Brahmanical institutions and upholding universal rights, but, at the same time, blighting the poetry of life and literature. And thirdly, we have seen a regenerated corrupt Brahmanical system triumph over Buddhism, and partially restore the poetry of earlier days, but fail essentially in the working of its fourfold system of Caste.

The old Brahman was not so wanting in abstract belief as in obedience to law and knowledge of God's will. The Buddhist tried to give the law, but it was law without God, and resulted in barren formalism. The Buddhist was republican but not spiritual, the old Brahman spiritual but exclusive, and thus we may compare them with those terrible insects of India known as white ants. Periodically they are clothed with wings, burst from their dark homes and soar upwards; unguided, they fly equally toward sun or lamp or rushlight: many perish in flame; others fall exhausted, and, crawling home without wings, again become an industrious community, but incapable of flights toward heaven. And thus we close these studies, standing like weather-bound travellers on a mountain-top,—

> "Wrapt as in the cloud
> In which light dwelt before the sun was born."

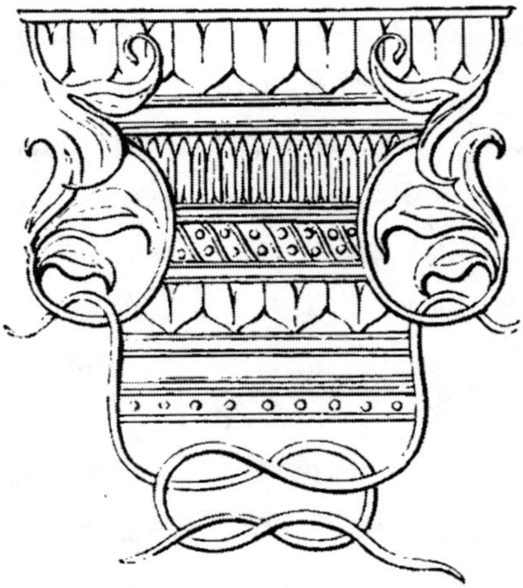